*Religion and State Formation
in Postrevolutionary Mexico*

Religion and State Formation in Postrevolutionary Mexico

BEN FALLAW

Duke University Press *Durham and London* 2013

© 2013 Duke University Press
All rights reserved

Designed by Amy Ruth Buchanan
Typeset in Minion by Keystone
Typesetting, Inc.
Library of Congress Cataloging-
in-Publication Data appear on the
last printed page of this book.

For Mónica and Amy María

and in memory of

Hernán Menéndez Rodríguez

Contents

Acknowledgments ix
Abbreviations xi
Glossary xv

INTRODUCTION 1

CHAPTER 1. The Church and the Religious Question 13

CHAPTER 2. Catholic-Socialists against Anti-Priests in Campeche 35

CHAPTER 3. "The Devil Is Now Loose in Huejutla": The Bishop, the SEP, and the Emancipation of the Indian in Hidalgo 63

CHAPTER 4. Beatas, Ballots, and Bullets in Guerrero 101

CHAPTER 5. "Un sin fin de mochos": Catholic Cacicazgos in Guanajuato 157

CONCLUSION: The End of the Religious Question 219

Notes 227
Bibliography 295
Index 317

Acknowledgments

Over the past decade, the support of many people and institutions enabled me to research and write this book. First and foremost, I gratefully acknowledge the American Council of Learned Societies and the late Charles Ryskamp. Their generosity made it possible for me to conduct fieldwork in Mexico during the 2002–3 academic year. At Duke University Press my editor, Valerie Millholland, ably seconded by Miriam Angress and Gisela Fosado, patiently saw this project through to its completion. I hope that it was worth the wait.

Many scholars read and commented on parts of the book. Long discussions with David Nugent about Latin American history and politics were the seed of this project. Silvia Arrom, Roberto Blancarte, Kristina Boylan, Michael Ducey, Wolfgang Gabbert, Paul Gillingham, Alan Knight, Jennie Purnell, Ute Schüren, and Rich Warren commented on various chapters. Matthew Butler helped me get a firmer grasp of the history of the Church in Mexico. Benjamin Smith read and provided valuable feedback on the entire manuscript. Two anonymous readers at Duke University made this a much better book. Despite all their sage advice and counsel, this work undoubtedly contains errors, and they all are my own.

I am indebted to several colleagues' kindness for help in researching this volume. Years ago Mary Kay Vaughan insisted I go to the federal education archives, and for that I am in her debt. Peter Reich, a true pioneer in the Church archives, lent me a copy of Paul Murray's survey of the Church in Mexico. Finally, Frans Schreyer generously shared his field notes as well as important insights into the Nahua of Hidalgo and Guerrero.

In Mexico City, the staffs of several archives provided invaluable professional assistance. At the Archivo Histórco del Arzobispado de México, Father Gustavo Watson, Marco Antonio Pérez Iturbe, and Berenise Bravo Rubio helped me locate important documents. I gratefully acknowledge the aid of Maestra María de Jesus Díaz, director of the Biblioteca Francisco Xavier Clavijero of the Universidad Iberoamericana. In the Secretariado Social Mexicano, Father Manuel Velázquez Hernández, a sociologist and activist, and his staff were wonderful hosts and good company. Like many scholars of postrevolutionary Mexico, my research was enriched by the archives of the Fideicomiso Archivos Plutarco Elías Calles y Fernando Torreblanca. I greatly appreciate the professional courtesies of its director, Lic. Norma Mereles Torreblanca de Ogarrio, and her most diligent and personable staff. At the Archivo Histórico de la Secretaría de Educación Pública, Roberto Pérez Aguilar was a model archivist. Finally, I acknowledge the efforts of the staff of the Hemeroteca Nacional and Archivo General de la Nación, above all the legendary Don Juventino González Pimentel.

Over the past few years my research assistants at Colby College—Kate Bellerose, Patrick Campbell, Julie Guilbaut, Abbott Matthews, Sarah Trankle, Andrew Wall, and Rachel Watson—put in countless hours preparing the manuscript for publication.

I dedicate this book to three people. The first is the late Hernán Menéndez Rodríguez. His zeal to reveal the Church's hidden role in Mexico's modern political history inspired me to begin this project. The other two are my wife Mónica and our daughter Amy María. They lovingly sustained me over the past decade. I remain eternally grateful to them both.

Abbreviations

ACJM   Asociación Católica de la Juventud Mexicana, or the Catholic Association of Young Mexican Men; one of the three groups founded to re-Christianize Mexico by countering the revolutionary project, its involvement in the Cristero War led the episcopate to firmly subordinate it to the ACM

ACM   Acción Católica Mexicana, or Mexican Catholic Action; the umbrella group for all officially sanctioned Catholic lay groups, founded in 1929, it absorbed most organized, formal lay organizations

AHPEC   Archivo Historico Plutarco Elías Calles

ANPF   Asociación Nacional de Padres de Familia or National Association of Parents; another Catholic parents organization founded to oppose socialist education

ANPLE   Asociacion Nacional Pro-Libertad de Enseñanza; another Catholic parents groups founded to oppose socialist education, it was semi-autonomous, and some local chapters were implicated in segunda violence

CCM   Confederación Campesina Mexicana; founded in 1933 by supporters of Lázaro Cárdenas, it was the forerunner of the peasant wing of the corporatist structure of the ruling party

CEM   Conferencia del Episcopado Mexicano, or Mexican Episcopal Conference, the governing body of the Church in Mexico

CNC   Confederación Nacional Campesina, or National Peasant Confederation

CPRG   Confederación de Partidos Revolucionarios de Guanajuato, or Confederation of Revolutionary Parties of Guanajuato, party founded by civilian classical Liberals in Guanajuato by combining local parties

CRD   Conflictos Religiosos por Diócesis

CROM	Confederación Regional Obrera Mexicana, or Mexican Regional Workers Confederation; founded in 1918, it was Mexico's leading labor confederation until the mid-1930s
DEF	Dirección de Educación Federal; the office responsible for supervising all the federal schools in a particular state, overseen by the equivalent of a superintendant
ENR-H	Escuela Normal Rural in Hecelchakán
EPL	Ejército Popular Libertador, or Popular Liberating Army, a group which claimed to command the segunderos in some states in the mid-1930s
ICAM	Iglesia Católica Apostólica Mexicana, or Mexican Catholic and Apostolic Church, a schismatic, nationalist, and pro-revolutionary splinter group of the Roman Catholic Church
JCFM	Juventud Católica Feminina Mexicana, or Mexican Catholic Female Youth, the young women's wing of the the ACM
LNC	Liga Nacional Campesino, or the National Campesino League, a national agrarian organization in the 1930s
LNDL	Liga Nacional Defensora de la Libertad, or the National League for the Defense of Liberty; the principal lay Catholic organization supporting a second Cristero War, it was marginalized by the Mexican episcopate
LNDLR	Liga Nacional Defensora de la Libertad Religiosa, or the National League for the Defense of Religious Liberty, prinicipal lay Catholic organization supporting the Cristero War
PAN	Partido de Acción Nacional, or Party of National Action; the right-of-center opposition party founded in 1939, its leadership and ideology mainly Catholic
PNR	Partido Nacional Revolucionario, or National Revolutionary Party; the ruling party founded in 1929, it eventually became the Partido Revolucionario Institutional in 1946
POA	Partido Obrero de Acapulco, or Workers Party of Acapulco
PRI	Partido Revolucionario Institucional, or Institutional Revolutionary Party, the successor of the PNR as the ruling party
PSA	Partido Socialista Agrario, or Socialist Agrarian Party, the ruling revolutionary regional party in Campeche, affiliate of the PNR
PSG	Partido Socialista Guerrerense, or Guerreran Socialist Party; founded by Adrián Castrejón, it sought to become the sole revolutionary regional party by mobilizing agrarian support
SEP	Secretaría de Educación Pública, or Ministry of Public Education

UCM   Unión de Católicos Mexicanos, or Union of Mexican Catholics; the older men's wing of ACM, it replaced and absorbed the Knights of Columbus

UDCM Unión de Damas Católicas Mexicanas, or Union of Mexican Catholic Ladies, known as the Damas Católicas; the most important formal lay organization of women in postrevolutionary Mexico, founded in the early 1920s, it was formally absorbed into the UFCM of the ACM during the 1930s

UFCM Unión Feminina Católica Mexicana, or Union of Mexican Catholic Women, the older women's wing of ACM

UNPF Unión Nacional de Padres de Familia, or National Union of Parents, the religious equivalent of the Parent-Teacher Association in the United States; founded by the Church to oppose the national revolutionary regime's education policy shortly after the promulgation of the Constitution of 1917

UNS   Unión Nacional Sinarquista, or National Sinarquista Union; founded in 1938, a conservative, extremely nationalistic, and allegedly apolitical movement that disguised its links to the Church; its right-wing ideology, centralized structure, and military-like discipline caused foes to charge it was fascist

Glossary

acapadores	middlemen who brought up the harvest for resale in larger markets
acordada	constabulary
agraristas	recipients of or petitioners for land grants from the federal government
antifanatical	efforts at eradicating elements of Catholicism deemed excessive, wasteful, backwards and superstitious
apareceros	tenant farmers
apertura	historical opening
Arreglos	"arrangements" between federal government and episcopate to end the Cristero War, they restated the Mexican polity's secular nature and prevented the state from interfering in the Church's internal affairs
asistentes eclesiásticos	chaplains/guides appointed by Catholic Action
atentados al pudor	sexual assault
ayuntamiento	town council elected to govern a municipio (both the town or city designated the county seat and the entire county, including the county seat and administratively subordinated villages and hamlets); at times governors would overturn elected ayuntamientos and directly appoint a council
beatas	activist Catholic laywomen
besamanos	submissive kissing of hands
cacicazgos	domain of cacique

caciques	petty bosses who rule outside and above the law and formal institutions, mediating between the grassroots level and overarching political, economic, and social systems
caciquismo	rule by caciques
campechano/a	resident of the state of Campeche
cargo system	a civil-religious hierarchy in indigenous communities historically linked to a cofradía, it often controls social, political, and economic lives
clericales	pro-Catholics
cofradía	colonial lay brotherhood devoted to the cult of a saint, indigenous communities modified it to make it the basis of the cargo system
comisario	roughly justice of the peace, the lowest ranking civil officer with jurisdiction over hamlets, small villages, and haciendas who lacked municipal status and was administratively subordinated to the county seat of a county (both termed *municipio*); a comisario could be either elected or appointed from the county seat
comodines	sellouts
compadrazgo	godparentage
corrido	folksong
corvée	unpaid labor draft exacted from indigenous people by local authorities
costeño	resident of coastal region
costrumbres	customs
coyotes	corrupt government officials
creyente	believer
Cristiada	Cristero War (1926–29)
cristeros	rebels in the first Cristero War (1926–29)
cuadrilla	hamlet or smaller village under the jurisdiction of the county seat (municipio)
Damas Católicas	See Unión de Damas Católicas Mexicanas in the Abbreviations
decente	moral, proper
defanatization	efforts to eliminate Catholic practices deemed excessive, wasteful, backwards, and superstitious

defensive segunda violence	spontaneous mob attacks (at times involving women and even children) against perceived enemies of or offenses to Catholicism
defensas rurales	agrarian militia raised and armed by the federal government from loyal peasants
defensas sociales	paramilitary police raised by state or local authorities, often from conservative elements or even white guards
delahuertistas	followers of Adolfo de la Huerta's rebellion against President Álvaro Obregón and his candidate for the presidency, Plutarco Elías Calles, in December 1923–May 1924
delegados municipales	justices of the peace
diezmos	Church tithes, usually 10 percent of income
la educación	roughly, good morals
ejidatarios	peasants who received collective land grants
ejidos	collective land grants made by the federal government after a petition signed by eligible recipients was investigated and approved by federal bureaucrats. At times interference by state or local officials or appeals by affected landowners could delay grants for years.
escobaristas	supporters of Gonzalo Escobar's March 1929 coup
faena	labor service. See also *corvée*
gente de razón	a colonial term referring to whites
gobiernistas	pro-government
Green Party	a clique of civilian classical Liberals who dominated regional politics in Guanajuato; see the Confederación de Partidos Revolutionarios de Guanajuato (CPRG) in the Abbreviations
gremios	similar to the colonial confraternities, these lay fraternities or guilds oversaw religious practices in Campeche and Yucatán
guanajuatense	resident of the state of Guanajuato
guardias blancas	paramilitaries organized by landowners, usually to oppose agraristas, at times designated as *defensas sociales*
guerrerense	resident of the state of Guerrero
hacendado	landowner
Hidalguense	resident of the state of Hidalgo

indigenism	nationalist ideology valorizing the indigenous past as the font of national identity, while encouraging the incorporation of contemporary indigenous people on the state's terms
jefe máximo	maximum chief
jefes políticos	prefects appointed by Mexico City
juez	judge
juntas vecinales	neighborhood councils that took over custody of churches closed under anticlerical legislation
levitical	a community where the Church defined social, educational, and often political life
ley de cultos	anticlerical regulations passed by states to enforce article 130 of the Constiutiton
licenciados	lawyers
liderismo	domination by charismatic strongmen
liviana	flighty or flirty
maestros rurales	rural teachers in SEP service, they often organized peon unions and peasant agrarian petitions
mancuerno	political alter ego
Maximato	a historical period in Mexico from 1928 to 1934 that was named after former president Plutarco Elías Calles; as the *jefe máximo* (national boss), he functioned as a superexecutive more powerful than presidents Emilio Portes Gil, Pascual Ortiz Rubio, and Abelardo Rodríguez.
mayordomías	stewardships devoted to the cult of a local saint, a high office in the cargo system
medieros	sharecroppers
militares	soldiers
milpa	a small field that is used throughout Mesoamerica for growing maize and other complementary crops
mocho/a	overly religious
municipio libre	municipal democracy
obreras	female workers
offensive segunda violence	premeditated, organized attacks by gangs of men against perceived enemies of Catholicism
organizadoras	female catechists

Padres de la Familia	literally, Parents of the Family, name or variant adopted by a number of Church front groups opposing socialist education
parcelas	private plots
la patria potestad	domestic patriarchy
pláticas	chats
plebecito	primary election
Porfiriato	the era of Porfirio Díaz's government from 1876–1911
posadas	nine days of Catholic religious celebration from December 16 through December 24 that reenact Mary and Joseph's journey from Nazareth to Bethlehem
prestanombres	fictive owners
primacias	gifts, such as the first fruits from a tree or first egg from a chicken, customarily given to the clergy
el pueblo	the people
Psychological Revolution	Plutarco Elías Calles's proclamation in July 1934 calling for an educational, social, and cultural revolution to secularize the minds of the next generation of Mexicans through socialist education
quemasantos	saint burning
rancherias	hamlets; small communities
Ranchero group	a coalition of landowners, lawyers, and military men who had long controlled Guerreran politics
recristeros	veterans of the first Cristiada who fought in the Segunda (second Cristero War)
Red Shirts	organizations of leftist, ardently anticlerical youth and young adults started by admirers of Tomas Garrido Canabal of Tabasco
Reds	the Green's rival party, supported by most agraristas and organized labor in the state. It gained the support of Plutarco Elías Calles; nationally, referred to the informal group of supporters of Calles who opposed President Ortíz Rubio in 1930–32.
retablo	miracle
Revolutionary Family	the inner circle of the leaders of the postrevolutionary regime
riquillos	"little rich men," a derogatory term used by leftists to refer to the local bourgeoisie

rodriguista	supporters of Matías Rodríguez
Rosary Belt	a term used by Carlos Monsivaís to describe the center west Bajío (the states of Colima, southern Guanajuato, Jalisco, Michoacán, Nayarit and southern Zacatecas) that has long enjoyed a reputation for exceptional religiosity
Segunda, the	the second Cristero War in the 1930s
segunderos	fighters in the Segunda, the second Cristero War
serranos	highlanders
sexenio	the single six-year term served by a president
Sinarquismo	a national conservative and Catholic organization avowedly apolitical and covertly linked to the institutional Church, it defended private property, opposed the left and Cardenismo. Its extremely nationalist ideology and militaristic organization reminded many of fascism.
teoixpan	domestic altars
tequitlato	an office in indigenous civil-religious hierarchy responsible for organizing labor drafts
Terciarios	Third Order of the Franciscans, an elite lay organization that often collected taxes for the clergy
tienda de raya	the company store on a hacienda or mine
trabajo comunal	communal work often owed in indigenous communities
uniones libres	free unions
voto morado	literally, "the purple vote"; figuratively, the Catholic ballots cast in supposedly revolutionary politics
white guards	See *guardias blancas*
Whites	partisans of President Pascual Ortíz Rubio in 1930–32, in the struggle against the pro-Calles Reds
white terror	violence carried out by landowners against agraristas
Zapatismo	the legacy of revolutionary caudillo Emiliano Zapata (d. 1919), an ideology of agrarismo and decentralized democracy
zahorines	traditional Nahua spiritual specialists

INTRODUCTION

The overthrow of dictator Porfirio Díaz in 1911 began a decade of bloody strife and social upheaval known as the Mexican Revolution. By 1920, the triumph of a faction of warlords and civilian politicos ended the revolution's armed phase.[1] As the Partido Revolucionario Institucional (PRI, Party of the Institutionalized Revolution), it held power until the year 2000. While almost every other Latin American nation experienced long periods of military rule or divisive social conflict during the Cold War, the PRI ruled without recourse to systematic repression. If not strictly democratic, the PRI regime was stable, inclusive, and favored by the United States.

Over the past two decades, scholars seeking to explain the PRI's longevity and apparent popular support have moved away from Marxist-inspired socioeconomic determinism. Instead, they have closely examined the ruling party's negotiations with diverse popular groups. Two complementary concepts drawn from Antonio Gramsci's political theory, "hegemony" and "civil society," have become increasingly prominent in postrevolutionary historiography. The former term posits that successful state formation requires both coercion and consent. Only negotiation and compromise with key social sectors creates hegemony. The concept of hegemony encouraged scholars to look beyond narrow institutional politics to the broader category of political culture. Consequently, Mexico's civil society—politically active groups in society that enabled the state to rule—received much closer attention.[2] By the end of the 1990s, a generation of scholars, especially those identified with the New Cultural History of Mexico, had opened up promising new vistas on the process of postrevolutionary state formation.[3] The academic gaze shifted to the participation of subaltern groups in politics, especially peasants and women, in politics.⁴ Three important sectors in civil society, however, have largely been overlooked: Catholic associations, the press, and business.⁵ Originally this project set out to examine all three, but it narrowed to focus just on Catholics because of their crucial role in several key aspects of state formation. The religious question—meaning the place of the Church in a Catholic country after an anticlerical revolution—profoundly shaped the process of postrevolutionary state formation. To avoid overgeneralizing regional idiosyncrasies, I researched four states: Campeche, Hidalgo, Guerrero, and Guanajuato. Chronologically, I limited my research to the eleven formative years from the end of the Cristero War in 1929 until late 1940, when the new president, Manuel Ávila Camacho, presumably resolved the religious question by stating that he was a believer.

I argue that Marxist revisionists of the 1970s and 1980s and more recent postrevisionist scholarship have overlooked the pervasive influence of Catholicism in complicating postrevolutionary state formation. True, by the late 1930s, most Catholics had grudgingly accepted the regime eventually known as the PRI, and many regional affiliates of the ruling party could not govern without the collaboration of some Catholic leaders. To be sure, the institutional Church partnered with the postrevolutionary state at critical historical moments, for instance, when suppressing a second Cristero revolt and supporting the nationalization of oil. Ultimately, however, the institutional Church's long-term strategy was to indirectly undermine the postrevolutionary state, albeit culturally and socially rather than directly challenging it militarily or electorally.⁶ Ironically, the regime's dependence on elections for legitimacy allowed Catholics to hinder key parts of postrevolutionary state formation. Time and time again, Catholic voters elected officials who nullified anticlerical regulations, opposed federal schools, and even resisted agrarian reform.⁷ President Lázaro Cárdenas's rightward tilt after 1937 resulted in no small part from Catholic opposition, opposition that continued even after most anticlerical restrictions had ended. Even after Cárdenas left office, this remained an uncivil society.⁸

Definitions and Methodology

This is a study of Catholics and Catholicism in postrevolutionary state formation as opposed to a religious or social history of Catholicism.⁹ Census data from the 1930s indicates that all but 2 percent of Mexicans self-identified as Catholic.¹⁰ Determining actual religious beliefs, however, is complicated by a number of methodological and epistemological difficulties. This is especially true in the case of political leaders. Take the case of Governor Francisco Ramírez Romano of Nayarit (1927–28). Educated in a Jesuit college, he later joined the Freemasons, perhaps to advance his political career. Once governor, he toed the state's anticlerical line by jailing priests and lay leaders. At the same time, he also privately maintained close relationships with Catholic leaders, including the head of Nayarit's Knights of Columbus. When his tailor found a scapular in his suit and denounced him, Ramírez Romano was politically discredited. In 1930, he went to the archbishop of Guadalajara, recanted his anticlericalism, and asked for a letter of introduction and money. The archbishop demurred, fearing another "unpleasant surprise" from this unreliable ally.[11]

Filiberto Gómez, a key political leader in the state of Mexico, provides another example of how nominally revolutionary elites often kept a foot firmly planted in both camps. Gómez corresponded warmly with Archbishop Pascual Díaz. During the Church-state conflict of the early 1930s, Díaz recognized Gómez's past "good will" although he warned him that should he give in to pressure from Plutarco Elías Calles (president, 1924–28; maximum chief or *jefe máximo*, 1929–35) and harass Catholics, "the blow would cut into the Church of Christ."[12] Díaz summed up the dilemma of revolutionary politicos like Gómez who were Catholic offstage but anticlerical in public life: "even though a person privately wants to work for good, political obligations push them to do the contrary." After all, the prelate lamented, "before everything else, they are politicians."[13]

Defining state formation has its own peculiar challenges. Following Gramsci, many historians now see the state as much more than a set of formal institutions. In other words, the state is less a thing than a process. Gilbert Joseph and Daniel Nugent productively defined that elusive yet pervasive process of state formation as a "repertoire of activities and cultural forms that have provided modes of organization, social practice and identity."[14] Rituals and routines, then, enabled the postrevolutionary state to rule without constant reliance on coercion.[15] Many scholars have convincingly shown how the postrevolutionary state intended to carry out a cultural revolution by incorporating popular aspirations and values, allowing it to reach deeply into everyday life.[16]

As my research continued, it became clear that many Catholics were not averse to supporting some aspects of postrevolutionary state formation, specifically routine governance that protected private property and the patriarchal family. However, most Catholics rejected agrarian reform and the extension of federal schooling. Most contentious of all, of course, was revolutionary anticlericalism. Together, I term these three elements—agrarian reform, federal schools, and anticlericalism—the revolutionary project. By separating governance from the revolutionary project, I could reconcile Catholics' seemingly contradictory position vis-à-vis the postrevolutionary state.[17]

Eventually, I focused on six topics to explain how Catholics and Catholicism both facilitated and frustrated postrevolutionary state formation in the 1930s: anticlerical legislation, gubernatorial elections, socialist education, the Segunda (a second Cristero War in the 1930s), agrarian reform, and indigenism.

Anticlerical legislation provides an obvious starting point to understand the religious question. In the early 1930s, almost every Mexican state passed harsh *ley de cultos* (anticlerical regulations) which licensed priests to strictly control their numbers, location, and activities. Some such laws even prohibited parochial education and banned public religious practice. Catholics responded in numerous ways, among them by voting.

At first glance, examining Mexican elections to understand Catholic political behavior seems counterproductive. After all, balloting was often fraudulent, and the electoral process was in theory closed to counterrevolutionary candidates. In fact, elections served a vital role in Mexico's revolutionary democracy, a system with both exclusive and inclusive traits. Key elected officials, including many governors, generally came from a relatively small clique known as the Revolutionary Family and were ultimately nominated by its paterfamilias (Plutarco Elías Calles from July 1928 to July 1935, then Lázaro Cárdenas until November 1940).

Once tapped, however, candidates had to turn out the vote in order to claim office. Alcohol and money were commonly used to boost electoral turnout, and at times voters were transported in buses or trains across state lines. Electoral chicanery was not without risks, though, because the press and defrauded candidates could object. Fraud and apathy among the population made legitimate votes all the more valuable because they were harder to nullify or ignore. Candidates and their key campaign aides relied on intermediaries who mobilized clients and captive corporate groups—ideally worker and peasant associations, but in practice often Catholic associations. These electoral compromises were not always honored, and electoral brokers often sought political offices, contracts, or other favors for themselves.

Nevertheless, widespread bargaining between candidates and brokers meant that electoral results often expressed genuine social demands.

Ironically, electoral bargaining represented one of the few ways politically excluded "reactionary" groups like Catholics could have their demands redressed. In state after state, many crucial brokers were in fact Catholic. Catholic men voted frequently, and pious women, although denied suffrage, actively participated in electoral campaigns as well. What I term the *voto morado* (literally, the purple vote; figuratively, Catholic ballots cast in supposedly revolutionary politics) mattered immensely in many states.[18]

A close examination of Catholics' electoral participation sheds light on their role in state formation. It also brings into sharper focus the religious question in what Michael Erwin calls "middle politics."[19] Not just regional and local officials, but also "military leaders, the business community, the Church, urban-based workers, and even students, not to mention regional caciques," dominated this sphere.[20] Historical studies based solely on a narrow range of primary sources, such as letters from peasant communities to presidents, underestimate the extent to which middle politics mediated relations between the state and subaltern groups. Certainly, in spite of a degree of manipulation, peasants generally accepted mediators who represented them to distant authorities.[21] To avoid lapsing into what Quetzil Castañeda called the "ventriloquism of representing the subaltern voice," I focus on why and how popular groups made tactical alliances with mediators rather than trying to re-create their worldview.[22]

Nonviolent Catholic resistance to federal schools serves as my third focus. Vaughan's pioneering study of schooling in the 1930s in the states of Puebla and Sonora suggests that Catholic responses to the Secretaría de Educación Pública (or SEP, the Ministry of Public Education) ranged from violence to participation.[23] My research suggests that the impact of Catholic resistance to federal schools was much greater than previously thought and was never really neutralized by a hegemonic pact with the postrevolutionary state.

A close reading of Catholic anti-SEP discourse and a careful examination of Catholic networks that convened illegal attendance strikes, set up underground parochial "home" schools, and covertly distributed the bishops' pastoral letters show that women played crucial roles in both. While I agree with Kristina Boylan that Catholic women were neither counterrevolutionary dupes of the clergy and *latifundists* nor motivated by a backward-looking Marianism, their attempts to revitalize the Church brought them into direct conflict with the revolutionary project.[24] While they might have sought to refashion this project over the long run, in the short run they sought to thwart or capture it.

Activist Catholic women were animated by Catholic values, energized by the Church's radial strategy of decentralized resistance, and tenuously linked to hubs of clergy and formal lay leaders. Religious networks that resisted socialist education exerted considerable pull over civil society at a time when the institutional Church was debilitated and the postrevolutionary state was still feeble. Moreover, these largely autonomous groups made up mainly of Catholic women participated in electoral campaigns, opposed agrarian reform, and at times supported the Segunda, or second Cristero War. The latter is my fourth focus.

For much of the 1930s, *ejidos* (collective land grants), federal schools and teachers, and other government agents were attacked in the name of defending the Catholic Church. Even the boldest and best armed never threatened to overthrow the state by seizing strategic towns or defeating the army. Instead, they menaced soft targets and then melted away into hamlets and hills before the army arrived.[25] Scrutiny of segunda violence in Guerrero and Guanajuato suggests it was of two different sorts: offensive and defensive. The former involved well-armed, all-male paramilitary bands operating with premeditation and strategic purpose. Offensive segunda violence was often linked to landowners and often blurred into white terror (violence aimed at ending agrarian reform or unionization). Defensive segunda violence, on the other hand, was usually a spontaneous, localized reaction to a specific provocation, such as iconoclasm or rumors of teacher immorality. Perpetrators often included women and even older children. Generally speaking, defensive violence proved much less lethal than offensive violence.

Segunda attacks against *ejidatarios* (peasants who received collective land grants) alerted me to a fifth area where Catholics and Catholic belief profoundly undermined state formation: land reform. Although the institutional Church tried to prevent its formal lay organizations and clergy from supporting segunda violence, it also condemned agrarian reform as an unacceptable affront to the natural right of private property. Moreover, affinity, kinship, and clientelistic connections linked many Catholic lay leaders and priests to landowners. Shared economic interest helped unite them: tithes were still collected in much of Mexico, and agrarian reform imperiled them. Antiagrarianism in the institutional Church, then, was not just ideological or cultural. It has been underappreciated because economic factors have been downplayed in much of the recent historiography of modern Latin

America.[26] Writing of the colonial "spiritual economy," Kathryn Burns warns historians against neatly dividing "spiritual" and "economic" factors.[27] This is a concern for postcolonialists as well. By exploring Catholic antipathy to agrarian reform, I take up William Sewell's challenge to pit the imperialistic paradigms of meaning (Geertzian culture), scarcity, and power relations (Foucauldian discourse) against each other. I posit that all three are at play in Mexico's postrevolutionary religious question.[28]

Initially, I assumed the Church in Mexico was a white or mestizo institution. As I examined how Maya, Amuzgo, Otomí, and Nahua Catholics reacted to the revolutionary project, my sixth and final focus emerged: indigenism. Revolutionary indigenism valorized the Mesoamerican past as the font of national identity and promised Indians modernity as part of state formation.[29] As a result, postrevolutionary state formation deeply divided some indigenous communities, pitting younger men and some women who fought in revolutionary militias, supported land reform, and at times demanded schooling, against elders who were tied to the syncretic Catholic *cofradía* (lay religious brotherhood). Fully examining the religious question required taking into account revolutionary indigenism's impact on religious practice, and indigenous Catholics' participation in the conflict over it.

Because most Catholic resistance was extrainstitutional, finding archival sources proved challenging. Actors carrying out illegal activities such as truancy strikes and segunda violence had good reason to cover their tracks. The institutional Church's documents referred to these processes obliquely if at all. State actors noted their impact but were usually only dimly aware of the actors and ideologies behind them.[30] I aggregated information gleaned from three different types of archival sources (the Mexican government, the Church, and the U.S. State Department) as well as periodicals and published secondary sources. Mosaicing these sources fleshed out middle politics and shed light on the ideological underpinnings and social foundation of Catholic resistance.

In terms of Mexican archival sources, I drew on the Dirección General de Gobierno collection in the Archivo General de la Nación, specifically on complaints of violations of anticlerical legislation and detailed reports of gubernatorial and mayoral elections. Documents at the Fideicomiso Archivo Plutarco Elías Calles y Fernando Torreblanco proved indispensable in sorting out gubernatorial elections. Finally, the Secretaría de Educación Pública's archives contained a rich, at times almost ethnographical trove of inspectors' and superintendents' reports on rural communities and the place of Catholicism in them.

To try to get away from state-centric narratives of the religious question, I utilized several Church archives. The archives of the Secretariado Social Mexican and Acción Católica Mexicana yielded a wealth of information about lay activists. The Archivo Histórico del Arzobispado de México was especially useful, as it houses the correspondence of the two leaders of the national episcopate, Pascual Díaz and Luis María Martinez. The private archive of a key civilian leader of the *cristeros* (rebels in the first Cristero War) and champion of the *segunderos* (fighters in the second Cristero War, or Segunda), Miguel Palomar y Vizcaya, sheds light on Catholic advocates of armed struggle and the institutional Church's attempts to suppress it.[31]

To complement Mexican archival sources, I drew on Mexican newspapers and the U.S. State Department's consular reports. Each had its own fortes and foibles. A North American diplomat said of his informants, "among foreign residents in Mexico the longer the residence, the less reliable the information." Mexican or foreigner, their information was often distorted by "racial, political, or business bias."[32] Still, consular officials took a keen interest in the religious question and tried to keep a finger on the pulse of regional affairs, including elections and the Segunda. The most famous (and easily available) Mexico City daily newspapers, *Excelsior* and *El Universal*, had comparatively little to say about these topics. However, in the national *hemeroteca* (periodical archive), I stumbled on two semiweekly national newspapers, *Hombre Libre* and *La Opinion*, filled with articles that often reflected Catholic sensibilities.

Questioning Religion in Scholarly Literature

For the most part, the scholars who researched postrevolutionary Mexico's religious question thirty or forty years ago could not tap the archival sources mentioned above. But their conclusions still echo in scholarship today. Jean Meyer, Lyle Brown, and Albert Michaels depicted Church-state relations as evolving from conflict provoked by Calles (1926–35) to mutual accommodation under Cárdenas (1935–40). To court popular Catholic support for his progressive agrarian and prolabor policies, they argue, Cárdenas sought a truce with the high clergy. By rejecting revolutionary anticlericalism, the story goes, Cárdenas pacified the countryside, garnered the Church's support for his landmark nationalization of Mexico's oil in March 1938, and denied opposition politicos Catholic votes. In other words, the ruling party's social peace was predicated upon a high-level mutual understanding between Mexico's populist president and Church prelates.[33]

More recently, Marjorie Becker sought to correct the materialism of the Marxist-inspired revisionism by dwelling on the symbolic and aesthetic in Catholicism. However, she essentially confirmed the revisionists' idea that Cárdenas solved the religious question by ending controversial anticlerical policies.[34]

Vaughan's pathbreaking analysis of federal education made a theoretically innovative and empirically grounded argument that federal schools were crucial sites of cultural negotiation between the postrevolutionary state and Catholics.[35] Peter Reich leveraged recently opened Church archives to look at a very different kind of negotiation: pacts between revolutionary elites and the high clergy at the state and national levels. For him, this "hidden revolution" yielded a mutual accommodation that circumvented legal and institutional anticlericalism. Ultimately Reich, like Vaughan, argued that by the end of the 1930s, consensus and cooperation prevailed over conflict in Church-state relations.[36] In a series of articles, Adrian Bantjes reached a diametrically opposed conclusion, demonstrating how revolutionary anticlericalism provoked pervasive Catholic resentment and resistance. Bantjes called for a new, broader definition of political culture, one sensitive to religious conflict and cognizant of the human cost borne by Mexican Catholics during the Church-state conflict.[37] In different ways, Vaughan, Reich, and Bantjes each set new standards for methodological innovation and theoretical sophistication, but they required reconciliation. This study sets out to understand how Catholics could both fight a Kulturkampf and at the same time collude and cooperate in the creation of a postrevolutionary state.

To do so, I focus on the regional level to capture both national and grassroots perspectives. My approach to Catholicism follows those of Vanderwood and Rugeley, who examine the interplay of regional cultures, localized sacralities, and individual priests and lay leaders.[38] While the level of analysis is regional, my study examines the religious question of the 1930s in four quite distinct states. Three of the best regional studies of Catholics in regional politics—those of Jennie Purnell, Matthew Butler, and Chris Boyer—all focus on one state, Michoacán. Purnell argued that each community's decision to rebel in the Cristiada resulted from a complex series of historical factors, including local religious practice, petty political factionalism, popular notions of property rights, and interaction with individual officials and clergy.[39] Butler's detailed microhistories of rural parishes convincingly explained how localized social constructions of Catholicism and relations with priests determined whether peasant communities supported the Cristero insurgency, embraced the postrevolutionary project, or remained neutral.[40] Christopher Boyer stressed how deeply the ideology of Catholic nationalism ran in much of Michoacán.[41] Butler's and Purnell's monographs ended with the Cristiada's termination in 1929, while Boyer's ended in 1935—before the remarkable re-Christianization of much of Mexico took place in the late 1930s.

The Argument

To cast the religious question in a new light, I begin by examining its national context and considering it from the Catholic perspective in chapter 1. Rather than representing the Church as a single monolithic institution, I analyze key constituents such as bishops, priests, and formal lay organizations like Mexican Catholic Action (Acción Católica Mexicana or ACM, the umbrella group for all officially sanctioned lay groups). State repression and institutional weaknesses hindered the operation of the ACM in many regions until the end of the 1930s. Consequently, Rome and episcopal leadership authorized decentralized resistance via front groups like a supposedly independent civic organization for parents known as the UNPF, or Unión Nacional de Padres de Familia (National Union of Parents).

Chapter 2 explores the religious question in the southeastern state of Campeche. Inspired by Tomás Garrido Canabal's Tabasco and Marxist-inflected Catholicism, the SEP made Campeche's Maya villages an important laboratory for the revolutionary project. Federal educators opened Mexico's most radical normal school, set up peasant cooperatives, angled for influence over regional elections, and tried to shake Catholics' faith. Catalyzed by iconoclasm and the specter of a collectivized economy, Campeche's Catholic mestizo ranchers and merchants fought back. Informal anti-SEP lay groups, as well as semiofficial syncretic *gremios* (guilds), channeled resistance against federal teachers. Several key Catholic leaders were also local bosses in the nominally revolutionary regional socialist party. The Catholic–Socialist axis bested the radical teacher-peasant bloc in the decisive 1935 gubernatorial election.

Chapter 3 explores how Bishop José de Jesús Manríquez Zárate built his newly minted Diocese of Huejutla (Hidalgo) to showcase social Catholicism. He ministered to his Nahua *inditos* while blessing the tithes and labor drafts that sustained a racialized social hierarchy. To counter his Catholic indigenism, federal teachers used his diocese as a revolutionary testing ground for their brand of indigenism. The SEP's point man, Inspector Francisco Zárate, founded schools and advanced agrarian reform. But his iconoclasm and treatment of female students seemed to confirm Catholics' worst fears about federal teachers' true intentions. As a result, Catholic mass mobilization complicated efforts to dismantle *cacicazgos*. Ironically, Cárdenas's hand-picked governor allied with local politicos who were protecting Catholics, which sealed the fate of the revolutionary project.

Beatas (pious laywomen), the voto morado, and *segunderos* in the famously fractious southwestern state of Guerrero are analyzed in chapter 4. Geographically fragmented, desperately poor, and ethnically divided, *bronco* (wild) Guerrero long defied national and Church authorities. During the 1930s, the revolutionary project floundered, and the decentralized Catholic strategy of resistance thrived. Beatas helped elect pro-Catholic, antiagrarian candidates. Catholic networks led by clergy, *hacendados*, and elected officials coordinated truancy strikes against schools and repressed *agraristas*. They also eluded Church discipline. A close reading of segunda attacks reveals two distinct types of violence, offensive and defensive. In the former, male bands (some bi-ethnic) led by mestizo landowners deployed antiagrarian and antiteacher violence strategically against the revolutionary project; in the latter, Catholics (including Indians) of both sexes and all ages reacted spontaneously to specific insults to religious beliefs. By the end of the 1930s, Catholic authority reasserted itself through the ACM.

Chapter 5 examines a series of Catholic cacicazgos in Guanajuato that coexisted with a dense web of formal Catholic groups. Together, they delegitimized the revolutionary project, especially federal schooling, and encouraged segunderos. Ex-cristero Salvador Azanza, scion of a pious landowning dynasty, used his social standing and ties to the federal military to carve out a fiefdom across the northern half of the state. Azanza championed conservative Catholic interests by surreptitiously aiding segunderos, personally assaulting two SEP inspectors, and murdering agraristas and a key Cardenista leader with impunity. Attempts to expand *ejidos* (collective land grants made by the federal government) and SEP schools in Ciudad González led to a bloody skirmish with Catholics on March 28, 1936, that left nineteen dead and raised a national outcry. President Cárdenas sermonized against fanatics martyring revolutionaries yet accelerated the state's retreat from anticlericalism. At the same time, Cárdenas redoubled agrarian reform in northern Guanajuato, hoping land and an end to Jacobinism would refill schools and legitimize the postrevolutionary regime. Yet his overtures to

Catholics were largely spurned, and ejidatarios had to be imported from neighboring states.

I conclude by arguing that the religious question was never satisfactorily answered by Mexico's postrevolutionary politicos. By the late 1930s, Cárdenas had presided over a dismantling of the most egregious anticlerical legislation, and socialist education was on its last legs. Many key Catholic leaders were ensconced in the state, as electoral brokers drew on Catholic sociability and symbols to barter for political spoils. At the same time, this was in many ways an uneasy and incomplete truce. While the institutional Church acquiesced to the postrevolutionary state's governance and suppressed the Segunda, Catholics retained a lasting antipathy to key elements of the revolutionary project, such as agrarian reform and revolutionary schooling. Consequently, Mexico's predominantly Catholic civil society denied the revolutionary ruling party generalized consent.

CHAPTER 1

The Church and the Religious Question

Behind the monolithic, ultramontane façade of the Church in Mexico, deep divisions lurked. Moderate prelates' dominance riled confrontational bishops. Foreign regulars' clout rankled Mexican diocesan priests. Ex-cristeros resented episcopal peacemaking. Rome's radial strategy that sanctioned dendritic resistance to the revolutionary project unintentionally widened these rifts by undermining the Church's hierarchical structure and encouraging lay autonomy.

After surveying the national Church-state conflict from 1910 to 1940, this chapter maps these internal fault lines and describes Mexico's episcopate, clergy, and formal lay organizations. Next, it analyzes how priests and the ACM (the umbrella group for all officially sanctioned Catholic lay groups) set up semi-clandestine task forces to coordinate supposedly autonomous front groups, and why and how these groups so often escaped supervision. Lastly, it considers how Mexico's spiritual geography shaped regional outcomes.

Origins of the Religious Question

Scholars of postrevolutionary state formation often explain postrevolutionary religious conflict with state-centered narratives. This approach crowds out Catholic perspectives, plasters over divisions in both the revolutionary camp and the Church over the religious question, and erases the agency exercised by individual clergy and lay leaders.[1] It often glosses over how Catholics' approach to the religious question was shaped by their historical experience. The Revolution's partisans labeled the Church a conservative remnant of the Porfiriato; Catholics, however, pointed to Díaz's positivism and freemasonry.² For them, the Revolution interrupted the Church's Mexican renaissance.³ Moreover, this Porfirian transformation predisposed Catholics to reject the Revolution.

The "global new Catholicism," to use Christopher Clark's phrase, had many dimensions. Although it continued Pius IX's ultramontane authoritarianism, the Church now engaged rather than rejected modernity. To regain social influence, it educated the best and brightest young men, not just seminarians. Through parochial schooling with a vocational bent, it reached out to those left behind by economic development. Pope Leo XIII's Rerum Novarum (1893) promised a systematic response to illiteracy, disease, and poverty. Social Catholicism encouraged charitable works, promoted mutualism, and expanded education. Revitalized lay groups provided a Christian remedy for the shortcomings of soulless, laissez-faire capitalism and so indirectly countered Liberal attempts to compartmentalize religion. By the end of the nineteenth century, the Church was appropriating key parts of modernity, including the use of mass media to influence civil society and the recognition of women as social actors.⁴

A new generation of young bishops educated at Rome's Pius Latin College brought this global revolution to Mexico. The Vatican believed these so-called Romans, seconded by European regulars, would educate, discipline, and generally professionalize the often-wayward, native-born priesthood. Lay activists, typically middle- and upper-class women, gained new authority and added responsibilities under social Catholicism. These determined women helped defend the *patria*, property, and the patriarchal family.⁵

Neo-Christendom, to use Anthony Gill's expression, came to terms with some socioeconomic changes, but it also reinvigorated political conservatism.⁶ Rather than bless a Catholic party, the Church preferred to influence elections via discreet episcopal pressure on elites who would in turn sway civil society.⁷ The Church's "traditionalizing effect" countered the spread of liberalism, inhibited "social pluralism," and buttressed regional oligarchies.⁸ In Mexico, bishops supported Porfirian capitalist development and authoritarian political stabilization. Overmyer-Velázquez documents how Oaxacan archbishop Eulogio Gillow disciplined the working class via mutualist labor circles, guilds, reenergized parochial schooling, and charities. In the city of Oaxaca, social Catholicism and modernized pious associations created "social identity and regional pride" that greased the wheels of Porfirian material progress.[9] In Yucatán, Archbishop Martin Tritschler y Córdoba forged a lasting alliance with the peninsular oligarchy headed by Olegario Molina, who was both governor and Díaz's minister of development. The henequen boom underwrote churches, schools, orphanages, and mutualist labor associations in Yucatán. Tritschler, however, remained discreetly mum on the brutal debt peonage practiced on henequen plantations.[10] In many dioceses, social Catholicism sanctioned the científicos' positivist project without humanizing it.

After the collapse of the Porfiriato, many revolutionary military officers, labor leaders, and intellectuals went after the Church with a vengeance.[11] Venustiano Carranza's Constitutionalists alleged that the Church had propped up Díaz and then endorsed General Victoriano Huerta's reactionary regime (1913–14) through its conspicuous consecration of the nation to the Sacred Heart on January 6, 1914.[12] To Catholics, the revolutionary Constitution of 1917 was frankly antireligious, denying the Church and its clergy legal status, imperiling parochial education, and persecuting the majority's faith. Yet presidents Carranza (1917–20) and Alvaro Obregón (1920–24) preferred not to enforce the Constitution's anticlerical provisions in order to preserve social peace. Obregón did punish perceived Catholic provocations, but he preferred moderate, measured secularization to incendiary direct attacks.

During the early 1920s, the Church set out to recover its influence over everyday life by reviving social institutions and official lay groups.[13] President Plutarco Elías (1924–28) broke Obregón's tacit truce with the Church and urged governors to enforce Article 130 of the Constitution by drafting state-level ley de cultos. These anticlerical regulations imperiled the Church's postrevolutionary recovery and outraged Catholics. Bishops protested by declaring a sacramental strike in mid-1926. In the Bajío (and elsewhere), some Catholics took up arms. Although Rome and some bishops hesitated to condemn the insurgency, their eventual loss of authority and the human cost of the conflict led them to seek an end to the war.

The *Arreglos* (arrangements) that ended the Cristiada (Cristero War) fell far short of the victory cristeros craved. From the state's perspective, the Arreglos settled the religious question once and for all: Mexico would be secular, and the state would no longer meddle in the Church's internal affairs. In return, the Church would suppress the cristeros and support the government. Initially, the ruling revolutionary party seemed anxious to reconcile with Catholics. With the apparent approval of Calles, now the country's ultimate executive as jefe máximo, interim president Emilio Portes Gil (1928–

30) nullified the most restrictive elements of anticlerical legislation.[14] His successor, Pascual Ortiz Rubio (1930–32), called upon all citizens, regardless of ideology, to join the ranks of the ruling party, the PNR. This left the door open politically to Catholics.[15] In January 1930, speculation mounted that Catholics would even take seats in congress.[16]

The Mexican episcopate's co-leaders—the archbishop of Mexico City, Pascual Díaz, and the papal delegate and archbishop of Morelia, Leopoldo Ruiz—signed the Arreglos over the objections of hard-line Catholics and a few bishops.[17] Now, with peace secure, Díaz and Ruiz seemed inclined to accept the regime's discreet overtures as a way of broadening the Church's influence in the political sphere. Archbishop Díaz's Christmas 1930 pastoral instructed Catholics to convince "competent authorities" to rescind anticlerical legislation. It reminded them to act as individual citizens exercising their civil rights and not as a Catholic bloc.[18]

Maintaining this blurry boundary between citizenship and creed mattered. The Church had long seen direct involvement in elections as politically risky and potentially corrupting of Catholic leaders.[19] The Constitution still prohibited all political activity by religious organizations, and clergy could be legally prosecuted for such violations. Archbishop Ruiz lamented in 1935 that the Church had "been deprived of all power."[20] In the eyes of the prelates, however, separation of Church and state was only relative. Their reading of the Constitution allowed Church representatives to encourage Catholics to participate in politics as citizens as long as the Church stopped short of directly endorsing candidates.[21] To influence politics legally, the Church sanctioned civic action: the education of Catholics as individual citizens without formal, explicit Church direction.[22]

The institutional Church fully expected that Catholic citizens would be guided by clergy, shaped by parochial education, and informed by the ACM. Civic action stressed defending parental control over children's education, protecting private property rights, and demanding freedom of religion. Catholics would vote as citizens to support candidates who opposed not just anticlericalism, but also key elements of the revolutionary project such as ejidos, federalization of schools, and left-leaning unions. Although priests had to remain "outside and above all political action," the laity would act decisively in elections and protests "inside the limits of Catholic morality."[23] Through this "licit" (peaceful, legal, moral) civic action, the Church would settle the religious question by persuading civil society to reject the revolutionary project. Ortiz Rubio's invitation to Catholics to resume their place in public life gave the Church a golden opportunity to do just that.

Revolutionaries, particularly those close to Calles, saw Catholic civic action after the Arreglos as pure Jesuitical perfidy. They feared Catholics would use the ballot box to win what the cristeros had lost on the battlefield. By 1931, the charge of crypto-Catholicism was a point of contention in a bitter dispute within the ruling party between Calles's supporters (Reds) and partisans of President Ortiz Rubio (Whites). The Reds alleged the Whites were betraying the Revolution by allying with the Church. The example of fiery anticlerical governor Tomás Garrido Canabal of Tabasco nudged other governors to pass harsh new legislation on the Church. With Calles's tacit support, in mid-1931 the Reds toppled White governors in Jalisco and Durango. The message from Mexico City was clear: governors who failed to zealously enforce anticlerical legislation would be next.[24] When the Church ostentatiously celebrated the four hundredth anniversary of the Virgin of Guadalupe's first miracle on December 12, 1931, the Reds blamed Ortiz Rubio and the Whites.[25] The Arreglos that apparently had resolved the religious question were unraveling, and another Church-state confrontation loomed.

The new wave of revolutionary anticlericalism was not just orchestrated from above. It welled up from the ruling party's base, too. Key leaders in the SEP, the federal army and other agencies, civilian politicos, and *agrarista* (recipients of or petitioners for land grants from the federal government) and labor leaders advocated a hard line. In September 1932, Calles finally replaced Ortiz Rubio with a trusted military man and millionaire, General Abelardo Rodríguez. While personally no radical, Rodríguez took a tougher stance than Ortiz Rubio on the religious question.[26] The new president supported stricter anticlerical education and threatened to oust governors gone soft on the Church.[27]

In retaliation, Pope Pius XI's angry encyclical *Acerba Animi* (September 1932) accused the state of duplicity and tyranny and called on Mexicans to "continue defending the sacrosanct rights of the Church." President Rodríguez exiled Archbishop Ruiz, and many state governments passed their own tough new ley de cultos.[28] By early 1935, only four or five of Mexico's thirty-four bishops were still in their dioceses, and hundreds of priests had fled or gone into hiding.[29]

Renewed anticlericalism roiled regional politics. Governors had to stiffen anticlerical regulations or risk their own removal, yet many relied on Catholic votes. As one U.S. consul put it in 1931, "It may be good politics in Mexico City to attack an official for sympathy to the Church but it is poor politics in Durango. . . . The recent charges against [Governor] Valdez as a church sympathizer will almost certainly force Church feeling to become an element in local politics."[30] The adoption of socialist education in late 1933 further inflamed Catholics by tasking schools with eradicating "fanaticism" —roughly defined as superstitious, unpatriotic, wasteful, and backward. In July 1934, Calles visited Guadalajara and called for a Psychological Revolution to make socialist education mandatory and defanaticize Mexico's youth.

Catholics, already alarmed by coeducation, feared that the new curriculum included sexual education.[31] In hindsight, such concerns seem greatly exaggerated; in 1932, the prospect was dashed by a huge wave of Catholic demonstrations. Even in officially atheist Tabasco, teachers steered clear of it.[32] Nevertheless, Catholics were convinced socialist education would lead to the sexual abuse of children.[33] Conservative newspapers in Mexico City often printed lurid tales of teachers promoting nude sunbathing and worse.[34] Such narratives reflected widespread anxiety regarding the dissolution of parents' authority over children, teachers' authority over students, and even men's authority over women.[35] In fact, almost all federal teachers supported the patriarchal family structure (including the glorification of motherhood) and discouraged free unions outside of marriage.[36] Catholic anxiety about sex in the federal classroom was not entirely specious, however.

Socialist education seemed to pose an existential threat for many Catholics. For some, it justified a second insurgency. According to David Raby, during the 1930s segunderos (Catholic combatants in the Segunda) killed three hundred federal teachers.[37] As with most insurgencies, we do not know for sure when the Segunda began or ended. Especially in parts of the Bajío region, some cristeros never laid down their arms, and others accepted amnesty in 1929 only to take up arms again against socialist education in the 1930s. Some of these recristeros fought until the early 1940s.[38] The Segunda peaked in early 1935, coinciding with the strictest anticlerical restrictions and the rancor provoked by socialist education.[39] Too weak and disorganized to capture strategic targets or wage set-piece battles, the segunderos fought a classic guerrilla war: opportunistically congregating into larger bands, they swarmed isolated federal schools or ejidos, then dispersed into the surrounding civilian population before government forces arrived. Only a handful of segunda leaders campaigned continuously or commanded more than a few dozen men: Lauro Rocha in the Altos of Jalisco; José Velasco in Aguascalientes;

Enríque "El Tallarín" Rodríguez in Morelos and Puebla; and Trinidad Mora, Florencio Estrada, and Federico Vasquez in Durango's rugged Mezquital.[40]

Was the Segunda a Catholic insurgency? Its would-be national command, the EPL (Ejército Popular Libertador, or Popular Liberating Army), its self-appointed civilian front, the LNDL (Liga Nacional Defensora de la Libertad), and Rocha all denied it.[41] However, segunderos could not fight without Catholic support, their proclamations echoed Catholic dogma of natural rights, and their discourse mirrored Catholic fears of revolutionary tyranny.[42] Because these connections endangered the Arreglos and their own authority, Díaz and Ruiz marginalized the LNDL and punished any clergy and lay leaders linked to the revolt.[43] The Church, however, refused to condemn individual segundero combatants. For instance, Archbishop Ruiz rejected another Cristero War in November 1934, but the next month he said of violence that "neither the Episcopate nor the Clergy ought to meddle in it, either by promoting it or prohibiting it."[44] The Vatican seemed even more ambiguous. In March 1937, Pope Pius XI wrote that citizens could not passively submit to assaults on basic religious liberties. Still, the pontiff barred both clergy and official lay groups from supporting the Segunda and warned that violence must be proportionate and cause more good than harm.[45]

What explains this contradictory position of condemning the Segunda and all Church involvement in it while refusing to condemn segunderos? The first pastoral letter (April 12, 1936) of José Garibi Rivera, moderate archbishop of Guadalajara, offers some insight. He forbade his priests and official lay groups from "taking part in either warlike or political activities, but as to violent resistance to evil, [this] author prays he will not incite anyone but it is beyond his mission to say whether it is licit or not." He went on to add that socialist education was "pagan" and "immoral and shameful," and that its spread was "rooting out the faith from the hearts and minds of both teachers and pupils."[46] On the one hand, the Church hierarchy hoped to preserve the Arreglos to prevent renewed anticlerical legislation or another Cristiada as well as retain a modicum of control over radicals in both the clergy and laity. On the other hand, Church dogma stated individuals could defend their natural rights by force as a last resort. For the Church, socialist education threatened one of the most precious of natural rights: that of parents to religiously educate their children.

To channel resistance to socialist education in a nonviolent direction, the Mexican episcopate under Díaz and Ruiz sought to mobilize widespread, peaceful civil protests without running afoul of constitutional prohibitions.

To that end, in 1934 Díaz secretly ordered priests to covertly use Catholic Action as well as other (unspecified) groups to organize boycotts of any school that adopted the controversial new methods.[47] This campaign against socialist education was in full swing when a dramatic shift in national politics seemed to rescind Callista anticlericalism.

In June 1935, President Lázaro Cárdenas broke with his former mentor Calles and distanced himself from some of the jefe máximo's strongest anticlerical policies. Cárdenas pointedly removed Tomás Garrido Canabal, Mexico's greatest anticlerical, from his cabinet. Perhaps in response, in January 1936 the Church stopped threatening to excommunicate parents who sent children to SEP schools. At the same time, Díaz called for strengthening boycotts to defeat socialist education once and for all. The episcopal leadership also reached out to the working class "to counter the modern errors."[48] In other words, the Church called on Cárdenas to nullify every state's ley de cultos, end state-sponsored anticlericalism, and entirely remove socialist education from the SEP curriculum. It also planned to mobilize the working class against revolutionary corporatism.

For his part, Cárdenas delayed decisively resolving the religious question, although in early 1936 the president strongly hinted that he would abandon the most extreme forms of Callista anticlericalism. In February 1936, Cárdenas supported defanaticization while calling for respect for religious beliefs.[49] On March 4, 1936, Cárdenas returned to Guadalajara, where Calles had called for a Psychological Revolution, and criticized the jefe máximo as strident and narrow-minded: "the government shall not incur the error of previous administrations by treating the religious question as the preeminent problem that subordinates other aspects of the program of the Revolution."[50] This seemingly marked a turning point in Church-state relations. A few days later, on March 9, 1936, Catholics occupied and reopened many churches. Cárdenas ordered no action be taken to dislodge them.[51] The president would later say his official policy all along had been to let the local situation dictate the outcome of the religious question in each state.[52] International pressure might well have played a role in his decision.[53] In any event, during 1936 and 1937 Church-state tension slowly lessened on the national level.

Cárdenas continued to be cautious in directly addressing the still touchy religious question, in spite of consistent demands from Catholics for more concessions. A missive from Chihuahua's faithful in March 1936 spoke for many: "the Catholic pueblo anxiously awaits the liberty of religion offered by you."⁵⁴ Yet Cárdenas refused to remove objectionable constitutional amendments, merely calling for the harshest anticlerical legislation passed by the states to be modified.⁵⁵ The bloody events in Ciudad González, Guanajuato, in March 1936 (see chapter 5) forced Cárdenas to move a bit quicker. Following Cárdenas's cues, the Supreme Court struck down Chihuahua's strict ley de cultos in 1937, and it granted a stay against Campeche's in November 1938. This led to the slow and uneven nullification of some state and federal anticlerical legislation.⁵⁶ In another important decision, Cárdenas permitted parochial schools to legally operate on January 10, 1938, reversing SEP policy that had long riled Catholics.⁵⁷

Still, many Catholics blamed the president for dawdling and even duplicity.⁵⁸ On a deeper level, Cárdenas never abandoned Calles's goal of defanaticizing Mexico; instead, he rejected Calles's means as counterproductive. Indeed, Cárdenas's expansion of agrarian reform and the SEP, support for organized labor, toleration of the Communist Party, and state-directed mobilization of youth and women would thwart the Church's own social project; Cardenismo conflicted with Catholic values of private property, patriarchy, and parental control over education. In April 1937, the president stated that "the salvation of the Indian lies in the school, not the church."⁵⁹ Still, Cárdenas firmly rejected direct confrontation with the Church. Regionally, from mid-1935 to the end of his term, the president's allies displaced the most radical Callista anticlericals in part by tapping Catholic support. On this basis, the president and the institutional Church uneasily shared common ground.

For its part, the institutional Church quickly and positively responded to Cárdenas's conciliatory gestures without forgetting its opposition to much of the revolutionary project. When Díaz died in May 1936, Rome replaced him with Luis María Martínez. He hailed from Cárdenas's home state of Michoacán and got on well with the president personally. Under Martínez, the Mexican bishops supported Cárdenas's March 1938 nationalization of foreign oil, refused to back Saturnino Cedillo's coup in 1938, and declined to endorse Almazán's challenge to the ruling party in the 1940 presidential election.⁶⁰ By proclaiming that he was a *creyente* (believer), Manuel Ávila Camacho (1940–46) became the first openly Catholic president since the Revolution; his simple statement ended the religious question for many. In fact, many of Ávila Camacho's policies echoed the Church's calls for social harmony.⁶¹

During the last half of the Cárdenas administration, many localities did indeed witness a harmonious resolution of the religious question. Luis González y González's microhistory of San José de Gracia, Michoacán, recounts Lázaro Cárdenas's triumphant visit in 1937. The much beloved padre of San José, Father Federico, united agraristas and Catholic foes to welcome the president. Cárdenas and Father Federico embraced and went arm in arm into a private meeting that lasted over an hour.⁶² Only a closer look at a broader sample of communities and states can establish the extent of reconciliation, however. Moreover, to fully understand Catholics' reaction to the revolutionary project during the 1930s, we must account for the deep divisions within the Church.

Inside the Church: Actors and Interests

Let us start at the top. At the apex of the Church hierarchy in Mexico sat thirty-four archbishops and bishops.⁶³ Compared to their nineteenth-century predecessors, they were younger, better educated, and (for the most part) graduates from Rome's Pío Latino College and therefore much more closely attuned to the Vatican's message.⁶⁴ While all Mexican, they tended to hail from the Bajío, the west-central region long noted for its Hispanic culture and mestizo ethnicity. More than a few were sons of European migrants, and many were related to other priests, nuns, and bishops. The saintly bishop of Veracruz, Rafael Guízar y Valencia, hailed from the Abajense city of Cotija, Jalisco. Thanks to his mother, he grew up fasting twice weekly and saying the rosary every night. Bishop Guízar's famous kin included José M. González Valencia, bishop of Durango, and his nephew, Luis Guízar Barragán, bishop of Campeche and Saltillo. A female relative founded the Guadalupanas de Cristo Sacerdote, and his oldest sister, Maura Guízar Valencia, was beatified.⁶⁵ Martín Tritschler y Córdoba, archbishop of Yucatán (1900–42), was born to another clerical dynasty, this time in Puebla: brother Guillermo became bishop of San Luis Potosí and then of Monterrey.⁶⁶

In spite of these common bonds, the bishops had been divided by the Cristero War. Except for a few doves like Tritschler, many bishops chafed at Díaz and Ruiz's policy of moderation after the Arreglos.⁶⁷ For embittered cristeros and their sympathizers, José de Jesús Manríquez was the Bishop of the People, while Díaz and the pacific archbishop Martin Tritschler of Yucatán were *comodines* (sellouts), *gobiernistas* (pro-government), or just plain cowards.⁶⁸ The Segunda reopened these internal rifts in the episcopate and put bishops and priests at odds as well.

Generally speaking, priests were more likely than bishops to countenance violence; some even ministered to bands of combatants. When some Veracruz clergy threatened to do so, the bishop threatened rebels with excommunication.[69] But Father Rafael Rúa, diocesan vicar of Veracruz, and some other priests refused to sever ties with segunderos, arguing that they restrained rebels from committing atrocities.[70] In Zacatecas, the bishop threatened to excommunicate segunderos, but in 1936 a segunda leader claimed at least some clergy were helping arm their band.[71] In Durango, Father David G. Ramírez, archdiocesan secretary, wrote *la Guerra Sintética*, which glorified the Cristiada. Another *duranguense* priest, Father José Buenaventura Montoya, died while serving as chaplain to excommunicated segunderos.[72] While bishops tried to break up any ties between the institutional Church and the rebellion, a minority of priests resisted.

Clerical discipline represented a serious, persistent problem for the Church. Since the seventeenth-century Tridentine reforms, bishops had been charged with reforming their clergy.[73] Spurred by Rome, Mexico's bishops imported European and regular priests, opened new diocesan seminaries, and raised moral expectations for the clergy (honoring Lent, internalizing shame, celebrating marital responsibility). Lynch points out that Porfirian bishops were as preoccupied with pastoral visits to monitor wayward priests as they were with battling liberalism.[74]

The armed phase of the Revolution greatly complicated the task of disciplining the clergy. Ramírez Rancaño argues that when bishops returned to their dioceses in 1918, they lacked enough suitable seminary graduates. Consequently, they had to tolerate undereducated, lax priests (some autoconfirmed sacristans or acolytes) who saw the ministry not as a vocation but as a commercial venture.[75]

We still know precious little about the lives of Mexico's modern magistrates of the sacred.[76] French chargé d'affairs Ernest Lagarde filed a long, detailed letter on the sad state of the Mexican Church in 1926. He found its rural priests in miserable condition, fallen into poverty and almost entirely dependent on the upper class. Mexican priests bitterly resented the fact that the best posts—urban parishes with reliable incomes—went to foreign regulars.[77] The Cristiada's conclusion in 1929 probably bettered the Mexican priesthood's precarious condition, but bishops still relied on regulars, and demand never kept up with supply. There were four hundred Jesuit priests in Mexico in 1931, an increase of fifty since 1925.[78] In the four states examined here, however, the vast majority of priests hailed from areas close to the parishes that they served and grew up in white or mestizo landowning and commercial families.

The clergy's social origins explain in part why priests generally were so set against agrarian reform.[79] Church dogma often reinforced the political inclinations they brought to the seminary. The Church might criticize capitalism for widening class divisions and corroding morality, but it defended private property as a natural right threatened by state intervention in the economy.[80] Priests' families feared losing haciendas to agrarian reform. North American journalist Ernest Gruening reported that with a few exceptions, the clergy in the 1920s bitterly opposed agrarian reform as well as federal schooling as "socialist," "Protestant," "atheistic," "bolshevik," and "Masonic."[81] The opposition was not just ideological, social, and cultural. Agrarian reform threatened the precarious economic condition of penurious priests who depended on "voluntary" tithing.

After the nineteenth-century Reform outlawed tithes, *primacias* (customary gifts known as the first fruit), and a host of other religious taxes, they were quietly revived in some dioceses during the Porfiriato.[82] In Yucatán, for instance, magnate and governor Olegario Molina allowed the Church to collect "voluntary" tithes assessed on the new Porfirian boom crop of henequen.[83] In Jalisco, the Church's income from tithes went up two and a half times during the Porfiriato, helping the clergy buy back property lost to Benito Juárez's nineteenth-century liberal reform.[84] R. H. Tierney, U.S. spokesman for the Church in Mexico, admitted in 1914 that central Mexican farmers were expected to tithe, although he claimed that contributors decided the amount. In some dioceses, tithes supported the bishop's staff (including canons, the cathedral's priests that became key administrators), seminaries, and educational and social institutions. They also subsidized priests in poor parishes lacking sufficient sacramental fees.[85] This meant that the priests in the poorest parts of Mexico stood to lose their livelihood should agrarian reform take place, because the compliant *hacendados* (landowners) and rancheros would turn over their land to (supposedly) anticlerical ejidatarios. The institutional Church feared for its future in rural Mexico without tithing; in 1924, it instructed provincial clergy to dutifully collect tithes "with due prudence."[86]

Callista anticlericalism compounded the clergy's problems. By 1935, the state-level anticlerical legislation had legally lowered the number of priests to between 190 and 500. Of course, due to evasion and widespread toleration of unregistered priests, the actual number was much higher. During the mid-1930s, the ratio of priests to parishioners dropped from 1 per 3,400 to 1 per 5,000—about where it had been in Benito Juárez's era. In the United States the ratio in 1940 was 1:620; in Mexico during the Porfiriato it had been 1:1,600.[87]

The dearth of clergy made lay leadership all the more important. Since the late nineteenth century, the Church had counted on a cadre of trained laypeople to second the clergy. This group was, like the population of observant Catholics as a whole, predominantly female. Vatican I's emphasis on curbing male sexuality, Victorian privileging of female morality, and the elite men's retreat from the pews "feminized" the laity during the late nineteenth century.[88] The combination of modernized Marianism and social Catholicism gave "respectable" (middle- and upper-class) women new authority over the private sphere and expanded their domain from worship, charity, and education to issues like the living wage and moral conduct. Beyond this spiritual windfall, Matthew Butler sees female lay leaders gaining new access to "scarce networks of extrafamilial sociability and an organized voice in the social and political spheres by placing women in the vanguard of the postrevolutionary drive to re-Christianize the social order."[89] The Church relied on these women to mobilize and regiment the laity during the Revolution.

Even before the Revolution was over, the Church chartered the Unión de Damas Católicas Mexicanas to defend women, children, and Catholicism itself from an antagonistic state and a "pagan" popular culture. Its appeal to "the High and Sublime Mission of Mothers of Families" mainly honored patrician women.[90] At about the same time their male counterparts, the Knights of Columbus, as well as the ACJM were founded. Together, these three groups were to re-Christianize Mexico by countering the revolutionary project.[91]

On Christmas Eve 1929 the Damas, Knights, and ACJM were folded into the Acción Católica Mexicana (ACM), an umbrella group for all official lay organizations.[92] The episcopal leadership hoped centralization of lay organizations would prevent another Cristero War. The chieftain of LNDL, Miguel Palomar y Vizcaya, was outraged. Given the "state of war between Jesus Christ and Satan," Palomar fumed, prohibiting violence "mutilated" the ACM—"they might as well call it Catholic Inaction."[93]

Besides catechization and social works, the ACM was charged with implementing the doctrine of civic action. Ideologically, ACM resolutely rejected agrarian reform but restricted itself to purely rhetorical warnings about capitalism's excesses. True, social Catholicism placed the social utility above the natural right of private property in theory, but its main message was one of social harmony, mutual aid, and material and moral self-improvement.[94]

The ACM absorbed a host of organizations ranging from Sacred Heart popular libraries to the Scouts (their motto: "piety, order, discipline, brotherhood, cleanliness, bravery, loyalty, honor and faithfulness"). In fact, many supposedly subordinate groups retained a great deal of autonomy throughout the decade of the 1930s.[95] The ACM's three pillars were the Damas, now rechristened the Unión Feminina Católica Mexicana (UFCM, Union of Mexican Catholic Women); the ACJM; and the Knights of Columbus (now the Unión de Católicos Mexicanos, or UCM). A fourth group rounded out the ACM: the newly minted Association of Mexican Catholic Young Women (Juventud Católica Femenina Mexicana, or JCFM.) Judging by 1925 national enrollments for Damas Católicas (23,000), Knights of Columbus (5,000), and the ACJM (7,000), the ACM was still a largely female-dominated organization.[96] Indeed, high clergy fully expected women to take the lead; the men never really caught up.[97]

In most dioceses, the ACM struggled until the end of the 1930s. An inspector of virtually all its chapters found "some good (Mexico City, Guadalajara, San Luis Potosí, Aguascalientes, León), others mediocre, the rest failures."[98] In 1933, the ACM ran smoothly in only ten dioceses, faced considerable problems in six more, was still embryonic in seven, and did not exist at all in eight.[99] Persecution by government authorities explains many of its woes. The Cristiada had taken a real toll on the ACM's three key forerunners: the Damas, the ACJM, and the Knights. Together they lost half of their membership during the war, and fourteen of the thirty-two Damas regional centers had to close.[100] Calles's Psychological Revolution renewed harassment in the mid-1930s. Around November 1934, official ACM publications were censored for at least six months, and the Church suspended the training of new activists; many leaders and even rank-and-file members of the ACM were arrested. At this point, the national ACM admitted it had yet to be organized in most dioceses, and most Catholics did not comprehend its mission.[101]

Even after systematic state suppression eased in late 1935, serious internal problems persisted. Because the Damas, ACJM, and Knights chapters had strong esprit de corps, many of their members resented their merger into the bland, centralized ACM. The Knights/UCM suffered the most and never fully recovered during the 1930s.[102] In the episcopate's eyes, the ACJM remained suspect because of its links to the Cristeros; in 1934, Archbishop Díaz worried that the ACM could not prevent the ACJM from backing segunderos.[103] The Damas/UFCM fared best, but it too chafed under ACM control. In Morelia, the UFCM's *señora presidenta* was an admirable administrator, but she repeatedly clashed with the ACM's regional leader, who happened to be her husband. Meanwhile, the ACJM there had been in open revolt against the ACM and its own chaplain for most of the 1930s.[104]

Tensions between the clergy and the laity in the ACM were not confined to this archdiocese. Catholic Action's vertical, pyramidal structure was to promote priestly influence and proper training of the laity, but many bishops failed to appoint and support the *asistentes eclesiásticos* (chaplain/guides) required at the national, regional (diocesan), and local (parochial) levels.[105] Luis Bustos complained that lay leaderships were paralyzed because they had to "wait for directions of the chaplains, which is a mistake."[106]

The ACM intended to restore the Church's influence over the rural and urban poor. Here, too, there were a number of daunting challenges. In 1933, the ACM's national magazine urged outreach to ejidatarios' children, now estranged from the Church.[107] This in turn meant bridging a social and at times ethnic gap, as the ACM recruited mainly from the nonindigenous middle and upper classes. The social origins of its membership reflected institutional guidelines (members had to be literate and pay considerable dues), and unintentionally encouraged the Church's retreat from social justice.[108] While the Church nurtured the ACM, a Catholic federation of trade unions all but disintegrated in the 1930s.[109] With its emphasis on social harmony, it rejected any discussion of economic fairness, even the eight-hour workday.[110]

This elite bent put the ACM at a disadvantage, because its schools, charitable missions, and cooperatives were intended to undermine the revolutionary project's popular appeal. The UFCM, by far the most important branch of the ACM, opened night and Sunday schools for "servants or female workers" to better themselves and earn more. This would keep women away from SEP schools, which endangered "customary morality." Learning reading, writing, math, religion, and home economics would help them "make the house attractive . . . for working families . . . harmed by disorderliness." The ideal teacher of servants was none other than their employer: "the señora . . . with love for this other social class so despised today, the workers."[111] Because "respectable" women did not work in the formal economy, the UFCM/Damas's organizational matrix reflected a gendered and hierarchical social order: sewing workshops to help clothe the poor and catechism classes for the unlettered.[112]

However, the revolutionary project's anticlericalism so antagonized poor Catholics that the UFCM cadre could mobilize cross-class coalitions in many communities. Moreover, Kristina Boylan's work on UFCM cadres in Jalisco convincingly rejects the idea that its activists were reactionary or victims of false consciousness. Their activism ruptured conservative boundaries limiting women to auxiliary status. And they were imbued with a new sense of social mission that managed to meet the real needs of many members of underprivileged groups in spite of the ACM's condescending discourse.[113] Rome itself encouraged the Damas to reach out to peasants and workers by adopting a new strategy for the entire ACM, one that moved away from a carefully organized, vertically controlled model to a looser, horizontal confederation of more autonomous groups.

The Radial Strategy

The Damas/UFCM chapters were scattered bright spots in the otherwise dark picture of the ACM during most of the 1930s. The combination of state harassment, internal tensions, clerical indifference, and uneven social support (the gender gap, class and ethnic tensions) hindered its growth. The Church hierarchs and key lay organizers like Luis G. Bustos needed to overcome these shortcomings to mobilize a broad cross section of civil society. Making a virtue out of necessity, they relaxed the formal, top-down structure of the ACM. Instead, they relied on decentralized, informal cells—directed when possible by priests—to mobilize the Catholic base and escape the state's supervisions. In August 1934, Archbishop Díaz ordered priests to use the ACM and other, unspecified lay organizations to mobilize *el campo civico* (civil society).[114] In 1937, Pope Pius XI himself recognized this strategy when he called on Mexico's ACM to serve as a "radial center of light" coordinating "other initiatives" to defend the family and "public morality." These auxiliary Catholic groups, such as parents' associations, according to the pope, deserved "a just autonomy and fitting liberty of action necessary to accomplish their specific aims."[115] Mexico represented another opportunity to refine this strategy of decentralized resistance first tested in Italy, where Leo XIII's social Catholicism created a "dense set of capillary networks that mirrored—and sapped the strength from—secular institutions."[116]

By acting as the hub for supposedly independent front groups, the Church could mobilize society against SEP schools without risk of reprisal and coopt existing, spontaneously formed popular groups. Camacho Sandoval's perceptive study of the campaign against socialist education in the Bajío state of Aguascalientes shows it was led not by priests but by "communications networks among relatively autonomous Catholic groups." This weblike structure allowed Catholics not only to run "home schools" and coordinate attendance strikes, but also to shelter fugitive priests and persuade Catholic workers to reject unions.[117]

Attempting to rein in these grassroots mobilizations, the Church revived a religious equivalent of the Parent-Teacher Association in the United States, the Union Nacional de Padres de la Familia (UNPF). Founded by the Knights of Columbus to defend parochial schools against the Constitution of 1917, the UNPF declined in influence after Carranza and Obregón largely acceded to its demands. It helped mobilize Catholics against Calles's anticlericalism in 1926. In early 1934, the UNPF threatened a national attendance strike and "economic and social boycott" of SEP educators to halt any discussion of sexual education. The national daily *Excelsior*'s coverage popularized the idea of truancy strikes and shunning teachers, turning a bluff into a template for future mass action.[118] In public discourse, the UNPF obscured its link to the Church and reached out to moderates in the revolutionary camp by invoking the liberal notion of freedom of conscience.[119]

Thousands of parents' groups sprang up in a kind of viral campaign in response to controversy over sexual education and the adoption of socialist education. Clandestine cells probably existed in most towns by 1935.[120] The press, homilies, and rumors, not the ACM's organization matrix, spread the Church's message. However, the literate, socially advantaged leadership that captained civic organizations covertly linked to the Church channeled popular mobilizations. Due to the fact that parents' groups claimed to be secular elements in civil society, the two most respected national daily papers, *Excelsior* and *El Universal*, covered their activities and spread parts of their message without risking governmental reprisals. The tabloid press in Mexico City went even further: in October, *Omega* published a UNPF declaration strongly criticizing the new curriculum; *El Hombre Libre* denounced socialist education as one step on the road to state tyranny.[121]

The widely circulated booklet *A Fact, A Secret, A Danger!* exemplified the propaganda campaign waged by Catholic parents' groups against the SEP. It targeted the key constituency of the Church's radial strategy, elite matrons ("Read it to your husband, your children, and all your servants!"). *A Fact, a Secret, a Danger!* claimed socialist education was part of a global Communist plot, calling Mexico the Russia of the Americas. Behind it all lurked the shadowy (and apocryphal) Atheist Apostles.[122] By conflating socialist education with sexual education, *A Fact, a Secret, a Danger!* raised the specter of the seduction of innocent children in the SEP classroom.[123]

Alarmist propaganda like this energized the radial strategy by stimulating truancy campaigns against federal schools among all social classes. Yet this strategy had its drawbacks. It is debatable whether the institutional Church exercised much control at all over the UNPF on the grassroots level. Unlike the ACM, the UNPF had no clerical commissars to guide it, train its leadership, vet its propaganda, or approve its tactics. Murky organizational structures further complicated the institutional Church's attempts to oversee parents' groups. A plethora of such Catholic parents' groups operated under a variety of designations. In the state of Mexico, for instance, the UNPF operated as the Unión de Madres de Familia (Union of Mothers).[124] Nationally, the Church supposedly merged the UNPF with the Asociación Nacional de Padres de Familia (ANPF, or National Association of Parents), subordinating both to the ACM upon the foundation of the latter in 1929.[125] To further muddy the waters, the UNPF had links to the shadowy Asociación Nacional para Libertad de Enseñanza (ANPLE, or National Association for Freedom in Teaching), which operated at times under other names and had links to the pro-Segunda LNDL, which had been proscribed by the bishops.[126] This confusing multitude of groups all claimed to have Church sanction, and they all mimicked the UNPF's tactics. They distributed information door-to-door and kept teachers under surveillance to detect leftist ideas or any hint of sexual education. If warranted, they organized attendance strikes, encouraged the faithful to shun foes, and set up "home schools."

The radial strategy also stimulated two phenomena that deeply preoccupied the institutional Church: segunda violence and the conversion of Catholic leaders into electoral brokers. On the first count, these cells' autonomy and the virulence of antisocialist education sentiment contributed to the Segunda. Many of the men and women involved in defensive segunda violence were part of some of the groups mobilized and motivated by the radial strategy. In some cases, participants in offensive segunda violence were probably part of Catholic networks mobilized by the radial strategy as well. Paradoxically, even as the ACM sought to expel segunderos from lay organizations, the radial strategy opened a back door for them.

Similarly, the radial strategy undermined Church prohibitions on electoral activity by Catholic lay leaders and organizations. Jesuit Miguel Dario Miranda, the ACM's first chaplain, stated unequivocally that "Catholic Action is completely out of politics," and the ACM instructed its local organizers in 1940 to steer clear of discussing electoral politics to "avoid confusion."[127] But the ACM never really was in a position to enforce these norms until the late 1930s, and their impact was at best equivocal. Roberto Blancarte found that in the 1940s, Catholic activists skirted the ACM's prohibition on electoral activity as part of "double militancy," resigning from the ACM temporarily to take part in politics.[128] When ACM leaders participated in clandestine task forces opposing SEP schools, evasion of Church restrictions against electioneering was even easier. For example, in 1935 the UNPF in Nieves, Zacatecas, was accused of "twisting its noble mission of education to do politics," throwing its lot in with "politicians always hunting for opportunities."[129] The pervasiveness of this double militancy becomes evident only when we closely examine regional politics.

The Religious Geography of Mexico: Levitical and Otherwise

Adoption of the radial strategy and the spread of the UNPF and parallel groups changed the way Catholics responded to the revolutionary project. Geography also shaped their reaction. While Mexico of the 1930s was a Catholic nation, not all regions were Catholic in the same way. The center-west Bajío has long enjoyed a reputation for exceptionally strong Catholic belief; Carlos Monsiváis calls it the Rosary Belt. Catholics in Rosary Belt states like Querétaro and Jalisco are known for their exceptional religious fervor, and they generally followed the orthodox liturgical practices endorsed by the institutional Church, as opposed to syncretic or folk traditions with strong indigenous and African strains.[130] Jean Meyer argued that in contrast, the north was a focus of North American imports like Protestantism, freemasonry, and other anti-Catholic ideas.[131] Catholic chronicler Antonio Rius worried that Gulf ports like Tampico were centers of "pleasure and perversion."[132] These salient geographical variations profoundly shaped the religious question.

Alan Knight argued that local variations in religious history, such as the degree of the Church's Porfirian recovery, rank among the most important predictors of regional receptiveness to the revolutionary project. In general, the more *mocho* (religiously observant) highlands proved more obstinate, while the less devout lowlands proved more fertile ground for teachers and agraristas.[133] Knight noted the need to go beyond these generalities to look at local variations. I use the term *levitical* to describe communities where the institutional Church still educated future elites, standardized religious practice, instilled obedience to clerical authority, and insured that Catholicism was still deeply ingrained in everyday life, present in everything from bell-ringing to popular processions in public space.[134]

Identifying regions as levitical, however, is not always so easy. Roberto Blancarte, examining the circulation of *Cultura Cristiana*, a four-page magazine spreading the Church's doctrine, cites it as a rough proxy for the Church's strength in 1942. Most went to just three foci: Mexico City (27,000 copies), the dioceses of the Rosary Belt (11,600 in Guadalajara; 8,000 in Morelia; and 4,400 in León), and Puebla (8,000), while less than 500 each circulated in the northwestern (Sinaloa, Sonora) and Gulf and southern (Campeche, Yucatán, Chiapas, Huajuapan, Papantla, Tehuantepec) dioceses.[135] The general pattern was confirmed by ACM lay commissioner J. M. Maya's 1944 report on the number of lay people it took to support each priest. The highest ratio of parishioners to priests was found in Chiapas (24,529 lay people per priest), Huejutla (23,684:1), Tehuantepec (20,000:1), Sinaloa (18,954:1), Sonora (13,454:1), Tamaulipas (10,282:1), and Campeche (9,378:1).[136] Less levitical regions tended to have younger, and generally speaking poorer, dioceses. Of the eight new dioceses created in booming Porfirian peripheries in 1891, only Colima, Nayarit, and Chihuahua inherited strong administrative infrastructures; the new dioceses of Saltillo, Sinaloa, Tehuantepec (southern Veracruz), Cuernavaca, and Tabasco had weak institutional foundations, as did that of Campeche, created four years later.[137] Within these larger subnational patterns, geographer Moisés de la Peña pointed out a gap between the more levitical towns and the wayward countryside. By comparing births to parents married in Church to births to couples living together in *uniones libres* (free unions) in 1939, he found cities more levitical than the countryside (15 percent children born to uniones libres versus 35.5 percent born to parents married).[138]

Conclusion

There was no single Church in Mexico; clergy high and low, lay leaders both formal and informal, clashed with each other as well as with agents of the revolutionary state. Tension between levitical and folk/syncretic Catholicism remained unresolved. Rather than fracturing the Church along these old fault lines, the revolutionary project tended to unite Catholics. As demonstrated in chapter 2, even in a quite unlevitical region like Campeche, Catholic sentiment and Catholic forms of sociability frustrated attempts at revolutionary transformation. At the same time, the institutional Church had few means to shape regional outcomes because the radial strategy undermined institutional control of the grassroots.

CHAPTER 2

Catholic-Socialists against Anti-Priests in Campeche

In late May 1934, revolutionary politicos and federal teachers inaugurated Nunkiní's newly restored *plaza principal*.[1] For months, Mayan peasants had rebuilt curbs and gardens, drained standing water, and weeded the town square to promote public health, instill orderliness, and encourage civic pride.[2] Teachers planned a simple event to celebrate. Young and old from Nunkiní and nearby villages recited poetry and performed music. Speakers lauded the Revolution, and a few probably attacked fanaticism. Suddenly, a rainstorm blew up. Because the crowd was too large to take shelter in the town hall, leaders of the assembly demanded that town officials turn over keys to the church, which had been recently closed under Campeche's ley de cultos.[3]

Once inside, revolutionary politicians and *maestros rurales* (rural teachers in SEP service) ritually assaulted Catholicism. Some donned clerical vestments and mounted the pulpit to shout anticlerical slogans. To the tune of "The International," others began smashing icons. Most peasants, however, left the sanctuary. Some went to rouse their neighbors to defend the church. Catholics later claimed that Nunkiní's population peacefully surrounded the building and respectfully asked the intruders to leave. Teachers claimed an angry mob burst through the door and chased them out. In any event, iconoclasm provoked widespread indignation among many *campechanos*, and only federal soldiers' presence protected maestros from violent reprisals.

Campeche was among Mexico's least levitical states.[4] Yet the Nunkiní incident helped unite Catholics and Socialist caciques (petty bosses) of the nominally revolutionary Partido Socialista Agrario (Socialist Agrarian Party, hereafter PSA) against the revolutionary project.[5] To understand the religious question in Campeche, I start by explaining why federal teachers directly attacked Catholicism, then examine their revolutionary alternative. Supplanting syncretic Catholicism, however, required the cooperation of Campeche's regional politicos. In the following two sections, I explore their contradictory stance on the religious question and the subregional variations between north and south.[6] In spite of the Church's profound institutional weakness in Campeche, Catholicism was deeply embedded in regional symbolic systems and socioeconomic structure. This gave the revolutionary project's foes a crucial advantage in the watershed 1935 gubernatorial election, as I show in the next section. I then turn to the Church in Campeche, exploring its counterintuitive combination of bureaucratic weaknesses and popular support. I conclude by explaining the Socialist-Catholic alliance's legacy, which both frustrated the SEP's revolutionary project and undermined the institutional Church.

The SEP and the Revolutionary Project in Campeche, 1934–1935

Nunkiní's ill-fated *quemasantos* (saint burning) marked the first stage of an ambitious plan to radically transform northern Campeche into a revolutionary laboratory. Federal teachers focused on the poor southeastern state for a number of reasons. The SEP perceived the state as only nominally Catholic because of Maya syncretism and the Church's regional debility.[7] A conservative national paper called Campeche the "eternal bulwark of Liberalism" in late 1934.[8] Indeed, since the mid-nineteenth century, institutional Catholicism had been in decline in Campeche.[9] It seemed particularly weak in Nunkiní, the cradle of the PSA. Fernando Enrique Angli Lara, a key organizer of the cultural conference, was the party's midwife.[10]

As a federal congressman, Angli Lara also helped craft the constitutional reforms adopting socialist education.[11] Under the new pedagogical doctrine, the maestro would oversee a structural and cultural transformation by organizing ejidos, unions, and cooperatives. In the words of Mary Kay Vaughan, "the educators' notion of modern Mexico appeared to be the antithesis of indigenous society, which was seen as insular, religious, and subsistence-oriented, abjuring the modern market and the Patria."[12] To implement this revolutionary transformation, SEP doctrine stressed defanaticization: the elimination of backward, wasteful, and irrational religious practices. Nevertheless, the SEP expected its teachers to refrain from attacking Catholicism per se. The long-serving director of the SEP in Campeche, Claudio Cortés, however, believed that "the liberation of the peasant" demanded defanaticization.[13] For Cortés and many of his cadre, the noble goal of freeing peasants justified direct attacks on Catholic belief and symbols.

The SEP project in Campeche was unusually ambitious, in part because its leadership was exceptionally radical, well resourced, and competent compared to the national educational bureaucracy as a whole. Before 1934, inspectors had come up through the ranks after accruing years of experience. Rapid growth in the SEP, however, forced it to increase the inspector corps from 209 in 1934 to 349 in late 1935, and the ratio of teachers per inspector grew rapidly as well. As a result, inspectors had to dispense rudimentary in-service training to their teachers, who usually lacked a normal degree—some only had a few years of schooling.[14] In the mid-1930s, pay for *maestros rurales* was dismally low, only sixty cents per day, contributing to an annual turnover rate of 40 percent.[15] Across Mexico, the SEP's apostolic aspirations were undermined by a multitude of mundane problems: newly minted inspectors and superintendents lacked local knowledge, woefully underqualified maestros often did not stick out the school year, and state and local officials refused to help.

In Campeche, however, the SEP's leadership and teachers alike were largely homegrown, unusually long-serving, and exceptionally leftist. Native son Cortés served as federal superintendent of Campeche for years on end in spite of the SEP policy of annual rotation. After promotion to inspector general of the entire southeast district, he remained in the city of Campeche. Some inspectors were Maya-speaking natives of the state, making them more effective than monolingual outsiders. The SEP in Campeche could also count on the graduates of Escuela Normal Rural in Hecelchakán (hereafter ENR-H). Co-founded by Angli Lara, the ENR-H's faculty included many Communists. They mentored a cohort of young teachers whose class consciousness went hand in hand with rejection of Catholicism.[16]

The ENR-H enhanced the SEP's capacity to transform Campeche. Other factors helped, too. Historically, federalization of education had begun much earlier (1922) and advanced more quickly in Campeche than in the rest of Mexico. The SEP pumped money into the state, including substantial investments in a large network of peasant cooperatives. Campeche's state government, on the other hand, was poor and weak. Its economy collapsed with the dyewood bust around 1904 and never really recovered; modest chicle and henequen exports were declining even before the Great Depression. In 1933, the entire state budget amounted to 447,000 pesos, while the SEP's budget in Campeche was 234,000.[17] For all these reasons, the SEP enjoyed a remarkable degree of influence and authority in Campeche.

Campeche's maestros rurales had strong connections with the Garrido Canabal regime in neighboring Tabasco, a linkage that intensified their defanaticization campaign. Superintendent Luis Álvarez Barret, another ENR-H alumnus, set up a radio with loudspeaker to broadcast Garrido Canabal's speeches in Campeche's capital, and he convinced many teachers to put on the Garridista red shirt.[18] Cortés demonstrated his "complete adhesion" to Garrido Canabal by firing teachers who attended church (even for marriages) or displayed Catholic icons in their houses.[19] Angli Lara was another self-described "keen garridista." As head of the federal Ministry of Agriculture and Development in Campeche, he implemented the plans of its new secretary, Garrido Canabal. For Angli Lara, material improvements like drilling wells justified iconoclasm: "we burn saints, but we give water."[20] Garridistas in Campeche found a powerful patron in Francisco Múgica, commander of the army garrison in Campeche and Yucatán for most of 1934. Múgica had aggressively advocated for anticlericalism since the Constitutional Convention of 1916–17. Now he hoped to Tabascanize Mexico by spreading Garrido Canabal's ideas, beginning with Campeche.[21]

Tabasco's example, radical *normalistas*, and Múgica influenced federal educators in Campeche to adopt explicitly anti-Catholic policies. While building a new, revolutionary society, the SEP in Campeche never worked from a single blueprint. Federal officials in Mexico City never explicitly defined socialist education; some teachers and inspectors looked to Garrido Canabal's Tabasco, others to the USSR or even freemasonry and spiritism for inspiration.[22] Drawing on diverse ideological sources, SEP leaders generally agreed on four ambitious goals for northern Campeche: realizing defanaticization, creating a cooperative economy, awakening class consciousness, and instilling a new revolutionary identity.

When it came to defanaticization, SEP leaders told their teachers that progress required breaking all contact between peasants and the institutional Catholic Church (both clergy and elite lay catechists) and ending fanatical practices such as syncretic Catholic festivals. A harsh crackdown by state authorities on the Church would give teachers a window of opportunity to amass grassroots support and realize a sweeping social transformation.

In 1934, the SEP enacted this two-step strategy in Campeche. In Bolonchenticul, Iturbide, and smaller villages, federal teachers invoked state laws and hectored officials to suspend folk Catholic festivals in 1934. During Holy Week 1934, peasant allies of the SEP in the town of Dzitnup and the village of Pocboc used "direct intervention" to expel lay catechists; supporters in Hecelchakán forced the bishop to cancel a pastoral visit. Intervention and then education would encourage peasants to abstain from fanatical practices like fiestas. For Cortés, syncretic fiestas were "against the peasant economy." He also objected to their raucous, even bawdy elements: girls cross-dressed, people danced suggestively (and so "perverted the sexual instinct"), and participants recited *bombas*, poems spiced with Maya and Spanish double entendres.[23] Cortés displayed what Carlos Martínez Assad termed *modernizing Puritanism*: the belief that material progress required sobriety, simplicity, and self-discipline.[24]

Cooperativism stood as the second pillar of the revolutionary project in Campeche. Teachers managed an impressive number of peasant consumer and producer cooperatives, coordinated via the Confederation of Revolutionary Cooperatives. In the past, peasants had sold their corn crop long before harvest to pay debts and taxes. Middlemen gave them only about a third of its value in Mérida or Yucatecan henequen estates. Now, producer cooperatives shared a granary (a nationalized church building) and voted when to sell maize. Tax exemptions and federal credit raised peasant income. Cooperatives also pooled resources to buy cattle and pigs; Maya members' beef consumption tripled. They also cut prices between 20 and 50 percent on imported staples like sugar, coffee, beans, and butter. The SEP's cooperatives in Campeche proved to be more democratic and efficiently run than others elsewhere. A share of communal profits, typically one-fifth of a family's corn harvest, went to a communal fund to buy medicine, pay for school maintenance, and underwrite infrastructural improvements.[25]

The SEP believed the cooperative economy would create new, revolutionary social relations. Cooperatives would cut Mayan peasants' patron-client ties to mestizo merchants and landowners, ties sustained by debt and sanctioned by *compadrazgo* (godparentage). Teachers hoped that localism (and localized Catholic practices like pilgrimages and patron saints) would be replaced by Mexican patriotism, just as deference to petty elites and priests would be erased by class consciousness. Campeche's mestizos legitimized their superiority by stigmatizing Maya cultural practices as inherently inferior. However, the SEP dismissed ethnic inequality as just another result of economic inequality. Consequently, federal teachers in Campeche followed national policy that rejected bilingual education and considered speaking Spanish a patriotic, modernizing act. By supplanting Yucatec Maya language with Spanish, teaching the history and geography of Mexico, and spreading Western norms of housing, clothing, and recreation, SEP doctrine predicted Maya peasants would progress into Spanish-speaking proletarians. At the same time, inclusion of many Communists in the inner circles of the SEP in Campeche gave it an internationalist vision and a pro-Moscow tilt that downplayed indigenous culture.[26]

The fourth and final goal of the SEP plan was to create a new sense of community among peasants. When first explained to peasants by SEP teachers, categories like nation and class often came across as rather hollow and abstract, lacking Catholicism's everyday meaning. The SEP's revolutionary martyrs (Emiliano Zapata, Felipe Carrillo Puerto) lacked the immediacy of the saints. Compared to the synesthetic glories of a syncretic Catholic festival, secular ritual seemed dry and uninspiring; Benjamin Smith documented revolutionary Masonic lodges' "abstemious and apparently rather solemn festivals at the summer and winter solstices," featuring orange juice, sandwiches, and crepe papers.[27] The liturgical cycle of semiprofane festivals and pilgrimages gave life meaning for petty elites and peasants alike.[28] To usher in the anticipated post-Catholic era, the SEP had to decide how to deal with campechanos' ingrained religious values.

Christian Socialism and the Dilemma of Defanaticization

Campeche's federal teachers were divided over whether defanaticization required removing all religious sentiment or merely Catholicism's refractory elements.[29] For the most part, SEP leaders in Campeche deeply disliked the Church. To honor Lázaro Cárdenas's inauguration (on December 12, 1934), Inspector Francisco Ovalle lectured Sabuncuy's Catholics on "The Origin of the Religion and the Ills That It Has Caused in Every Epoch."[30] His colleagues blamed the Church for encouraging alcoholism through ritual consumption during festivals. Classroom murals depicted the Church's nefarious role in inflicting historical injustices and perpetuating a "general colonial ideology."[31]

For Inspector Luis Espinosa, however, religion oppressed "our race" but was ultimately redeemable.[32] Early Christianity, he argued, strongly resembled socialism, and "true" or "primitive" Christianity's altruism and austerity could help federal teachers create an egalitarian, collective mindset.[33] Espinosa interpreted the Sermon on the Mount, in which Christ said that the meek shall inherit the earth, as a precursor to historical materialism. Dissident and utopian thinkers in the Catholic tradition, men like Christian humanist Thomas More and the now-forgotten Dominican Tommaso Campanella (1568–1639), inspired him too. Historically, Espinosa argued, the militant Church perpetrated the Crusades, the Conquest, and the Inquisition's persecution of early "heretical and secret primitive Christian organizations." The inspector thus conflated the early, underground Church with reform movements like the Cathars and (perhaps) even early Protestantism. Here Espinosa's ideas paralleled other revolutionaries who opposed the institutional Church but believed Jesus to be the first socialist.[34] Campeche, Espinosa hoped, would be the first place to realize what he termed "Christian" or "Utopian Socialism."[35]

Espinosa's ideas also reflected a familiar trope of the SEP: the revolutionary teacher as a modern, secular successor of the colonial missionary friar. From its origins, the SEP frequently compared itself to colonial Franciscan missionaries. In 1923, SEP chief José Vasconcelos chose the term *cultural missions* to describe the mobile teams of teachers dispatched to remote indigenous communities; Claudio Cortés spoke in 1927 of "spiritually conquering" the Maya.[36] The ENR-H, run as something of a commune itself via joint student-faculty governance, gave its pupils a year of training in agricultural methods before sending them out to rural schools to form "small agricultural communities."[37] Like the first missionaries, ENR-H normalistas hoped to transform indigenous people's mentality by sharing in their daily life.

Espinosa's ideas promised to resolve the SEP's dilemma by supplanting Catholicism's transcendent message, cultural practices, and ethical code with a revolutionary blend of Christianity and Marxism.[38] They were never systematically implemented, however, probably because of Garrido Canabal's unyielding opposition to any religious sentiment. Instead, the SEP's formal cultural program celebrated what historian Adrian Bantjes terms the revolutionary nationalist creed. Cultural Sundays and Red Sundays featured plays about the evils of alcohol and the priest, along with songs and dramatic recitations.[39] This did generate a degree of popular support. Decades later, aging campechano peasants remembered learning rousing revolutionary songs like "El Himno Agrarista" (The agraristas' hymn), "Sol Redondo y Colorado" (The red, round sun), and "Bandera Roja" (Red flag) taught by ENR-H normal school graduates.[40] Civic observances in campechano federal schools yield some glimpses into the revolutionary future. Federal schools honored national heroes like Hidalgo, Juárez, and Obregón, and Superintendent Cortés also honored Campeche's hero of the war against the French Empire, Pablo García. Cortés interpreted García as an embodiment of José Vasconcelos' Cosmic Race: "he was not a member of any of the pure races into which skin color divides the human race."[41] The exaltation of *mestizaje*, while an important nationalist theme, precluded a potential source of symbols much more meaningful to indigenous students and their parents: Maya culture.

Teachers, unlike the first friars, remained remarkably uninterested in mastering indigenous language and folkways. Many never learned Yucatec Maya, and they were often patronizing (at best) toward indigenous Campechanos. Samuel Pérez, head of the cultural mission based in the ENR-H in 1934, bemoaned the "infantile mentality of the Maya Indian, where psychologically speaking the instincts of combativeness and exhibitionism dominate."[42] In a moment of revolutionary self-criticism, teacher Ramón Berzunza Pinto, covert leader of the Communist Party in Campeche, faulted leftist organizers because too often

> they limited themselves to transplanting the same mottos, using the same phrases, and employing the same means of struggle that were used with indigenous peoples nationally in general, without duly adapting them through conscientious examination to particular indigenous groups, given the distinctive features of each [indigenous group's] differences in language, social organizations, customs and culture.[43]

Revolutionary indigenism exalted an abstract Indian past as the fount of national identity, but it advocated modernization on terms dictated by the mestizo state.[44] The federal teachers' failure to Mayanize the revolutionary project represented a missed opportunity.

As it was, the SEP's plan for diffusing a new communal ideology hinged on rooting out the Church's influence. National events favored a frontal assault on the Church in 1934: an admiring Lázaro Cárdenas visited the ENR-H in March; in October, Múgica advocated an "open attack." After that, reactionary resistance would presumably crumble.[45] Superstitions would be forgotten, sports would replace drinking, and acts of theater and patriotic ritual organized by the teacher would supplant sacred spectacle.[46] No wonder the archbishop of Yucatán, Martín Tritschler y Córdoba, compared the rural federal teacher to an "anti-priest."[47]

The Politics of Anticlericalism: The PSA and the Catholics

Curbing the Church required the aid of the PSA because only the state government could enforce Article 130, which regulated religious practice via a ley de cultos. The party had long held the exclusive revolutionary franchise in Campeche and had supported some mild anticlerical measures in the past.[48] But it was unenthusiastic about enforcing them.[49] National authorities at the time leaned on states, and the powerful garrison commander, General Múgica, had already made it clear that he had little use for the PSA, whose governors had "never done anything for the people." Under stiff pressure, Governor Benjamín Romero Esquivel and the PSA acted.[50]

Between June 21 and September 21, 1934, Campeche's government passed harsh new laws directed against the Church. After having previously capped the number of priests at nine in 1932, the government lowered it to five and then to three. At the same time, legislation restricted the bishop and remaining priests to practicing in a handful of churches, denying the rural population the sacraments and preventing pastoral visits. Only the largest urban churches could collect enough alms to maintain their buildings. Federal teachers tried to suspend popular fiestas to spare the population their "stultifying effect." Following verbal (and probably illegal) orders issued August 1, 1934, Campeche's state police chief fined women catechists of ACM a whopping five hundred pesos when they tried to enter churches to teach children. Coupled with a September 1934 law curbing parochial education, these acts crippled religious schooling. Priests had to pay a special professional tax, on top of which municipalities could charge four to eight pesos for permits for religious marriages. In December 1934, state authorities expelled the only priest from the southern town of Carmen, then ousted the few remaining clergymen in Campeche and sent the bishop packing to exile in Yucatán for good measure. Campeche's state government had already shuttered almost every church on September 21, 1934. Unlike many states, there was little margin for extralegal religious practice until March 1936.[51] One priest who tried to return to Campeche from refuge in neighboring Yucatán was quickly jailed.[52]

Campechano Catholics initially let official lay organizations take the lead in opposing the legal crackdown, likely reflecting archbishop Tritschler's directions from Mérida. Middle-class matrons, probably Damas Católicas, undertook a petition drive to repeal the ley de cultos, gathering thousands of signatures from men and women with Maya and Hispanic surnames. This convinced the federal Ministry of Government that Campeche's harsh new anticlerical regulations were in fact unconstitutional in October 1934. Nevertheless, on December 11, 1934, President Lázaro Cárdenas refused to take action on the matter. The state and federal governments each said only the other could take action. The official Church strategy of lay-led, licit (peaceful) opposition was to no avail, however. Moreover, the petition drive, like the boycott of all public events, including the cinema, was mainly the work of elites. Reaction by peasants is harder to assess, although outside observers noted "much agitation" across the state. When Catholic demonstrations turned violent in September 1934, several people died in Hecelchakán and the city of Campeche.[53]

As long as General Múgica leaned on him, Governor Romero feared following other governors and opening up secret negotiations with lay Catholic leaders. Moreover, the kind of back-channel pressure on the governor that might have wrung out some concessions never amounted to much. Campeche's aristocracy, the henequen barons who had the most clout over the PSA, had decamped en masse to Mérida. There was no Segunda, meaning state and federal officials did not have to yield on anticlerical regulations to discourage violent resistance.

However, the national shift in Church strategy from lay-led licit civil action organized by official lay groups like ACM to the radial strategy, which relied on unofficial, decentralized Catholic networks, held true in Campeche as well. The suspension of public Catholic services and the expulsion of priests, as well as the SEP's anticlerical offensive, riled Catholics. They feared that the Church would wither away as revolutionary communes flourished. After lobbying and civic action failed, Campeche's Catholics found other ways to counter the revolutionary project. Their responses, though, varied geographically.

The Geography of Catholic Resistance

Sweeping geographic generalizations about regional religious sentiment are risky; Alan Knight posits that while differences are often pronounced even within a single state, all political culture is essentially local.[54] The town of Bolonchenticul was known as a Catholic island in the generally unlevitical central *municipio* of Hopelchén, while the town of Palizada was more liberal than surrounding villages.[55] Still, the general pattern of a solidly Catholic south and divided north holds true in Campeche.

Broadly speaking, the southern municipios of Carmen and Palizada historically had been more churched than the rest of Campeche. The Porfirian boom in dyewood helped build a lasting institutional matrix, and the Church still had a strong following across society in the south in the early 1930s. Consequently, the SEP project floundered there. Widespread popular recalcitrance forced federal teachers to soften or abandon anticlericalism entirely in the south. Indeed, many federal teachers in Palizada and Carmen municipios ignored SEP directives on the religious question. Because the SEP federalized state-run schools in towns, it would have incorporated many Catholic teachers (above all women) in the south. A quemasantos scheduled in Carmen for the Day of the Revolution on November 20, 1934, had to be canceled because most teachers and state government officials balked and Catholics shrewdly secreted their crucifixes and saints.[56] That month, the embattled SEP inspector for the Third (southern) District, Francisco Ovalle, condemned the

> totally adverse social environment. . . . The labor of the home is very difficult to counter in the schools. The students, from the youngest to the oldest, dare to insult the *señoritas profesoras* (female teachers) for their antifanatical work. . . . Little have they achieved, and it is worse as of late.[57]

The SEP never fully grasped the factors stiffening Catholic resistance in the south, nor did it spend much time trying to overcome them.[58] Instead, it shifted resources northward.

Comparing subregional differences yields some important insights into the nature of Catholic opposition to the revolutionary project. In the south, middle- and upper-class laywomen initially led the fight. In Carmen, it was Josefa de la Cebada de Azcue and other women of notable families who pamphleted, petitioned, and prayed to repeal the ley de cultos and stop socialist education. Most of Carmen's elites, and people of more modest origins as well, seconded her efforts.[59] But in the north, gender, ethnic, and social divisions already existed; many Maya men responded favorably to the SEP's revolutionary mission, further widening these fissures. Moreover, proximity to the City of Campeche-Mérida road, a commercial axis for centuries, probably predisposed northern towns to accept liberal ideas.[60]

Four factors likely contributed to Catholic resistance in the south. First, class differences here were generally not exacerbated by ethnic inequality. In the north, conversely, the sisal plantations left a lasting historical memory of brutal ethnic exploitation of Maya peasants through debt peonage.[61]

Second, in the early 1920s, the southern elites lost a bitter struggle against the PSA, which was based mainly in central and northern Campeche. Backed by the great Yucatecan socialist leader Felipe Carrillo Puerto and Plutarco Elías Calles, at the time the national minister of the interior, the PSA eliminated the Carmen and Palizada bourgeoisie from regional politics. The PSA saw the southern "reactionaries" as their only serious political rivals, because the southern chicle and dyewood enclave economies were linked to powerful foreign capitalists like the Hearsts. Campeche Socialists gunned down José María Roura, scion of one of Carmen's "most distinguished families" in 1922; a year later Senator Francisco Field Jurado, Palizada's native son, was slain outside his Mexico City law offices after criticizing Obregón.[62] For southern elites, the struggle against the SEP's revolutionary project of the 1930s was just another battle in a long war against the Revolution.

Third, by the mid-1930s, some Tabascan exiles who had fled Garrido Canabal's iconoclastic regime had resettled in Carmen.[63] Their presence hardened Catholic southerners' suspicions of the SEP's project and stiffened their resistance to it.

Fourth, advocates of the revolutionary project in the south never exploited the serious social divisions that existed among Catholics. During 1930, in the city of Carmen, the priest publicly denounced poor women who were not married sacramentally as adulterers and scolded them for not giving more to the Church. He punished the poor women's gremio by refusing to bless their beloved standard carried on pilgrimage should they not come up with a seventy-five-peso fee for mass.[64] By attacking all religious practices wholesale, federal teachers unintentionally united rich and poor women against the SEP.

For all these reasons, the SEP's campaign gained more traction in the north than in the south. It is true that much of the provincial middle class in the north, in particular women, and (ironically) more than a few female teachers in state schools, reacted negatively. Conversely, among the Mayan peasantry in the northern subregion, especially men, the link between defanaticization and economic improvement through cooperatives gave the SEP a foothold.[65] In the north, teachers successfully equated the priest with other "exploiters" like the mill owner who once charged high prices to grind corn, the rancher who sold meat at high prices, and the store owner who bought corn futures low and sold basic necessities high. The considerable expenditures on folk Catholic festivals and the sacramental fees, teachers argued, would be better invested in schooling and the cooperatives.[66] Some Mayan peasants, especially women, did not renounce what John Coatsworth has called Catholicism's "psychic splendors," and so were not convinced.[67] But many did withdraw from public folk Catholic practices.

The SEP harped on the political and socioeconomic inequality that persisted long after the Revolution. The same mestizo families who owned the few grain mills, stores, and ranches in each community traditionally led Catholic confraternities, sent children to seminary, and sold alcohol at fiestas. These same local notables controlled municipal politics via the PSA. The SEP's director in Campeche denounced a conspiracy between the provincial bourgeoisie and the Church ("Capital and Religion"), on the one hand, and the PSA's "false so-called Socialists" on the other. The unchecked authority enjoyed by the PSA boss—typically both a merchant and a landowner—looked to Marxist maestros like feudalism; one exasperated SEP inspector called it *señoritismo* (petty lordism).[68]

In response, federal teachers advocated a direct assault on the peasantry's exploiters on all fronts: political, socioeconomic, and religious. At the defanaticization campaign's peak, the teachers' discourse incited open class warfare: one federal teacher penned the song "Death to the Bourgeoisie" ("The thieving and evil boss is finished, Long live Labor!").[69] When federal teachers attacked clericalism as feudal, many peasants readily grasped this radical discourse as an essentially accurate description of real, palpable inequality. Of course, dislike for the individual priest did not necessarily translate into repudiation of Catholicism, and responses to revolutionary anticlericalism were shaped by gender and class as well as by local politics. The confrontation between supporters and opponents of the teachers' radical project in the 1935 gubernatorial election made the religious question's complexities abundantly clear.

The 1935 Gubernatorial Campaign

Given the close ties between the Church and local elites, success for the SEP would hinge on breaking the PSA's stranglehold on Campeche's electoral politics. Fortunately for teachers and their peasant supporters, the gubernatorial election of 1935 was contested by a strong opposition candidate, Angli Lara. Backing him was a risky strategy for the federal educators, as the SEP officially prohibited its teachers from electoral involvement. However, Ramón Berzunza Pinto, a young firebrand and recent graduate of the ENR-H, used the leftist teachers' union, Bloque de Maestros Revolucionarios, to unabashedly back Angli Lara.[70] Angli seemed to enjoy the right national connections. One mentor, General Múgica, was now in Mexico City as Cárdenas's secretary of communications and public works. Another, Tomás Garrido Canabal, was secretary of agriculture and development.[71]

Between Angli Lara and the governorship stood Ángel Castillo Lanz. The diminutive ex-tailor, a former governor and current federal congressman, was Campeche's Callista boss (jefe mínimo).[72] Castillo Lanz ordered Governor Romero to throw the full weight of the PSA apparatus behind an unpopular veteran party hack, Eduardo Mena Córdoba.[73] The jefe mínimo's machine and Catholic sentiment kept Campeche's capital city and the south solidly behind his man, Mena Córdoba. To triumph, Angli Lara would have to win decisively in the north.[74] Petty Socialist bosses there resented and feared federal teachers and cooperatives, and they eagerly backed Mena. Catholics in the subregion bitterly opposed Angli because of his close ties to ENR-H and his complicity in the *garridista* invasion of Nunkiní's church. Mena Córdoba's wife led the state capital's Damas Católicas to turn out the *voto morado* there.[75]

Like most regional revolutionary parties, the PSA depended on caciques to control the countryside. Unlike larger and more radical regional revolutionary parties, the PSA lacked a cadre of party intellectuals or press to instill ideological purity. Mena Córdoba's hybrid coalition was exemplified by four key local PSA leaders: Ignacio Reyes Ortega, Máximo J. Mex, Juan Barbosa, and José León Montero. All four were party stalwarts and staunch defenders of the faith.

Ignacio Reyes Ortega, long a confidant of the jefe mínimo and perennial cacique of Calkiní, alternated between state congress and town hall for years on end. Reyes was a member of a handful of light-skinned, relatively wealthy families who monopolized economic and political power for decades. In fact, his white grandparents had fled Yucatán during its mid-nineteenth-century Caste War. Barely literate in Spanish, Reyes spoke fluent Maya. This helped him found the PSA branch in Calkiní as a young man back in 1921, promising to help build huts for poor Mayan ex-peons migrating to Calkiní after the abolition of brutal debt servitude on nearby henequen haciendas. He was soon managing Calkiní's municipal fund for an electrical plant (enemies charged he embezzled the money). In the early 1930s, federal teachers challenged the entrenched privileges of Reyes's family and similar clans. As late as 1929, social inequality was starkly symbolized by a rope physically separating white and mestizo townsfolk from darker-skinned, poorly dressed Maya laborers and servants at town dances in Calkiní.[76]

While not particularly pious, Reyes was brother-in-law of the influential local priest, Lorenzo García Ortega. The location of the federal school in Calkiní's ex-convent antagonized prominent, pro-Catholic families; its decoration with murals with nationalist and indigenist themes was a further provocation. The foundation of a Masonic lodge also offended Catholic sensibilities; social shunning forced most brothers to resign in 1933. To challenge federal teachers, Reyes assembled a network of state teachers and policemen to mobilize Catholics in smaller towns and villages in Calkiní municipio. Reyes's allies visited Bacabchen and San Antonio Sahcabchen, warning residents that federal teachers were planning another quemasantos should Angli win. His supporters in Nunkiní invaded Hecelchakán and rang the church bells to summon a mob to forcibly take down the red flag atop the ENR-H, a symbolic and intimidating assault on this bulwark of the leftist teachers.[77]

Another leader of the Socialist-Catholic coalition was Manuel J. Mex. A veteran PSA operative, he ran the city of Campeche's charcoal and firewood cooperative—reportedly for personal profit. During the Cristero War, while serving as the PSA's secretary general, Mex telegraphed its support to Calles for "enforcing our laws that the clergy tried to trample."[78] By the end of the 1930s, however, Mex was an important lay Catholic leader, serving on the state ACM directorate. Mex turned against the SEP because he feared Campeche's schools would be Tabascanized. To oppose maestros rurales, he worked closely with Bernabé Euán Euán of Pomuch. A revolutionary veteran who had fought against Huerta's counterrevolution, Euán helped found the PSA in 1920 and went on to serve as Pomuch's mayor and alternate to state congress. When Nunkiní's federal school required Euán's son to don the Garridista red shirt, Euán started an attendance strike.[79] Given their Maya *apellidos*, Mex and Euán's roles speak to the bi-ethnic nature of the anti-SEP coalition.

Support for Mena Córdoba in Hecelchakán was spearheaded by PSA cacique Juan Barbosa Barahona. His clique fought against the ENR (the normal was based in the town) for years, and Catholicism was its ideological lifeblood and social glue. At the time of the gubernatorial vote, Barbosa had ruled the town for fourteen years and served as general secretary of the Campeche state branch of the PNR. As with Mex and Euán, Barbosa's key allies included Catholics and PSA powerbrokers. Many Catholics were outraged by the ENR-H's direct insults to their faith, but a closer examination of resistance to the revolutionary project in Hecelchakán reveals its multicausal nature. State congressman and *curandero* (natural healer) Alvaro Quintal had been ruined by competition from the ENR-H's resident doctor. Another Barbosa ally, Domingo Ortíz, resented the toll SEP prohibition campaigns took on his cantina. Barbosa's core supporters were the mestizo families (the Ortega, Vera, Mendoza, Ortegón, and Ruiz) of merchants and butchers economically undercut by SEP-run cooperatives. These same clans demanded the reopening of Hecelchakán's church and a resacralization of the town's public life threatened by the ENR-H. The specter of another quemasantos raised by Barbosa convinced many peasant Maya women to join the local mestizo notables and their wives in opposing Angli Lara.[80] Their efforts insured that Hecelchakán's male Catholic voters boosted Mena Córdoba's electoral tally.

José León Montero was yet another established northern cacique who turned to Catholic support to best the Angli Lara-SEP-cooperative coalition. León owned the only corn mill in Bécal, a sizeable town in Calkiní municipio. His maternal kin, the Monteros, were prosperous ranchers and fervent Catholics. Bécal's SEP school and its associated cooperative, La Lucha, threatened these families' economic and political dominance. In spite of being elected mayor on the PSA slate for the 1929–31 term, León was an active Catholic who was literally the standard-bearer of his gremio. Not surprisingly, he had led the fight against the SEP teachers since 1934; during the 1935 campaign, he helped turn out the vote for Mena Córdoba by stoking Catholic resentment of federal teachers.[81]

Across northern Campeche, most Socialist bosses ably played on Catholic fears. Caciques also capitalized on their own or family ties to traditional, semi-official religious organizations like the gremio as well as to newer, official Catholic groups like the Damas Católicas and Catholic Action.[82] It is difficult to qualify this grassroots mobilization against the revolutionary project as purely instrumental, even though Catholicism in northern Campeche towns was bound up with socioeconomic inequality. After all, mestizo notables' sense of status depended upon the Church. In Campeche's postcolonial society, notions such as respect and decency were defined primarily through Catholic values, and religion culturally encoded the mestizo petty bourgeoisie's status. Similarly, syncretic Catholic practices like the fiesta sponsorship via gremio leadership increased elites' social capital.[83] So too did compadrazgo, which religiously sanctioned patron-client relationships. But we should not reduce mestizo elites' defense of Catholicism to the protection of privilege. The intensity of SEP's iconoclasm genuinely outraged many veteran PSA activists.

Complex motivations united ardent Catholics and psa leaders. Mena Córdoba's campaign drew on supple networks of patron-client relationships, resentment of the sep's socioeconomic leveling, and ire over federal teachers' anticlericalism. Multiple motives behind Catholic hostility to the sep project suggest that the voto morado's endorsement of Mena Córdoba was but one part of a larger Catholic strategy in which mestizo elites and not the clergy took the lead.

Campeche's Catholics Confront Revolutionary Teachers

Socialist caciques' success in capitalizing on Catholic support to blunt the revolutionary project seems counterintuitive. Campechano Catholics were never known as orthodox or clericalized.[84] Observant Catholics in neighboring Yucatán considered campechanos to be nearly agnostic.[85] Archbishop Pascual Díaz, the co-head of Mexico's episcopate, spoke of "[Campeche's] diocese where for years disdain for religion has existed."[86] The Church's institutional weakness in Campeche was obvious and persistent.

The Diocese of Campeche was small, poor, and young. Its creation in 1895 resulted not from any inherent geographical logic but from the efforts of the Porfirian regional strongman, Joaquín Baranda. Above all, Baranda sought to deny the Yucatecan clergy's claims over the fledgling state carved from Yucatán thirty-seven years earlier. He did so by achieving the creation of a new diocese in the newborn state, in spite of the institutional Church's weakness there.[87]

Leadership was a perennial concern; from 1895 to 1938, the diocese had no fewer than six bishops. None were natives; most hailed from the distant Bajío. Before the Revolution, Campeche's bishops did their best to create a model Vatican I diocese by importing priests, monks, and nuns from Spain and levitical Puebla, founding a new seminary and a few new schools, and opening a hospital. To reform the lapsed laity and replace ragged confraternities, the diocese instituted new lay religious associations, mainly for women. Rather than being a rock on which modernizing bishops could build a stronger Church, the diocese served as a stepping-stone for better posts elsewhere—at least for those bishops hardy enough to survive tropical diseases.[88] Frequent turnover and lack of local knowledge—above all, ignorance of Yucatec Maya —deprived the diocese of strong, effective leadership from its prelates. Of course, even a long-serving native would have found the diocese's institutional penury and the dispersed, somewhat recalcitrant populace trying.[89]

During the postrevolutionary national Church-state conflicts, Campeche's bishops charted a cautious course. Bishop Francisco González (1922–31) went into exile with the rest of the episcopate during the Cristiada. His conciliatory attitude reflected his personality as well as his diocese's debility.[90] This, then, was the shaky structure inherited by another imported bishop, Luis Guízar (1932–38), scion of a Michoacano clerical dynasty. The new bishop proved to be just as moderate as González. Throughout 1932, tightened anticlerical enforcement prevented him from carrying out pastoral visits. When he did manage to reach the remote Chenes backcountry in mid-1933, malaria struck him down. He spent most of 1934 recuperating in exile in Mérida.[91]

Campeche's priests were always too few for the diocese's dispersed churches, and they tended to cluster in Champotón, the city of Campeche, and Carmen. At its high point in 1905, the diocese counted twenty-nine priests, mostly campechanos. The Revolution took its toll. Carrancistas expelled European priests and all nuns, which crippled attempts to catechize the laity and professionalize the native clergy. There was not much of a recovery in the 1920s. By the early 1930s, only eight priests remained. In 1932 just one priest, Lorenzo García Ortega, covered all twenty-five northern parishes.[92]

Since the Revolution, priests had been few in number and lightly supervised due to distance, episcopal reticence, and political disruptions. Surviving priests probably hailed almost exclusively from Campeche's mestizo provincial middle sectors; no Maya last names appear in the clergy's ranks. Because of their cultural proximity to Maya peasants and bicultural mestizos and whites, most probably spoke some Yucatec Maya and comprehended syncretic folk Catholicism. In the Chenes, one priest even used Mayan beliefs to teach Christianity.[93] Campeche's clergy did not command the respect of Indian faithful the way priests in central Mexico did, nor were mestizo townspeople eager to support a larger clerical establishment.[94]

Heterodox when it came to liturgy, Campeche's clergy stuck closely to Church doctrine when it came to opposing revolutionary reforms. Catholic teachings predisposed Campechano priests to oppose the revolutionary project: private property was sacred, and parents' right to control education was sacrosanct. Friendship, kinship, and a common aversion to revolutionary social leveling united Campeche's *curas* (priests) with mestizo elites against teachers and cooperatives. Father Julian Gonzalo Balmes counted strongmen León and Reyes among his closest friends.[95] The infamous incident at Nunkiní and Angli's campaign only strengthened these bonds.[96]

Any assessment of Campeche's diocese must take into account the unusual severity of anticlerical regulations in the state. The diocese's few remaining clergy were exiled in late 1934, and the official (and female-dominated) Church lay groups, like the ACM and UNPF, withered under intense state harassment during the mid-1930s. The latter's members exerted a strong influence, however, by joining informal groups opposing revolutionary teachers under Rome's radial strategy.

During the worst of the Church-state conflict in the mid-1930s, Campeche's rural Catholics were led mainly by mestizo lay elites and mobilized by semi-official Catholic lay organizations. Male notable leaders are easy to identify, given their prominence and the federal teachers' copious complaints about them. Reconstructing deeper patterns of Catholic sociability and their mainly female leadership is much more difficult, considering their often loose organizational structure and semiclandestine nature.

Still, a few defining characteristics of Campeche Catholicism seem clearcut. In the handful of larger towns, the institutional Church was stronger, and women of middle- and upper-class families were still important. Early on, bourgeois lay women like Carmen's "well-known señoras and señoritas" led. After churches closed, the well-to-do hosted religious services in their own homes. In 1931, members of Carmen's upper class were confident enough of political protection to open up their doors during worship and to parade religious images in the streets.[97] Even after priests trickled back into Campeche, churches were not always available. Therefore in the larger towns like Carmen, the city of Campeche, Dzitbalché, and Champotón, high-status families still hosted services. Elite families with their retinue of kin, neighbors, and hangers-on would have been the logical core for lay mobilizations against the revolutionary project—and in favor of sympathetic politicos.

Although the clergy needed the elite laity's cooperation to keep the Church alive during the period of intense persecution, they feared the elite's growing control over the Church. After the end of Garrido Canabal's regime in Tabasco, the Church hierarchy was dismayed by the "frightening relaxation in the discipline of the Church." When circumstances permitted clergy to end services in homes and reopen churches, lay complaints multiplied: "more than a few people stubbornly want mass where they want, at the time they want."[98] When Campechano elites assumed temporary leadership over their community's religious life, then, they reaped both a social and a spiritual windfall.[99]

If the spacious homes of the wealthy and devout were the matrix for

Catholic resistance in Campeche's larger urban areas, gremios served as the likely hub for Catholic groups in smaller towns and villages. Considering their centrality to public religious practice and their proliferation across the peninsula, there simply were no alternatives to gremios. For decades, these semi-official groups scheduled pilgrimages and often raucous fiestas in honor of their communities' patron saints. Like so much else in Campeche, gremios have been largely overlooked by scholars, but we can draw insights from research on the gremios in neighboring Yucatán. Terry Rugeley's pathbreaking study on nineteenth-century religious practice in southeastern Mexico reveals that gremios were founded by "humble artisans of the cities and towns" in imitation of the colonial confraternities of high society. The old colonial brotherhoods and sisterhoods that survived the Bourbon Reforms and independence eventually succumbed to the Liberal Reform and social deterioration brought on by the Caste War of Yucatán, but the gremios weathered these storms better. After all, they were more modest and much more autonomous from the institutional Church. Consequently, the secularizing Bourbon and then postcolonial states found it hard to regulate or suppress them. For common folks, gremios provided not just spiritual outlets; they also fulfilled important social functions such as insurance against burial expenses and, in some cases, against sickness.[100]

Most likely, Campeche's priests and lay stalwarts revived gremios during the Porfirian reconstruction of the Church. But Catholics watched them decline again as they fell victim to revolutionary-era restrictions. Anthropologist Ron Loewe's study of gremios in Maxcanú, located in western Yucatán bordering Campeche, suggests that around 1925 the Church rebuilt them to help restore conservative, neocolonial values after the Revolution. The suffragan diocese of Campeche might well have done the same. In any event, lay leaders soon took the initiative to bolster gremios. Doubts about their doctrinal purity lingered in the clergy's minds, but priests lacked alternatives—gremios seemed to be the only means of restoring the institutional Church's social authority and expunging the syncretic fiestas' most profane tendencies. In larger towns, male gremios were defined by profession, thus reproducing ethnicity and class distinctions. Hacendados and merchants processed in their gremio, followed by "their" peons (who were excluded from formal membership). Women also had their own gremio, although in Maxcanú it eventually split into two separate entities, one for wealthier mestizo inhabitants, the other for poorer Mayan ones.[101]

Gremios in Campeche would have reflected larger social divisions, too, and they also gave men one of the few religious outlets at a time of a growing feminization of Catholicism.[102] During the course of the nineteenth century, gremios across the state of Yucatán were feminized as men dropped out.[103] But Campechano men kept marching behind their gremio's banner. The lack of secular alternatives for networking and status acquisition for men in the stagnant society and economy of Campeche might explain why. Or was it the lucrative gaming and cantina concessions associated with fiestas? In any event, gremios reproduced mestizo socioeconomic privilege in the religious realm and kept elite men in the pews in Campeche.

The gremios' male leadership gave them more autonomy vis-à-vis the institutional Church than other lay organizations, which in turn heightened lay-clergy tension. At times, the Church hierarchy assigned the gremio one saint, while the community demanded another.[104] The fiesta's profane practices were another contentious issue for the institutional Church. Anthropologist Robert Redfield believed that during the 1920s and 1930s, fiestas were rapidly turning from holy days into holidays on the Yucatecan peninsula; de la Peña argued that fiestas in relatively large, mestizo towns like Carmen, the city of Campeche, and Dzitbalché were already largely devoid of much religious content by the 1930s.[105]

The gremios' idiosyncratic structure and unorthodox religious practice distanced them from the clergy. Unlike Catholic Action, gremios lacked an official chaplain to guide leadership and discipline the rank and file, although priests could exercise a degree of control. They also stubbornly refused to accept standardized terminology and the top-down organization characteristic of modern, orthodox lay groups like the ACM. Although gremios in larger, more mestizo towns were led by men with the secular-sounding Spanish title of *diputados*, Yucatec Maya terminology persisted longer in villages and hamlets where the *yum* (owner) or *kuch* (burden bearer) oversaw fundraising and pilgrimages.[106] De la Peña admired the Campechano gremios' frugality when compared to the colonial cargo system of central Mexican Indians; gremios did not burden officeholders with the heavy expenses needed to underwrite fiestas.[107]

This flexible structure prevented the institutional Church from consistently exerting clerical authority or homogenizing religious practice. The close links between the mestizo gremios and the upper stratum of provincial communities also explain why these confraternities channeled Catholic resistance to the SEP's revolutionary project under the radial strategy. Not only were gremios the most important lay organization in towns and villages, but during the ideologically charged period of 1934–36, the gremios were also one of the main legal targets for suppression by radical federal teachers and allied campesinos who joined cooperatives. Moreover, the male mestizo elites who led the gremios were under attack by the very same foes on socioeconomic and political fronts simultaneously. When León defended his gremio, he was also battling teachers and peasants who organized the cooperative La Lucha that threatened mestizo elites' control of Bécal's main product, its famous woven hats.

Still, categorizing male mestizos' motives for defending the Church is difficult. Defining them as purely religious or political or economic is impossible. Given the gremios' ambiguous relationship with the clergy, it is questionable whether the expulsion of the priests and the end of normal sacramental life was in and of itself sufficient motivation to drive Catholics into confrontation with the SEP. Probably, it was the shock of the assault on Nunkiní's icons combined with two other disruptive anticlerical measures—banning clerical visits to towns and villages to hold mass during the gremios' fiestas and the closing and sealing of church doors, disrupting pilgrimages—that incited Catholics to resist so strongly. Significantly, this resistance was led by mestizo men whose economic and social stake in fiestas was imperiled and by mestizo women whose notions of respectability rested in part on Catholic rites and beliefs.

Why, then, did Maya peasants defend a social order that subordinated them? The same anticlerical offenses that rankled mestizo ranchers and shop owners also incensed them. More so than mestizos, Maya peasants were reluctant to accept priests as unquestioned authorities over all aspects of life. They did, however, value them as supernatural specialists, without whom festivals were incomplete. Denied access to the venerated images sheltered in the closed churches, the festival lacked its umbilical connection to the sacred realm. The *novenas*, or nine days of pilgrimages, and other religious practices organized by gremios that preceded the fiestas lacked their earthly locus after churches were shuttered. No wonder that in the central Campeche community of Hool, many Maya peasants wrote to express their great distress that a priest had been barred from the annual fiesta and that the gremios' pilgrimage to honor the town's miraculous Virgin had been halted after a federal schoolteacher complained of the "fanatical pueblo."[108]

Closure of churches greatly distressed peasants because syncretic rites required access to these hallowed precincts. To make matters worse, after padlocking churches on September 22, 1934, the state government ignored its legal responsibilities to communities across the state to turn over the keys to *juntas vecinales* (neighborhood councils).[109] Palizada's faithful repeatedly and fruitlessly begged for the keys to the church to allow the festival of the Virgen del Carmen to take place.[110] Interruption of traditional practices pushed mestizo and indigenous Catholics into alliance with Socialist caciques. At the same time, the expulsion of clergy and the ACM's problems in Campeche created a vacuum in the state's religious life, one which local male mestizo elites filled.

Following national strategy, Bishop Guízar reinforced the authority of upper-class lay leaders. In October 1934 he organized all male, mainly mestizo committees in Campeche's twenty-two largest communities to care for closed churches. The Church's larger strategy was to rely on these lay notables to oversee the spiritual life of Catholics in each community until the worst of Callista anticlericalism blew over and priests could come home.[111] It also continued the diocese of Campeche's attempts to retain male lay leadership. During Lent in 1933, Bishop Guízar personally oversaw "an intense religious movement" in the city of Campeche's cathedral that brought men to church "in spite of the traditional idea in these places, that religion is something only for weak-willed women."[112] The revolutionary state's crackdown scuttled Bishop Guízar's campaign. At the same time, the SEP's radical project gave men their own reasons to rally to the Church's defense.

Aftermath: Mena Córdoba's Victory and the Religious Restoration

Anticlericalism united Socialist caciques and Catholic brokers in an unlikely coalition in many Campeche communities. Mena Córdoba capitalized on this tactical alliance to wrest the 1935 ruling party (PNR-PSA) gubernatorial election away from Angli Lara. To be sure, Catholics alone did not win the election for Mena Córdoba. The jefe mínimo and Mena Córdoba bribed electoral observers sent from Mexico City, and Mena Córdoba cultivated President Cárdenas's chief political operative at the time, Emilio Portes Gil. The PSA used the police and civil courts to harry federal teachers and for good measure imported voters from Yucatán by train and from Tabasco by boat. Still, the voto morado proved priceless for Mena Córdoba's victorious electoral equation. In the capital city, Campeche's largest single precinct, Catholic voters provided a decisive share of Mena Córdoba's ballots. His promise to reopen churches undoubtedly swayed many. Catholic women, led by Mena Córdoba's wife, motivated male family members to cast their votes. Many men inducted into the ACM's chapter by the bishop must have backed Mena as well. In the end, Angli's federal teachers and cooperative members lost everywhere except for their stronghold of Hecelchakán. They bombarded Mexico City with well-founded complaints of intimidation and fraud. Angli Lara lamented that "the fanatics and the reactionaries defeated the revolutionaries."[113] Without the Catholics' electoral boost, Mena Córdoba could never have convinced national authorities to accept his questionable victory.

In spite of Catholics' decisive role in his election, Mena Córdoba reneged on his promise to open churches immediately. Like Governor Romero before him, he blamed Mexico City for the delay; meanwhile, for several months he continued to expel priests trying to return.[114] On March 4, 1936, President Cárdenas, in well-publicized remarks, said that he would no longer make anticlericalism a priority. When Campeche's Catholics physically occupied many churches on March 9, 1936, President Cárdenas tolerated the technically illegal seizures. After a slow but steady relaxation of anticlerical regulations, nine legal and at least twenty-six unlicensed priests were practicing in Campeche by late 1939.[115]

In spite of Governor Mena Córdoba's failure to honor his word, the alliance between PSA politicos and Catholics endured. Several priests endorsed Mena Córdoba's candidates over their leftist opponents in December 1936 *ayuntamiento* (town council) elections. Priests preached that should the governor's candidates not prevail, the churches would be closed again. Plainclothed state policemen protected a Catholic demonstration against federal teachers.[116] Catholics once again played a key role in helping a rickety PSA machine fend off the challenge of leftist teachers and their peasant allies in the north.

The PSA electoral machine and its Catholic allies continued to battle federal teachers and *cooperativistas* throughout 1936 and 1937. The restoration of Catholic services did little to diminish resentment of federal teachers. In late 1936, a visiting priest took up money to aid Franco's counterrevolution in Spain with the help of Socialist caciques León and Reyes. By now, some Catholics probably saw the battle against godless Communism in Campeche as part of a global war. Cárdenas himself came to Campeche in July 1937 to try to negotiate a truce between Mena Córdoba and leftist teachers; in return for accepting land reform and two (of nine) state congressional seats, federal teachers agreed to accept the governor.[117] But the PSA, bled by the Left's attacks, fatally splintered when Governor Mena Córdoba and jefe mínimo Castillo Lanz split in 1938. A cynical reading of Mexican history would conclude that Cárdenas kept leftist teachers just strong enough to smash the PSA but too weak to take power. In truth, Cárdenas was rarely well informed enough to carry out such precise calculations.

In any event, outsider Héctor Pérez Martínez, a former dentist, a politically connected journalist, and reportedly a member of the Communist Party, prevailed in the 1939 gubernatorial election. With the help of many SEP leftists, Pérez Martínez broke the PSA's monopoly on regional politics. Once in office, he largely ignored federal teachers and cooperatives and angled for advancement in the national capital; in 1948, President Miguel Alemán rewarded Pérez Martínez with the plum cabinet position of secretaría de gobernación.[118] Sadly, the SEP's cooperatives were eventually taken over by the most entrepreneurial or politically connected of their members.[119] Over time, leading leftist teachers received a *cuota de poder*—their share of the political pie—in the consolidating national political system and an expanding SEP bureaucracy. By the 1940s, most teachers were uninterested in utopian communes.

In the end, defanaticization in Campeche went out like a lamb. Priests returned, and churches reopened only twenty months after the Nunkiní incident. The defanaticization campaign, however, had some unanticipated long-term effects on Catholicism in Campeche, beginning with the ACM. In the early 1930s, the bishop and a few priests had made Catholic Action a top priority.[120] The crackdown on the Church from late 1934 to early 1936 stunted the ACM's growth; the ban on lay catechists in particular greatly complicated outreach to peasants.[121] Even after restrictions were relaxed, only one of the ACM's local councils was reconstituted by 1938.[122] Luis G. Bustos, Catholic Action's key lay organizer in Mexico, visited Campeche in 1941 and blamed the ACM's poor condition on the lack of clergy; priests could barely meet minimal sacramental demands, he lamented, much less undertake the exacting organizational and educational requirements of forming ACM cadres. This, he speculated, had left the field open to leftist ideas; the young men in particular were "completely lost."[123]

The end of harsh restrictions sparked an outburst of religious fervor, but it proved to be short-lived. The number of clergy dropped from a high of at least thirty-five at the end of 1939 to only eleven in 1944. This time, the dramatic fall in priests was due not to revolutionary anticlericalism but to

Catholic apathy and the institutional Church's poverty. Only six out of thirty-four other dioceses in Mexico had a lower ratio of priests to Catholics in 1944.[124]

Defanaticization first provoked widespread popular opposition, then a "bounce" in religious expression when it ended. During this outpouring of Catholic sentiment, the laity willingly supported a relatively large number of priests. (There was probably a pent-up demand for the sacraments of baptism and marriage that yielded a bonanza of fees.) But Campeche's religious life eventually regressed to the spiritual mean. The gremios marched again, and the profane fiesta resumed. Campechano laity, mestizo and Maya alike, felt they could get by without the expense and intrusion of a large clerical establishment. Without tithes, the Church in Campeche could not afford that many priests.

Ironically, the rise of a Socialist-Catholic alliance not only frustrated post-revolutionary state formation, but also set back the institutional Church's strategy to use ACM and other organizations to make the state more levitical. The fact that Campechano Catholics proved unwilling to support many clergymen clearly confirms this. This does not mean Campeche was less Catholic per se; rather, it was unwilling to give up its regionally specific religious practices at the behest of Rome or Mexico's episcopate. Campeche's Catholics treasured their customary folk Catholic celebrations, and the gremios' syncretic revelry economically benefited rural caciques. Their undesirability was perhaps one of the few points of agreement shared by the SEP and the institutional Church.

Politically, the chaotic mid-1930s in Campeche revealed not just the unpopularity of anticlericalism (across society in the south, among many women and male mestizos in the north), but also how Catholics could find common ground with regional politicos who wanted to keep Mexico City at arm's length for quite different reasons. This unlikely coalition, which combined casting ballots with a host of other tactics, showed that there was no single Catholic strategy of resistance. As the subsequent chapters reveal, Campeche's Socialist-Catholic alliance differed significantly in ideology, tactics, and degree of success compared to other examples of regional resistance, such as the segunderos and truancy strikes.

The rise of Campeche's Catholic-Socialist alliance demonstrates the risk of analyzing conflicts over religion in purely cultural terms. Focusing only on the dramatic, symbolic, and aesthetic in Catholicism or anticlericalism can be just as simplistic as reducing them to superstructure.[125] Cooperatives converted peasants to the SEP's project in part through its economic appeal; mestizo caciques defended the Church for reasons not purely spiritual. Campeche's Church-state conflict of the mid-1930s stands as one example of how Catholic belief affects, and in turn is affected by, political and economic interests and social status.

CHAPTER 3

"The Devil Is Now Loose in Huejutla"

The Bishop, the SEP, and the Emancipation of the Indian in Hidalgo

Bishop José de Jesús Manríquez y Zárate of Huejutla has gone down in Mexican history as a flamboyant fringe character famous for his intemperate condemnations of the Revolution.¹ His Sixth Pastoral Letter (March 10, 1926) accused Plutarco Elías Calles of trying to "turn [churches] into synagogues of Satan." For antagonizing the state and the Church hierarchy, Manríquez endured the longest exile of any Mexican bishop, from 1926 to 1944.² During his Texas exile, he endangered the Arreglos by baiting Calles and tried to foil the Cárdenas-episcopal rapprochement by inciting segunderos against "the Beast." Throughout the 1930s, Manríquez was the bishop the national episcopal leadership longed to muzzle, the Catholic the anticlerical revolutionaries loved to hate, and the man the *cristeros* lionized as the "Manly Bishop."³ There is another side to Manríquez: the indigenist bishop whose diocese became a pivotal battlefield in the Church-state conflict.

This chapter first sketches Hidalgo and the Huastecan subregion. It then explains how Manríquez and white and Nahua supporters built his diocese and how SEP teachers tried to counter them. As the revolutionary project floundered in 1934, the growing national Church-state conflict inflamed resistance to federal teachers and their local allies. Inspector Francisco Zárate González intensified the upstate defanaticization campaign by staging a quemasantos on June 3, 1935—although his motivations were far from transparent. As a counterpoint to the conflictive upstate, the chapter briefly examines the comparatively quiescent downstate. Lastly, it summarizes the religious conflict in Hidalgo and explores how the struggle over the religious question in Manríquez's diocese sharpened his ferocious opposition to the revolutionary state and intensified his ardent Guadalupanism.

Hidalgo's political and natural geography shaped the conflict between Manríquez and the SEP's secular missionaries. In 1869 Benito Juárez created Hidalgo, a "spoils" state, to reward Liberal loyalists who fought against Conservatives and the French in the western Huasteca (a zone of high semitropical valleys).[4] This remote region long protected the northeastern approaches to the nation's capital and bordered Veracruz's oil fields; Mexico City closely monitored it because of its geostrategic value. To round out the new state, Juárez aggregated other areas to the mountainous upstate: the southern plains around Apam, dominated by large, pulque-producing haciendas; the semi-arid Valley of the Mezquital; and the central mining and industrial zone surrounding Pachuca, the state capital. Collectively, these regions are termed here the downstate. Hidalgo's geographic heterogeneity made it an ethnic and linguistic patchwork. The upstate had between fifty thousand and seventy thousand monolingual Nahuatl speakers around 1921. The downstate Mezquital was home to about as many monolingual Otomí speakers.[5]

To church Hidalgo, Rome established the new Diocese of Tulancingo in the sleepy downstate city in 1863.[6] As in Campeche, turnover at the top undermined the Diocese of Tulancingo's growth. Between 1885 and 1921, it had no less than six bishops. By the Revolution, Tulancingo was for the most part politically and economically irrelevant. The Church never experienced a dramatic Porfirian renaissance in Hidalgo as it did in Yucatán or Oaxaca, although it was stronger here than in Campeche.[7]

The Revolution reversed some of the Church's gains in Hidalgo, although the clergy escaped the systematic Carrancista persecution. Taking advantage of President Obregón's conciliatory policy, Bishop Vicente Castellanos y Núñez imported Spanish and French missionary priests. The Europeans clashed with Mexican priests, and the Church's reconstruction lagged in Hidalgo.[8] Calles's presidency witnessed an uptick in Church-state tensions. From his pulpit, Father Trinidad Vargas, the priest of Acaxochitlan (near Tulancingo), called presidential candidate Calles anti-Christian.[9] Catholics mounted a petition drive in April 1926 against Calles's call for stricter anticlerical legislation, to no avail. Still, rising Catholic antipathy toward the Callista regime did not lead to widespread insurgency during the Cristiada, because revolutionary politicos shied away from head-on confrontation with the Church.

Since 1925, Calles had relied on Colonel Matías Rodríguez Melgarejo (governor until 1929, strongman with de-facto control over the governor until 1935) to manage Hidalgo's middle politics. Of humble, indigenous origin, Rodríguez fought first for the Constitutionalists and then for the Sonorans. In the early 1920s, he entered politics as a radical populist and a CROM (Confederación Regional Obrera Mexicana, Mexico's leading labor confederation) ally with an early reputation for governing honestly. However, he never commanded a centralized party structure, instead relying on a coalition of loyal caciques and limited agrarian reform to control downstate politics.[10] But he never really governed the upstate.[11] Eventually, Rodríguez came to terms with Wenceslao Martínez, Huejutla's perennial mayor, and used him as his upstate intermediary.[12] The Hidalgan superintendent of SEP said of the upstate in 1930 that "socially [it is] very backwards . . . the state government has practically abandoned the region . . . it only is worried about collecting taxes."[13] To mask political weakness, Rodríguez relied on radical revolutionary rhetoric.

Brash anticlerical slogans allowed Callista politicos like Rodríguez to burnish their revolutionary credentials. He once lambasted the Church for spreading a "rancid conservative mentality of God and the Boss."[14] Nudged by Calles, he passed a strict new ley de cultos, which banned parochial schools, expelled foreign clergy, and permitted only one priest per municipality (Pachuca and Tulancingo kept two). Yet he never consistently enforced the new law.[15] Remarkably, between 1925 and 1929 Catholics built or renovated seventy-one Catholic churches, cast nine new bells, and lost only a few buildings to nationalization.[16] Rodríguez did arrest a few prominent lay leaders to prevent an Hidalgan Cristiada, yet he never systematically persecuted the Church.[17] After his gubernatorial term ended in 1929, Rodríguez prolonged his hold over Hidalgo via Ernesto Viveros (governor, 1930–34). As national Church-state tensions rose, Viveros accommodated, rather than confronted, Catholics.

During the Rodríguez and Viveros administrations, local officials generally left anticlerical legislation unenforced. Some town councils sympathized with aggrieved Catholics. Actopan's mayor admitted sacramental marriages took place in private houses, but he somehow never caught Catholics in the act.[18] Clandestine masses took place in Pachuca even during the Cristiada.[19] In Metztitlán, local officials bent over backward to assist violators of anticlerical law. The state attorney general overlooked unlicensed foreign priests ministering in the wealthy Gutiérrez family's private chapel. State congressman Ambrosio Díaz protected the collection of some twenty-five thousand pesos in alms, allowed priests to run a parochial school in his own house, shielded nuns who taught catechism classes, and permitted public religious processions. When reminded of the new ley de cultos, Díaz asserted his local prerogatives: "he is Congressman and he commands from Pachuca to Huejutla."[20] In the downstate, the state and local authorities crafted *compromisos* with Catholics knit together by faith, apathy, and self-interest. As a result, the subregion largely escaped conflict generated by the renewed national Church-state tensions of the mid-1930s. The upstate, however, was another matter.

"Hay que respetar la religión": Mestizos, Nahua, and the Church in the Upstate

In 1923, Manríquez was consecrated the first bishop of the newly minted Diocese of Huejutla. Rome hoped the energetic thirty-nine-year-old native of León, Guanajuato, would use social Catholicism to revive the Church in the upstate. Catholicism in the new diocese was highly syncretic because it had the highest concentration of Nahuatl speakers in Mexico.[21] This made it the logical place for a second "Indian" diocese after the Mixtec Diocese of Huajuapan de León (Oaxaca).[22] The bishop had his work cut out for him: Huejutla's cathedral was collapsing; the episcopal palace had yet to be built; and the diocese had only eighteen priests, many of them aged and infirm.[23] The bishop and his admiring biographers dramatically recounted his early travails. On his first pastoral visits, he was seared by "an African sun" and shocked by "savage" and "diabolic" Nahua syncretism. Upstate mestizos did not have much use for the institutional Church or its dogma either.[24] Undaunted, Manríquez learned Nahuatl and catechized thousands of peasants in impromptu open-air classes. Nahuatl-speaking catechists (mostly mestizo women) formed the core of the ACM. The Nahua, who (in Manríquez's telling) once feared him as just another white exploiter, soon adored their Totatzín or Papacito (little father). From distant hamlets they flocked to his "indigenized" Natividad del Indio (Indian Christmas) and Pascua del Indio (Indian Easter). The bishop also set up a cooperative store for his *"inditos"* ("little Indians"). These steps, he explained, built a strong "Indian Church" in the heady days of the 1920s. After his long exile ended in the 1940s, Manríquez modeled national Guadalupanism (he advocated Juan Diego's beatification) on his indigenist Catholicism, insisting "pure Indians" come to the jubilee celebration of his consecration.[25]

Although friendly biographers stress Manríquez's empathy with the long-suffering Nahua, the bishop had a contradictory relationship with indigenous communities. Before investigating the diocese's inner workings and its intra-ethnic relations, a discussion of its social and political context is in order. The diocese's foundation coincided with a subregional postrevolutionary political settlement. While the new era of conservative stability ended the chaos of the Revolution's armed phase, it also precluded radical social reforms. Self-exiled Porfirian landowners came home in the early 1920s. To revive their fortunes, they forged alliances with the upstate's new political elite of smallholders and petty intellectuals. Ranchero revolutionaries forged lasting understandings with surviving hacendado clans like the Andrade and the Azuara. In many locales, upwardly mobile indigenous elites and elders were included as junior partners in these arrangements. Religion sanctioned this settlement. The Church's conservative modernizing project in the Huateca accommodated, rather than challenged, the new political order. Although not exactly a preferential option for the rich, Manríquez's Church did preach respect for property and progress through education, mutual help, and social harmony. In other words, it addressed the indigenous "problem" without jeopardizing the privileges enjoyed by Spanish-speaking whites or Nahua notables. Catholicism thus helped stabilize the new postrevolutionary political equilibrium in the upstate, one that protected the subregional economy of ranching and commercial farming. Ultimately, the subregion's religious and economic systems rested on the extraction of labor rents from Indians.[26]

Bishop Manríquez's brand of Catholic progress did not fundamentally challenge the upstate's hierarchal socioeconomic structure—at least in the short run. By loudly proclaiming his indigenist mission, Manríquez's ministry effaced an older, much more radical Christian tradition in the Huasteca: between 1879 and 1882, Huastecan Nahua revolted in neighboring San Luis Potosí, inspired in part by Father Mauricio Zavala's agrarista social Catholicism.[27] Rather than ignore indigenous Christians, the bishop made them a special missionary focus. When the new diocesan seminary opened in December 1923, five of its first students were Nahua. Moreover, the bishop crafted an indigenous liturgy, convened pilgrimages from Nahua communities to Huejutla's new cathedral, and opened a special Sunday school for them. His pride and joy was an Indian-only special confraternity (Los Hermanos Custodios) reserved for the best indigenous catechists.[28] Their elaborate ceremonial dress and ornate staffs reflected Manríquez's indigenist pretensions.

In the final analysis, however, Manríquez's claims of transforming the upstate seem overstated. Rather than integration and equality for the Nahua, Manríquez created a parallel and generally subordinate set of indigenous lay institutions. Ultimately, he viewed Nahua Catholics with condescension and concern. Really replacing Nahua syncretism with orthodox Catholicism would have required many more priests and more time. In Mexico's first indigenist diocese in Oaxaca, the seminary became a place of intellectual ferment where mestizo clergy embraced Catholic indigenism to restore the Church's influence in Mixtec communities. This diocese, however, had seven productive years of peace before the Revolution. In Huejutla, conversely, the postrevolutionary state closed the seminary just three years after it opened. And there is no evidence that Huejutla's seminary turned out more than a few (if any) indigenous priests for years.[29]

Moreover, many of Bishop Manríquez's indigenist initiatives disrupted long-established Nahua religious practices. To encourage peregrinations to his cathedral, he removed the beloved Nuestro Padre de Jesús from a country chapel and brought it to Huejutla. Indigenous villages now had to come to the cathedral on their Candlemas pilgrimages and request the bishop's permission to bring the icon for brief visits to their village for nocturnal adoration.[30] Such bold assertions of the institutional Church's power over cherished local customs undoubtedly provoked resentment among many Nahua Catholics.

Manríquez's claims to have remade indigenous religious practice by eliminating syncretic rites and winning over reluctant whites and mestizos were exaggerated. The upstate remained far from levitical. For instance, the ratio of sacramental marriages to "free unions" remained low.[31] Clergy remained much more attuned to the needs of mestizos than to those of Nahuas. Given the seminary's shortcomings, the bishop's clergy were still embedded in what Claudio Lomnitz-Adler has called the regional culture of the Huasteca: the complex interplay of political economy and symbolic systems that allowed ranchero mestizos to naturalize the exploitation of Nahua peasants.[32] Priests spoke Nahuatl, however, and even if they looked down on folk Catholic rites and disapproved of Nahua syncretism, they still understood Huastecan religious folkways. Father Arturo Arellano, the seminary's first rector, was Manríquez's resident "expert on the psychology of the Huastecos."[33] Another priest, Mateo Ochoa, spoke perfect Nahuatl, ran a profitable still, and fully shared the macho lifestyle of the rancheros; a fearful federal teacher said of him, "This priest is a man with hair on his chest, with his pistol in his belt, his carbine and a pack of dogs, he hunts animals and menaces the helpless peasants of the region." While their ministry reproduced ethnic inequality, the clergy's intimate knowledge of indigenous culture gave them a key advantage over their adversaries in the SEP, many of them monolingual outsiders.[34]

That said, Manríquez's clergy did try to promote some changes in the religious life of the upstate. Like their counterparts in the first Indian diocese, Huajuapan de León (Oaxaca), the clergy of the diocese of the Huasteca encouraged the cult of the Virgin of Guadalupe to renew popular faith and roll back secular liberalism. In both places religion had a strong indigenist bent.[35] Father Arellano called Our Lady of Guadalupe the first "aboriginal catechist" who "achieved [the Indians'] miraculous conversion and evangelization."[36] Of course, Catholic indigenism in Huejutla, unlike that in Huajuapan de León, never had the time and institutional strength needed to put down deep roots. Consequently, the bishop's claims to have purified indigenous Catholicism by removing superstition should be taken with a grain of salt.

Nevertheless, Nahua Catholics revered the Church. They needed priests' sacramental office to complete their festivals and required access to the sacred spaces of churches and their holy objects like statuary (such as the sequestered Nuestro Padre de Jesús). Still, indigenous peasants did not necessarily accept clerical authority over aspects of everyday life or priests' demands that they give up their *costumbres* (customs).[37] Recent ethnographic work on the Huastecan Nahua of Veracruz found syncretic home altars still being tended, guardian stones still looking over the hearth, and discreet offerings to spirit guardians still being made in the *milpa* (small fields of maize).[38] Huastecan Nahua Catholics likely learned to hide syncretic rituals from itinerant priests in the 1920s and 1930s, just as Nahua Catholics concealed Mesoamerican paper guardians behind store-bought pictures of saints decades later.[39] Lack of diocesan clergy meant priestly visits to smaller communities were few and far between, especially during the critical years of 1934 and 1935. At best, no more than half a dozen clergy tended some seventy thousand Nahua (and half again as many mestizos).

For all the talk of a new Indian Church, the bishop and his priests cherished colonial customs such as the *besamanos* (submissive kissing of hands) and jealously collected primacias and *diezmos* (tithes). Some priests reportedly exploited their status to act as agricultural brokers. Manríquez's kin reportedly profited from the Indians' ritual offerings to their saints, apparently through his Church-run cooperatives. In the absence of a well-developed cargo or *cofradia* system, indigenous elites took it upon themselves to organize and sponsor pilgrimages and fiestas.[40] Manríquez's diocese reinforced the power of older, prosperous Nahua elders to ensure the smooth operation of long-standing religious systems that had spiritual ends—but with undeniable economic and social dimensions.[41] Manríquez did oversee some innovations from exile in the mid-1930s, ordering Father Arellano to organize lay groups and revive confraternities for catechization and social needs. While they included some Nahua, most of their leadership came from elite mestizo families.[42]

Reliance on mestizos as intermediaries to guide Nahua was yet another conservative feature of Manríquez's diocese. When the bishop invited Ildefonso Velázquez Ibarra to open the Free Normal School, Huejutla's first secondary school, students were mostly middle class. White and mestizo elites of the subregion welcomed the bishop's school because they no longer had to send sons as far away as Pachuca or Mexico City. The school also allowed Catholics to claim their own notion of progress apart from the postrevolutionary state; students practiced hands-on learning in the form of field trips to gather insects and flowers and fielded the first basketball team in the upstate. The curriculum was secular, too, but most students followed the example of headmaster Velázquez, who attended mass weekly.[43] By subsidizing the upstate's only secondary school and encouraging new forms of sociability there, the Church spread its presence in urban, middle-class society yet did little for the Nahua, whose educational deficit was much greater.

Between 1923 and 1926, Manríquez built a new diocese under trying circumstances. He ministered to indigenous Catholics and took modest steps to address their marginalization. But Manríquez's Catholic indigenism never supplanted Nahua syncretism nor did it threaten the conservative social status quo. Generally speaking, it reinforced the Church's dependence on a socioethnic hierarchy that subordinated most indigenous Huastecans. The "Indian" diocese was thus symbiotically linked to upstate elites by its clergy, religious practice, and lay institutions.

Many ties bound priests and provincial elites tightly together: education, shared economic interests, and common social privilege. Merchants, landowners, and politicians sent their sons to seminary and sought leadership positions in Catholic lay organizations for prestige and piety. Catholic sodalities generated social capital for elite clans and reinforced ties to priests. For example, Molango elected prosperous rancher Moisés Angeles mayor in 1933, while his brother led the La Vela Perpetua and Guardia de Honor sodalities overseen by Father Luis Marín.[44] Rodríguez's cacique (boss) of the Sierra town of Zacualtipan, mayor and state congressman Trinidad Arteaga, was a priest's brother and president of the Sacred Heart of Jesús confraternity. While honoring the Niños Heroes, Arteaga led cheers to the Virgin of Guadalupe.[45] Given the overlap of local officialdom and lay leadership, it is not surprising that mestizo authorities often spurned anticlerical legislation and considered religious conformity a guarantee of social peace, thus advancing their own careers. In banning an anticlerical demonstration in 1933, Antonio Sosa, the mayor of Huejutla, explained, "religion must be respected because it is moral, and I don't want problems."[46]

Huastecan politicos' support for the Church resists reduction to one cause, either cultural or socioeconomic. Upstate Catholicism was not just superstructure, the ideological carapace of latifundia, as revolutionaries charged.[47] However, we must recognize that Manríquez's clergy, like the mestizo landowners and politicos, depended on unpaid labor drafts. Typically, all adult Indian men owed one day a week of *faena* (labor service) or *trabajo communal* (communal work), although the name and exact nature of drafts varied from place to place. On top of fulfilling this neocolonial obligation to Church and state, landless, mostly indigenous peasants also had to pay labor rents charged in return for access to land. All upstate Nahua communities were obliged to perform unpaid labor services to the mestizo-dominated municipal government.[48]

In fact, Porfirian progress was subsidized by unpaid Nahua corvée labor. Mestizo-dominated *ayuntamientos* (town councils) expanded the old colonial practice to build and maintain new roads and public buildings without taxing prosperous white residents. Porfirian development expanded uncompensated indigenous labor drafts because sugar and livestock haciendas privatized national and communal land. Wealthier, politically connected leaders of Nahua communities facilitated sharecropping arrangements in which land-starved Nahua communities sent poor young men as laborers and women as domestics to hacendados in return for land access.[49] Nahua elites, the same group that upheld communal religious obligations, were thus complicit in this system; some apparently became ranchers themselves. In 1937, a defender of the status quo denied that Indians were enslaved and claimed that many Indians were better off than *gente de razón* (a colonial term referring to whites).[50]

Ironically, the Revolution strengthened rather than dismantled the practice by constitutionally enshrining *municipio libre* (municipal democracy). Many smaller mestizo towns gained self-rule and escaped administrative subordination to larger ones; the newly autonomous burgs imposed labor levies on surrounding Indian hamlets.⁵¹ After the upheavals of the Revolution's armed phase, mestizo rancheros and indigenous elites reconstituted these swaps of labor drafts (levied on young indigenous men) in return for communal access to land.

Poor peasants did not necessarily perceive these neocolonial exactions as exploitation or servitude. Local political authorities and landowners represented them as reciprocal. Moreover, wealthier, older Nahua who governed and supervised the religious life of indigenous communities supported and at times benefited from these arrangements.⁵² But for the federal teachers who made their way into the upstate in the 1920s, these unpaid labor drafts and rents seemed nothing less than slavery; their existence cried out for revolutionary emancipation.

From Liberation to Defanaticization:
The Revolutionary Project's Anticlerical Turn, 1927–34

The Huasteca's proximity to Mexico City, its strong Nahua culture, and the Church's growing presence made the upstate of Hidalgo the logical place for the SEP to open its first cultural mission in October 1923. Starting in the Sierra town of Zacualtipan and then working its way from town to town, the cultural mission served as a mobile laboratory for rural education. Pioneering missionaries included Rafael Ramírez, soon the SEP's leading pedagogue.⁵³ A second mission arrived in 1925 and a third in 1927. The SEP officials were struck by the upstate's geographic isolation, social inequality, chronic misgovernance, low literacy in Spanish, and the stubborn survival of forced labor drafts.⁵⁴ The SEP would remedy these social ills by invoking revolutionary indigenism: "the Indians are legitimate owners of the land, while, we, the mestizos, we are nothing less than the descendants of those who despoiled them of their land." At the time, opposition by local landowners and politicians, as well as fears of provoking another Huastecan Caste War, prevented the SEP from taking further action.⁵⁵

Nevertheless, the SEP opened its first federal school in the upstate in 1927. Teachers reported witnessing overseers, whip in hand, forcing indigenous peons to perform uncompensated labor, strengthening the indigenist narrative of poor Nahua awaiting emancipation.⁵⁶ Maestro Bonfilo Galván opened his school in Orizatlán and boldly helped Liga Nacional Campesino (a national agrarian organization) activists initiate land reform. Landowners and local officials reacted by massacring agraristas in September 1927. Galván barely escaped "martyrdom."[57]

The SEP's plans to liberate the Nahua stalled until interim president Abelardo Rodríguez passed progressive education, labor, and agrarian legislation. By 1933, beleaguered upstate *maestros rurales* (the SEP's rural teachers) could finally initiate land reform and halt illegal labor drafts.[58] The new federal superintendent in Hidalgo, Chiapan Federico A. Corzo, was an expert on "civilizing" Indians with strong anticlerical sentiment hardened by a stint in Tejeda's radical Veracruz.[59] Corzo encouraged inspectors to bend SEP policy prohibiting confrontational defanaticization tactics. One inspector asserted that "the Church was on the side of the rich to exploit the poor" and condemned the syncretic Catholic fiestas as "anti-economical," while another posited that indigenous liberation demanded "aggressive combating of surviving idolatry and individualistic prejudices."[60]

To spearhead the SEP in the upstate, Corzo counted on Inspector Rubén Rodríguez Lozano. Ideologically, the twenty-seven-year-old Zacatecan was a moderate classic liberal with little love for either Communism or strident anti-Catholicism. No political neophyte, Aguascaliente's governor, Rafael Quevedo, promoted him from third-grade teacher to state superintendent for making stump speeches. In 1937, he helped Cárdenas topple Saturnino Cedillo as SEP superintendent of San Luis Potosí, and he advised right-wing president Gustavo Díaz Ordaz (1964–70).[61] In the upstate, he proved to be an energetic advocate for the SEP's revolutionary project. Half secular missionary, half manager, Rodríguez Lozano turned forty mostly young and undertrained men and women posted in remote, Nahuatl-speaking hamlets and villages into passable pedagogues and revolutionary vanguards.[62] He spoke only Spanish (like many teachers) and considered indigenous culture exotic and backward. Posted in Campeche in 1933, he expected that the Maya's "primitive customs" and "special religion, shaped by ancient rites" would be remedied via "defanaticization . . . incorporation . . . material improvement of the pueblos, hygienic improvement of the home, technical improvement of agriculture, [and] spiritual improvement of ideas and knowledge."[63] He saw the Huasteca Nahua as even worse off due to labor drafts, requiring the eradication of "fanaticism, exploitation, and tyranny that victimized the Indians."[64]

To that end, Inspector Rodríguez Lozano's teachers pushed prohibition, oversaw adult literacy drives, and staged patriotic civic ceremonies. He deputized his teachers to enforce agrarian and labor laws. In a few months, Rodríguez Lozano and his teachers filed paperwork to set up forty ejidos and forwarded seventy-five complaints for violation of federal labor laws. Above all, Rodríguez Lozano pushed teachers to end the "slavery" of labor drafts.[65] Revolutionary emancipation, however, would cripple the hacienda economy, local governance, and the Church in the Huasteca, dividing Nahua communities. Rodríguez Lozano was stirring up a hornets' nest.

From the start, Inspector Rodríguez Lozano and his teachers met stiff resistance from mestizos and some Nahua. Requests to municipal and state officials to help schools and support agrarian and labor reforms were resisted, sometimes violently, with teachers fearing being ambushed. Rodríguez Lozano, though, proved to be resourceful and hard to intimidate. Although the inspector came armed with legal authority to close all parochial schools, he shrewdly let Manríquez's Free Normal School run, holding it hostage to guarantee the oligarchy's cooperation. He convinced the military zone commander, General Evaristo Pérez, to provide armed escorts to him and his most imperiled teachers. When Rodríguez Lozano saw the scarred back of a peasant macheted by a landowner in Piedra Hincada, a large Nahua village in Orizatlán municipality divided by a long agrarian dispute, he bypassed the legal system and sent federal troops to jail the guilty landowner. When Inspector Rodríguez Lozano refused entreaties to free him from Huejutla's mayor, state congressman, and local judge, more death threats followed. Superintendent Corzo was so concerned that he tried to give Rodríguez Lozano an old pistol owned by General Felipe Angeles.[66]

Rodríguez Lozano hoped that his public bravery in the face of intimidation from Huejutla's local elites would have a positive demonstration effect, rallying the Nahua. The SEP's narrative celebrated enlightened missionaries of modernity, battling reaction and superstition to uplift indigenous people. But how did Nahua communities actually respond to the revolutionary project intent on defanaticizing? Unfortunately, the historical record provides limited insight, although the silences suggest SEP failure when it came to extirpating superstition.

The inspector and his teachers faced long odds from the start. In the first place, history warned upstate Nahua from aligning too quickly with these liberators from without. The Revolution's *apertura* (historical opening) closed in the early 1920s when the old hacendados and the revolutionary elites restored labor drafts and precluded far-reaching land redistribution in the

1920s.⁶⁷ Indigenous peasants had good reason to fear violent retribution and initially remained aloof from the well-meaning outsiders.⁶⁸

Moreover, the inspector failed to grasp the intricacies of small Nahua communities. Instead, he generally followed the SEP and imagined Huastecan society as divided into two monolithic blocs: landowning whites and mestizos and the long-suffering indigenous peasantry that they oppressed. This perspective overlooked the alliances linking white and mestizo landowners with Nahua authorities and the existence of indigenous smallholders. Indian officials and landowners both had a stake in maintaining labor drafts and the political status quo. When the inspector realized that the indigenous *tequitlato* who oversaw these labor drafts at times whipped, jailed, and expelled Indians who refused to serve, he tried to abolish the office as a colonial relic. Mestizo municipal governments countered by naming tequitlatos to the civic office of *juez* (judge), making it a constitutional post and so beyond the reach of federal officials.⁶⁹

Rodríguez Lozano tried to mobilize poor, landless indigenous people against local elites—even if they were Nahua. The Nahua poor did not necessarily view their elders or even white petty elites as oppressors—provided they protected clients and respected religious obligations. Schryer's ethnography shows that poor Nahua honored corvée obligations to maintain reciprocal bonds with patrons.⁷⁰ Some landless young Nahua men (and perhaps women, too) did come to reject labor drafts and ally with federal teachers. However, the SEP's lack of local knowledge prevented it from leveraging such supporters. In particular, the SEP's ban on bilingual instruction and reliance on teachers and inspectors lacking Nahuatl were profoundly counterproductive. In 1927, a SEP administrator fruitlessly criticized monolingual pedagogy, pointing out its "poor results" because only 1 percent of Huastecan Nahua children understood Spanish.⁷¹ The SEP closed several schools in the Huasteca in early 1935 because teachers could not speak what they called Mexicano (Nahuatl); another noted that priests invariably could speak Nahuatl perfectly.⁷²

Nevertheless, Inspector Rodríguez Lozano rejected bilingual education in hopes of accelerating acculturation to the dominant mestizo culture. It was not just a matter of linguistic assimilation, as his teachers convinced some "inditos" (in his words) to adopt Western-style pants and shoes to "elevate them to the level of the bourgeoisie, [so] they will no longer be humiliated." They also hoped that performing dramas with indigenous students would erase ethnic inequality once their charges could "hear the applause of the whites."⁷³ In the school and on stage, Rodríguez Lozano glimpsed a bright future for his Nahua students. They were more likely than their parents to share his vision, embrace Spanish, and accept new social mores, judging by the experience of the Nahua communities of Tepoztlán, Morelos, between 1928 and 1944.⁷⁴

Nevertheless, this kind of progress came slowly in the Huasteca. Most federal schools never overcame widespread truancy and a general reluctance of many in indigenous communities to cooperate. Poorer Nahua families could not afford to lose their children's labor by sending them to class. The story of a young teacher, José Cabrera, illustrates many of the challenges SEP teachers faced. Cabrera learned Nahuatl on his own and braved charges of being a Communist. For two years, his school in Cuautenahuatl (municipio Huautla, near Huejutla) was a success. But eventually Cabrera had to flee when wealthier Nahua families retaliated against his attempt to organize an agrarian petition by threatening him.⁷⁵ Rather than leading a victorious class struggle against indigenous kulaks, teachers could not overcome internal inequalities that fractured even the smallest Huastecan Nahua communities.

There were some significant successes. In some villages in Yahualica and Orizatlán municipalities, federal teachers implanted the revolutionary project in the space of only a few months. By early 1934, they had gained enough popular support and political power to end labor rents and drafts, suppress the tequitlato, and convince some to abandon traditional dress—changes that undoubtedly seemed traumatic and deeply threatening to older Nahua.⁷⁶ Buoyed by these victories, Inspector Rodríguez Lozano claimed in May 1934 that the SEP's campaign of liberation was gaining ground.⁷⁷ Many triumphs proved ephemeral, however, as mestizo elites and conservative Nahua convinced many parents to turn against the teachers. Facing these reverses, Inspector Rodríguez abandoned his moderate stance on the religious question and turned to direct defanaticization.

The SEP curriculum tasked teachers with undermining fanaticism through subtle, indirect means. In the large Sierra town of Molango, the federal elementary school modeled these methods by commemorating the deaths of national heroes Benito Juárez, Miguel Hidalgo, and Alvaro Obregón with civic ceremonies. Its basketball club played those of other communities to "strengthen the friendship among the pueblos." In the process, games would draw adults away from cockfights—and church. The strategy of the SEP envisioned these "social fiestas" as incrementally defanaticizing with "tact and moderation, in order to not create sterile hatreds . . . until reason and justice completely hold sway; killing with a sure blow . . . the harmful control that the priest exercises."[78] But most federal teachers opened under-resourced schools in smaller, Nahuatl-speaking communities. The best they could do was follow SEP directives to scientifically explain natural phenomena to slowly chip away at superstitions.[79] Nahua peoples' reactions to these *pláticas* (chats) are difficult to gauge, but the significant silence of official reports on their impact suggests results were disappointing. Rodríguez Lozano and his teachers blamed mestizo clergy and lay leaders for their own failures and believed expelling them would lead to the definitive defanaticization of Nahua pupils and parents. Behind all the Catholic resistance, Rodríguez Lozano fumed, was Bishop Manríquez.[80]

From his Texas exile, Manríquez kept in close contact with his beloved diocese via his family. Sister Paula Manríquez, nephew José Amador Manríquez, and another in-law, Margarita Amador (who once published a Catholic women's magazine in Huejutla), set up camp just across the state line in Tamazunchale, San Luis Potosí.[81] Protected by conservative Potosino strongman Saturnino Cedillo, his family relayed messages from the bishop to his clergy. His kin also sheltered fugitive priests and lay leaders, and Manríquez coordinated their frequent forays back to Hidalgo into which they brought sacramental services and instructions.[82] Manríquez kept such close tabs on his diocese that Inspector Rodríguez believed the bishop had actually snuck back into Mexico in mid-1934.[83] Frequent reports allowed the bishop to closely follow the SEP's progress in his diocese.[84] Reacting to revolutionary anticlericalism, Manríquez charged in April 1934 that federal teachers were "of the Devil."[85] His priests followed his example; in May 1934, Father Luis Marín of Molango, as well as the priests of Xochicoatlán and Huazalingo, condemned socialist education from the pulpit.[86] The fugitive priest of Huejutla, Father Salvador Borja, denounced teachers as "Demon's Spawn."[87]

Bishop Manríquez's polemical attacks on socialist education intensified as the SEP's revolutionary project advanced in the upstate. In August 1934, just as SEP schools reopened after summer recess, Manríquez penned his "Third Message to the Civilized World." It decried Calles's Psychological Revolution as nothing more than a "Jewish-Masonic plot." Once again, he equated socialist education with ultimate evil: "will ye even allow the bolshevik monster to make its way into the temple of the conscience of your children, to destroy the religion of your fathers and to plant therein the

Devil's own flag?"[88] His "New Argument and Protest" a few weeks later charged that federalization of education benefited "Jews, coyotes [corrupt government officials], and other exploiters." It defended his Indian diocese by singling out revolutionary indigenism for special scorn:

> Now more than ever we see the Indian sad and mistrustful. He does not want to hear any about incorporation, nor improvements, nor farces . . . [the Indians] want to be left in peace to work their land with the sweat of their brow. The Indians' only true friend was the Church that brought spiritual relief, sharing their suffering, and working to bring them out of the shades of barbarism.[89]

Manríquez's widely circulated diatribes alarmed Catholics across Mexico and the United States about the supposed threat posed by socialist education. Their timing and content were clearly calculated to reverse whatever headway Rodríguez Lozano and his teachers had made in early 1934.

The bishop's demonization of the SEP spurred truancy strikes and social shunning of teachers in his diocese just when Rodríguez Lozano and his teachers seemed to be gaining a toehold in some Nahua communities. At the same time, the bishop provided a convenient scapegoat for the SEP's difficulties. Moreover, his incendiary language convinced Inspector Rodríguez Lozano to take drastic measures against Catholicism. To combat fanaticism, Rodríguez Lozano required the solid support of his teachers.

He recruited them locally for the most part, following SEP policy. Upstate mestizo families had long sent many sons (and some daughters) to the normal school in Molango.[90] While cultured and hardworking, they still sprang from their local gentry, and the enthusiasm of many waned as the revolutionary project threatened to flatten social hierarchy; Rodríguez Lozano came to despise the upstate insular mestizo elites as a reactionary "caste" and to suspect many local teachers' loyalty.[91] With a few notable exceptions, female *serranos* (highlanders) proved especially reluctant to implement even subtle forms of defanaticization in the classroom. The SEP eventually fired several for leading catechism classes and attendance strikes in Calnali, Xochiacoatlán, and Molango.[92] To replace them, the SEP recruited "foreigners" for upstate classrooms.[93] Manríquez charged that "the main agents of socialism in my diocese are outsiders, coming principally from Tabasco and Veracruz, because the men of this region do not easily support these things."[94] These radical outsiders helped Rodríguez Lozano organize Huejutla's Society of Teachers, Workers, and Indians in November 1934 to push the revolutionary project forward and finally free the Nahau. Their first step: rousting Manríquez's clandestine clergy.[95]

By now, Rodríguez Lozano had found enough homegrown allies in Huejutla to do just that. Religious dissidents identified with the revolutionary project because of years of harassment by local authorities.[96] In 1928, Huejutla's mayor jailed a Protestant just for evangelizing.[97] Teachers of the SEP seemed to be avenging angels, and revolutionary anticlericalism promised to open new missionary opportunities. Tabascan Pentecostals volunteered for revolutionary literacy campaigns in indigenous areas, discreetly proselytizing in Garrido's vaunted atheist republic.[98] Closer to Huejutla, the anticlerical Group "Benito Juárez" opposed the pro-Catholic local politicos of Tianguistengo as "consummate CRISTEROS" and idealized Calles, a man "educated by the light of Protestantism, a dynamic force called to transform the world."[99]

Other spiritual traditions had their own axe to grind with Huejutla's Catholic authorities, like schoolteacher Francisco M. Moreno's Clear Truth chapter of the Escuela Magnético Espiritual de la Comuna Universal (Magnetic Spiritual School of the Universal Commune), a pan-American spiritist movement. In 1932, Moreno denounced Father Salvador Borja as "all powerful" and said all of Huejutla's society kissed his hand.[100] Guillermo Castro, perhaps a spiritist, denounced the priest for raking in a small fortune by illegally holding marriages in his house. Mestizo and Nahua alike long sheltered Borja, and only a knowledgeable, long-time resident like Castro or Moreno could have fingered Borja to the SEP. Tipped off, federal troops captured and expelled Borja from Huejutla under the threat of death.[101] Spiritists, along with Protestants, generic freethinkers, and disgruntled Catholics never amounted to much more than a beleaguered minority. But they gave Rodríguez Lozano valuable local knowledge in Huejutla and likely recruits for his schools. Their push from below, as well as Manríquez's provocations, explain Inspector Rodríguez's embrace of more drastic means of combating fanaticism.

Regional and national politics, too, favored harsher measures against fanaticism. During the summer of 1934, Calles declared a Psychological Revolution, and SEP superintendent Corzo hectored Governor Viveros to tighten Hidalgo's ley de cultos.[102] By the end of September 1934, Inspector Rodríguez wrote that "we no longer have priests in this region that can exploit the people."[103] Teachers took "radical actions" to best "the Cristero Manríquez y Zárate and his family." Little by little, Rodríguez Lozano reported, teachers and their partisans ran out the remaining clergy; by late November 1934 he announced, "now there are no priests and there is no religion."[104] In the space of a few months, federal educators in the Huasteca had moved from tactful moderation to imposing a Tabascan, post-Catholic outcome.

As in Campeche, the law and regional politics complicated defanaticization. The SEP could denounce but not legally prosecute violations of the Constitution's Article 130; it needed the state government to strengthen and enforce its own ley de cultos. Under intense pressure, Governor Viveros reduced the number of licensed clergy in the Diocese of Tulancingo (which included the downstate and part of the upstate) from forty-three to just thirteen and squeezed the Diocese of Huejutla even tighter. Even though Viveros dragged his feet on enforcement, the law enraged Bishop Manríquez. Defying the Mexican episcopate, he preemptively closed his churches and sent his priests underground rather than accept any new state regulation.[105] For his part, Corzo used the new ley de cultos to harry Catholic leaders in late 1934: "fanatical Catholicism was strongly attacked by many of our teachers and some of our inspectors," and priests had been "beaten down" in much of Hidalgo—but not yet in Huejutla.[106]

While the SEP's conscientious vanguard denounced public processions and priests who practiced outside the law, their complaints underscored the fact that few mayors prosecuted Catholic parents for boycotting schools to protest socialist education.[107] Worse still, most teachers shied away from the fight against fanaticism. Frustrated by foot-dragging, Superintendent Corzo fired a few "fanatic" teachers. When this failed to inspire, in February 1935 Corzo followed an unconstitutional secret directive from the SEP and forced teachers to sign controversial pledges affirming that their "beliefs were not those of any sect or religious creed" and promising to defend "scientific truth."[108] Many teachers quit rather than sign; one inspector was fired for refusing. The opposition press seized on the "atheist oaths," further inflaming Catholic sentiment.[109] Corzo was soon transferred, but his example encouraged Inspector Rodríguez Lozano to move against the Church outside the law and SEP policy.

Throughout the fall of 1934, the inspector asked federal troops to expel clergy. On the Día de la Raza (October 12, Columbus Day), he organized a mass rally to cow Catholics. Huejutla's town square—long an elite space—was filled by SEP teachers with hundreds of Nahua peasants from surrounding villages. For Rodríguez Lozano, their presence demonstrated unified indigenous support for the SEP and "frightened" the hacendados.[110] Six Nahua communities that marched were free at last: "they do not let themselves be exploited." These indigenous peasants rejected labor drafts, but their emancipation was not only structural but also spiritual: in these half-dozen villages, Huejutla's mestizo catechists and priests were no longer welcomed and "religious fanatics have no influence." Echoing the language of federal educators in Campeche, Rodríguez Lozano stated that his teachers won the "faith" of the peasants by demonstrating the benefits of "economic liberation" only after expelling priests and catechists.[111] By November 1934, Rodríguez Lozano's teachers had "liberated" another eighteen communities.[112]

Inspector Rodríguez Lozano used iconoclasm, albeit on a small scale, to shake the old belief system of indigenous people. In November 1934, one teacher used his power as a labor inspector to fine a hacendado for violating the federal labor code and then encouraged an indigenous worker to destroy a cross. Didactic iconoclasm drove home the message that destroying fanaticism dissolved class and ethnic inequality. Smashing sacred objects would (it was thought) rouse indigenous people to turn against religion by demonstrating its supposed inefficacy.[113] The priest, now shown to be useless, would be ignored along with other exploiters—or so the teachers hoped.

By November 1934, Rodríguez Lozano's talks with Nahua villagers had taken on a sharper tone as well. Religion's only truth, he informed them, was "a perfect masquerade." As in northern Campeche, Huastecan teachers and students painted schoolhouse walls with anticlerical murals mocking Christian symbols. When it came to defanaticization, Rodríguez Lozano wrote that "we believe ideas are valued more for their repetition than their subtlety." Only when the priests were gone would Indians realize that school was "the only way to improve."[114] Superintendant Corzo lauded Rodríguez Lozano for working a miracle in Huejutla, "where it was once not possible to speak of agrarianism." Progress came, Corzo believed, only after the inspector "achieved the exile of the priests of the region."[115]

Rodríguez and his vanguard of determined teachers claimed to have emancipated two dozen hamlets by the end of 1934. The question remains, though: how much did federal teachers really change indigenous culture? Some peasants probably abandoned syncretic Catholic rites entirely. Years later, Nahua who joined the leftist agrarista movement in the 1970s in fact did so.[116] The crackdown on the institutional Church in the second half of 1934 probably interrupted the public, collective religious life of Nahua communities by stopping pilgrimages and suspending fiestas. Although this alienated many, it might have allowed some, especially the younger men and women already at odds with village patriarchy and priests, to drift away from syncretic Catholic celebrations and into the teachers' circle.

Still, most peasants continued to honor the religious rituals deeply rooted in Mesoamerican beliefs. Even without a public cult, they could make private offerings at the home altar, the hearth guardian stone, and the cornfield. So-called superstition possessed important practical functions for farmers. Nahua people closely watched nature to gather practical knowledge: they could "read" the clouds in the morning to predict rain in the afternoon. But this native empiricism was inseparable from religious beliefs. In the Nahua worldview, the natural was supernatural, but not irrational.[117] When confronted by teachers intent on defanaticization, indigenous people feigned compliance while covertly continuing traditional spiritual practices. Most federal teachers were probably only dimly aware of the centrality of these religious practices in the lives of indigenous peasants. Nahua Catholics in the Veracruzano Huasteca hid their core ritual life from a resident schoolteacher for three decades, just as they had done from clergy for centuries.[118] Faced with the survival of Nahua religious practices, teachers tolerated superstitions as long as the public, collective services officiated by the Catholic priest ceased and mestizo catechists were shunned. Indeed, Rodríguez Lozano reported to his superiors that "the Indian of this region is not Catholic but just superstitious," suggesting that he adopted this distinction between tolerable Mesoamerican and proscribed orthodox Catholic religious practice.[119]

When Rodríguez Lozano left Huejutla in early 1935, the SEP's revolutionary project still had a long way to go. True, he had made headway in some two dozen communities, and pro-revolutionary agraristas and religious dissidents enjoyed an unprecedented degree of freedom of action.[120] Yet most local and state politicos' attitudes had hardened against the SEP. Catholics were seething, and attendance strikes were spreading. In most communities, labor drafts and rents were still collected, and land reform remained stalled. Trying to suture the social divisions that the revolutionary project had opened inside Nahua communities, Rodríguez had come to believe that emancipation of the indigenous required the extirpation of Catholic influence. The religious question had been radicalized but not resolved. It would fall to his successor to finish the struggle.

The Inspector, the Bishop, and the Nahua

In March 1935, Francisco Zárate González took over the SEP's zone headquartered in Huejutla. When it came to the religious question, few SEP inspectors took as hard a line as Zárate. Trained to teach in the rational education method inspired by Spanish anarchist Francisco Ferrer Guardia in Salvador Alvarado's radical military administration of Yucatán in 1915–17, Zárate had been promoted by Governor Felipe Carrillo Puerto (1922–23) to school inspector and rural political organizer. Zárate took to heart Carrillo Puerto's Ninth Socialist Commandment: "flee from religion, especially Catholicism, like the worst plague!" During the 1920s, he likely went to garridista Tabasco with other Yucatecan rational educators.[121] Given this professional formation, Zárate believed that implementing SEP socialist education required "finishing off once and for all the Clergy, the Rich, and the Caciques."[122] When it came to the religious question, he was particularly belligerent: "as long as priests and churches exist the masses cannot be redeemed."[123] Indians were especially vulnerable: "the Indian prefers to go without eating, in order to pay for a mass or to take a *retablo* [miracle] of silver or gold so that the saint will do them a favor." He saw only one way forward: "remove [Indians] from religious practices, from fanaticism, from superstition and from witchcraft."[124] Defanaticization demanded direct action, but like his mentor Felipe Carrillo Puerto, Zárate understood the utility of bilingual education to advance education. He probably had picked up a smattering of Nahuatl after over a year in Hidalgo, visiting homes and conversing with indigenous Huastecans outside of the classroom. But Zárate never really overcame the apathetic façade Nahuas projected to threatening outsiders: he claimed that "the Indian does not have friendship; they do not even visit each other."[125]

Zárate's previous posting during 1934 in the Sierra district of Calnali only strengthened his anticlerical zeal. Upon arrival, he tried to jail the beloved local priest, Luis Marín, for baptizing without civil registration.[126] Freed by politicians fearful of the voto morado, the priest bitterly attacked socialist education from his pulpit as "foreign teaching brought to corrupt and to deceive" and threatened to excommunicate parents who refused to boycott it (his brother Vicente ran an underground parochial school). To reach surrounding Nahua communities, Father Marín organized middle-class mestizas into the Liga Sociedad Hermana (Sisterly Social League). The Sisters brought Nahua to hear Sunday homilies in favor of boycotting the SEP and reminded peasants to pay tithes and perform the "voluntary" communal labor for the parish.[127]

Zárate viewed his foe Father Marín in crudely Marxist terms: a parasitic figure exploiting the lower class by collecting tithes and primacias, pocketing fees for baptism and marriage, and buying real estate under assumed names.[128] However, Marín was not just a puppet of the mestizo landowning elite. In the 1940s, Father Marín braved the wrath of powerful mestizo caciques by opposing the draft of Nahua into their paramilitaries.[129] Marín tolerated unorthodox traditional religious practices against Bishop Manríquez's wishes. Nahua Catholics had long thronged to the grounds of Calnali's San Marcos church to honor their patron saint in a raucous, profane festival: they took in cockfights and horse races and danced the *huapango* for three days (April 25–27) in the church's atrium.[130]

The fiesta's exuberant syncretism (especially binge drinking) struck Zárate as especially egregious fanaticism. Ending the Indians' blood sports, sloth, and superstition would turn them toward literature, team sports, and other healthy, secular pastimes.[131] To prevent the 1934 fiesta, Zárate nationalized the church's atrium for an athletic field. When he personally confronted Father Marín to enforce the order, a melee ensued. The Liga Hermana told Nahua that the inspector wielded a bottle, stick, or knife against the popular padre. When opposition to federal schools spread, Zárate blamed "ignorant and fanatical indigenous people."[132] By trying to end the San Marcos festival, he threatened the principal sacred event for Nahua Catholics in Calnali's indigenous neighborhoods and surrounding hamlets.[133]

Zárate's confrontational tactics also provoked political blowback, as fear of the voto morado and the pull of personal and pious connections to the clergy turned upstate politicians against the inspector. State congressman José Mercado, Marín's compadre, jailed Zárate. Rather than punish the priest and his party, *rodriguista* governor Víveres recommended that Inspector Zárate "walk in harmony" with Father Marín. Zárate found few local allies. He pinned his hopes on Calnalí's new mayor, Felipe J. Sierra. But Sierra's anticlericalism was an attempt to damage a longtime political rival who sheltered the fugitive Marín in his house. Sierra tolerated illegal Catholic processions through the streets and stood as a godfather to a political ally. Furthermore, Zárate's potential allies among the Nahua peasants mistrusted Sierra because in the past the mayor had stolen their communal landholding.[134]

Eschewing consensus building and popular mobilization, Zárate resorted to litigation (and likely intimidation) to drive Marín out of town—probably into hiding in a nearby Nahua hamlet. Zárate's successor declared priestless Calnali "a magnificent environment" in the spring of 1935.[135] Later that year, however, the voto morado elected Gregorio Ortega mayor. Ortega attacked SEP supporters as "government spies" and welcomed another priest to Calnali.[136] Zárate's victory proved pyrrhic, and he was spoiling for another fight with fanatics when he arrived in Huejutla.

Catholics had gained the upper hand there during the 1934 *posadas* (nine days preceding Christmas). When classes resumed with the new year, attendance strikes paralyzed federal schools, forcing Inspector Zárate to close seven of them (one-fifth of the zone).[137] By early 1935, he was firing teachers whom he suspected of being Catholic.[138] Facing numerous setbacks, Zárate focused on Xochiatipan, sensing that its extreme class and ethnic polarization might facilitate popular, pro-SEP mobilization. After the Revolution, three upwardly mobile, interrelated mestizo landowning clans, the Bustos, the Martínez, and the Pérez, had displaced Porfirian magnates atop Xochiatipan's society and subjected the town to endless feuds: an epic 1954 shoot-out between the Pérez and the Bustos was later immortalized in a *corrido*. In May 1935, Zárate risked his own life by personally visiting to demand that mestizo rancheros immediately end unconstitutional labor drafts. Miguel Pérez, top dog at the time and a leading despoiler of Nahua land, threatened to hack Zárate into mincemeat (*en picadillo*) if he ever returned. Zárate later narrowly escaped an attempted ambush. Never one to turn the other cheek, Zárate armed a pro-SEP Nahua hamlet in the municipio to check Pérez's "reign of terror." Still, the inspector would not return until August—this time with a bodyguard of soldiers.[139]

At about the same time, SEP teachers faced off against the macho Father Mateo Ochoa in the Nahua hamlet of Pilcuatla (Tlanchinol municipio). Ochoa visited frequently in 1935, leading public processions, preaching against socialist education, and reportedly pocketing the princely sum of one hundred pesos for mass during Holy Week. The beleaguered maestra rural blamed the priest for the failure of her "social labor" (agrarian reform, prohibition of labor drafts, and home visits to discuss hygiene). However, she held class in the community's former chapel, and the SEP's seizure of sacred space undoubtedly alienated many peasants. In April or May 1935, residents demanded her key to the building and then converted the school back to the center of communal cult. The SEP blamed the charismatic, Nahuatl-speaking priest, not popular sentiment, for her defeat and asked that troops arrest

Father Ochoa in secret to prevent the indigenous pueblo from taking reprisals against her.[140]

As the school year ended in May 1935, Zárate's failures were manifest. Like Rodríguez Lozano before him, Zárate believed that fanaticism reinforced structural inequality, above all labor drafts. Defanaticization required patience and the enthusiastic support of state and local officials to enforce the ley de cultos. Zárate had neither. Setbacks in Tlanchinol and Xochiatipan and continuing attendance strikes across his zone highlighted the limits of revolutionary change.[141] Prohibiting Huejutla's Holy Week celebrations, like his campaign against Calnali's fiesta the previous year, promised Zárate a rare public triumph against "reaction." But when Zárate denounced illegal bell ringing, alms gathering, and masses, district attorney Antonio Sosa jailed Zárate. In revenge, Zárate invoked federal regulations to close the beloved Free Normal School and two unlicensed parochial schools, and for good measure he impounded part of the bishop's cathedral for a museum.[142]

Zárate and his most anticlerical federal teachers (José Valencia, Emilia Hernández, Federico Bautista, R. Sara Sierra, Rosaura Sierra, Serafina Vite, María Castelán García, Fidel Vite) planned an even bolder act of defanaticization: a quemasantos, in defiance of SEP regulations. Judging by their last names, his teacher-collaborators were locals. Several might well have seen their schools closed due to Catholic campaigns or hailed from religious dissident backgrounds. Most had participated in Rodríguez Lozano's commemoration of the Día de la Raza in October 1934 and were able to marshal hundreds of Nahua supporters from emancipated hamlets. Anticlericalism was center stage at the June 3 rally; led by teachers, peasants marched into Huejutla's plaza and proceeded to smash and burn an estimated five hundred icons.[143] After his Holy Week incarceration, Zárate, teachers, and allied Nahua removed dozens of roadside shrines by torching them, desacralizing Huejutla's hinterland and denying the diocese a valuable source of alms.[144] In a bold challenge to the social hierarchy, supporters of maestro José Valencia in "liberated" and agrarista Piedra Hincada took down most of the crosses from above the doors in streets in Orizatlán, the mestizo county seat. Anticlericalism here did not dim the SEP's appeal—the community would later honor Valencia by naming a school for him.[145] In La Laguna village, some Nahua brought the teacher their own crosses. But most Nahua would never have willingly surrendered the small crosses that represented dead relatives on family domestic altars (*teoixpan*).[146]

Even if the quemasantos destroyed mostly mestizos' icons, it showed some

Nahua supported the SEP's project, including anticlericalism. Liberated in the eyes of the SEP, they were lost souls in the eyes of the Church. Manríquez fumed that armed teachers now occupied his diocese and that "the Devil is now loose in Huejutla."[147] The June 3 quemasantos, like Rodríguez Lozano's Dia de la Raza rally, allowed the SEP to claim a popular mandate for the revolutionary project. Zárate and his supporters would later rationalize the anticlerical ritual in various other ways: a spontaneous protest against Zárate's jailing during Holy Week; a demonstration against the landowning caciques of Xochiatipan, Oriztlán, Yahualica, and Huatla; and a grassroots movement demanding that the ley de cultos be enforced.[148] Zárate himself explained it as a daring coup against Bishop Manríquez in a letter to President Cárdenas.[149]

Such explanations failed to cover up an embarrassing truth: at the time Zárate faced prosecution for sexually assaulting (*atentados al pudor*) a young female student. Supporters undoubtedly dismissed the charges as trumped up. After all, foes had jailed Zárate twice before (in Calnali in 1934 and during Holy Week 1935 in Huejutla), and Bishop Manríquez and Father Marín of Calnali both baselessly berated Zárate for pushing sexual education.[150] But three factors strongly suggest Zárate was in fact guilty.

In the first place, the case required a prominent family to risk social stigma. Would the family have risked damaging a daughter's reputation in such a public legal gambit? Second, there is the matter of Zárate's own musings on indigenous culture penned almost a year later. He criticized the tyranny of indigenous fathers who exercised *la patria potestad* (domestic patriarchy) by arranging children's marriages—for him, yet another symptom of a defective culture lacking sentimentality. The only glimmers of hope for him were the *indias*—"the most sociable" of all—eager to talk while washing clothes or hauling water from the river.[151] Zárate had apparently been striking up conversations with quite a number of them; he routinely sought out young indigenous women in situations that allowed for a degree of emotional intimacy—if not more.[152] Third, eighteen years before in Yucatán, Zárate faced accusations for kidnapping a young female student.[153] The quemasantos was less a blow against conservative resistance than a cynical tactic allowing Zárate to deflect the charges of sexual assault as a plot by Manríquez.

The stratagem shielded Zárate. In Hidalgo as in Yucatán, Zárate escaped conviction.[154] His superior disciplined him for a lesser charge of illegally docking his teachers' pay and scolded his "militant politics" and "extreme crusade against fanaticism."[155] But he kept his job, perhaps an attempt to protect the SEP's reputation and the maestros rurales' hard-won gains in the Huasteca.

After it appeared on the front page of the sensationalistic, right-leaning national newspaper *Hombre Libre*, the allegation of rape against Zárate hardened Catholic opposition to federal education across Mexico.[156] Two months later, a letter to *Hombre Libre*'s editor accused Zárate of assaulting a second young girl, as well as tyrannizing Huejutla by banning catechism classes and bell ringing and "stirring up" peasants to illegally occupy land.[157] Catholic activists successfully conflated Zárate's sexual assault with anticlericalism and land reform. After Zárate's scandal, many Catholic readers of *Hombre Libre* came to see the entire revolutionary project as an existential threat not just to the Catholic faith but also to children's innocence. And in the upstate, defense of morality was also defense of the socioeconomic status quo.

Of course, Zárate's apparent guilt in no way substantiated all of the alleged sexual misconduct Catholic propaganda attributed to federal teachers. Moreover, compared to the army or the revolutionary political class, the SEP was a veritable model of probity and professional conduct. It was less patriarchal than other federal agencies (many women worked as teachers and, in a few cases, inspectors), and its teachers often advocated fairly conservative social mores—advocating marriage over free unions and championing the commemoration of Mother's Day.[158] However, Zárate's case was not unique. A small minority of male teachers and inspectors did in fact use their official positions to seduce or sexually assault female students with impunity.[159] In 1927 an internal SEP investigation discovered that ten young female students and faculty were pregnant due to the ex-director and another teacher at the Hidalgo state normal school in Molango.[160] In the 1920s, a teacher in the Yucatecan village of Chan Kom "disgraced" one girl of seventeen and molested another after trapping her in the schoolhouse.[161] In 1931, one SEP inspector reportedly raped a maestra rural in Chihuahua; in February 1936 another eloped with an indigenous student in Puebla.[162] These infamous incidents discredited all teachers in the eyes of some and provided grist for the propaganda mills of Catholic activists. The perception of teacher impunity further fed popular outrage. Katherine Bliss argues that the postrevolutionary state's inability to control the predatory sexual behavior of its male politicians, policemen, and soldiers compromised its attempts to "moralize" society.[163] Dissolute male schoolteachers and inspectors were an even greater danger to the revolutionary project because of their routine contact with children.

Zárate's scandal undoubtedly played a major role in consolidating Catholic opposition to the SEP and undermining the authority of the federal government in the upstate. His June 3, 1935, quemasantos also marked the end of the anticlerical campaign due to national events. When Inspector Zárate's message to Cárdenas describing it arrived in Los Pinos in early June, tension between Cárdenas and Calles was mounting.[164] A fortnight later, President Cárdenas boldly broke with Calles and replaced the Callista loyalists in his cabinet, including Tomás Garrido Canabal, the great advocate of iconoclasm.

Still, Cárdenas strongly supported the SEP, enabling upstate federal teachers to strike and force local authorities to free Zárate from jail. New SEP superintendent Leobardo Parra exonerated "comrade Inspector" Zárate and funneled arms to teachers and Nahua agraristas.[165] By the end of 1935, Zárate's superiors claimed that his jailing was unjust and described the strike and quemasantos as nothing less than a "resounding triumph" against latifundia and caciquism. At the same time, the slow relaxation in Church-state tensions nationally meant that Bishop Manríquez and the clergy were no longer identified as enemies by the SEP.[166]

Easing religious tensions did not lead to success for the revolutionary project in the upstate. Setbacks in 1935 in the Huasteca were compounded by reverses in the Sierra town of Molango, ironically a liberal stronghold historically. Molango's gentry supported Benito Juárez and then Francisco Madero, swayed by its Masonic lodge, the Guardians of the Sierra. But in the mid-1930s, Molango's officials and landowners supported an attendance strike led by Father Sánchez and his mestiza catechists (including two federal maestras rurales). In nearby Xochicoatlán, another unlicensed priest and another federal maestra rural organized another crippling boycott of SEP schools.[167] In fact, so many federal schools had to close in 1934 and 1935 that the SEP quietly merged the two upstate districts (Calnali/Sierra, Huejutla/Huasteca) into one.[168]

Nationally, the SEP was downplaying its moderate policy of defanaticization by 1936, a decision driven not only by national events but also by the success of Catholic campaigns in places like upstate Hidalgo. In his annual plan for 1936–37, Rodríguez Lozano, now inspector in the downstate Hidalgan zone of Tula, pledged to fight fanaticism. Yet he now lumped it in with other "social ills" like alcoholism and carefully specified that his fight would be nonconfrontational in line with SEP doctrine.[169] In 1938, Rodríguez Lozano was promoted to federal superintendent of neighboring San Luis Potosí, where he hosted an indigenous conference in Tamazuncaule, the roost of Manríquez's family. He asked President Cárdenas to create a special federal intendancy with an indigenist mission just for the Potosina Huasteca (in many ways the secular equivalent of Manríquez's diocese).[170] Cárdenas's silence on the matter suggests the president no longer considered the Huasteca a promising place for revolutionary change. Absent consistent pressure from the postrevolutionary state, the labor drafts that the SEP considered the principal impediment to indigenous emancipation persisted for decades.[171] Even after Cárdenas and the SEP struck defanaticization from the revolutionary agenda, popular suspicion of schools and ejidos lingered in the upstate.

Counterpoint: Downstate Quiescence

Hidalgo's downstate largely escaped the intense conflict between apostles of revolutionary change and foes united by Catholicism that roiled the upstate in the mid-1930s. Understanding this absence of conflict requires reckoning with a number of factors, beginning with the Church's very different institutional profile in the subregion. The downstate Diocese of Tulancingo lacked both consistent clerical leadership and abundant resources. Bishop José Luis María Altamirano y Bulnes (1932–37) moved on to Michoacán after five years.[172] The diocese's clergy operated without much direction from above or interference from the revolutionary state. Priests showed little enthusiasm for Rome's reforms; in fact, three attempts to found ACM in the diocese fizzled between 1930 and 1936.[173] By June 1936, Tulancingo's ACM was finally organized, but the bishop anticipated a dim future: "it is barely beginning, and in conditions not very favorable."[174] Indeed, the ACM never grew into a strong hub group for civic action against the revolutionary project.

Instead, it was the largely autonomous *Padres de Familia* (Parents of the Family, a Church front group opposing socialist education) based in the state capital of Pachuca that took the lead. In August 1935, it frightened state officials by staging a massive demonstration by men, women, and children against Hidalgo's ley de cultos.[175] Across the downstate, Padres chapters conveyed episcopal orders to boycott federal schools, shun federal maestros, and set up home schools.[176] Still, downstate Catholic resistance to the revolutionary project was geographically uneven and generally weak. Some areas witnessed no Catholic mobilizations at all. In a few locales, however, some local

Padres ignored explicit Church prohibitions against illicit resistance.[177] Catholic resistance to the revolutionary project turned violent in only three downstate locales: the towns of Singuilucan and Tepeji del Rio and the Tenango de Doria district. A closer examination of these three areas sheds light on the exceptional conditions that produced segunda violence in the downstate.

A mountainous region on the eastern edge of Hidalgo bordering the states of Veracruz and Puebla, Tenango de Doria proved remarkably resistant to the revolutionary project. Neither highland Otomí villages nor mestizo towns in the valley were well schooled until the SEP began operating in the district around 1930. By 1935, a bloc of radical federal teachers was at loggerheads with the district's Callista cacique, Modesto Licona. Licona protected numerous underground parochial schools and four priests (only one licensed). During the fall of 1935, long-serving Father Adrián Cerón officiated in Licona's own house and led an effective boycott of SEP schools. In retaliation, federal teachers encouraged peasants to defy Licona's electoral dominance. In late March or April 1936, supporters of Licona and Father Cerón dynamited the federal school in the hamlet of Huasquilla (San Bartolo Tutotepec municipio). Federal maestro rural Leodegario Solís Gómez fingered Father Cerón and his gang of "fanatics" as responsible, and Mexico City leaned on local authorities to squeeze the clergy in response. Fiery anti-SEP homilies from Tenango de Doria's priests denounced the crackdown, apparently encouraging the same gang to kill maestro Solís a few weeks later. Although a defiant Licona freed seven suspects in the killing, federal pressure forced the cacique to expel the four priests he had protected, leaving both factions sullen and seeking revenge.[178]

Four factors spurred offensive segunda violence in Tenango de Doria. First, close ties between local political (Licona) and religious (Cerón) elites gave segunderos de facto impunity—Solís's alleged killers walked out of jail. Second, strong preexisting religious tensions predisposed Catholics to react violently to confrontational federal teachers: in 1926, several thousand schismatic Catholics affiliated with the Iglesia Católica Apostólica Mexicana (ICAM) tried to seize three churches in the district.[179] At the time of Solís's murder, the Assembly of God was evangelizing in the district.[180] Third, anti-clerical regulations damaged the economy, further inflaming local sentiment over the religious question. In July 1936, peasants from Agua Blanca (Iturbide municipio) complained: "the customs here, once known for being upright and honest, today are disorderly and in general decline, respect and *la educación* [roughly, good morals] are on the point of disappearing into anarchy." To make matters worse, the ley de cultos banned annual fiestas that also served as the main market for Otomís and mestizos: "there is no liveliness in the pueblos, the town square is almost deserted, local business is passing through a black crisis . . . religion gives life to all . . . like electricity moving through the machinery in a factory."[181] Fourth, the prospect of land reform riled local elites. The gang of segunderos that killed Solís was probably originally organized by landlords to oppose the creation of ejidos.[182]

A similar dynamic stoked violence in Singuilucan. In this magueygrowing town on the plains of Apan, the dominant Espejel clan blocked revolutionary change by installing a wealthy landowner, Luis Lopé, in the town hall. His *defensa rural* (a paramilitary rural police) terrorized maestros and agraristas and even dared to assassinate a federal bureaucrat in nearby Tulancingo. The Espejel backed Father Francisco Arceaga, whom agraristas suspected was the true "director of politics in the area," dominating elections and convincing peasants to reject ejidos. Though he was expelled two years earlier for legal violations, the Espejel and allied gentry protected Arceaga's clandestine masses, parochial school, and covert monastery.[183]

In another town near Tula, Tepeji del Rio, religiously motivated violence had targeted agraristas and federal maestros since 1931. Socialist education reignited smoldering divisions between revolutionaries and their Catholic foes, reactivating antirevolutionary vigilantism around Tula. By October 1935, federal teachers in several villages had received so many threats that they asked for federal troops to protect their schools, fearing segunda violence primed by attendance strikes.[184] As in Tenango de Doria and Singuilucan, the violence in Tepeji del Rio was overdetermined, resulting from local political competition, the lingering effects of past religiously tinged conflicts, and individual teachers' determination to fight rather than accommodate Catholic opposition. Still, conflicts over the religious question remained isolated in the downstate because the Diocese of Tulancingo shied away from direct confrontation with the state, and neither the Rodríguez regime nor the SEP in the subregion enforced anticlerical measures.

The Otomí pueblos of the impoverished, semi-arid Mezquital region drew considerable attention from federal educators. Alfonso Fabila, who led a SEP cultural mission there, claimed that "the influence that the priest once had, the teacher now possesses."[185] But for the most part, inspectors did not see the institutional Church as a major threat in the subregion. In 1935, when Rodríguez Lozano directed a downstate district in the Mezquital, his anticlericalism was only rhetorical; he told the Otomí children that the Conquest was "the clergy's first betrayal."[186] There was no polarizing figure comparable to Manríquez here, nor were there obvious forms of ethnic exploitation like labor drafts embedded in religious practices in the Mezquital. For the most part, then, downstate teachers shied away from direct attacks on Catholicism. Absent conflicts over the religious question in most of the downstate, other goals of the revolutionary project were realized in Otomí communities.[187]

Local politics in the downstate discouraged anticlericals' attempts to confront the Church. A few complaints from Masonic lodges and anticlerical organizations in the subregion trickled into Mexico City's secretary of gobernación (secretary of the interior), alleging that priests performed unregulated marriages, led public processions, held masses in private houses, and ran underground parochial schools.[188] Labor leaders from the historically strong Hidalgo Miners Confederation and the railroad workers took an aggressive stance on the religious question, perhaps because of their unions' anarcho-syndicalist tradition. These radical urban workers tried to encourage peasants to organize and reject Catholic influence. But state authorities generally refused to cooperate, and many of the unions' rank and file were deeply divided over the religious question.[189]

Generally speaking, the religious question never weighed on gubernatorial elections the way it did in Campeche in 1935. Catholic brokers did intervene in elections at times. In 1929, opposition candidate José G. Parres mounted a strong challenge to the Matías Rodríguez machine, thanks in part to "understandings and arrangements" with the "clerical reaction." In Apam, Hidalgo, for instance, a noted Knight of Columbus and wealthy merchant, Victoriano López Bello, headed his campaign.[190] Perhaps this opposition strategy encouraged Rodríguez's local lieutenants to placate Catholics in order to neutralize the voto morado. In the 1933 gubernatorial election, Matías Rodríguez backed his son-in-law, Ernesto Viveros. Viveros used his opponent's Protestantism to try to amplify Catholic turnout in his favor.[191] For the most part, Matías Rodríguez's loose confederation of caciques generally either ignored or actively accommodated Catholics. In 1935, the mayor of Cardonal (Mezquital Valley) permitted illegal religious services in a legally closed church thanks to the protection of his "intimate friend," the state secretary of government.[192] Such informal pacts discouraged anticlericals from confronting Catholics for fear of retaliation.

In the downstate as in the upstate, the SEP leadership, diocesan institutions, ethnicity, and anti-Catholic dissent shaped conflicts over the religious question. But in this subregion, in sharp contrast to the upstate, these factors generally discouraged politicization of the religious question. In Hidalgo as in Campeche, a watershed gubernatorial election would give Catholics a lasting advantage and doom the SEP-led coalition for revolutionary change to slow marginalization.

Cardenismo, the Election of 1936, and the End of the Revolutionary Project in the Upstate

After Cárdenas's June 1935 break with Calles, Catholics across Mexico looked hopefully to Mexico City for relief from anticlerical regulations. In September 1935, a priest exiled by a federal teacher from the downstate hacienda El Candelario presciently promised that "soon the Catholic question will be arranged and then I will come back."[193] Until late March 1936 Cárdenas moved slowly on the matter, allowing governors to deal with the sensitive religious question themselves as Cárdenas's political operatives focused on removing regional bosses loyal to Calles. Hidalgo's April 1936 gubernatorial election gave Emilio Portes Gil, Cárdenas's electoral czar, the chance to break Callista Matías Rodríguez's hold on state politics. To do so, Portes Gil backed his old friend Javier Rojo Gómez for governor.[194] Though only forty years old at the time, Rojo Gómez had served and then abandoned three governors between 1920 and 1935.[195] Rojo Gómez cultivated a radical image, representing himself as a left-wing populist and bashing the Church. During the Cristiada, state congressman Rojo advocated drastic limits on the size of the clergy, although his colleagues refused to act. An early and vocal champion of the SEP's Huastecan project, he charged that upstate landlords enslaved Indians. True to form, in his 1936 gubernatorial campaign he styled himself an ardent Cardenista, championing workers and agraristas against his former mentor, Matías Rodríguez, whom he now denounced as a reactionary and tool of Calles.[196] To ensure Rojo Gómez's triumph, high-ranking Cardenistas in the SEP summoned Inspector Rubén Rodríguez Lozano to Mexico City to undertake a covert political mission. Working in his downstate district of Tula, Inspector Rodríguez Lozano oversaw Rojo Gómez's electoral campaign, using federal teachers with influence over indigenous communities, ejidatarios, and workers in the huge Cruz Azul cement factory to turn out the vote for Cárdenas's man.[197]

With Mexico City's help, Rojo Gómez steamrolled Matías Rodríguez's demoralized and divided supporters in the April 1936 polling.[198] No candidate, not even Camerino Solís, a Knight of Columbus, successfully courted Catholic electoral brokers, suggesting Cárdenas's break with Calles helped depress the voto morado in Hidalgo.[199] Rojo Gómez's triumph played a decisive role in ending the religious conflict in a way that favored the Church in Hidalgo. The new governor had no quid pro quo with Catholic voters, but Rojo Gómez's downstate local allies had come to terms with landowners and caciques in many key communities in order to dismantle Rodríguez's machine. These local pacts effectively nullified the revolutionary project because the strongest advocates of anticlericalism (federal teachers, labor and agrarian organizers) were effectively marginalized in the Rojo Gómez regime. Downstate agraristas who backed Rojo Gómez soon complained of corruption and machine politics on ejidos under the new administration.[200] Organized labor in the subregion soured on Rojo Gómez as well; the formidable miners union of Real del Monte walked out of the ruling party in Hidalgo and eventually backed the opposition Almazán presidential candidacy in 1939–1940.[201] In the upstate, Rojo Gómez's decision to cut deals with powerful ranchero bosses ended the SEP's anticlericalism once and for all. Using Juvencio Nochebuena (a wily rancher and retired general) as his intermediary, Rojo Gómez cultivated support among upstate rancheros that had long defended labor drafts against the SEP.[202] Among his new allies was Honorato Austria, an exceptionally violent boss whose victims included numerous family members, a federal army officer, a judge, and the mayor of Lolotla. At the peak of his power, Austria could summon a private army of over a thousand retainers and deal directly with national figures like Calles, Cárdenas, and Saturnino Cedillo. An exasperated federal teacher compared his power to "a strong ring of iron that the Revolution cannot break."[203]

By endorsing caciques like Austria and Nochebuena, Rojo Gómez stymied revolutionary change in the upstate. Although state-sponsored anticlericalism waned during his term, Rojo Gómez kept his distance from Catholics and refused to rescind Hidalgo's ley de cultos. Furthermore, his upstate ranchero allies were far from pious. In the 1920s, Honorato Austria had a priest bound, kidnapped, and dumped in Molango after the cleric crossed him. In 1946, Father Marín (Zárate's old foe) opposed Francisco Austria Martínez's forced induction of Nahua into his paramilitary. In reprisal, this member of the Austria clan brought in a Methodist minister dressed as a bishop bearing two bogus papal bulls to try to steal away the priest's followers.[204]

For the most part, however, the Austria clan cultivated good relations with most priests, but they were also on good terms with *zahorines* (traditional Nahua spiritual specialists). The Austria, like their bitter rivals the Cabrera and the Olguín clans, had much to lose if they riled local Catholics by persecuting important priests.[205] The Austria and other mestizo notables had political, economic, and social stakes in maintaining the religious status quo. The SEP's vaunted liberation of the Huastecan Nahua meant abolishing tithes and labor drafts, prying apart Catholic social networks, and suppressing Catholic sources of social capital like parochial schools. This would have leveled the subregion's socioethnic hierarchy with the mestizo bosses at its apex.[206] The ascendancy of Austria and other caciques meant that federal teachers faced an uphill fight for the rest of the Cárdenas presidency. True, maestros rurales had some popular support (probably of younger and poorer male Nahua campesinos and some religious dissidents like spiritists and Protestants) and some pull in Mexico City.[207] But Rojo Gómez's accommodation of Austria and his ilk compromised the SEP's revolutionary project, including what was left of the defanaticization campaign. The loose confederation of Huastecan and Sierran strongmen who consolidated their power in the mid-1930s under Rojo Gómez would hold on to power in the subregion until the 1970s.[208]

By late 1936, the banishment of Callistas meant that national support for anticlericalism had declined greatly, and the SEP responded accordingly. In the reports filed by eight inspectors in 1936 and 1937, six make no mention of defanaticization at all.[209] One advocated scientific knowledge to fight ignorance but followed the Cárdenas line of postponing defanaticization until after structural socioeconomic reforms.[210] Federal cutbacks in rural education meant the SEP could not open many new schools. Ironically, even newly created ejidos, the pride and joy of Cárdenas, were frequently left without one.[211] With the Church-state thaw on the national level, the number of unlicensed Catholic schools set up to encourage boycotts of federal classrooms had dwindled by the late 1930s.[212] But hard feelings among Catholics lingered for years. One downstate teacher complained of threats from "fanatics . . . inspired by a priest enemy of the social school." In the upstate, the situation was even worse, as priests in the Sierra reportedly advocated violence against teachers, and federal and local authorities did nothing to protect them.[213]

From the armed phase of the Revolution until the mid-1930s, the religious question had played at best a secondary role in Hidalgo. However, between 1934 and 1935 it came to dominate upstate politics; the revolutionary project's fate hinged on defanaticization. Rather than simply responding to national events, regional actors and institutions drove the conflict in the subregion. The stakes were high because Bishop Manríquez and his SEP counterparts, Inspectors Rodríguez and Zárate, hoped to turn the upstate into a testing ground for rival indigenist projects. In the eyes of the SEP vanguard in the upstate, Catholicism was part and parcel of the system of ethnic inequality exemplified by labor drafts. Eradicating religion would emancipate Indians. For Catholics, defanaticization and iconoclasm threatened not just the faith but morality itself; Zárate's immoral behavior seemingly confirmed Manríquez's dire predictions. Catholic discourse melded agrarian reform with the moral panic over teachers' allegedly widespread scandalous conduct. Most Nahua peasants refused to firmly support either the SEP or the Church project. Their reticence only hardened the inspectors' and the bishop's uncompromising stands.

Federal teachers failed to create a popular coalition transcending ethnicity and class largely because of widespread popular resistance to anticlericalism. My point is not to reduce opposition to the revolutionary project to instrumentalist exploitation of Catholicism. Religious belief and practice was part and parcel of local markets, definitions of community, and even electioneering. In the final analysis, the SEP could not isolate and uproot "fanaticism" deeply embedded in everyday life. Resistance to the federal schools in this not particularly mocho region can be explained not only by Manríquez's aura, caciques' defense of privilege, and the diffused nature of Catholic belief, but also by the reckless conduct of Inspector Francisco Zárate González.

Still, the Church in Hidalgo did not emerge from the catacombs to reconquer lost souls in the last years of the Cárdenas *sexenio* (the single six-year term served by a president). Instead, its anemic institutions struggled to reassert their authority over their own apathetic laity and often strong-minded clergy. Revolutionary politics still posed problems: the state's ley de cultos was a dead letter but was still on the books, leaving the Church in legal limbo. As late as early 1938, state authorities refused to open more churches, license more priests, or allow much public worship. Cárdenas refused to break the deadlock, saying it was a state matter.[214] Mini-Arreglos with local power brokers often proved fragile, and the Church remained anxious to gain lasting legal protections and recognition. These were not idle fears: in June 1936, Bishop Altamirano of Tulancingo made a pastoral visit to a town with the mayor's permission, but the federal prosecutor nevertheless arrested the bishop, a priest, and the mayor for violating the ley de cultos. A federal judge absolved the clergymen but let the mayor languish in jail for months.[215]

Although the robust persistence of older lay sodalities gave the institutional Church a social presence, lack of priests and an underperforming ACM hindered both Hidalgan dioceses for years to come. In 1945, the Diocese of Huejutla had only one priest per every 23,000 of its 450,000 Catholics, the third worst ratio in Mexico.[216] With few priests and an absent bishop (the Church finally replaced Manríquez in 1939), Catholic Action in the Diocese of Huejutla deteriorated even more. As late as the mid-1940s, there were only about 350 members (all female). Consequently, Sinarquismo emerged as the strongest voice for lay Catholics. Although it was nonviolent and its upper leadership was under the nominal control of the Church hierarchy, it was unyielding in its opposition to the revolutionary project. In the upstate, it appealed to many mestizo rancheros bullied by the Huastecan bosses now defended by the postrevolutionary regime.[217]

Tulancingo's diocese recovered slowly but solidly in the late 1930s. Priests' numbers rebounded in the late 1930s, with one priest per 5,700 inhabitants; by 1945 the ratio was among the best in Mexico. Even in Tulancingo, however, priests could not—or would not—find time to help start an ACM chapter. Almost all the ACM members were female, and the UCM (the ACM branch for older men) did not come into being until years later.[218] In the mid-1940s, the ACM in the diocese had only 2,469 members and only five functional municipal councils (including one in Singuilcan).[219] Much more research needs to be done into grassroots Catholicism in the state, but if there was a revival of the Church in Hidalgo starting in the waning years of the Cárdenas sexenio, it took place largely outside of formal structures and probably built on older lay associations.

If there was a victor in the religious conflict in Hidalgo, it was Bishop Manríquez. Because of him, the clash in the upstate had ramifications across Mexico. Even without the battle against the SEP in the Huasteca, Manríquez almost certainly would have rejected the temperate and reserved approach of the episcopal leadership when it came to the postrevolutionary state. But the bitter conflict in his beloved Indian diocese made Manríquez more belligerent and confrontational, goading him to couple apocalyptic warnings about diabolical bolshevism with thinly veiled references to the righteousness of armed struggle.

From his Texas exile, Manríquez did all he could short of publicly supporting the Segunda to prevent a lasting state-Church reconciliation. After the Calles-Cárdenas break, he thundered that "the tyrant is gone but tyranny remains." He feared that Cárdenas's concessions on the religious question would trick Catholics into accepting the "pure communism" of socialist education.[220] To stave off this Machiavellian quid pro quo, Manríquez again reminded Catholics in *El Socialismo* (1936) that the Church would never condemn believers who took up arms as a matter of conscience.[221] Some segunderos, convinced by Manríquez that Rome really backed them, disparaged Manríquez's episcopal superiors as craven sellouts.[222] The national episcopal leadership finally stripped him of his miter in 1939. Unrepentant, Manríquez continued to plot with LNDL (Liga Nacional Defensora de la Libertad) leader Miguel Palomar y Vizcarra to revitalize the Segunda, meeting with rightist opposition figures ranging from José Vasconcelos to fascist Gold Shirts jefe Nicolás Rodríguez to find a figurehead to lead a second Cristiada.[223]

The upstate conflict undoubtedly hardened the bishop's counterrevolutionary stance. Referring indirectly to the Zárate scandal, Manríquez said of federal teachers, "Corruptors of children and youth abound in all parts, by brute force they inculcate people with Socialism and they are the terror of those regions."[224] Why he did not identify Zárate by name remains something of a mystery. Perhaps it would have prompted anticlerical attacks on individual clerics' sexual mores.[225]

In any event, hard-line Catholic leaders opposed to the institutional Church's conciliatory line seized on the bishop's notion of a moral crusade against socialist education to prevent schoolhouse perversion. Manríquez's confrontational messages roused the faithful against the revolutionary project across Mexico. In 1929, women in Guanajuato went door-to-door distributing Manríquez's September 22, 1928, pastoral letter as the flyer "Current Events that All Good Catholics Should Know."[226]

Because of Manríquez's status as a bishop, segunderos across Mexico invoked on his existential exhortations to legitimize violence. A segundero in Guanajuato quoted the "Manly Bishop" Manríquez on the dangers of sexual education in 1932: "If we are reasonable, if we still have one ounce of dignity, if we do not want our wives and daughters to become prostitutes, and if we do not want our sons to join the vanguard of the army of atheists, it is time for Defenders [of the Church] to redouble our efforts in the armed struggle."[227] On January 27, 1936, a band of segunderos attacked the federal school of Ibarrilla, near León, Guanajuato. The gang held a kind of drumhead court marshal, trying the teacher under "the commandments of the Archbishop [*sic*] of Huejutla." Only the arrival of federal troops saved her from torture or killing.²²⁸ Manríquez's defense of his Indian Church against the SEP's indigenist project helped inspire the Segunda across Mexico. Later, Manríquez's Catholic indigenism turned to the canonization of Juan Diego, the indigenous man whose vision of the Virgin of Guadalupe was the most important religious event in the Americas, a goal finally realized on July 31, 2002.²²⁹

CHAPTER 4

Beatas, Ballots, and Bullets in Guerrero

On Sunday, September 25, 1932, General Gabriel R. Guevara scored a resounding victory in Guerrero's gubernatorial election.[1] The political unknown upset Ezequiel Padilla, a candidate strongly backed by the governor, General Adrián Castrejón. Even though Calles and influential generals endorsed Guevara, he prevailed mainly because of the voto morado. A key political operative, Ladislao Alarcón, was the brother of a priest who campaigned with the slogan "Viva Cristo Rey!" When a thunderstorm blew up in the capital of Chilpancingo during the polling, Catholic women kept men from leaving until they had voted for Guevara. Governor Castrejón blamed Guevara's strength in Chilapa on "associations of *beatas* and fanatics" who brought "ignorant campesinos" to the polls.[2] Although Guevara was endorsed by what I term Guerrero's Ranchero group: a coalition of landowners, lawyers, and military men who had long controlled Guerreran politics, his counterintuitive combination of Mexico City clout and the voto morado underscores an important unwritten rule of postrevolutionary politics: Calles favored some gubernatorial candidates but expected them to muster a modicum of electoral support in order to claim their office. In Guerrero, the Ranchero group could not deliver sufficient votes for Guevara. Instead, it was the voto morado that permitted this Callista praetorian to claim victory.

Guevara's campaign capitalized on rampant Catholic anxiety about the revived national Church-state conflict and leveraged long-standing local alliances between the Ranchero group and Catholic mediators. For years, Catholics leaders (both lay and clergy), ideas, and at times even symbols helped the Ranchero group cling to political power against agrarista candidates. Female Catholic activists (derogatorily called *beatas*) influenced elections and helped organize boycotts of federal schools. Some Guerrero Catholics resisted the revolutionary project not with ballots but with bullets as segunderos. Even after Church-state tensions decreased nationally, Cardenista agrarian reform targeting Guerrero in the late 1930s was doomed in no small part by Catholic resistance.

To understand how *guerrerense* Catholics confronted postrevolutionary state formation, I begin by examining how Guerrero's geography and revolutionary history empowered the Ranchero group, and I explore its symbiotic relationship with the Church. I then turn to the historical, cultural, and gendered dimensions of Catholic participation in postrevolutionary politics in Guerrero. Next, I analyze segunda violence, probing its complex connections with Catholicism by contrasting offensive and defensive attacks in the state. Then I turn to the religious question in the late 1930s, focusing on how the Church reconquered lost ground and helped frustrate agrarian reform. I conclude by explaining why the Church's institutional weaknesses paradoxically facilitated Catholic resistance to the revolutionary project in Guerrero.

Casting the Voto Morado: Regional Geography, Revolutionary History, and the Ranchero Group

Guevara was an unlikely governor; he lacked both previous political experience and military distinction. During the Cristero War, he fought agraristas more than Cristeros in Jalisco.[3] Nevertheless, by nominating Guevara, the Ranchero group shrewdly exploited the army's clout and Calles's desire to restore social order and economically rebuild the poor, chronically ungovernable southwestern state. Guevara owned the state's first tractor, making him a model modern farmer. Recent national political shifts also favored Guevara; Calles wanted to weaken Governor Castrejón's principal protectors, President Ortiz Rubio and the head of the military, Joaquín Amaro, by defeating Castrejón's candidate, Padilla. Most importantly, as a soldier Guevara seemed to be the right person to quell Guerrero's rampant social conflicts with an iron hand. Presidents from Díaz to Cárdenas often preferred military men to tame the *bronco* (wild) state.[4] Shortly before his election, Guevara promised Calles: "Guerrero will not represent a problem that impedes the smooth functioning of federal institutions or a worry for you, on whose shoulders weigh all national problems."[5]

Still, Guevara needed a popular electoral mandate to legitimize his rule. Guevera's stump speakers were mostly young intellectuals (including Octavio Paz, who would go on to be one of Mexico's leading writers). With their limited appeal, they could not match the strong agrarista vote for Castrejón's proxy, Padilla. Pacting with Catholic brokers gave Guevara electoral parity. Catholic electoral mobilization in 1932 was not a political innovation, however. It represented the intensification and strategic coordination of long-standing patterns of informal collaboration between Ranchero group politicos and Catholic electoral brokers.

To understand the voto morado's power in the state, we need to recognize how regional geography fractured Guerrero's middle politics and shaped religious practice.[6] Rugged topography segmented the state into four distinctive subregions: Ambos Costas (the Twin Coasts) comprising the Costa Grande (Big Coast) and Costa Chica (Little Coast); the central and northern valleys; the Tierra Caliente (the Hot Country) in the northwest; and la Montaña (the Wilderness) in the northeast.[7] Guerrero's birth in 1849 did not obey geographic logic, but rather served to reward Liberal caudillo Juan Álvarez, who had long controlled the Costa Grande (the districts of Montes de Oca, Galeana, and Tabares), stretching from the port of Acapulco and its hinterland northwest to the border with Michoacán. The coastal plain was only ten to twenty-five kilometers wide, and it was overshadowed by the western reaches of the ridges and valleys of the Sierra Madre del Sur. Porfirian tropical export booms (sugar, palm oil), as well as cattle, enriched landowners and merchants, especially Acapulco's three Spanish commercial houses. Their enclave economy funneled exports to Mexico City, North America, and Europe. Not until 1928 did the completion of the Acapulco-Mexico City road break this mercantile oligarchy's hold.[8] The other half of the Twin Coasts was the Costa Chica (Allende and Abasolo districts), stretching from Acapulco southeast to the Oaxaca border. Plantations and a few mills long dominated its economy. Predominantly mestizo, the Costa Chica harbored a considerable number of Afromexican and Amuzgo communities, as well as a few Tlapaneco and Nahua ones. Acapulco, the Twin Coasts' premier city, monopolized finance and transportation; foreigners imported technology and at times became businessmen and landowners. Mexico City, not Chilpancingo, mediated the Twin Coasts' major political problems.[9]

To create Guerrero, Mexico City added three regions to the Twin Coasts: the Tierra Caliente (Mina and parts of Aldama districts), the central (Guerrero and Bravos districts) and northern (the remainder of Aldama, Alarcón, and Hidalgo districts) valleys, and la Montaña (Zaragoza, Morelos, and Álvarez districts). Porfirian mining, tropical agricultural, and ranching booms brought prosperity to the Tierra Caliente's elite and accelerated acculturation of Nahua villages. Trade tugged the subregion toward Michoacán and Mexico City. Poor and remote, la Montaña was pried reluctantly from Puebla. Limited economic growth did little to erase deep socioethnic divisions or endemic poverty. Nahua, Tlapaneco (Me'phaa), and Mixtec villages were still under the thumb of Hispanic mocho merchants in la Montaña's towns. The northern and central valleys were a world apart. Predominantly mestizo, several sizeable Indian communities survived in the subregion's highlands and in some urban areas. The valley's principal towns, however, shared little in common. Government was Chilpancingo's only real business. Chilapa was the diocesan see. Iguala was the state's largest town, principal railhead, and commercial dynamo. Taxco was an old mining town in slow decline.[10] The high degree of internal segmentation further complicated attempts to govern Guerrero.

Subregional rivalries were another obstacle. Porfirian growth created not one unified state but several modernizing enclaves linked to other states in Mexico and other nations.[11] Guerrero's landowners and merchants never flocked to a single dominant city like Mérida or Guadalajara for credit, political favors, and status. Geographic barriers, ethnic divisions, and elite recalcitrance inhibited basic state functions like taxation, public education, and law enforcement. As Paul Gillingham put it, the state in Guerrero was a façade.[12] To make matters worse, revolutionary fighting opened new sociopolitical fissures. Zapatismo made inroads in many indigenous villages seeking land and freedom from oppressive *jefes políticos* (prefects appointed by Mexico City). Great landowners decapitalized and lay low politically. As in upstate Hidalgo, chronic social violence enabled Guerrero's rancheros to fill the political vacuum by forming paramilitaries (albeit as white guards on the Twin Coasts).[13] One faction of self-made *militares*, petty professionals, and yeomen farmers aligned with the victorious Constitutionalists and became the Ranchero group's nucleus. Mentored by Joaquín Amaro, the Sonoran dynasty's favored general, and his key lieutenant, Guerrero native Andrés Figueroa, Ranchero group members served as governor year after year: Héctor F. López (1925–27), Guevara (1932–35), José Inocencio Lugo (1935–37), and Alfredo F. Berber (1937–41). As classical liberals, members of the Ranchero group considered secularization a precondition for progress— but not a priority. And they jealously defended local prerogatives against

Mexico City.[14] As Alan Knight noted, revolutionary-era rancheros had a Jekyll and Hyde character: peaceful and democratic, they turned violent if not reactionary when agrarian reform loomed.[15] When it came to land reform, Guerrero's rancheros had good reason to worry.

Zapatismo and Article 27 of the Constitution encouraged guerrerense peasants to petition the national authorities for land after the armed phase. Politically, agrarianism was a big tent in Guerrero, encompassing pen-pushing career politicians like Desiderio Borja and Ezequiel Padilla, Tierra Caliente and central valley Zapatista captains, and activist workers of the anarcho-syndicalist Partido Obrero de Acapulco (POA, or Workers Party of Acapulco). Agrarismo remained a fractious confederation bound together by shared values and common interests. Unity and leadership posed perennial problems; even when they had the upper hand under Governor Castrejón (1928–32), agrarista leaders undermined his corporatist Partido Socialista Guerrerense (PSG or Guerreran Socialist Party).[16] In spite of widespread peasant support, agrarista leaders were incapable of sustained, coordinated regional political action.

Nevertheless, the agraristas' strong base forced Ranchero group generals, *licenciados* (lawyers), and landowners to seek the support of Catholic mediators as an electoral and social counterweight. Governors Eduardo Neri (1921–24) and Hector López (1925–27) used Father Margarito Escobar of Chilapa as a nexus to the institutional Church. A favorite of Chilpancingo's high society, Escobar's cousin was Neri's mayor of Chilpancingo. Such connections facilitated a Church-state reconciliation through Escobar's good offices. In return, Neri permitted Father Escobar to hold illegal outdoor masses in the state capital; López protected Escobar from prosecution even during the Cristiada.[17] Numerous but nebulous Ranchero-Catholic personal pacts tried to corral Catholic support for Ranchero candidates, culminating in the 1936 alliance between the Ranchero group's leader, Governor Lugo, and Bishop Díaz.[18]

The voto morado's power was evident in the June 1926 federal congressional elections. Clergy in the fourth district (Iguala) openly endorsed Alfonso Nava.[19] Nava shared a spot on Ranchero governor López's slate with Agustín Vieyra, a member of Chilapa's LNDLR (Liga Nacional para la Defensa de la Libertad Religiosa), the Cristeros' political arm.[20] Vieyra's alternate, Pascual Nogueda, was an ex-seminarian and "hardcore clerical" who counted on the "unconditional and decided support by all of the pro-Church elements."[21] Catholic candidates sometimes opposed the Ranchero group; in la Montaña,

Juan B. Salazar was literally crowned with St. Michael's coronet while campaigning—this "candidate of the clergy" was sponsored by his adoptive father, a priest.[22] Even as independents, however, Catholic candidates never supported agraristas, and the voto morado usually aided Ranchero politicos.

Ironically, the voto morado became even more important for the Ranchero group during the Cristero War. General Claudio Fox implemented a brutal counterinsurgency campaign to reopen the strategic Mexico City–Acapulco corridor menaced by Cristero bands and the Vidales brothers' agrarista insurgency. Fox forced civilians into resettlement camps where some starved—and executed suspected collaborators and surrendered combatants. Exploiting his military power, Fox elbowed out Ranchero group officials to impose his own mayors, congressional slates, and, eventually, interim governor in early 1928.[23] Then Fox nominated General Adrián Castrejón, a key subordinate, for governor in 1929. Amaro and Calles concurred.[24] The weak interim president at the time, Pascual Ortiz Rubio (1930–32), strongly backed Castrejón to pacify Guerrero and wean him away from Calles.[25]

Castrejón had Mexico City's mandate, but he also had widespread agrarista support in Guerrero. Known as "el Gran Indio" for his ethnic heritage and Zapatista past, the native of Apaxtla joined the Sonorans' 1920 revolt against Carranza and was rewarded with a formal military education and a fast track upward in Amaro's army. As governor, Castrejón hoped to transform agrarismo into a true political party, the PSG, through centralization, ejidal grants, and rural schooling, imitating governors Lázaro Cárdenas in Michoacán and Adalberto Tejeda in Veracruz.[26] Ranchero group and Catholic opposition to agrarismo stoked chronic social violence and electoral conflicts, debilitating Castrejón. In the end, corruption, economic depression, and unpopular forced labor drafts undermined Castrejón's administration.[27]

In spite of Castrejón's political failure, the revolutionary project was not completely spent in Guerrero. The SEP grew substantially in Guerrero as the number of primary schools more than doubled from 195 to 480 during Castrejón's term. By 1933, however, the SEP had run up against daunting barriers: difficult geography, lack of resources, and Catholic opposition. Guevara's victory in the watershed 1932 election halted progress in land reform and federal schooling. Interim president Abelardo Rodríguez (1932–34) accelerated agrarian reform, enabling federal teachers to file seventy-five agrarian petitions during the 1934–35 school year in Guerrero. In response,

Guevara's bureaucracy stalled pending ejidal grants, while landowners and local officials armed paramilitaries and allied with Catholic leaders.[28]

Regional political strife, deep-seated social conflicts, and long-standing electoral ties to the Ranchero group overdetermined Catholic opposition to Castrejón, the SEP, and agrarian reform. Guerrerense Catholics also remembered Castrejón's role in Fox's counterinsurgency, especially the alleged arrest and execution of Father (later Saint) David Uribe Velázquez and the psychological torture of other priests.[29] Still, as governor, Castrejón was no Garrido Canabal. Although he bowed to Callista pressure and passed a new ley de cultos in 1931 (prompting Vatican condemnation), he minimized its impact.[30] His administration ignored unlicensed priests, including Bishop Leobardo Díaz, who came home to conduct public pastoral visits and hold outdoor masses. Castrejón reached out to Father Escobar, offering more concessions in hopes of winning the voto morado. Nevertheless, only one priest endorsed Castrejón's man, Ezequiel Padilla, in the 1932 election.[31] Castrejón's conciliatory attitude could not overcome stubborn resistance by a long-term coalition of clergymen and Ranchero politicos, one ironically enabled by the Diocese of Chilapa's institutional underdevelopment.

The Church, Middle Politics, and the Roots of the Catholic-Ranchero Alliance

The Diocese of Chilapa was cobbled together from disparate parts in 1862. Although it inherited fragments of four other dioceses, nearly half its parishes (including the see city, Chilapa) came from Puebla. Its first native bishop, Ramón Ibarra y González (1890–1907), tried to modernize and centralize his sprawling diocese. He built Guerrero's first railroad to ship stones for the cathedral (a replica of Puebla's) and opened Guerrero's first meteorological and seismic laboratories in the new seminary.[32] Ibarra regularized tithing to expand sacramental service—and tried mightily to train and discipline his wayward clergy. He also set up the first modern social Catholic institutions in Guerrero: schools, charities, and a few indigenist institutions like the Misioneros Guadalupanos to supplant syncretism.[33] In neighboring Oaxaca, Archbishop Eulogio Gillow had much more success in implementing a similar project. Centralized, well-funded Church institutions bestowed "social identity and regional pride" and greased the wheels of Porfirian material progress in Oaxaca.[34] Ibarra, however, lacked Gillow's two key assets: a unified regional bourgeoisie's economic backing and Porfirio Díaz's patronage. Consequently, Bishop Ibarra could never overcome formidable geographical impediments, vexing ethnic divisions, and the guerrerense lower clergy's jealous defense of customary prerogatives.

Whatever success Guerrero's institutional Church enjoyed in professionalizing the clergy and standardizing sacramental practice was found mainly in "little levitical" urban islands: Chilapa, Iguala, Olinalá, Azoyú, Ometepec, and some smaller towns. It was there that "priests, seminarians, nuns and public processions" enjoyed pervasive influence over social life and education.[35] Nearby towns with similar socioeconomic profiles often had much lower levels of orthodox devotion. In the central valleys, for instance, Quechultenango was liberal, while Mochitlán was (fittingly enough) mocho.[36] Local elites' attitudes toward the Church often spelled the difference. Spiritual motives aside, some notables sponsored the Church's late-nineteenth-century reconstruction to spread a new, modern morality more amenable to liberal capitalism (obedience, temperance, thrift) and to provide much-needed social services.[37]

The Revolution undid much of the Church's Porfirian progress. Madero's insurgency, Huerta's coup, and the Carrancista revolt inflicted considerable collateral damage on the Church's infrastructure, finances, and priesthood. In 1913, armed gangs robbed the bishop and ransomed his successor. During the Carrancista occupation of Guerrero in 1914, the Church escaped systematic persecution, but many priests (especially European regulars) fled, and the seminary and many parochial schools closed. Just as the Diocese of Chilapa was cautiously rebuilding after renewed social strife triggered by the Agua Prieta and *delahuertista* (followers of Adolfo de la Huerta) revolts, the Cristero War struck.[38]

Not until Leobardo Díaz Escudero was consecrated bishop of Chilapa on November 5, 1929, did the diocese finally begin its long-postponed postrevolutionary reconstruction. Born to a landowning la Montaña mestizo family in 1880, Díaz experienced Ibarra's neo-Christian project at its zenith as a young priest. The Revolution took a toll on Díaz as agraristas claimed land farmed by his family. The Cristero War was even worse. General Fox ordered him, his brother (also a priest), and eight other priests shot, and only the miraculous downing of a telegraph line spared the "Padres of Chilapa." As bishop, Díaz literally rebuilt the Church, reconstructing the cathedral that tragically burned to the ground in 1930 and founding a second seminary in

Iguala.[39] More importantly, his diocese reopened long abandoned chapels in remote hamlets where priests had not trod for years.

Social origins, historical experience, and personal conviction strongly disposed Díaz to oppose the revolutionary project. While he avoided directly challenging the revolutionary state or endorsing armed resistance, he worked tirelessly to extirpate any hint of revolutionary ideology in Guerrero; in 1937, his diocese edited an anti-Communist newspaper that crusaded against federal schooling. In 1939–40, the bishop defied the episcopate and backed opposition candidate Juan Andreu Almazán, a fellow la Montaña notable, for president.[40]

Because Díaz's diocese had limited institutional resources to parry the revolutionary project, it had to rely on his obstreperous homegrown clergy. In 1921, the diocese had only about fifty priests to tend to the needs of almost 650,000 faithful, living mostly in small, remote villages.[41] Díaz resorted to roving, mostly regular "missionary" clergy to restore liturgical orthodoxy and resolve a sacramental backlog dating from the Revolution's outbreak. They visited towns for a few days, married, baptized, and held mass, then moved on to stay one step ahead of authorities.[42] Such stopgap measures did little to regularize sacramental life or discipline parish priests.

Reasserting episcopal control over his clergy after decades of negligence was Bishop Díaz's greatest challenge. Judging by the contentious issue of priestly celibacy, it was a slow, uphill struggle. In the early 1940s, at least four indigenous communities killed or expelled priests for violating women.[43] Clerical constancy proved especially difficult, as most priests were recruited from ranchero clans not known for Foucauldian self-governance. Seminarians from Tierra Caliente and la Montaña reportedly brawled to defend their *patria chicas*' honor.[44]

Schism was another perennial preoccupation for Bishop Díaz. The charismatic, dynamic Macario Roman Salgado was excommunicated for heresy in 1922, refused to vacate his church, and eventually resumed his long and successful vocation in Iguala.[45] In 1941, a bogus priest operated under various names in Taxco and Acapulco before detection.[46] Father Moisés Carmona Rivera, ordained by Díaz in 1939, broke with Rome after Vatican II and set up his own schismatic church. (Carmona blamed an attempted assassination on the bishop of Acapulco.)[47] Yet the Iglesia Católica Apostólica Mexicana (ICAM) failed to expand its one foothold in Tepecoacuilco municipio in the mid-1920s, when the institutional Church seemed at its weakest.[48] To keep his clergy in the fold, Díaz accorded his priests considerable independence.

Autonomy apparently enhanced priests' influence in the Catholic archipelago, where mestizo Catholics paid tithes, feared excommunication, and took Church injunctions against agrarian reform and socialist education to heart.[49] Few (if any) guerrerense priests sympathized with the Revolution; many were so hostile that they severely tested ecclesiastical injunctions against partisan politicking.[50] Consider the case of Zumpango del Río (central valleys), where a SEP inspector in late 1933 complained of "the reigning fanaticism" because of virulent priestly admonitions against his schools and land reform.[51] Many guerrerense priests preached that accepting land taken from owners by federal agrarian law was sinful.[52] The priest of the small town of Chichihualco (Leonardo Bravo municipio) proclaimed in 1932: "If to heaven you wish to go, on land that is not yours do not sow."[53]

Clerical hostility to the ejido and SEP schools reflected the Church's dogmatic defense of private property and the parental prerogative to decide how to educate children. The economic motive should not be ignored, however. Guerrero's priests openly collected tithes well into the 1940s (if not later).[54] When ranches and haciendas lost land to ejidos, priests feared their income would drop. It is not clear, then, where theology ended and material interest began. Some priests combined tithe collection with allegedly lucrative roles as *acapadores* (middlemen who bought up the harvest for resale in larger markets). Their defenders argued that these priestly brokers ensured that corn was sold locally to prevent hunger.[55] The fact remains that priests in rural Guerrero were deeply implicated in an economic system that relentlessly squeezed cheap labor and economic surplus out of the peasantry.

Geography, history, and regional culture distanced Guerrero's priests from the institutional Church, and drew them close to yeomen farmers, merchants, and petty officials of the Ranchero group. In many locales, priests anchored strong coalitions that opposed agrarian reform and SEP schooling. Why did clergy personally front conservative coalitions instead of strictly following the institutional Church's radial strategy of apolitical, licit resistance via lay proxies? To begin with, thick, multi-stranded ties bound priests to mestizo notables in many levitical islands, and the Church in Guerrero never really institutionalized and controlled such links through the ACM. In April 1930, Bishop Díaz tasked Guerrero's newly minted ACM with the "moralization of society": tending the indigent, catechizing children and lapsed adults, distributing Sacred Heart icons to sanctify homes (and supplant syncretic household saints), and subsidizing poor seminarians. Yet the ACM's membership actually declined during the decade of the 1930s, and only one out of four members was a man. An outside inspection in 1941 revealed a stagnant ACM in Guerrero; Bishop Díaz blamed the lack of available clergy to train the laity.[56]

The Damas and older female sodalities like the Hijas de María were extremely active, but they acted outside official Church supervision. These, then, were the beatas that so troubled Castrejón in the 1932 election. Ironically, the nineteenth-century Liberal Reform energized pious women, as they volunteered to administer parishes after the Church's disestablishment banned government subsidies.[57] In the 1930s, beatas forged informal networks based on their parish organizations and sodalities to resist the revolutionary project across Guerrero.[58] For instance, the mestiza matrons of Chichihualco's Society of Catechists "intervened" against the ejido by reminding clients, debtors, and employees of agrarismo's threat to Catholic values.[59]

To impose Rome's radial strategy and channel the efforts of these largely autonomous groups of beatas, Bishop Díaz inaugurated the UNPF in Guerrero in February 1932.[60] Although its chief, Aurelio Mendez, was male, its organizers and home school teachers were overwhelmingly female. They mimicked the UNPF methods, but refused Church instructions to formally surbordinate their parents' organizations into the national UNPF. The beatas' truancy campaigns lowered attendance considerably from 1933 to 1934. By 1935, only one out of four children in Guerrero went to school, and attendance kept falling until at least 1938.[61]

Even after the SEP retreated from radicalism on the religious question, Catholic women campaigned against federal schools and ejidos. As Kristina Boylan points out, the ACM's female leaders in a very different state, Jalisco, were not all aristocratic matrons, nor did they want to roll back the Revolution in order to restore the Porfiriato. Instead, they were creating a Christian commonwealth to minister to all social stations, often challenging gendered expectations in doing so.[62] That said, Guerrero's beatas hailed disproportionately from the upper and middle classes, and their ideology was firmly conservative. Their jaundiced view of the revolutionary state was colored not just by their gender and very real faith, but also by their social location. ACM members were wealthy enough to pay relatively high dues and possessed enough social capital to serve as examples to *los de abajo*. Many owned houses large enough to shelter fugitive clergy and host underground parochial home schools. Because of their high social standing, it was hard to shut the door when Damas Católica called.[63] Catholic resistance in Guerrero was led by the provincial upper crust—"well known" residents of Acapulco organized covert masses in the home of the Galeana clan, one of Guerrero's first families.[64]

Generally speaking, beatas were Spanish-speaking and relatively well off. Few, if any, were indigenous. Still, they bridged the social, linguistic, and geographic gaps that distanced the institutional Church from the poor, illiterate, and often indigenous Catholics in underchurched hamlets and popular barrios.[65] Across Guerrero, female catechists lectured peasants about the evils of SEP schools and land reform.[66] By 1941, Guerrero's ACM had founded affiliates for indigenous men aimed at halting the spread of Protestantism, probably by institutionalizing connections forged by informal lay groups in the 1930s.[67]

The institutional Church's cross-ethnic outreach to Indian Catholics in Guerrero faced formidable challenges. In 1940, over 90 percent of Guerrero's one hundred thousand or so monolingual speakers of indigenous languages were concentrated in just thirty-six municipios (including the entire la Montaña region) but divided into four distinct ethnicities—a testament to Guerrero's pre-Conquest past as Mesoamerican middle ground on the periphery of the Aztec Empire.[68] To further complicate matters, only the Amuzgo (seven thousand strong) were unified geographically (in part of the Costa Chica). About fourteen thousand Tlapanec speakers were scattered across la Montaña and Costa Chica. Among them lived twenty-four thousand Mixtecs. The Aztecs had expanded into Guerrero's Tierra Caliente and northern and central valleys before the Conquest, planting Nahuatl-speaking colonies and Nahuatizing Chontals. Many Nahua were Hispanized during the Porfiriato, but about forty thousand Nahuatl speakers remained in 1940.[69]

The Church long sought to impose liturgical orthodoxy on all four indigenous groups with only limited results. In the southern half of la Montaña, Nahua and Tlapanec Catholics still venerated carved stone saints resembling pre-Columbian deities. Pilgrimages to Tlapa and (especially) to Xalpatláhuac had few Christian elements. Priests never exerted much control over either folk saints or indigenous peregrinations. Civil-religious cargo hierarchies (*mayordomías*, or stewardships) sustained this syncretic cult in most indigenous villages. Most mayordomías could trace their lineages back to colonial cofradías (confraternities, a name often applied to them), although a winning lottery ticket in 1926 helped found a mayordomía dedicated to the Virgin of Guadalupe in the 1940s.[70] The cargo system aided the institutional Church by maintaining chapels and accommodating circuit-riding priests, but also sustained localized syncretic practices by funding the annual fiesta of the patron saint and organizing processions and pilgrimages.[71] Mayordomías were also the axes of the social, political, and economic lives of indigenous communities. Their officers negotiated sacramental fees with priests and stewarded corporate land that underwrote sacred obligations. Some Tlapanec mayordomías even lent out corporate funds at high interest rates.[72] In the *cuadrilla* (hamlet), the cofradía's current (fiscal, mayordomo, *topil*) and past (*principales* or *pasados*) officers monopolized political life, controlling the only civic office of *comisario* (justice of the peace), and enforcing custom, not secular law. In Nahua Tepecoacuilco, the principales (many prosperous) made sure thieves were still roped up and thrown in the river and that parents continued to arrange their children's marriages. In Jalaca de Catalán, the civil comisario was mayordomo for the Virgin of Guadalupe, and the PNR delegate was also the Cross's steward; both collected money for the Church.[73] As in Hidalgo's upstate, indigenous patriarchs often allied with mestizo politicos and clergy in the county seat. These elders saw no need to choose between spiritual obligations and revolutionary politics.

Federal teachers tried to force indigenous leaders to do just that. A zealous maestro rural determined to enforce the ley de cultos denounced as a criminal and a fraud the indigenous comisario who tried to end a drought by leading religious processions carrying his cofradía's santo.[74] Material competition heightened such conflicts. The SEP required host communities to feed teachers and build and maintain schools, so the maestro rural demanded the same share of the communal surplus and claimed the same labor draft that had traditionally gone to support syncretic celebrations and the chapel. Nahua villagers in the Tierra Caliente preferred to volunteer their labor to expand the church rather than to erect a federal school; topiles and mayordomos in the Costa Chica chose to sweep and repair chapels rather than construct classrooms.[75]

Still, not all members of indigenous communities were opposed to revolutionary change.[76] During the Revolution's armed phase, la Montaña priests warned their indigenous compadres, probably elders, that the Zapatistas would stop traditional pilgrimages; nevertheless, many younger indigenous men fought Zapata, then returned home to challenge the village status quo.[77] Similarly, in Nahuatl-speaking Chilacachapa (Cuetzalá municipality in the northern valleys), the Revolution opened generational (and perhaps class) rifts. Many young men embraced agrarismo and followed homegrown Zapatista chieftains Jesús Salgado and future governor Adrián Castrejón. After Castrejón joined the Sonoran regime in 1920, they took up arms to help put down the delahuertista and Cristiada insurgencies in Guerrero. In 1927, when a National Agrarian Commission engineer finally showed up in Chilacachapa, he could not communicate because he spoke no Nahuatl. Elders condemned such federal agents as "robbers" and "enemies of the religion" in a defense of the cofradía's land and their patriarchal authority. Agrarista Nahua, however, charged that the principales shielded their reactionary protectors, the Rabadán family, a Porfirian petty dynasty that still ran Cuetzalá's city hall as late as the 1980s.[78]

Generational conflicts pitting younger men (and some women) who identified with Zapata, agrarian reform, and the Revolution against elders probably erupted in other indigenous communities. In Amojileca (Chilpancingo municipio), principales opposed the federal school, but young women refused their civic-religious obligations to the Church and instead supplied building materials and labor to the federal teachers.[79] The opening of these intravillage rifts demonstrates that not all indigenous communities were closed to revolutionary change.[80] However, in order to build widespread grassroots support, federal teachers would have to negotiate the potentially explosive religious question.[81] By the early 1930s, the fate of the SEP's project was inseparable from the Church-state struggle in Guerrero.

Guevara and Catholics against the Revolutionary Project, 1933–1935

As in Campeche and Hidalgo, the revolutionary project's success—including anticlerical reforms—hinged on the SEP's ability to sink roots in indigenous communities and win over state and local politicos. Unfortunately for them, Governor Guevara depended on Catholic brokers for his election and deepened his alliances with them in ayuntamiento elections during his term. In at least fifteen larger municipios, the pro-Guevara slates that bested pro-Castrejón agraristas were headed by Catholic leaders often linked to wealthy landowners and merchants. Castrejón blamed these "beato-burgueses" for his political reverses. Electoral disputes often escalated into violent social conflicts. Guevara's administration allowed landowners to deputize paramilitaries as *defensas sociales* (paramilitary police). These constabularies intimidated agraristas in nearby hamlets, but the ex-Zapatistas and veteran counter-Cristero militias held their own. Religious conflicts often exacerbated social and geographical rifts in municipios, as priests and Catholic lay activists in the mestizo county seat clashed with agraristas and teachers in indigenous hamlets.[82]

Iguala stands out as a sterling example of the historical collaboration between conservative politicians and Catholic mediators that propelled Guevarista town council slates to victory in 1933 and 1934—and battled the revolutionary project to a standstill. The pro-Guevara ballot in Iguala's municipal election included ex-cristero Andrés Mendiola and former supporters of the Huerta counterrevolution (1913), the delahuertista coup (1923), and Antonio I. Villarreal's right-wing opposition presidential campaign against Lázaro Cárdenas (1934). Father Macario Roman Salgado blessed the whole slate.[83]

Iguala's Catholic political brokers (Father Roman Mendiola among them) enjoyed three key electoral advantages: a strong Church presence in the everyday life of rich and poor alike, widespread antipathy to the revolutionary state, and robust Catholic corporatist organs. For decades, Iguala was a key social laboratory for the diocese. During the 1870s, an enlarged and energized clergy ended penitential processions of flagellants and weaned the faithful away from the old syncretic cult of the saints by encouraging new, orthodox forms of household and parish piety. Catholic matrons consecrated their families to the ultramontane Sacred Heart and helped priests venerate the holy sacrament in churches instead of honoring household folk saints. The diocese's second seminary opened in Iguala during 1931, and seminarians helped priests and lay auxiliaries establish a quotidian presence in townsfolks' lives through new pious organizations like Nocturnal Adoration. The clergy was unusually mindful of Iguala's working poor, founding the Association of Saint Joseph to offer free medical care.[84]

Catholic political brokers also mobilized Iguala's voto morado from all social stations by tapping into strong local resentment of the army, an institution closely identified with the revolutionary state. Iguala's wealth and strategic location made it a magnet for the federal military, and it had been garrisoned since 1915. During the armed phase of the Revolution, Maderista paramilitaries, captained by the famous Ranchero clan of the Figueroas, disbanded the Damas de Caridad, perhaps to punish the Porfirian aristocracy. Then, in 1915, Constitutionalist General Amaro forcibly relocated the church's cemetery outside of town. General Claudio Fox occupied Iguala's parsonage and destroyed a beloved image of St. Francis. When his troops surprised a priest holding mass, Fox had him shot before horrified Catholics. Father David Uribe Velázquez, once a priest in Iguala, was executed during the Cristiada; he was later canonized. In 1929, a soldier interrupted a Holy Week mass by yelling that the church was about to be burned down.[85]

At about the same time, the exiled bishop of Tabasco, Antonio Hernández, took refuge there, bringing tales of his sufferings at the hands of Garrido Canabal to Iguala's faithful. The sense of persecution by a tyrannical, anti-Christian central government was seared into the collective memory of Iguala's Catholics by revolutionary soldiers. Catholic political operatives tapped the reservoir of antirevolutionary sentiment again and again.

To politically mobilize the poor, Catholic mediators did not have to start from scratch. Rather, they could use existing Church organizations to marshal the voto morado. During the 1920s, Father Roman co-directed the Melchor Salgado Club, which usually prevailed in municipal elections. The priest founded a society for Catholic laborers in nearby Teloloapan to stem the rising agrarian tide, and from the pulpit he repeatedly endorsed allies for elected office. Foes alleged Roman was still "preaching rebellious doctrine" and collecting tithes in 1935.[86]

Spatial, class, and ethnic barriers limited the voto morado's power in Iguala's municipio (county). The division between the Ranchero group and agraristas tended to follow the division between Catholics close to the institutional Church and clergy on the one hand and adepts of syncretic Catholicism on the other. Mayordomías still thrived in Iguala's indigenous barrios like Chontal Juanacate. Juanacate's principal agrarista leader, an ex-mayor and retired Zapatista colonel named Pedro Padilla, was the Holy Cross cofradía's steward. Padilla had a strong following in Iguala's hamlets, where priests rarely visited.[87] Padilla's participation in folk Catholic rites, however, alienated defanaticizing teachers. At the same time, revolutionary anticlericalism gave Iguala's "beato-burgueses" another political advantage by associating Padilla's agrarismo with the federal military's excesses. This, in turn, allowed beatas of Damas de Caridad and the Asociación de la Medalla Milagrosa (Association of the Miraculous Medallion) to turn out the voto morado for Ranchero group candidates in Iguala.

Catholics in bustling Iguala, remote central valley villages, and towns on the Twin Coasts countered the revolutionary project in a number of ways during the Guevara administration. Pro-Catholic slates took many town halls through popular election or intervention by the state government, meaning the clergy could openly resume their preeminent role in civic life and restore public ritual. Opponents faced jail, fines, and selective taxation. The Ranchero group's regional resurgence in late 1932 and 1933 was clearly energized by the spillover of the growing national conflict over the religious question. Specific dynamics varied from place to place, but overall the Ranchero group's drive to take back town halls and halt land reform fused with Catholic rejection of anticlericalism and federal schooling. Given the SEP's federal status and advocacy of agrarian reform, resistance from the provincial bourgeoisie and clergy was inevitable. But their rancor only intensified due to the SEP's determination to defanaticize. To understand how teachers went from being a revolutionary vanguard to an embattled rearguard requires a closer look at the often contradictory dynamics of Callista anticlericalism in Guerrero.

During 1933 and 1934, Calles's desire to decisively settle the religious question forced Governor Guevara to tighten anticlerical restrictions. In 1934, barnstorming presidential candidate Lázaro Cárdenas visited and berated Guevara for tolerating open religious processions in Chilapa.[88] The SEP opportunistically pressured the governor to squeeze the Church in hopes of breaking resistance to federal schooling. The governor responded by expelling several especially troublesome priests and, in October 1934, passing a new ley de cultos slashing the number of licensed priests from forty to fourteen. Yet Guevara's administration enforced it unenthusiastically and irregularly. The governor's dealings with Catholics could be fairly described as two-faced. On November 3, 1934, he stood as godfather for the mayor of Acapulco, Carlos Adame, while a federal deputy stood in for an absent acolyte. Yet a few weeks later, Guevara allowed the officiating priest to be arrested and fined five hundred pesos for violating the ley de cultos.[89] In April 1935, authorities expelled Acapulco's one licensed priest but ignored two unlicensed Catholic clergymen.[90] State officials pled chronic governmental incapacity, but in fact Guevara could not govern without Catholic support in key towns like Iguala, so frequently dragged his feet in enforcing his own ley de cultos. After Calles proclaimed his Psychological Revolution and the SEP's presence expanded, the competing demands of Mexico City and guerrerense Catholics could not be easily reconciled.

Fortunately for Guevara and his Catholic allies, the SEP's project in Guerrero was never as coherent or as focused as it was in northern Campeche or upstate Hidalgo. Guerrero's normal schools never turned out a cadre of radical teachers like Hecelchakán's normal.[91] Poorer than virtually every other state, Guerrero had only 150 schools when federalization of the educational system began in 1922, and the 15 poorest municipios had none at all. Rather than taking over existing urban schools from the state government and then focusing resources on rural areas, the SEP had to build schools in town and country under difficult conditions.[92] Among Guerrero's indigenous people, only the Tierra Caliente Nahua readily accepted formal education. Teachers of the SEP generally preferred to live in town, spending as little time as possible in the Indian hamlets they served.[93] The SEP's Spanish-only policy made matters worse.[94] As a result, the SEP's progress in indigenous Guerrero was slow indeed.

Moreover, the SEP tried to open dozens of new schools in indigenous communities at a time when the religious question was polarizing guerrerense society. Anticlerical zeal varied from educator to educator; a few federal inspectors and teachers did extirpate so-called fanaticism; more were moderate and tactful, sticking close to the SEP line to avoid directly offending Catholic belief. Yet national controversy over the religious question inflamed Catholics in Guerrero no matter how cautiously federal teachers handled it. Even the SEP's policy of coeducation seemed to be a moral threat to Catholics in this heated atmosphere.[95]

The political resurgence of the Ranchero group in Guevara empowered Catholic defiance of SEP expansion at a vulnerable moment. In Tepecoacuilco municipio in the northern valleys, the Guevarista town council that served in 1933–34 allowed the Brotherhood of the Father of Jesus and the Daughters of Maria to hold processions to stoke resistance to the revolutionary project, and above all, to SEP schools. A federal teacher who took incriminating photos of a local demonstration was threatened.[96] In mid-1935, pro-Guevara authorities in Mochitlán and Quechultenango (central valleys) allowed priests to brazenly flout the ley de cultos by freely propagandizing against federal schooling and openly coordinating truancy strikes. In the Tierra Caliente cities of Arcelia and Coyuca, as in the Montaña towns of Olinalá and Huamuxtitlán, priests—aided by lay leaders—launched successful boycotts of federal schools and publicly held fund-raisers to rebuild abandoned churches.[97]

The Ranchero group provided political and judicial cover for Catholic attendance strikes against SEP schooling. Federal educators demanded strict enforcement of truancy laws and Guevara's ley de cultos, but local authorities rarely complied. Other problems plagued the SEP in Guerrero. Consider the case of SEP inspector Isidro Rivera, sent in early 1933 to open rural schools in the Nahua hamlets surrounding Chilapa. Rivera blamed his teachers' failures on the Church, not only because of fanaticism but also because too many feast days prevented peasants from working or sending children to school. When he closed two parochial schools in Chilapa to break attendance strikes, he provoked a strong popular backlash. Perhaps Calles's proclamation of a

Psychological Revolution in July encouraged him to double down rather than to fold. When schools reopened in the fall of 1934, he dreamed of transforming his district along the lines of Rodolfo Elías Calles's Sonora, a regional revolutionary laboratory inspired by Garrido Canabal's Tabasco.[98] Inspector Rivera admitted frankly that too many of his own teachers were Catholic and refused to defanaticize via direct action. Nevertheless, he visited nearby hamlets to assemble and hector peasants about "fanaticism, alcoholism and sloth" to overcome their "ancestral indifference." Progress meant not just secularizing but also Hispanizing. His dreams of turning Chilapa into a Garridista utopia evaporated when his assemblies fizzled. One by one, peasants stood up and walked out.[99] Mestizo and indigenous Catholics forced the SEP to retreat from radicalism not by taking up arms, but by voting with their feet. Because local elected officials rarely lifted a finger to help teachers, there was little they could do.

Resistance to the SEP in Guerrero was not always nonviolent. In September 1935, Superintendent Guillermo Bonilla Segura predicted that the return of the clergy to public life would lead to the election of "fanatics," reinforcing peasants' "rebellious attitudes" toward teachers and eventually leading to violence against them and "friends of the schools."[100] Remarkably, in the spring of 1935, the state army commander, General Vicente González, issued oral orders to teachers to let up on the Church to calm Catholic resistance.[101] Threats against teachers became so widespread by 1936 that the army commander in Guerrero pledged to break up armed gangs menacing schoolhouses.[102] During 1936, the SEP accused priests in Tixtla and in the hamlet of San Marcos (near Acapulco) of directly inciting mobs that nearly lynched teachers. In San Marcos, peasants attacked the teacher, shouting "long live the priest de San Marcos!" While the army occasionally managed to kill segunderos, it could never protect more than a handful of teachers at one time. In fact, several local garrison commanders, allied with landowners who were in turn linked to segunda gangs, resisted federal schools and agrarian reform.

Guerrero's Segunditas

In January 1935, Guerrero's EPL declared war against the "socialist" government to stave off "the destruction of Religion, the perversion of children and youth of Mexico, and the trampling of private property that would open the door to hated Communism."[103] We know relatively little about guerrerense segunderos, but most had not awaited the EPL's proclamation, perhaps because few were recristeros (veterans of the first Cristiada) accustomed to a degree of military discipline.¹⁰⁴ The EPL of Guerrero sought to rally segundero bands by drawing on conservative nationalism, hoisting Agustín Iturbide's tricolor first unfurled in Iguala in 1821.¹⁰⁵ Although the EPL voiced sentiments shared by many segunderos and sympathizers in Guerrero, it never mustered more than two hundred men in the state.¹⁰⁶ Most guerrerense segunderos fought their own war in small bands.

Multicausal, low intensity, decentralized, and chronic, the Segunda in Guerrero was, in short, representative of the Segunda nationally. Segunda violence erupted in every subregion of Guerrero except la Montaña; the murder of federal teachers in December 1932 and February 1939 bracket nearly a decade of persistent bloodshed in Guerrero that also took the lives of several dozen agraristas, soldiers, and noncombatants.¹⁰⁷ To analyze the Segunda's highly localized nature, I will examine each of Guerrero's four subregions.

To make sense of these *segunditas* (subregionally specific episodes), I will continue to distinguish between offensive and defensive violence.¹⁰⁸ The former refers to premeditated attacks against perceived enemies of Catholicism. Some perpetrators of offensive violence were renegade members of informal Catholic groups campaigning peacefully against federal schools. Most were members of all-male gangs that operated for months on end, sometimes far from home. Often they received intelligence, logistical support, arms, and moral legitimization from extended networks that united landowners, Catholic activists, clergy, Ranchero politicos, and even federal military officers against agrarian reform. Sketchy archival evidence and several published studies that briefly mention offensive segunda violence suggest these gangs at times relied on terror tactics such as mutilation or sexual assault. Because gangs carrying out offensive violence often targeted agraristas, they functioned as white guards.¹⁰⁹ Isolating religious motives for offensive violence proves problematic, as it was usually driven in part by ethnic, class, and agrarian conflicts that long predated the Segunda.

The second category of segunda attacks, defensive violence, was more spontaneous than premeditated, communal as opposed to factional or conspiratorial, and reactive rather than instrumental. Often it was triggered by specific instances of anticlericalism, be they real (actual iconoclasm) or rumored (e.g., children allegedly molested by teachers). Perpetrators were often not only men, but also women and at times even older children. They probably believed that violence protected their community's moral core from godless government agents. A stunning example of defensive violence in the first Cristiada occurred in August 1927: the women of Chilapa stoned its mayor to death when he came to inventory a closed church.[110] The historical roots of defensive violence in the Segunda ran even deeper. It strongly resembled the colonial rioting studied by William Taylor. Both were spontaneous, short-lived, collective defenses of the community that did not directly challenge the legitimacy of the larger polity (although the colonial state was obviously an explicitly Catholic one).[111]

While the distinction between offensive and defensive violence can be seen across Guerrero, important subregional variations emerge, too, including one hybrid case. Below I track segunda violence in each of Guerrero's subregions to explain distinct outcomes. On the Costa Chica, SEP iconoclasm first provoked defensive segunda violence, followed by the Compadres' Segundita, offensive attacks perpetrated by Amuzgo and mestizo elites linked by Catholic godparentage. In the Tierra Caliente, offensive segunda violence reacted against growing SEP anticlericalism but soon evolved into antiagrarian repression as landowners and Ranchero politicos intervened. La Montaña, although the home of many former cristeros, remained largely peaceful due to institutional restraints, unique social factors, and an exceptional SEP cadre. In the northern and central valleys, segunda violence was localized, with a strong hybrid episode breaking out in Tlacotepec municipio. Finally, on the Costa Grande, two distinct kinds of segunda violence erupted. In the district of Montes de Oca, offensive segunda violence aimed principally to prevent agrarian reform, while close to Acapulco, conflict over religion was submerged in a bloody agrarian insurgency.

How can we explain the wide variation among and in some cases within subregions? Federal teachers' stance on the religious question is one key variable. A few teachers entered the classroom with strong anti-Catholic convictions; Guerrero's atheists and Protestants (2 and 1 percent of the population, respectively) were probably overrepresented in the SEP. As in Campeche, some teachers looked to the USSR or Garrido Canabal's Tabasco for iconoclastic inspiration.[112] In early 1935, one teacher greeted his students with the phrase "There is no God," to which they responded, "There never was one."[113]

Generally speaking, however, SEP inspectors set the tone for their teachers, and it was temperate. During the 1934–35 school year, only two of Guerrero's eight federal inspectors encouraged teachers to root out "fanatical" religious practice, yet segunda violence erupted in all but one subregion. So we must look to other factors to explain the Segunda's spread. As I argue, local political conflicts, agrarian struggles, as well as cross-class and cross-ethnic alliances, explain attacks on teachers and agraristas.

Costa Chica: The Compadres' Segundita

In the fall of 1934, Inspector Francisco G. Torres took over the Costa Chica zone, headquartered in San Luis Acatlán. During the 1931–32 school year, while teaching at a rural school in northern Guanajuato (see chapter 5), Torres provoked Catholic outrage by destroying a wooden cross.[114] In the Costa Chica, his maestros opened about thirty new schools in Amuzgo, Mixtec, and Nahua *cuadrillas* where students and parents spoke no Spanish. Like inspectors in northern Campeche and the Hidalgan Huasteca, Torres believed that education would help liberate indigenous wards by dismantling an unjust socioeconomic structure and promoting cultural mestizaje. And like them, Torres was shocked by social conditions he considered feudal and backward. The Mexican Revolution he idealized was remembered by the people of the Costa Chica as a time of chaos and looting. Inspector Torres hoped agrarian reform and the election of Lázaro Cárdenas would restore faith in the Revolution and facilitate defanaticization.[115]

The Amuzgo of his district, who were the most downtrodden of the three indigenous groups of the Costa Chica, were an early focus of the SEP. However, complex land tenure patterns and cross-class and cross-ethnic relationships frustrated teachers' attempts to mobilize the poor and indigenous against the mestizo and white rich. For example, Amuzgo Cozoyoapan (Xochistlahuaca municipio) was poor, but it had managed to hold on to enough communal land so that it could actually rent some to the Amuzgos of neighboring Xochistlahuaca. When the indigenous peasants of Cozoyoapan filed land reform petitions in the 1920s, it was not to reclaim land lost to haciendas, but to block agraristas in neighboring indigenous communities from claiming their land. Amuzgo elders in Xochistlahuaca and Tlacoachistlahuaca municipios had clientelistic ties with mestizo merchants and rancheros, and they tried to keep younger men from supporting Zapatismo and agrarismo. Since independence, ambitious mestizo farmers and merchants from larger Costa Chica towns had moved to indigenous communities, where they cultivated indigenous allies, at times married Amuzgo women, and claimed communal membership to claim communal land. Ironically, they began using the agrarian reform process to acquire even more after the Revolution.[116] It was difficult for teachers to pry apart these complex, vertical patron-client ties that muddied class and ethnic lines. Injecting the conflictive issue of anticlericalism further complicated the SEP's mission.

Still, Inspector Torres felt freeing the Amuzgo required erasing the Costa Chica's "intensely Catholic" nature. Children greeted parents saying "santo papí, santo mamá" (blessed father, blessed mother). Amuzgo elders bore icons as stewards of cargo systems, and as comisarios they fined citizens who refused to labor to meet religious obligations. Worse still, they refused to fine or jail parents who boycotted federal school. Bonilla, the SEP superintendent, told his inspectors that indigenous religious practice retarded revolutionary progress, and tacitly encouraged them to meddle in regional politics to combat pro-clerical elements and favor supporters of the federal schools.[117] When the priest of Ayutla sermonized against the SEP, Torres forced the mayor to threaten the cleric with prosecution if he did not desist. Still, Torres admitted that when he tried to start an "aggressive movement to demonstrate the harm and vanity of the Church's doctrine," most teachers dragged their feet.[118]

Maestro rural Francisco de Jesús, stationed in Yoloxóchitl (San Luis Acatlán municipio), did act. An admiring Torres said of him, "he has been intransigent when it comes to the fanatics." When Yoloxóchitl's Mixtec comisario took children to church, de Jesús had him stripped of his office, challenging a long tradition of indigenous self-governance. From the county seat of Tonalá, Mateo Gutiérrez oversaw an attendance strike that crippled several federal schools, including de Jesús's. The maestro retaliated by having Gutiérrez brought up on legal charges and by threatening parents with the same treatment. In the midst of this conflict, de Jesús set fire to a small cross in a *cobertizo* (a small, roadside shrine) on the outskirts of Mixtec Concordia, hoping to break Catholic resistance and shatter Mixtec reverence for icons. When Concordia's population discovered the desecration, residents tried to lynch de Jesús. The teacher barely escaped with his life by outrunning the mob, and Torres had no choice but to transfer him. This, then, was a clear case of defensive violence, a communal response to provocation.[119]

After de Jesús's iconoclasm, teachers stationed in nearby indigenous hamlets worried about their own safety and pressured Inspector Torres to prohibit quemasantos.[120] The SEP subsecretary Celso Flores eventually reprimanded Torres for abetting confrontational tactics. Prudence and caution were required, Flores insisted, because "the clergy and landlords want to get us into trouble with this problem, in order to get us to forget the economic problem."[121] Torres and a handful of determined teachers nevertheless felt obliged to shake indigenous communities out of blind obedience to priests, conservative elders, and so-called superstition in order to truly remedy socioeconomic inequality. De Jesús's provocative act and Torres's threat to punish the clergy and Catholic activists for truancy strikes touched off a wave of violence. In October 1934, at least two men abducted (and probably sexually assaulted) a girl from the school's sporting field in Amuzgo Cochoapa. When teacher Imelda Álvarez intervened to save her, the assailants beat her with rifle butts and left her for dead, then assaulted another federal teacher who came to her aid.[122] This was the first act of offensive segunda violence in the Costa Chica.

In March or April 1935, another of Torres's federal teachers confronted "fanaticism" in Tlacoachistlahuaca, a small mestizo town surrounded by ten Amuzgo, Mixtec, and Nahua communities. The SEP schools had struggled ever since rumors of miracles (likely a saintly apparition or folk prophet) had spread. In response, the teacher in one of Tlacoachistlahuaca's indigenous cuadrillas told students that crucifixes would burn just like any other object. At his urging, a pupil brought in a Catholic image, and the teacher ignited it. Students watched the act of pedagogical iconoclasm awestruck. When the anticipated divine retribution failed to arrive, Inspector Torres boasted that "the teacher had given a tremendous object lesson in defanaticization." Death threats soon followed, however, forcing Torres to transfer the maestro.[123]

At about the same time in Ometepec, the unofficial capital of the Costa Chica, another teacher adopted aggressive measures against fanaticism. Throughout the spring of 1935, teacher Custodio Sámano fought a running battle with Catholic students, parents, and Ometepec's mayor, Pantaleón Añorve. Sámano's foes demanded his removal for (unspecified) "immoralities." Matters came to a head when Sámano spanked a child for coming to school with a smudge of cinders on his forehead on Ash Wednesday (March 6) 1935. Outrage grew among Ometepec's Catholics, although Sámano apparently faced no retaliation.[124] Nevertheless, news of the incident further aggrieved Catholics, spurring more segunda violence.

Still, explaining why Torres's teachers faced violence or intimidation is hardly straightforward. Torres's reports were obviously biased, and reflected only limited knowledge of Catholic motives and not much curiosity about indigenous culture. I can only piece together fragmentary evidence to identify attackers and tease out motives.[125] In the October 1934 segunda violence in Cochoapa, in which a band of segunderos brutally assaulted a student and two teachers, the place of the attack—the federal school's athletic field—was significant. As Mary Kay Vaughan has shown, sports were an important part of the SEP's educational philosophy. Federal teachers saw athletics as not just healthy but also modernizing, instilling discipline, sobriety, and patriotism. Sports promoted a new sociability that could upset traditional social expectations for youth, as young men (and sometimes young women) took pride in their athletic accomplishments and turned their backs on their elders.[126]

It is no coincidence, then, that Catholic propaganda against socialist education frequently depicted the sporting field as a place of perversity. Federal teachers reportedly led students in nude calisthenics. Female participation in sports struck many as a moral outrage. In July 1935, *Hombre Libre* attacked the new ideas of masculinity forged on the federal schools' athletic fields when it ran a story claiming that an SEP national basketball tournament honored male players who were "bums" because their mothers and sisters had to work to support them while they practiced and played. In la Montaña during 1939, a priest sermonized that unless the community took down its basketball goals, their crops would fail. Father Rafael Altamirano, who helped introduce Sinarquismo to Guerrero, resolutely condemned sports in school as immoral.[127]

Catholic anxiety about the dissolution of long-standing gender and generational hierarchy by sports might well have fueled the violence on Cochoapa's sporting fields. Perpetrators were likely Amuzgos connected by clientelistic ties to the wealthy Ometepec mestizos. Mestizo catechists, probably female, would have transmitted Catholic propaganda against federal schools from Ometepec to Cochoapa, priming the band for violence.[128] Another religious link connected mestizo notables and Amuzgos: compadrazgo.[129] Across Guerrero, from Chilicachapa to la Montaña, compadrazgo cemented cross-ethnic alliances that were turned against agraristas and teachers.[130]

Behind the segunda gang operating in Cochoapa, Inspector Torres alleged, was Ometepec's mayor, Pantaleón Añorve, scion of a powerful landowning and mercantile clan long close to the Church. Back in 1922, the Añorve cofounded a Catholic school (with the help of a federal cavalry colonel) and staffed it with European Benedictines. A decade later, the Añorve sheltered itinerant missionary priests, helping to reestablish the Church's daily presence. Interestingly enough, Añorve and other town mestizos not only underwrote orthodox Catholicism; they also sponsored indigenous children's participation in the confraternities's fiestas, strongly suggesting that at times they participated in syncretic Catholic rites in Amuzgo communities.[131]

Because of the Añorve clan's alleged complicity in the Cochoapa attack, Torres charged that Ometepec's "great capitalists" had instrumentally manipulated religion.[132] His proof: perpetrators carried carbines provided by Antonio Morales, Francisco Meza, and other wealthy counterrevolutionary Ometepec notables.[133] Up and down the Twin Coasts region during the 1930s, landowners colluded with federal army officers (among them future governor General Alfredo Berber) to arm paramilitaries. Ex-colonel and perennial state congressman Rafael Sánchez was the nexus connecting army brass, littoral landowners, and paramilitary gangs.[134] The Añorves' motives likely were more complex than just extirpating ejidos. Just as Campeche's mestizo elites used the gremios to forge ties with Maya allies, the Costa Chica mestizo elites counted on compadrazgo and fiesta sponsorship to strengthen patron-client bonds with leading indigenous families. Tithing and religious donations reinforced the Añorve clan's status, and Catholic reverence for hierarchy and private property stabilized the postrevolutionary status quo. The SEP's anticlericalism threatened to undermine all these practices. Instrumentality aside, teachers' iconoclasm inflamed genuine religious sentiment on the Costa Chica.

Was this, then, Catholic violence? The institutional Church was not connected to this Ometepec gang, and the clergy played no known role. No official lay groups like the ACM or Daughters of Maria were active in the area. Informal task forces were propagandizing against the SEP there. In Torres's headquarters of San Luis Acatlán, Catholic activists set up a private religious school cleverly disguised with the name Benito Juárez.[135] Such civic organizations were covertly linked to the Church under the radial strategy, and they strongly denounced federal schools. Finally, there was a history of homegrown popular Catholic resistance to the revolutionary project that might have inspired Catholic support for the Ometepec gang's attack. During the first Cristiada, a ban on pilgrimages triggered a strong backlash, so that in December 1926 a large number of demonstrators shouted "Viva Cristo Rey!" and "Death to the Protestants!" to frighten officials.[136]

By mid-1935, the religious conflict in the Costa Chica eased as Torres and his handful of radical collaborators were transferred out of the district. No further incidents of SEP iconoclasm occurred.[137] Although the national Cárdenas-Calles break slowly eased tensions surrounding the national religious question, segunda violence did not dissipate and Añorve's Ometepec gang did not demobilize. Instead, it had a new target: Costa Chica agrarian strongman Nabor A. Ojeda.

Tierra Caliente: A Slow Segundita

In early 1934, Inspector Federico Cuanalo took over the Tierra Caliente zone, headquartered in the Porfirian boomtown of Arcelia. He hoped to support Hot Country agraristas without being distracted by the religious question, so he ordered his teachers to stick close to SEP policy of prudent defanaticization. Nevertheless, influential priests in Arcelia and Coyuca de Catalán, ably aided by lay activists, organized very effective boycotts against his SEP schools. Inspector Cuanalo lamented that fanatics "intimately connected to the clergy" commanded so many votes that local officials refused to support his teachers. The Arcelia town councilman responsible for education not only refused to prosecute truancy but also summoned a federal teacher to hear out his friend, the priest, and then the official insulted the maestro. In several isolated hamlets, federal teachers fled after receiving credible death threats. Charges that priests were ultimately responsible for them are impossible to confirm, but it does seem that the radial strategy mobilized much of civil society against the federal schools in the name of defending the true religion. Faced with this resistance, Inspector Cuanalo abandoned prudence in late 1934 and formed a local branch of Tomás Garrido Canabal's red shirts with the help of an ambitious young leftist politico.[138]

The inspector's plan to turn Tierra Caliente schools into little Tabascos riled Catholics, especially after *Hombre Libre* took an interest. The newspaper criticized SEP authorities who closed two parochial schools that served hundreds of schoolchildren in Chilapa at about this time and amplified Catholic accusations that the principal of Chilapa's federal high school, Dr. Acevedo, was in fact a "professor of sexual education" spreading "corruption and prostitution" in class. The SEP's dispatch of a reckless iconoclast, Tomás Cuervo, at the head of a cultural mission to criss-cross Guerrero in mid-1935 fed more rumors of Tabaquenization.[139]

Press reports fueled Catholic ire against SEP schools in the Tierra Caliente, even after federal teachers downplayed anticlericalism and abandoned red shirting in mid-1935. Tierra Caliente Catholics continued to view federal schools as outposts of atheism. In early 1936, angry villagers in El Cubo (also known as Villa Hidalgo, in the municipio San Miguel Totolapan) sent a clear message to the SEP teacher: they ripped open the school doors, then assembled in the nearby church and sang, drowning out the teacher's lessons with their hymn.[140] Such ritualized intimidation clearly threatened defensive violence. But there was also a long history of offensive segunda violence in San

Miguel Totolapan municipio. Local landowners, acting in cooperation with other Tierra Caliente hacendados and Governors Guevara and Lugo, used strategically coordinated white terror to put down a strong agrarian movement in the 1930s. Paramilitary gangs captained by Governor Lugo's relatives and his hacienda's overseer combated a strong agrarista movement headed by two dangerous foes: Rufino González, who had been a follower of the anarcho-syndicalist Escudero brothers of Acapulco, and federal congressman Desiderio Borja.[141] Just as in the Costa Chica, the expansion of federal schooling provoked defensive violence while also fueling Catholic support for gangs quelling agrarista mobilizations.

La Montaña: A Pacific Island

The segundita in the Tierra Caliente contrasted sharply with the calm in la Montaña, in spite of a strong Church presence and many ex-cristeros in the latter. Several factors explain la Montaña's remarkable quiescence. Potential recristeros were discouraged early on by preventive state action stifling problematic priests. On April 30, 1929, Governor Castrejón expelled Adalberto J. Miranda, Alberto Vivanco, and a third, unnamed priest because of their Cristero past.[142] Guevara's administration tolerated Father Agustín Díaz's presence in Tlapa, the Montaña's principal town, even when he sermonized that "the government by means of the rural teachers wants to destroy the religious beliefs of the people, and so this policy must be resisted by force." Federal teachers suspected Díaz and likeminded priests had "made common cause" with the hacendados to plot armed struggle. Absent hard evidence, maestros rurales pointed to the fact that landowning mestizo families had long sent sons to the seminary in nearby Chilapa. Bishop Leobardo and Father Agustín Díaz hailed from one such prominent clan. And priests in the subregion had long threatened peasants with hellfire should they ask for land.[143]

Guevara could ignore SEP demands to expel more priests from la Montaña as long as it remained peaceful. However, he drew the line when it came to known proinsurgent priests. The governor eventually re-expelled Vivanco when he returned to Guerrero and resumed suspicious activity. Vivanco took refuge in neighboring Oaxaca, and returned frequently to minister thanks to the protection of Guevara's key la Montaña ally, General Rafael Mendoza. A grateful Vivanco blessed Mendoza's protégé for state deputy.[144] Still, Vivanco steered clear of directly endorsing another Cristiada to avoid offending his political protectors.

The lack of violence in la Montaña was also due to the federal teachers' tact when it came to the religious question. The SEP inspector for the subregion, Salvador Gutiérrez, was a Communist, and he derided priests as lackeys of the *riquillos* (the petty rich). But he carefully limited his teachers' defanaticization to "indirect but efficient means" such as scientific explanations of natural phenomena and the promise of a "more just socioeconomic future."[145] Many of his teachers probably shared his hostility toward the clergy. Maestro rural Evelia Franco Nájera, a teacher from the Tierra Caliente serving in Atlixtac, blamed the priests for taking the side of the wealthy against the poor, indigenous majority. But following her inspector's instructions, she focused on raising class consciousness, not baiting Catholics. She also feared raising the ire of segundero chieftain El Tallarín, who threatened to come across the border from Morelos to avenge wrongs to Catholics.[146]

In this subregion, federal teachers mobilized communal support by advancing causes that united peasants with the SEP, like agrarian reform, and by avoiding divisive iconoclasm. Yet the religious question was never entirely absent. Agraristas in Amapilca (municipio Alcozauca) had doggedly fought a priest since 1922, accusing him of stealing their land with the help of relatives of Alcozauca native Bishop Díaz, whom they derided as "our oppressor."[147] Some Montaña peasant communities became anticlerical (though not necessarily anti-Catholic) because of long-standing agrarian struggles; Zapatismo's heritage played a role too. Here, at least, federal teachers did not have to resort to counterproductive direct attacks on religious sentiment. When SEP maestros denounced priests as exploiters, they found many believers.

The Montaña subregion escaped segunda violence through a combination of unique factors. Disciplined Communist teachers avoided provoking Catholics. Bishop Díaz and Ranchero group politicians like Governor Guevara and Montaña cacique Mendoza restrained potential segunderos, especially ex-cristeros. Finally, grassroots agrarian, Zapatista sentiment impeded the emergence of widespread cross-class, popular resistance to the revolutionary project that fueled the Segunda elsewhere in Guerrero.

Northern and Central Valleys: Several Segunditas, One Hybrid

The northern and central valleys were not nearly as quiescent. The single bloodiest incident in the Guerrero Segunda occurred on March 15, 1935. The federal army commander in Guerrero ordered Epifanio Nájera to take the *defensa rural* agrarian militia of Ojo de Agua de Progreso (Tlacotepec municipio, Bravos district) and arrest an unlicensed priest, Miguel Reza Miranda, in the town of Yextla in the neighboring municipio of Chichihualco (now Leonardo Bravo). The federal military only sporadically enforced anticlerical legislation, but Tlacotepec municipio abutted the capital of Chilpancingo, and at the time Governor Guevara was under pressure to prove his revolutionary credentials. The federal military used defensas rurales to carry out routine policing functions in remote areas. Because Nájera's men were pro-revolutionary agraristas, they could be counted on to round up the priest.

Nájera's militia surprised Reza in the middle of mass. Fearing violence, Nájera offered not to arrest the priest should he promise to stop ministering without a license. However, Reza's outraged parishioners turned on the intruders. Catholic witnesses remembered the attack on the defensa rural as a case of spontaneous, righteous fury; militia survivors accused Father Reza of inciting the faithful and charged that his brother fired the coup de grâce that killed Nájera. Sources agree that men and women alike of Yextla beat and shot several agraristas who failed to escape and then dismembered the bodies.[148]

In response, area defensas rurales and federales rushed to Yextla. They rounded up and detained many suspects, although Father Reza and his brother had long since fled. Surprisingly, state authorities released them five days later. To be sure, the rule of law was notoriously weak in Guerrero, but circumstances strongly suggest that Guevara stopped the investigation to avoid antagonizing Catholics and implicating political allies who protected Reza. Father Reza remained at large, and Guevara's authorities even returned the confiscated arms to the suspects.[149]

The Yextla massacre was but the first battle in a small war that raged in the hamlets around Tlacotepec municipio in 1935 and 1936. After the Calles-Cárdenas break in mid-1935 weakened enforcement of anticlerical regulation, several priests began to openly assert their influence in the municipio. They repeatedly clashed with agrarians, federal teachers, and the masons of Tlacotepec's Revolutionary Lodge. The anticlericalism of the SEP was not a factor here; back in the fall of 1934, conservative Inspector Sebastian Peniche López announced an "antifanaticism campaign" but never followed up.[150] Old local animosities, including religious tensions, socioethnic divisions, and agrarian conflicts, drove Tlacotepec's acrimonious segundita. When Catholic activists harried local anticlericals, it helped landowners liquidate agrarista leaders. At its peak, the struggle in Tlacotepec became a sort of ideological cleansing with strong class undertones. Father David Salgado visited many hamlets across the municipio, preaching against Tlacotepec's

Freemasons. The lodge had supported federal schools by forming local Pro-Education Committees and denouncing unlicensed priests. Tlacotepec's lodge was motivated by a detailed historical critique of Mexican clericalism with a strong indigenista subtext, in which the Church was culpable for the "Spanish rape" of pre-Columbian civilizations, including "the great Nezahualcoyotl." In the present, vampiric priests still sucked dry the peasants through tithes and fees.[151] Federal schooling, Tlacotepec's masons hoped, would finally drive a stake through the Church's heart.

Father Salgado struck back. In Los Hoyos village, he induced the defensa rural to try to kill lodge brother Tirso Adame, who had filed charges against and allegedly threatened the life of Salgado. Adame barely escaped a mob with his life in December 1935; two other masons fled after Salgado threatened them, too.[152] This then was hybrid segunda violence; attacks were planned as part of a coherent strategy as in offensive attacks, but carried out by almost the entire community as in defensive ones.

Salgado supplemented homilies against the school and the lodge with spectacle. On the Virgin of Guadalupe's day (December 12) 1935, he staged a public drama in the atrium of Tlacotepec's church. Satirizing socialist education, he reminded parents that they risked excommunication if they sent children to federal schools. Around Candlemas (February 2) 1936, Salgado and another unlicensed priest, Gabriel Ocampo, announced a new boycott of federal classrooms and demanded the return of their nationalized rectories from the SEP. More ominously, they secretly met to plot vigilante violence if demands went unmet. In March and April 1936, terrified federal teachers fled schools across the municipio.

Tlacotepec's segundita was especially bitter because of a long-simmering local struggle over agrarian reform and local power. In June 1935, a gang linked to Father Salgado and Tlacotepec elites tried to kill Justino Maldonado, the municipio's leading agrarista.[153] Since at least 1918, the Catholic leaders and landlords who backed Salgado had opposed Zapatista veterans headed by the Maldonado clan. In 1923, the Maldonados' agraristas backed the Sonoran regime in Mexico City and received good guns to fight against the delahuertista gentry of the county seat. Agraristas not only wanted rifles, they also wanted land. However, Tlacotepec's notables used connections in Chilpancingo via Congressman Rafael Leyva to bottle up many land grants. Leyva and then-governor Héctor F. López deputized a notorious pistolero, Ignacio Chávez, as police chief to bust Tlacotepec's agrarista movement. Uncowed, Flavio Maldonado gunned down Chávez. The agrarista *líder* cultivated good relations with federal engineers of the National Agrarian Commission, who finally created Tlacotepec's ejido. Over time, however, Flavio Maldonado, his son Justino, and his brother Enrique became small landowners in their own right. Foes called them caciques who ruled their "feudal domain" by "agitating" peasants and perpetrating violent acts, including rape, against foes.[154]

The religious question in Tlacotepec was inseparable from this long-festering agrarian conflict. During Castrejón's administration, the Maldonados' agraristas had the upper hand. When Guevara declared his 1932 gubernatorial candidacy, anti-Maldonado townsmen, ranchers, and Catholics in the county seat rallied to his cause. Led by Miguel Nava Alarcón, the brother of Tlacotepec's priest at the time, the Guevara campaign promised to free the clergy from legal shackles and break the Maldonados' hold. When the pro-Castrejón agrarista mayor questioned Father Melesio Altamirano's unregistered status, the priest strode into town hall in his robes with supporters at his heels and dared the mayor to take action.[155] By the time of Guevara's election, Catholics were on a collision course with the masons of Tlacotepec's revolutionary lodge and the Maldonado clan.

The Maldonados, masons, and maestros were defeated not only because of the Ranchero group's power and the chronic incapacity of the revolutionary state, but also because anticlericalism never spread widely among agraristas. After their rout by Salgado, brothers of the Revolutionary Lodge complained that priests had "deceived" the majority of peasants.[156] Agrarista widows accused Yextla's peasants of betraying their class—they were "not proletarians, but fanatical *clericales*."[157] Such charges speak to most peasants' pro-Catholic sentiment, while the class-conscious, ardently prorevolutionary agraristas remained a small, increasingly embittered minority. Anticlericalism acted as a wedge, isolating a revolutionary minority from the rest, while Catholicism acted as a kind of social glue, uniting wealthy townsfolk and poorer villagers.

At the same time, the segundita in Tlacotepec demonstrates that Guerrero's countryside was by no means solidly under the sway of the Church. Syncretic Catholicism survived even in predominantly mestizo central valleys. The agraristas of Ojo de Agua de Progreso and the brothers of the Revolutionary Lodge elaborated a largely organic anticlerical ideology that defined the institutional Church as the enemy. Even in small communities, anticlericalism was not necessarily an exotic ideology imported by interloping Jacobin teachers. Tlacotepec's anticlericals were a minority, but they were a native one. The uneven archival record makes it difficult to determine with any certainty if Tlacotepec was an outlier. At about the same time, in the hamlet of Xaltianguis (Acapulco municipio), teacher Wenceslao Jiménez and fellow-traveling free thinkers formed the Evolution Group to counter the Church's "false doctrine" that spread superstition: "No one can prove if life after death exists ... the best guide for man is nature"—not the clergy.[158] The existence of this group as well as Tlacotepec's lodge speaks to a simple fact: outside the levitical archipelago, Protestants, deists, agnostics, spiritists, and outright atheists found a small but sustainable social niche. By the same token, freethinking associations were less likely to survive in levitical areas. The challenge of these homegrown religious dissenters, coming on the heels of strict anticlerical restrictions, explains why Catholics felt besieged. Given the right circumstances, the faithful responded with violence.

In another central valley municipio not far from Tlacotepec, Apango (formally Martir del Cuello, in the east-central district of Guerrero), religious tensions also aggravated existing sociopolitical conflicts. As in Tlacotepec, Apango's clergy sided with the mestizo merchants and landowners against agraristas. In the county seat, the Díaz clan had held political power since the Porfiriato. In the Nahua villages and hamlets of the municipio, former Zapatistas sought the support of the national revolutionary state and Governor Castrejón to gain ejidal grants and political power. In December 1934, the Guevara administration restored the Díaz dynasty to local office in spite of its delahuertista, Cristero, and pro-Escobar past. By the early 1930s, the religious conflict had merged with the agrarian conflict in Apango. Agraristas in the Nahua hamlets of Zotoltilán, Oapan, and Hueyitlapan alleged that the pro-Díaz town council permitted expelled priests to return and resume public processions in spite of the ley de cultos. Worse still, Father Francisco Guerrero, a charismatic priest linked to landowners, came back from exile with Bernal García, a notorious shootist in the service of hacendados. Guevara deputized García to head Oapan's defensa rural.[159] Indigenous peasants witnessed the loss of their cherished arms, the formation of García's anti-agrarian paramilitary, the political empowerment of landowners, and the re-sacralization of public space as part and parcel of a local counterrevolution in Apango.[160]

The cuadrilla of Oapan had long been a center of revolutionary agrarianism. When it welcomed a SEP school, it became the target of offensive segunda violence. In March 1936, a gang shouting "Death to the Socialist School!" tried to kill maestra Cirenia Santos. She fought hand-to-hand against the segundero chief, suffering cranial blows before campesinos repelled the assailants.[161] Father Guerrero's role in the bloodshed is difficult to determine with certainty, but his condemnation of federal teachers and links to García's paramilitary strongly point to yet another case of clerical involvement in offensive segunda violence.

Ironically, when the state government finally expelled Father Guerrero from Apango in 1935, it was because of a sexual scandal.[162] The disgraced priest fled to the neighboring municipio of Zumpango, where he positioned himself on the antiagrarian side of a conflict strikingly similar to those in Apango and Tlacotepec. Allied with prominent citizens and their white guard, Father Guerrero opposed surrounding agrarista communities led by federal teachers.[163] Father Guerrero moved on to Tepecuacuilco, but in 1938, Governor Alfredo J. Berber, who generally accommodated Catholics, finally cancelled Guerrero's license after another sexual scandal.[164]

Segunda violence flared up in central valley municipios when the opening of SEP schools injected the religious question into an already combustible mix of class, ethnic, and factional conflicts. Key federal teachers saw Catholicism as counterrevolutionary even though they refrained from iconoclasm. Catholics for their part suspected that the federal schoolhouse endangered morals. In these central valley communities, the struggle over agrarian reform, electoral spoils, and anticlericalism tended to divide municipios along a single fault line. No matter what the specific mix of grievances, the revolutionary camp was almost always smaller and weaker than the conservative faction, due in no small part to the religious question. Charismatic priests like Father Guerrero, ably assisted by lay leaders, took advantage of the Ranchero group's return to power in Chilpancingo to restore the Church to the center of public life, usually working in tandem with local economic elites and conservative politicos. However, it was never a simple contest between mocho landowners (and their even more *mocha* wives) in the county seat battling poor agraristas in the hamlets. A number of factors overrode administrative, ethnic, and class divisions. Events in Tlacotepec clearly demonstrate that while peasants (mestizo and indigenous alike) might have resented the clergy, they still clung to Catholicism. This fact, along with the near monopoly on force enjoyed by foes of the revolutionary project, meant that teachers and agraristas repeatedly suffered from segunda violence and that the revolutionary project faced long odds in the central valleys.

Segunditas also erupted in the northern valley municipios of Huitzuco and Tetipac (Alarcón district). Like Tlacotepec and Apango, they were deeply divided between pro-Castrejón agraristas and conservative factions led by landowners and linked to the Ranchero group and the Church. Religious tensions were heightened after the SEP dispatched the veteran pedagogue and ardent anticlerical, Primitivo Álvarez, to serve as inspector of Taxco's district. During the spring of 1934, Álvarez set up the vanguard organization, Social Action for Public Good against Fanaticism, Ignorance, and Vice, to defanaticize the population. Echoing Garrido Canabal, Social Action demanded that Taxco's historic St. Prisca Church be turned into an art museum. Worried by Álvarez's support for agrarian reform and hoping to head off a Catholic backlash stirred up by talk of Tabascanization, the governor turned a deaf ear to the strident SEP inspector's demands. Priests safely sheltered in the houses of Taxco's leading families satanized Álvarez's maestros rurales as "masons or possessed by the devil." These clerical admonitions opened up, in Álvarez's words, a "deep social division," pitting outnumbered educators, unionized miners, and agraristas against "fanatics and reactionaries lodged in local governance" who looked on with "indolence and apathy" as priests propagandized. While an attendance strike emptied most SEP schools around Taxco, Catholic mediators backed pro–Guevara Ranchero politicos to block agrarian reform. When the SEP demanded action against clerical violations of the ley de cultos, the Guevara administration claimed it lacked actionable information.[165]

When Manuel S. Hidalgo took over as inspector in early 1935, tensions with Catholics seemed to ebb. Hidalgo encouraged teachers to defanaticize more discreetly by spreading a scientific worldview instead of prosecuting priests, yet Catholic resistance continued unabated. When Hidalgo closed several parochial schools and opened new SEP schools in nationalized rectories, boycotts of SEP schools mushroomed.[166] Inspector Hidalgo charged that interim governor Lugo and the "fanatics" in town halls hatched "a crusade against the [federal] Government." "Secret juntas of monks" planned the truancy campaign and, Hidalgo alleged, issued death threats if teachers fought back. Membership and leadership of this Catholic network remains shadowy, but eight unlicensed priests were probably its hub, while activist Catholic townswomen of Taxco, Noxtepec, and other mestizo towns were the spokes connecting it to villages and hamlets. No actual violence resulted from its campaign, but a recristero gang intimidated teachers. The likely link between the segunderos and this network overseeing the licit campaign against the SEP was Father Constantino Arizmendi Figueroa. During the first Cristiada, Arizmendi led a large cristero band that operated across Alarcón district.[167]

The cristero connection to segunda violence was especially strong in the small village of Noxtepec (municipio of Tetipac, but close to Taxco). In the spring of 1935, Noxtepec's teacher fled after receiving death threats, likely from recristeros. Undaunted, Inspector Hidalgo dispatched a new maestro, Martiniano Morán, to reopen the school in the fall of 1935. Like many effective federal teachers, Morán opened a very successful night school for adults. However, he did not generate new support for the revolutionary project as much as tap into existing agrarian and labor (miners) radicalism. Noxtepec's agraristas strongly backed Castrejón in hopes of much-needed ejido expansion, and some denounced pro-Guevara local authorities for sheltering an unlicensed priest and leading illegal processions of the local Virgin (a symbolic flashpoint since the Cristiada). For their part, authorities in the county seat of Tetipac bitterly opposed Noxtepec's agraristas and hosted Father Antonio Giles's advent service in 1935. In response, maestro Morán helped Noxtepec agraristas to protect and expand their ejido and set up a union.[168]

Geographic, agrarian, and anticlerical divisions overlapped, and the religious conflict strengthened conservative resistance to schools and ejidos. To realize revolutionary change in Noxtepec, Morán also aggressively enforced anticlerical regulations, making conflict with Noxtepec Catholics inevitable. Matters came to a head in the early fall of 1935. Father Giles, pistol in hand and twenty men at his back, invaded an agrarista meeting convened by Morán. A brawl ensued. Although no one was harmed, Morán claimed Giles threatened his life. The army and Governor Lugo dismissed the dustup as a purely personal conflict, but SEP persisted, forcing the governor to ban priests from Noxtepec until 1939.[169]

In other communities in the Alarcón district, conflicts between priests, landlords, and their supporters on the one side and agraristas and teachers on the other dragged on for years. Over time, offensive segunda violence by foes of the SEP and agraristas grew rather than declined in spite of the relaxation of anticlerical regulation. After teachers made inroads in several communities in the mid-1930s, the clergy and at least one well-organized gang of segunderos galvanized Catholic resistance that stymied teachers a few years later; the ascendant Figueroa clan tacitly approved.[170]

In Huitzuco (Hidalgo district, northern valleys), the SEP's project never really got off the ground. Federal schools were all but paralyzed by a wave of attendance strikes convened by unlicensed priests protected by pro-Guevara authorities. Lay activists even infiltrated the parents' group set up by the SEP. Teachers hoped to mobilize Huitzuco's Nahua hamlets that resented high sacramental fees, but it instead alienated them by prohibiting the traditional use of alcohol in syncretic religious ceremonies. Mestizo rum merchants and distillers readily exploited the rift between teachers and peasants.[171] Once again, anticlericalism undermined the creation of a grassroots revolutionary coalition.

Huitzuco's priests did not shy away from confrontation with the SEP, as events in the nearby village of Xilocintla demonstrate. An unlicensed priest based in Cocula began visiting in 1932, and was welcomed by friendly authorities. He openly decried parents who sent children to "irreligious" federal schools, predicting they were headed for hell. He organized the Daughters of Maria to coordinate a boycott of the school; even some teachers in the state educational system joined in. His censure also encouraged violent resistance: Xilocintla's SEP maestro rural fled after peasants repeatedly made death threats.[172] The situation became so bad that the army and state government finally gave in to SEP demands and expelled two unlicensed priests from Huitzuco. This calmed the situation, strongly suggesting that intimidation was part of a campaign directed by the expelled clerics.[173]

Sporadic, nearly lethal segunda violence broke out in northern valleys for roughly the same reasons as in the central valleys. In and around Taxco, SEP inspectors' anticlericalism triggered a Catholic reaction that at times turned violent (though stopped short of killing), but elsewhere SEP moderation did not prevent Catholic resistance from escalating into intimidation. If preexisting conflicts over land and power at times inflamed religious conflicts in a few areas, aggressive actions by priests like Antonio Giles and Constantino Arizemendi greatly heightened tensions elsewhere. In the end, however, the SEP's debility, the expulsion of bellicose priests, and the failure of agrarian and political challenges to the elite curbed segunda violence in the northern valleys, although antiagrarian violence continued. The Twin Coasts were another story.

Costa Grande I (Montes de Oca):
White Terror and Christianity by Fear

The Costa Grande was the bloodiest corner of Guerrero: chronic social violence pitting landowners, allies, and clients against agraristas began in the armed phase of the Revolution and never really ended.[174] There was no known anticlerical provocation from federal teachers in this subregion—embattled inspectors and teachers were too preoccupied with survival. Nevertheless, conservative coalitions drew on Catholic clergy, Catholic activists, and Catholic ideology to counter the revolutionary project. A closer look at the Costa Grande suggests that offensive segunda violence against agraristas and teachers was essentially the continuation of old agrarian and political conflicts.

The roots of the Costa Grande segundita run back to the bloody 1920s, when agrarismo's spread sparked a strong reaction. The tug of blood and the pull of shared social and geographic origins united Ranchero group politicos, landowners, and Catholic brokers into a network that deployed pistoleros against peasant radicals. Although Costa Grande politicos were far from pious and despised cristeros, they had much in common, both socially and ideologically, with Catholics. However, when it came to the religious question, there were significant differences between the Montes de Oca district (roughly the northeastern third of the Costa Grande) and the rest of Costa Grande, dominated by Acapulco. I first consider Montes de Oca, focusing on the pivotal role played by ex-governor Héctor F. López. A high-ranking revolutionary soldier, López was also the principal leader of a powerful conservative network at home in Montes de Oca.

Hailing from Coahuayutla, López boasted a distinguished revolutionary pedigree, fighting first for Madero and then Carranza. Military service under General Amaro earned him a place in the Revolutionary Family's inner circle. A descendant of a middling family of landowners in a mountainous, isolated municipio wedged against the Michoacán border, López apparently harbored no strong religious sentiment (as governor during the Cristiada, he jailed and harassed priests). His daughter Virginia, however, led a group of elite young women in the state capital that assisted Father Margarito Flores, a priest later killed for suspected cristero ties.[175]

Family and shared interests tied López to the Maldonado clan (no relation to Tlacotepec's Maldonados), latifundists who had long dominated the Montes de Oca district. General López married into the Flores family, and its patriarch Severino was a local bureaucrat who served as the Maldonados' perennial political operative. Flores took advantage of López's protection to direct a paramilitary gang that persecuted agraristas. For its part, the institutional Church never sanctioned this violence, but some of Flores's gunmen identified with (and quite probably operated as) cristeros and enjoyed a degree of support from Catholic lay leaders and even some clergy. The voice of Montes de Oca agraristas, lawyer Herminio Huato, denounced the López-Maldonado-Flores clique as "red-blooded *clericales*" because Father Manuel Herrera lent his moral authority to violence against agraristas and teachers.[176]

Agraristas in the Montes de Oca district were targeted long before the conflict over socialist education erupted. Impunity, meddling by state-level politicos, and even family vendettas fed social violence; the Flores family had long feuded with the rapacious mestizo Izazagas, who controlled area agrarista Defensas Sociales with the political and judicial protection of Desiderio Borja, Callista federal congressman and governor Castrejón's consigliere.[177] Growing religious tensions during the mid-1930s, however, drew Catholics and landowners closer, injected a sense of moral crisis to antiagrarian violence, and added federal teachers to the hit list of Flores's gang. Flores served as the nexus between landowners like the Maldonados and the Gutiérrez family, who had organized cristeros to check agraristas, and priests and lay leaders bent on closing federal schools. The nationalization of rectories and other Church buildings, when combined with anxiety about the phantom menace of sexual education in SEP schools, sharpened hostility against the federal teachers in the early 1930s. The Catholic campaign against federal schools encouraged death threats against several teachers in Montes de Oca, and maestro Margarito Ortega was gunned down from behind in December 1932. The SEP admitted that this "reactionary" counteroffensive undid most of its work in the district by late 1932.[178]

Two years later, SEP superintendent Guillermo Bonilla regretfully reported that "the Revolution has not been felt in the area." Landlord dominance rested on "fanaticism, which also blocks the work of the schools." Peasants refused to even speak of land reform because of clerical condemnation and white terror: "it was teachers alone against hacendados and Catholics."[179] Things changed little the rest of the decade.

Costa Grande II (Acapulco's Hinterland):
Agrarian Social Conflict Supersedes the Religious Question

Farther down the Costa Grande, in the Galeana and Tabares districts surrounding the commercial hub of Acapulco, landowners, Catholic activists, and Ranchero politicos countered a potent coalition of agraristas, federal teachers, and a small number of anticlericals throughout the 1930s. The SEP was stronger here than in the Montes de Oca district, although it never launched a sustained defanaticization drive.[180] This, along with stronger homegrown agrarismo, helps explain the relative success of the revolutionary project here. It also meant that Catholic leaders focused their resistance against the ejido, not the federal schoolhouse. In spite of the absence of significant anticlericalism in the 1920s and early 1930s on this stretch of the Twin Coasts, individual priests directly rallied Catholics against agraristas and other revolutionary agents. After agraristas gained the upper hand with help from the national Cardenistas administration in the mid-1930s, religiously sanctioned violence was subsumed into antiagrarian violence, and clergy and lay leadership lay low. By the end of the 1930s, however, the resurgent clergy had extended the Church's reach into the newly created ejidos.

Since the Revolution began in this part of the Costa Grande, the religious question intensified social violence by hardening the lines between revolutionary agraristas and their foes. Anticlericalism was a basic tenet of the anarcho-syndicalist Partido Obrero of Acapulco (Workers Party of Acapulco, or the POA for its initials in Spanish), the cradle of a generation of agrarista leaders on the Twin Coasts. During the Revolution's armed phase, several key *costeño* agrarista leaders denounced the clergy as lackeys of the landowners and Spanish merchants of Acapulco. Some of this anticlerical sentiment percolated down into agrarista communities. Hatred for priests was not an abstract idea for revolutionaries on the Guerrero littoral; they blamed Father Florentino Díaz for betraying costeño POA leader Juan Escudero to the delahuertista rebels who killed him in 1923.[181] In 1926, priests Vicente M. Cuevas and Manuel Herrera preached against the Partido Nacional Agrarista.[182] During the Cristero War, the Vidales brothers led a local agrarista insurgency and blamed Father Cuevas for identifying several men for assassination by federal soldiers. The major landowning and industrial families in the Costa Grande city of Atoyac strongly supported Father Cuevas. During the Cristero War, Governor Héctor F. López protected Father

Herrera, endorsing the mayor of Atoyac's defense of the priest as "useful . . . being a force for morality and progress of the people . . . he advises all to not make trouble, and that it is very useful to respect superiors, to empathize with our neighbors, and to not commit crimes amongst ourselves."[183] Whatever his personal beliefs, López saw the social and political utility of the clergy in curbing the spread of agrarismo.

López's decision to take the clergy's side on the Costa Grande reveals an important subrosa dimension of the religious question, namely, that some areligious revolutionary leaders nevertheless valued the institutional Church as a check on agrarianism and radicalism. In the eyes of Ranchero group politicos like López, the Church represented private property as a natural right and defended hierarchy as a moral necessity. For them, Catholicism legitimized the existing system of land distribution and class structure. López's affinity for Catholicism resembled that of the "Christians by fear," the anxious members of the nineteenth-century French bourgeoisie who wanted others to go to mass to stem the spread of radical ideologies.[184] Well-to-do politicos who otherwise advocated revolutionary modernization came to see anticlericalism as encouraging dangerous attacks on property and propriety. Consider Acapulco's Masonic lodge: it denounced "larcenous" clergy and policed violations of the ley de culto, but it also worried that the "Leninism" of coastal agraristas would unleash "chaos and anarchy."[185] Ultimately, many landowners, professionals, and politicians who identified with the Mexican Revolution came to see agrarian reform as a far greater threat than parasitic priests. For them, revolutionary anticlericalism threatened proper governance and the necessary social order, and the Church was the lesser of two evils.

The Ranchero group's Christianity by fear helps explain its counterintuitive decision to join forces with Catholic brokers on the Costa Grande. In López's native Montes de Oca district, Father Herrera went on to advise the Maldonado and Gutiérrez hacendados' white guard in the late 1930s; as a senator, López shielded the priest from prosecution.[186] Christianity by fear shaped local politics elsewhere in the Costa Grande, as in the 1929 mayoral election in Atoyac. Agrarista leader Feliciano Radilla, an heir of the Escuderos' and Vidales' radical tradition, was also a Protestant and close to Acapulco's María de la O, a fiery Communist and feminist leader who became an atheist after her husband died at a young age. From the pulpit, Father Herrera denounced Radilla and agraristas as anti-Catholic and openly opposed Radilla's slate for Atoyac's town council. Radilla and de la O tried to prosecute

Herrera for leading illegal processions, marrying and baptizing, and plotting a cristiada against Governor Castrejón. Their charges landed Herrera in jail briefly and nationalized his church's atrium, but only at the cost of deeply antagonizing Catholics.[187]

During his term, Governor Castrejón supported Radilla's unification of Costa Grande agrarianismo. In the second half of the 1930s, President Cárdenas helped Radilla survive repression by hostile state and local authorities. A covert army-landowner counterinsurgency claimed the lives of dozens of agraristas; Radilla proved to be as ruthless as his foes.[188] Given the lack of an enduring network linking Catholics and landowners in the Tabares and Galeana districts comparable to the Flores-López group in the Montes de Oca district, it is not surprising that local landowners generally relied on white guards and local federal military commanders, rather than segunderos, to halt agrarian reform. The absence of SEP iconoclasm here contributed to the diminution of the religious question as well. Consequently, around Acapulco and Atoyac the religious nature of violence was overshadowed—but never completely erased—by a bloody agrarian conflict.

Guerrero's Segunditas and Catholicism

These subregional cases reveal the complex, ambiguous, but undeniable relationship between segunda violence and Catholicism. In spite of significant local variations, several patterns emerge that suggest Catholicism played a substantial role in Guerrero's segunditas. First, peaceful boycotts of schools strengthened the influence of lay leaders and priests, many of whom were determined to oppose other aspects of the revolutionary project as well. Second, many Catholic clerical and lay leaders were embedded in social networks that defended local landowning and commercial elites. This in turn empowered perpetrators of offensive segunda violence aimed at schools and ejidos. Third, Catholic ideology that defined agrarian reform and socialist education as morally objectionable helped justify offensive and defensive violence.

Of course, given the absence of the rule of law and the deep social divisions in Guerrero, many would have died in the 1930s due to agrarian conflicts even without rising religious tensions. To be sure, the institutional Church did not directly sanction attacks on agraristas, teachers, or anticlericals. The peculiar weakness of the institutional Church in Guerrero probably encouraged segunda violence. The vertical hierarchy that allowed bishops to discipline priests and priests to guide the leadership of official and unofficial lay organizations was extremely weak. Chronic social violence and hyperlocalism prevented the bishop, priests, or ACM leaders from reining in amorphous, semi-autonomous groups and individuals who saw segunda violence as legitimately defending the Church. A handful of important priests did more than condemn socialist education and agrarian reform; they were also key participants in the social networks that fought segunditas. Priests like Melesio Altamirano, Antonio Giles, Francisco Guerrero, Manuel Herrera, and David Salgado jealously guarded their faith and local prerogatives by forcefully intervening against the revolutionary project. The institutional Church's radial strategy, coupled with its demonization of federal schooling, further loosened controls over lay groups and lower clergy and thus unintentionally facilitated the Segunda.[189]

Newspapers, flyers, and pastoral letters represent another link between Catholicism and segunditas. Catholic groups campaigning against federal schools distributed and read aloud pastoral letters and other official Catholic propaganda underscoring the dangers posed by the SEP and indeed the entire revolutionary project. The López-Flores-Maldonado network on the Costa Grande and Apango's coalition (the Díaz dynasty and Father Guerrero) tapped into an antirevolutionary discourse spun by the UNPF and the national opposition press using authorized Church teachings as one of its strongest threads. By highlighting the alleged outrages of the revolutionary government and federal teachers, these narratives undoubtedly encouraged the segunditas.

Press accounts and the propaganda of crypto-Catholic parents' groups effectively nationalized local incidents like the depredations of the allegedly perverse principal of Chilapa's high school and the red-shirting of Tierra Caliente schoolchildren. We have good reason to think that Catholic activists in Guerrero catalyzed resistance to the revolutionary project through such narratives. The Society of Catholic Guerrerans in favor of Mexican Catholicism published a letter in the Jalisco UNPF's newspaper in late January 1935 charging that SEP teachers were bent on combating the clergy.[190]

Key Catholic journalists in Guerrero did their part while working as stringers for Mexico City's opposition press, which frequently ran stories critical of federal schools. In May 1935, *Hombre Libre*'s correspondent in Chilapa criticized the SEP for closing two large parochial schools there, bashed the Guevara administration for jailing Father Rafael Altamirano, and alleged that a Jacobin mob stoned another priest's house.[191] Guerrero's readers of *Hombre Libre* were bombarded with a mix of factual and apocryphal stories from across the nation: Garridista parades, iconoclastic teachers, and children's loss of innocence in the classroom. This in turn raised Catholic fears about the ultimate intentions of the revolutionary project and, in particular, its maestros rurales.

Who were these journalists, and how were they linked to Catholic resistance? *Hombre Libre*'s provincial reporters in Chilapa lacked bylines, but two ACM standouts, Amando Salmerón Moctezuma and his son, Amando Salmerón Melo, probably penned them. The father was a former mayor of Chilapa; the son was the Guerrero correspondent for most Mexico City daily papers, including *La Prensa*. Together, they ran Guerrero's most prestigious photography studio in Chilapa. Given portraiture's importance for politics (the father photographed Zapata), they would have known volumes about regional politicking.[192] The Salmeróns' reports that stoked Catholic resistance were but one part of a multifaceted Catholic response to the revolutionary project, one that robbed federal teachers and agraristas of the support of much of civil society and helped inspire Guerrero's segunditas.

Segunda violence welled up from the grassroots and was encouraged and channeled by regional and local politicians, landowners, and in some cases even indigenous elders. Guerrero's segunditas, however, were never simply expressions of Catholic violence, and their uneven, unpredictable nature eludes any monocausal explanation. As we have seen, segunda violence unfolded in profoundly different ways from place to place. A number of its causal factors were part and parcel of the religious question: federal inspectors' and teachers' stances on defanaticization, some clergy's willingness to sanction illicit resistance, and dogmatic opposition to agrarian reform. But other causes of the segunda violence were clearly secular: landlords' capacity to mobilize indigenous and mestizo clients, class and ethnic conflicts, and family feuds. Still, without the involvement of clergy and lay leaders in networks that carried out offensive segunda violence—and without their dogmatic opposition to key aspects of the revolutionary project—violent attacks on agraristas, teachers, and anticlericals in the 1930s would have been less frequent and less deadly.

By the late 1930s, Guerrero's segunditas were either winding down or morphing into purely agrarian conflicts. By this time, the radical minority of SEP teachers and inspectors had abandoned the aggressive defanaticization of the Psychological Revolution. Cárdenas's gradual relaxation of anticlericalism prompted a shift in Catholic goals and tactics. Rather than petering out, Catholic opposition to the revolutionary project evolved in a less lethal direction. Instead of accepting the legitimacy of the postrevolutionary state in return for greater religious liberty, Catholic foes used largely licit, generally bloodless means to deny it the consensual support of civil society in Guerrero. Cárdenas's assumption that better relations with the Church hierarchy and the lowering of tensions surrounding the religious question would win over Catholics long wary of the revolutionary project simply did not hold true, at least in Guerrero.

The Spiritual Reconquest of Guerrero, 1936–1940

Guerrero's Catholics were neither depoliticized nor demobilized during the Cárdenas presidency. In broad terms, the voto morado became less important and defensive segunda violence waned, but neither abated entirely. During the latter 1930s, the institutional Church recovered, and focused on reestablishing the influence of clergy and lay leaders in underchurched areas, especially the countryside. The Church showed a particular interest in the ejidos created by Cardenista agrarian reform, considering them a particularly dangerous revolutionary intrusion into society. Formal lay organizations like the ACM revived in the late 1930s, but they were overshadowed by the Sinarquista movement, especially in rural areas. The Union Nacional Sinarquista (National Sinarquista Union), or UNS, was part and parcel of the Church's global strategy to reestablish its social authority in the wake of leftist revolutions. Its cell-like organization, militaristic drill, extreme right-wing nationalism, and explicitly anti-Communist ideology reminded many of fascism.[193] The institutional Church's resurgence reenergized Catholic campaigns to thwart federal schools, even though socialist education had largely vanished from the curriculum. As with the Segunda, however, the Catholic reconquest of society was significantly shaped by regional events.

Cárdenas's ouster of Calles in Mexico City had important regional ramifications in Guerrero. The Cardenista regime removed Governor Guevara for his Callismo on September 19, 1935, after an embarrassing gunfight between politicos at a bullfight.[194] To finish out his term, Cárdenas selected José Inocencio Lugo, a career military lawyer. As we have seen, Lugo enjoyed senior standing in Guerrero's Ranchero group and got on well with Héctor F. López. While personally loyal to Cárdenas, Lugo never purged the Ranchero group from state and local office; in fact, he relied on them to govern. Granted, Lugo removed forty town councils elected under and imposed by Guevara, but to replace them he appointed interim councils generally hostile to agraristas.

Moreover, he did not disarm landowner paramilitaries. Lugo's conservativism, however, was checked by a revitalized agrarista movement. Key national Cardenistas protected minor agrarista leaders in the Tierra Caliente and two key Twin Coast agraristas: Feliciano Radilla in Acapulco and its environs and Nabor A. Ojeda on the Costa Chica. Cárdenas tapped the two for national congress and jump-started the long-stalled ejidal grant requests on the Twin Coasts. Neither the Ranchero group nor their agrarista foes, though, were strong enough to prevail. Four years of bloody stalemate resulted.[195]

How did Catholics and Catholicism shape the regional conflict during the Cárdenas administration? State and local politicians aligned with the Ranchero group could now tolerate open violations of anticlerical regulations and strengthen alliances with Catholic political brokers. In doing so, they followed the example of interim governor Lugo, who reached an understanding with Bishop Díaz on March 20, 1936. The new governor halted the state government's half-hearted crackdown on the Church; in return, the diocese made its peace with the state administration. After three years, Bishop Díaz could safely make pastoral visits across his diocese. Closed churches reopened, exiled priests returned home, and priests in hiding resurfaced. The number of legal, licensed priests jumped from fourteen to forty-three, and the number of unlicensed ones protected by local authorities was probably much larger, including many roving regular "missionary" clergy.[196] Thirteen Jesuit missionaries based in Tlapa ministered to la Montaña in the fall of 1936, countering the influence of Communist federal teachers.[197]

The Lugo-Díaz pact enabled the spiritual reconquest of Guerrero and smoothed the way for the Ranchero group to hold onto Chilpancingo and many town halls. Rightly or wrongly, agrarian reform's shortcomings, governmental corruption and incapacity, electoral violence, and caciquismo colored Catholics' perceptions of Cardenismo. The Church's doctrine of civic action, order, and respect for patriarchy and private property presented a reassuring alternative to Cardenista popular fronts, ejidos, and social leveling. Although Ranchero politicos could no longer stir Catholic voters by campaigning against Tabascanization, they still benefited from the lingering residue of resentment left behind by anticlerical educators and agraristas. Church ideology and organization still influenced elections during the Cardenista era, even though Catholic voters did not always march lockstep behind the Ranchero group. Catholic counter-corporatism, to borrow Adrian Bantjes's useful phrase, defeated revolutionary agraristas in places like Iguala.[198] In at least one case, Catholic women's intervention was decisive; when the ruling party experimented with women's suffrage in the 1936 gubernatorial primary, Taxco's beatas voted as a bloc.[199]

The expiration of Lugo's interim term on April 1, 1937, threatened the Ranchero group's hold on the governorship. With Cárdenas's favor, the agraristas seemed poised to seize the power. In the ruling party's October 1936 gubernatorial primary, however, the Ranchero group managed to hold on to power after a chaotic campaign marked by widespread abstention and fraud. This time, the agraristas' blunders and internal divisions, not the voto morado, decided the matter. Agrarista leaders had consolidated a strong political base on the Twin Coasts and in the Tierra Caliente, but they tried to curry favor in Mexico City by nominating David Arizmendi, an outsider from Michoacán, Cárdenas's home state. The ploy backfired, alienating many in Guerrero. In the end, Cárdenas tried to placate the army (particularly zone commander General Vicente González) and put a stop to chronic violence by selecting yet another military man to rule the state, General Alfredo F. Berber.[200]

The new governor was also a protégé of key Ranchero leader Héctor F. López, whom he once served as private secretary. Major coastal landowners backed Berber. As a federal congressman (1934–36), Berber's alternate was Guillermo Miller, a reactionary Costa Chica landowner close to López. And as Guevara's interim mayor of Acapulco during the same time, Berber forged close ties with key antiagrarian landowners.[201] Cárdenas negotiated a truce between Berber and the de facto agrarista jefe, Nabor Ojeda, to promote "harmony and serenity." In hindsight, Cárdenas seemed quite naive. Berber broke his word and strengthened the Ranchero group by beefing up pro-landowner paramilitaries, even as Mexico City sent hundreds of rifles to agraristas.[202]

Berber's stance on the religious question is difficult to pin down. The new governor did not owe his election to Catholics, and during the Psychological Revolution he promised Garrido Canabal to fight against "fanaticism and vice."[203] But Berber understood the political utility of letting the pact Lugo negotiated with Bishop Díaz stand.[204] Consequently, the number of unlicensed priests climbed to well over sixty during his term, and Bishop Díaz and his priests enjoyed even greater freedom.[205] Cherished semiprofane religious festivals and public processions of beloved local saints joyously resumed.[206] If the institutional Church put out some green shoots, syncretic popular Catholicism bloomed.

In the coming years, the clergy and leaders of official lay organizations struggled to exert a degree of authority over guerrense Catholics. The institutional Church's main bridge to the laity, the ACM, recovered anemically, and its progress among male and indigenous Catholics was disappointing. By about 1940, the local chapters of the ACM existed in only one-third of the diocese's parishes, and only one-sixth had any male members. By necessity, the ACM wagered on the strong by building its base among women in conservative, levitical islands like the northern valley town of Taxco. It floundered in many underchurched areas, although it did set up a chapter in the coastal town of Ayutla, a flashpoint in the littoral agrarian civil war, and in little Apaxtla, Castrejón's birthplace. It even tried to reach out to Guerrero's indigenous communities. But for the most part results were meager.[207]

The Church remained a political force in Guerrero in the Cardenista era not only because of its institutional regeneration, but also because Bishop Díaz unyieldingly opposed SEP schooling as Communist and unchristian—even as Cardenismo retreated from defanaticization.[208] Given the ACM's halting progress, the institutional Church in Guerrero still relied on the often unruly clergy, older sodalities like the Daughters of Maria and the Damas, and semi-official lay groups to close federal schools and to redeem ejidatarios. While Díaz strictly followed the national episcopate's prohibition of any endorsement of another Cristiada, the institutional Church continued to work through decentralized networks and stubbornly independent priests through the radial strategy. Segunda violence diminished, but it did not disappear. The spiritual reconquest of Guerrero in the second half of the 1930s helps explain why many Catholics remained deeply suspicious of the Cárdenas regime, agrarian reform, and the SEP. The process and outcome of the continuing struggle between Catholics and Cardenistas varied greatly across Guerrero.

In the northern and central valleys, the national Cardenista regime tried to breathe new life into an agrarian reform that began in the 1920s but stalled after Guevara's triumph.[209] Absent a dominant líder, hard-pressed agrarista communities turned to petty caciques like Justino Maldonado and sought advice and support from SEP teachers. Maestros rurales found themselves caught between landlord-armed gangs and resurgent Catholic networks' boycotts. Events in the central municipio of Tlacotepec demonstrate how shifts in national and regional politics encouraged priests and lay leaders to intensify pressure against federal schools in 1936, and in the process undermine the Cardenista revolutionary project which was ramping up land reform at the time.

A new campaign against SEP schools lowered enrollment from two hundred to just forty in Tlacotepec. Father Gabriel Ocampo celebrated by ringing his church *timbres* to summon children to two parochial schools—and to literally drown out the federal school's bell. The school boycotts and the example of ideological cleansing advocated by Father Salgado encouraged some Catholics to intimidate teachers and their remaining allies. Federal teachers in Tlacotepec's isolated hamlets received threats, blamed the priests, and demanded army protection. Many fled their posts. Tlacotepec's pro-Catholic town council did not lift a finger to protect them, and town councilor Arturo Torres showed up drunk to the federal school and reportedly threatened maestros. His son, leader of a Catholic lay association, distributed a pastoral letter against the SEP. By 1938, most teachers hesitantly returned to Tlacotepec's hamlets, only to run up against the determined resistance still spearheaded by Father Ocampo. In Izotepec, the comisario beat a rural federal teacher after the two clashed. In 1939, the comisario of another Tlacotepec municipio, Chapultepec, backed efforts by his close friend Ocampo to expel its maestro rural. By 1939, the teachers' union complained that Ocampo had made it all but impossible to run federal schools in Tlacotepec municipio.[210]

Outright segunda violence and intimidation cropped up in other corners of the northern and central valleys, in places such as Tetipac municipio. During the Cardenista-era thaw in Church-state relations, Father Giles and other priests could once again openly hold services, but school boycotts and even death threats against federal teachers continued. As in so many other communities, there was clearly a coordinated effort by priests and lay leaders to convince peasant communities to shun SEP schools, and some Catholics broke Church prohibitions against illicit tactics. Federal teachers alleged that priests actively induced Catholics to physically attack them. Some charges were exaggerated, but in late 1937, a seminarian came to Tetipac and for six days straight preached against the federal schools. Duly inspired, one inebriated man waved a pistol and shouted insults at children playing on the federal school athletic fields on a Sunday. Tetipac's beatas seemed downright belligerent: Señora Francisca Estrada led female activists through the streets boldly crying out, "Follow the example of other pueblos, where they have run off the teacher!" Other beatas encouraged a defense of religion with bullets or stones. And as in Tlacotepec, the favorable local political equation emboldened Catholics and handicapped federal teachers and beleaguered local supporters. Many teachers abandoned their schools when the mayor of

Tetipac refused to protect them. Several maestros rurales in neighboring Pilcaya had to flee as well. The town council elected under Governor Berber and President Cardenas was so bold in favoring the Church that it flouted its open, friendly relations with Chilapa's seminary.[211] Across Tetipac municipio, restoration of the Church's moral authority over society isolated supporters of the revolutionary project and, in some cases, encouraged violent resistance to it.

Even in the town Noxtepec, where the SEP had gained its only foothold in Tetipac municipio in 1935 by allying with agraristas, Catholics turned the tables on their foes during the Cardenista era. Throughout 1936, rumors that a band of recristeros was roaming Tetipac's countryside spooked teachers. In December 1937, a teacher in a nearby hamlet fled after receiving death threats. In 1939, Father Benjamín Manzano dared to lead processions through town while dressed in his priestly robes; two federal employees marched behind him. Noxtepec's agraristas feared the worst; teachers felt their lives were in danger should they remain.[212]

Violence and intimidation played a role in the failure of the revolutionary project in the northern and central valleys, facilitating the Church's nonviolent, moral suasion that achieved the spiritual reconquest of Guerrero. The sympathy for the Church of many politicos aligned with the Ranchero group was also decisive. In Cuetzala (Aldama district), an ambitious politician encouraged Father Jesús Téllez and female ACM activists when they launched an attendance strike against the SEP school. (They resorted to handing out candy to keep children away from the classroom.)[213]

The revolutionary project stalled in central valley communities where Catholic peasants joined Sinarquismo. The movement's emphasis on order appealed to more than just the elite. Many poorer Catholics might have benefited from Cardenista economic nationalism but felt that its leftist values threatened what they held most dear: religion, the patriarchal family, and private property. Although the UNS movement claimed to be completely outside electoral politics and insisted that it was not linked to the clergy, local chapters were often led by men with political ambitions and, in some cases, by priests. By 1936, Quechultenango had been divided for years between agraristas linked to the SEP and their foes close to the clergy. Agraristas complained that the priest sabotaged ejidal grants and still collected tithes; meanwhile, his ally, the mayor, took part in (theoretically illegal) religious processions holding a candle and carrying a religious banner. Four years later, one ejido in Quechultenango had a Sinarquista majority.[214]

Sinarquismo gained a firm foothold in the central valley town of Chilapa, no miracle considering the Church's strong presence in the diocesan see city. Sinarquismo even colonized the revolutionary project in the community. During the Lugo interim administration, Ismael Salmerón was elected mayor for the 1936–37 term. After campaigning actively for the ruling revolutionary party's candidate, Ávila Camacho, in 1939–40, Governor Berber sent Salmerón to the state congress in 1941. At the same time that he was rising through the ranks of the ruling revolutionary party, Salmerón organized Chilapa's Sinarquista chapter, a considerable political advantage. A confidential federal report noted Salmerón had relatively strong support across society, not just among the elite.[215] As in Mexico as a whole, Sinarquismo in Chilapa appealed to small businessmen, farmers, and many peasants. And in spite of its apolitical mission, it was far from nonpartisan in practice. In short, the remarkable growth of Sinarquismo during the Cardenista era helped ensure that most of civil society in the central valleys remained Catholic and alienated from the revolutionary project.

The variety of Catholic reactions to Cardenismo evident in central and northern communities is remarkable. It seems safe to say that given the Church's generally weak institutional presence and underdeveloped formal lay organizations, individual priests like Gabriel Ocampo and Catholic lay leaders like Señora Francisca Estrada enjoyed wide latitude to influence politics. Catholic electoral brokers like Salmerón could summon the voto morado to great electoral effect. Segunda violence continued in some areas like Tetipac; school boycotts became even more common. Geographically, Catholic resistance was strongest in the levitical archipelago, but the "flipping" of Noxtepec from agrarista to Catholic suggests that the revolutionary project was losing ground even on ejidos.

The same was true in the Tierra Caliente. Catholics used a combination of tactics to counter the Cardenista project: organizing truancy strikes in some places while flexing its electoral muscles elsewhere. Significantly, the institutional Church focused considerable energy not just on shutting down SEP schools, but also on subverting the Cardenista ejido. In Arcelia, authorities protected licensed and unlicensed priests alike. By the fall of 1936, priests routinely visited hinterland hamlets to organize school boycotts. By year-end, the SEP was forced to close four deserted rural schools. In early 1937, almost every area federal school was empty. During a pastoral visit in April 1937 ostensibly to confirm children, Bishop Díaz forbade parents from sending children to SEP schools—and reportedly excommunicated federal teachers to boot. Díaz's foray into the Tierra Caliente seems to have been just one part of a larger strategy focused on reaching small rural communities, where the institutional Church's presence had long been weakest and where the SEP had been trying to open federal schools and create new ejidos. After all, Díaz made a point of telling the faithful in Tierra Caliente hamlets to not volunteer their labor to erect new federal schools. Instead, the bishop urged them to build chapels. Newly constructed small sanctuaries allowed visiting priests to establish the Church's permanent physical presence and extend the regular routine of sacramental life as well as facilitate lay organizing. Federal teachers were galled by the sight of poor women and their children across the Tierra Caliente hauling rocks to build places of worship instead of schools and offering turkeys, pigs, and sheep to the clergy instead of to them. Bishop Díaz's defiance, like the Lugo and Berber administration's reluctance to defend federal schools, emboldened priests. They now directly confronted isolated federal rural teachers while riding their circuits: one visited a rural school, condemned it as an "abortion," and waved written orders from the bishop in front of parents to take children out of school.[216]

Catholic women played a key role in the institutional Church's renaissance in many Tierra Caliente agrarista communities. In the municipio of Coyuca de Benítez, a hacendado's wife named Eusebia Mendoza de Terán convinced many women to persuade their ejidatario husbands to volunteer to build a chapel. She also formed a women's group, probably under the aegis of the ACM, specifically for campesinas on the ejidos.[217]

Such beatas did valuable advance work for the clergy. After years of absence, priests returned to small communities. Most peasant men and women alike welcomed them back to restore popular fiestas and offer the succor of baptism to sick children. The clerical surge reached many of the ejidos recently created by Cárdenas. The liturgical calendar of sacramental services was restored only after peasants resumed tithing and rebuilt chapels. The archival record of priestly visits to the ejido is frustratingly incomplete in Guerrero; I imagine that the clergy's grudging accommodation of land reform in some cases allowed them to reestablish their presence in agrarian communities. A SEP inspector from Jalisco in 1936 lamented that even though most peasants were agraristas and their "fanaticismo" was "latent," most remained loyal to the Church in their hearts even as they demanded ejidos.[218] Guanajuatan agraristas wrote to Cárdenas in 1938, "we are Mexicans and our pueblo since the time of ancestors has been Catholic."[219] Peasant women, perhaps working in concert with priests and upper-class women, probably helped bring about the unwritten understanding between priests and male ejidatarios to end clerical opposition to land reform in return for peasants' support for the Church. The kind of negotiations between priests and beatas like Mendoza de Terán and women and men in agrarian communities during the Cardenista era was a key part of the Church's renaissance.

Significantly, even when and where the ejido was accepted by Catholic peasants, the federal schoolteacher often was not. Scholars often point to the revival of the Church and the consolidation of agrarian reform as key parts of a larger hegemonic process, suggesting that Catholics accepted Cardenista socioeconomic structural reforms in return for religious liberty. Certainly, the national Cardenistas hoped as much, but there is scant evidence for that, at least in Guerrero. The Church not only routed federal teachers in many communities and established beachheads on ejidos across the Tierra Caliente during the last half of the Cárdenas sexenio; it also rebuilt its economic base by reclaiming its share of the ejidos' harvest. The priest was literally eating the teacher's lunch, a fact that the SEP in Guerrero found difficult to swallow.[220]

On the Twin Coasts, the Church's resurgence was less dramatic, but still notable. In Ometepec (Costa Chica), a strong Catholic undertow was apparent after the Cardenista high tide. Catholics remembered Inspector Francisco Torres's ill-fated anticlerical campaign in 1934–35, and landowners were spoiling for a fight with a strong agrarista movement headed by Nabor Ojeda. Paramilitary bands hounded teachers and agraristas. President Cárdenas had accelerated land reform in this subregion, and the institutional Church was on its heels here as in the Tierra Caliente. But it was soon off the ropes. Father Guadalupe Guevara of Ometepec condemned campesino communities along the Costa Chica who petitioned for land and dared to directly denounce President Cárdenas's agrarian reform. Many peasants listened. The ruling party's national peasant confederation was worried enough about Father Guevara's influence over ejidatarios to complain to Mexico City. Predictably, Berber once again refused to expel Guevara. Local lay organizations such as the ACM were strong enough in Ometepec to hold a Eucharistic congress there in early 1939.[221]

The Church did not pull its punches on the Costa Grande, either, in spite of Cárdenas's strong support for agrarian reform in the subregion. Up and down the Costa Grande, roving missionary priests based in Atoyac visited agrarista communities in late 1936 and 1937. Clergy focused on the thirty-six ejidos that Feliciano Radillà had organized. Although there were no documented links between Catholics and the landlords' death squads operating in the area, given the mutual hostility between Radilla's agraristas and littoral priests, it would have been surprising had at least some of the clergy not been peripherally connected to the networks backing segunda violence. The clergy's intervention on the Cardenista ejidos grew stronger after Radilla was assassinated in late 1940, an act generally attributed to Berber.[222]

The idea that the Church in Guerrero made its peace with the postrevolutionary state is even more dubious in light of the 1939–40 presidential campaign in Guerrero. General Juan Andreu Almazán, a native of la Montaña, challenged President Cárdenas's candidate, General Manuel Ávila Camacho. Almazán was an unlikely paladin of the Church. He had been a powerful member of the Revolutionary Family since the late 1920s. However, Almazán kept his distance from praetorian anticlericalism during the Cristiada and reportedly patronized more conservative subordinates in the army.[223] Still, he was loyal first to Calles and then to Cárdenas—until 1939. By then, he was one of the four or five strongest generals in the army and enjoyed a sizeable fortune thanks to close ties to the regional bourgeoisie of Monterrey. When he did finally break ranks with the ruling party and emerge as the public face of a heterogeneous coalition challenging Cárdenas's candidate, he had neither a coherent party structure nor a unifying ideology. Almazán never openly embraced the Church, but his support for freedom of expression and criticism of Cárdenas's leftist positions attracted much Catholic support across Mexico.[224]

Because Almazán was a native son, his campaign in Guerrero had an especially strong appeal. Ex-governor and senator Héctor F. López, long a key leader of the Ranchero group, played a crucial role. There is no doubt the voto morado gravitated to Almazán, especially after Bishop Díaz sidestepped the national episcopal policy of neutrality and tacitly endorsed him. Iguala's "Catholic aristocrats" were right behind him. Many Catholic brokers in Almazán's native la Montaña and elsewhere jumped on his bandwagon.[225] Almazán's strength in Guerrero suggests that Cárdenas governed with a lower degree of popular consent here at the end of his presidency than at its beginning.

Conclusion

By the time General Manuel Ávila Camacho announced that he was a "believer" shortly before his inauguration in late 1940, Catholics and Catholicism played a decisive role in frustrating the revolutionary project in Guerrero.[226]

During their long struggles for regional dominance, neither the Ranchero group nor their agrarista and SEP foes could claim a clear victory. Without the voto morado, beata activism, and segunderos' bullets, the Ranchero group could not have held on to power. True, agrarian grants continued, and the Ranchero group never found much favor in Mexico City after the collapse of Calles's regime. In fact, in 1941 the national ruling party ousted Berber for his disobedience. Nevertheless, the Ranchero group would never again face serious agrarian opposition in Guerrero; slowly but surely, its foes were either coopted, eliminated, or exiled.[227] The SEP in Guerrero was colonized by ambitious middle-class families who milked teaching posts economically and exploited them politically. Over time, the SEP in the state largely failed to execute its most basic task: teaching. The literacy rate actually fell during the 1930s.[228] Catholic organizing, Catholic ideology, and at times Catholic violence played crucial roles in undermining attempts by agraristas and federal teachers to realize the Revolution's radical potential. Although anticlericalism never played the defining role in the revolutionary project in Guerrero that it did in Campeche or Hidalgo, isolated incidents of iconoclasm and red-shirting provoked a formidable backlash that persisted for years, especially when inflamed by obstreperous priests and abetted by landowners and Ranchero politicos. Catholic activists, mainly women, kept alive the spirit of resistance to the government long after anticlerical regulations were relaxed.

The power of Catholics and Catholicism was often decisive at the polls. The voto morado tipped many elections in favor of the Ranchero group; none was more important than the 1932 gubernatorial election, which denied agrarista politicos regional dominance once and for all. Just as importantly, in local elections from Iguala in the north to Petatlán on the Twin Coasts, Catholic electoral brokers allowed Ranchero politicos to best agraristas at the ballot box.

Catholic priests and (largely female) lay activists used semi-official Church groups to eat away at the social influence of the ejido and the federal school. Dozens of rural schools had to close their doors when peasants boycotted their classrooms. Many never opened at all because communities refused to volunteer to build schools or even sell food to teachers. Segunda violence, though never endorsed by the institutional Church, was in no small part an expression of Catholic ideology and enabled by networks animated by Catholicism. Priests in the central valleys and on the Twin Coasts were key parts of networks that, wittingly or not, encouraged resistance to turn violent. On the Costa Chica (and probably elsewhere), compadrazgo encouraged offensive violence against teachers and agraristas. The multifaceted nature of Catholic resistance in Guerrero to anticlericalism, agrarian reform, and the revolutionary project as a whole forces us to rethink the conventional wisdom about postrevolutionary state formation in Mexico in the 1920s and 1930s. Cárdenas believed that once the revolutionary project downplayed anticlericalism, Catholics would acquiesce, and a largely secular civil society could consolidate. In fact, the easing of Church-state tension did not induce widespread Catholic support, at least in Guerrero. The resumption of religious processions, the restoration of the clergy's social prominence, and the renewal of the sacramental routine never convinced Catholics to accept Cárdenas' quid pro quo. Long after the ley de cultos was largely a dead letter and iconoclastic teachers were removed or repentant, the clergy, lay activists, and many mestizo and indigenous Catholics still resented the postrevolutionary state. During a wake for Pius XI in 1939 in Taxco, a center of resistance to socialist education, a female parishioner was arrested after shouting, "We have to free ourselves from the yoke of the government."[229]

Catholic opposition was not always decentralized and episodic. The institutional Church in Guerrero, for all its problems, demonstrated a kind of agility and resiliency that the postrevolutionary state never possessed. Guerrero's clergy excelled at implementing the Church's radial strategy because of the state's highly segmented society and its own autonomy. A cohort of charismatic priests used their moral authority and lay lieutenants to coordinate attendance strikes, hamstring agrarian reform, and marshal voters. The institutional Church showed the kind of administrative flexibility that the state never could. Rome realized the impossibility of governing such a geographically and ethnically divided region as Guerrero. It eventually set up a diocese for each of the fractured state's four subregions.

After Cárdenas, Guerrero's Catholics could claim that the revolutionary state now accepted their values. In 1943, the mayor of Huitzuco accused the priest Miguel Miranda of engaging in subversive behavior and illegally preaching in public by using a loudspeaker to deliver reactionary teachings audible outside his church. In the ensuing investigation, Father Miranda claimed that he was merely instructing the local ACM chapter. The broadcast, he argued, was "completely cultural," that is to say apolitical, and so constitutionally protected. Moreover, Father Miranda reasoned, his lesson on the value of "union, progress, and patriotism" reflected President Manuel Ávila Camacho's own morality. The charges were dropped.[230]

CHAPTER 5

"Un sin fin de mochos"

Catholic Cacicazgos in Guanajuato

On September 9, 1932, peasant delegates from across Guanajuato gathered in the "agrarista mecca" of Celaya to meet with Governor Melchor Ortega and federal agrarian officials.¹ The convention was the fruit of tireless efforts by SEP inspector Arnulfo Ochoa. For four years the gifted pedagogue had opened schools, founded peon unions, and helped peasants to petition for land across his northern district. The assembly followed a familiar formula: the revolutionary state offered land, credit, and tools in return for popular support. Yet it culminated not in the expected hegemonic dialogue of state and subaltern, but a startling act of violence. Salvador Azanza and Luis Martínez Vértiz waylaid Inspector Ochoa, physically assaulted him, and threatened him at gunpoint. Azanza was a former cristero. His confederate, Martínez Vértiz, was a leading Catholic and intimate of the bishop of León. Remarkably, the two were also key allies of Callista governor Melchor Ortega and would soon sit in the state and national legislatures, respectively.²

Centered on the town of Dolores Hidalgo, Azanza's Catholic cacicazgo hindered the revolutionary project across northern Guanajuato until the late 1930s.³ He called on a cadre of Catholic lay leaders and ex-cristero chieftains and found much popular support by representing himself as a defender of the faith. An exasperated anticlerical congressman lamented that in Guanajuato "there are few liberal elements but *un sin fin* (endless supply of) of *mochos* (excessively religious people)."⁴ Years later, Carlos Monsiváis memorably branded Guanajuato and other west-central states Mexico's Rosary Belt.⁵ The Cristiada, shadowy underground movements like the Legions and the Base, the Segunda, and Sinarquismo, all rejected the revolutionary project and tapped a deep reservoir of "traditional, nationalistic, Catholic and conservative" sentiment in the Rosary Belt.[6] As cacique, Azanza drew on the same ideology, but his relationship with the postrevolutionary state was ambiguous rather than purely antagonistic.

This chapter examines the religious question in Guanajuato during the 1930s to understand why opposition to the revolutionary project was largely defined by Catholic beliefs and mobilized by Catholic organizations but channeled through Catholic cacicazgos like Azanza's. Due to Azanza's importance and Cárdenas's own concern for northern Guanajuato, the chapter focuses primarily on this subregion. After analyzing Guanajuato's religious, political, and socioeconomic dimensions, the chapter then surveys the triangular conflicts and compromisos among Catholics, Governor Ortega's camarilla, and agents of the postrevolutionary state. By unraveling the web of paramilitaries, lay activists, and conservative politicians knit together by Azanza, the chapter shows how segunda violence and licit Church resistance sapped the revolutionary project. It then examines a bloody clash between Catholics and foes that left dozens dead in Ciudad González on March 18, 1936. The violence prompted Cárdenas to embrace détente with the institutional Church and restart agrarian reform in northern Guanajuato. Even after the demise of Azanza's cacicazgo, Catholicism frustrated Cardenista agrarismo. As a counterpoint to the north, the chapter then examines southeastern Guanajuato.[7] Here, the collapse of a weak Catholic cacicazgo fronted by David Ayala unleashed more fragmented Catholic mobilizations and sporadic segunda violence that emptied federal schools and delayed agrarian reform. More than any other single factor, it was Catholicism that frustrated the revolutionary project in Guanajuato. The voto morado, the Church's deep presence in civil society, and considerable Catholic support for segunda violence undermined Callista and then Cardenista projects, preventing the consolidation of a strong postrevolutionary state in Guanajuato.

Church and State in the Buckle of the Rosary Belt

Catholics often imagined Guanajuato as Mexico's spiritual center. The Church consecrated the nation to the Sacred Heart by erecting an eponymous monument at its geographic center, the hill of Cubilete near Silao, Guanajuato. For centuries, social, economic, and geographic forces strengthened the institutional Church and encouraged popular religious participation in

Guanajuato. To begin with, the Church benefited from colonial mining and cereal booms. The relatively early Hispanization of indigenous peoples reinforced clerical authority. During the late nineteenth century, railroads and hydroelectrification stimulated agriculture and manufacturing, which underwrote the Church's Porfirian expansion, especially in a southern tier of cities: León, Irapuato, Silao, Acámbaro, and Celaya. Subregional differences, though less pronounced than in other states, still mattered in Guanajuato. Its southern half was part of the fertile Bajío and boasted some industry and larger cities.[8] In northern Guanajuato, resistance by semi-nomadic indigenous peoples instilled a tradition of self-sufficiency and military prowess among mestizos; northern landowners tended to reside on their estates, and some could still raise armed retinues. Over time, the subregion's principal towns stagnated as mining declined. Although relatively underdeveloped compared to the south, the north was just as levitical.[9]

The Diocese of León was Guanajuato's institutional matrix (northeastern and southeastern corners excepted). Though young (erected in 1863), it inherited a strong colonial infrastructure—most importantly a well-established Jesuit contingent that ran ten urban missionary centers for workers, prisoners, and youth.[10] Thanks to Porfirian development and popular religiosity, the diocese boasted a formidable array of churches, monasteries, convents, schools, and charitable institutions staffed by a sizeable, well-trained, and disciplined clergy. In fact, the diocese was a veritable factory for bishops (including the first bishop of Huejutla); no other produced as many. At its head was Emeterio Valverde Téllez (1909–48), a cautious, moderate, and thoughtful bishop who encouraged catechism, education, and charity during his exceptionally long administration. Six years of bloody fighting between 1913 and 1919 took their toll on his diocese. Carrancista governors nationalized Catholic schools, hospitals, and asylums; expelled nuns from over twenty convents; and impeded the collection of tithes.[11]

The armed phase left the institutional Church in Guanajuato poorer and stripped it of much of its social and educational infrastructure (the nuns proved impossible to replace). It recovered in the early 1920s, only to face a new crisis upon the Cristiada's explosion. Sporadic uprisings erupted quickly in virtually every corner of Guanajuato, from large cities like Irapuato to highland villages. For the government, the Cristiada in Guanajuato was extremely costly to contain and impossible to completely defeat. The rebels, however, never seized the strategic initiative, nor could they break the federal government's will. In the end, Mexico City prevailed in Guanajuato through massive reinforcements (Cedillo's paramilitary from San Luis Potosí) and brutal counterinsurgency (deploying poisonous gas, shooting suspected subversives, and collectively punishing entire communities through forced resettlement).[12]

The Cristiada left a bitter memory in the state. Probably somewhere between 7,000 and 10,000 men fought as cristeros at some point. Thousands more, many of them women, provided logistical and intelligence support. After the Arreglos, veterans took home well-honed military skills.[13] Some renounced violence but never forgave the national revolutionary regime; they still saw agraristas and federal teachers as the enemy.[14] There was never any systematic persecution or effective disarmament of former cristero leaders in Guanajuato; in fact, many would take up arms again as recristeros. Others turned to politics, where the voto morado decided many elections.[15]

The institutional Church hoped the ACM would discipline the voto morado through civic action, demobilize and reintegrate cristeros, and insure that lay activists never again resorted to violence. The ACM in Guanajuato inherited three formal lay organizations (Knights of Columbus, Damas Católicas,and the ACJM) that the war profoundly transformed. On the eve of the conflict in 1925, the three mustered 6,500, mostly upper- and middle-class, members. Older, less structured devotional sodalities, ranging from the elite Terciarios (Third Order of the Franciscans) to the more humble Nocturnal Adoration, probably enrolled five or six times as many from virtually every social stratum. Parochial schools educated fifteen thousand students. Catholic workers' circles and cooperatives, once strong, never recovered from Cristiada persecution outside of a few bright spots like León and south-central Yurira, where the ACJM counted 300 worker-members and boasted a large headquarters including a library and lecture hall, night school, gymnasium, and sporting teams. Male lay leaders, ranging from the aristocratic Knights of Columbus to workers, were "disappeared" by the government during the Cristiada, and many others resigned in fear. Female organizations, however, generally fared better.[16] State repression of formal lay organizations unintentionally stimulated the growth of clandestine, semiautonomous associations of Catholics by forcing activists to go underground to organize.

The clergy faced numerous challenges in Guanajuato in the 1920s and 1930s. The government executed eleven Guanajuatan priests, shut the seminary, and exiled Valverde during the Cristiada. Bishop Valverde strictly followed episcopal policy but could not keep all priests and lay organizations out of the fighting—clerical hierarchy was clearly strained.[17] The institutional Church emerged from the war largely intact because of its broad socioeconomic base and its disciplined clergy's dedication. In spite of tight restrictions, clergymen proved adept at evading surveillance to maintain the minimal sacramental life of the Church. Father Jorge López even dressed as a miner and held mass in the shafts.[18] The diocese's economic base shrank but survived because priests used intermediaries to discreetly collect tithes as "voluntary contributions."[19] Two new convents were even opened in León. In 1930, the clergy still maintained strong influence over virtually every social segment in Guanajuato—even small, remote *rancherias* (hamlets).[20]

After the Arreglos, Bishop Emeterio Valverde Téllez began reconstruction anew. Via an intermediary, he negotiated with the governor for two hundred priests to practice outside of strict legal limits. Many mayors followed the governor's example and subverted the law.[21] The additional priests enabled Valverde to set up the ACM in Guanajuato, absorbing (on paper at least) the Damas Católicas and the Knights of Columbus (now the UFCM and UCM, respectively), as well as the ACJM. The Damas were always the ACM's backbone; by April 1930, its catechists, mainly well-to-do women, labored to restore the Church's presence in working people's everyday lives. Besides educational and charitable initiatives, it founded at least one group for *obreras* (female workers) and campaigned for modesty.[22]

The Revolution's failure to significantly alter Guanajuato's middle politics or the socioeconomic order facilitated the Church's recovery.[23] During the armed phase, agraristas and self-proclaimed Villista or Zapatista bands were quelled by town militia and white guards. Carrancista preconstitutional reforms floundered, precluding the subsequent rise of a more radical regional caudillo in the 1920s or 1930s. Instead, a clique of civilian classical Liberals dominated regional politics as the Confederación de Partidos Revolutionarios de Guanajuato (CPRG), or Greens for their ballot color. The Greens's moderation mirrored Francisco Madero's: they favored political democracy, property rights, and secular (but not anticlerical) education.

While the Greens enjoyed Alvaro Obregón's patronage, it was Catholic votes that helped them stay in power and stall the revolutionary project. In the December 1924 presidential election that pitted Calles against Angel Flores, pro-Green Catholics stoned foes, shouted "death to Calles and the Bolshevik Reds," and boldly planted the papal flag with St. Peter's golden key in front of a Flores urn in Acámbaro.[24] Catholic electoral brokers generally backed the Greens, although some cut deals with their regional rivals, the Reds, in the 1927 and 1931 gubernatorial elections.[25]

For their part, the Reds generally supported agrarian reform, labor, and anticlericalism. As Calles's favorites, the Reds tried to use the religious question to discredit the Greens, alleging that Green governor Enrique Colunga (1924–27) was "freemason out of convenience, liberal out of opportunity, governor due to a disgrace, and reactionary by conviction."[26] Partisanship aside, Colunga's acts of omission had aided the cristeros.[27] Many Green state congressmen and mayors maintained warm relations with the Church and gave priests permission to practice during the Cristero War—one even drove a doctor to nurse wounded cristeros.[28] Greens repeatedly coopted or neutralized the voto morado through negotiations, even if it meant defying Calles. In the words of Ernesto Hidalgo, opportunistic Greens were "with neither the Knights of Columbus nor [the CROMista anticlerical] Knights of Guadalupe."[29]

During the 1920s, the conservative, pro-Church, regional political equilibrium that favored the Greens in Guanajuato faced few serious challenges. A relatively small number of industrial workers (mainly railroaders and factory workers), freemasons, and radical intellectuals (teachers, petty officials, and professionals) criticized the Church and fruitlessly backed the Reds. As in Guerrero, the federal army armed some agraristas to fight the delahuertista coup (1923–24) and then the cristeros.[30] But Green administrations ruthlessly repressed agraristas and broke most CROM peasant and artisan unions, especially in the north.[31] In 1929, ejidos only existed around Celaya and in a few other pockets. The SEP superintendent summed up the predicament of agrarian reform in March 1929: "In some places where agraristas exist [the teacher] awakens aspirations in the peasant." But most campesinos are "fanatics above all in small communities where [cristero] rebels are supported."[32]

For beleaguered supporters of the revolutionary project in Guanajuato, change seemed to be on the horizon by 1931. Nationally, Calles and key national political operatives favored the Reds' gubernatorial candidate, Melchor Ortega, who was poised to end sixteen years of Green domination. Even in the benighted north, a new era in Guanajuato seemed to be dawning.

Catholics, Middling Politics, and the SEP in Guanajuato, 1932–1935

Who was this agent of revolutionary change in Guanajuato? Though a native guanajuatense, Ortega made his bones politically in neighboring Michoacán and in Mexico City, then wormed his way into the Revolutionary Family's inner circle via friendship with Calles. His nomination resulted from backroom deals cut by a renegade Green federal congressman, David Ayala, with federal agrarian and labor bureaucrats stationed in Guanajuato. Red leaders delivered railroad workers and ejidatarios, allowing Ortega to style himself a revolutionary champion fighting reactionary, corrupt Greens.[33] In a chaotic gubernatorial election on July 20, 1931, Ortega was denied victory in a questionable tally overseen by a sitting Green governor. Calles used the election's many irregularities as a rationale to overturn the vote, appoint a neutral interim governor, and give Ortega a second chance in September 1932. This time, Ortega claimed a popular electoral mandate as Callista champion of federal teachers, workers, and peasants.[34] In fact, his margin of victory came from the voto morado turned out by cagey Catholic brokers like David Ayala in the southeast and Salvador Azanza in the north.[35]

Ortega's campaign tapped the growing Catholic resentment of Calles's reopening of the religious question as well as a popular backlash against Green corruption. National events sparked the Church-state conflict in Guanajuato, but the state's religious and socioeconomic structures and contentious middle politics fanned the flames. Further complicating the matter, conflicts and compromises among politicians, Catholic brokers, and advocates of the revolutionary project varied from subregion to subregion and even from municipio to municipio.

When Church-state tensions rose nationally in 1932, most regional políticos and the institutional Church tried to contain the Church-state conflict in Guanajuato. Bishop Valverde and his metropolitan archbishop, Leopoldo Ruiz of Morelia, hoped to restrain recristeros and insure the tacit toleration of Governor Melchor Ortega (1932–35) for violations of anticlerical legislation. For its part, the Ortega administration tried to stall the revolutionary project, especially socialist education—a policy determined primarily by electoral logic.

While Ortega's jury-rigged coalition included many Catholic middlemen, it also had some labor and agrarista leaders. Revolutionary politics in a levitical state made for strange bedfellows. The Red ward heeler in León, a controversial anticlerical labor leader, put a prominent ACJM member on his slate as a "hook" to reel in Catholic voters.[36] In nearby San Francisco del Rincón, local Red politicos turned conspicuously churchgoing to draw Catholic votes.[37] The Reds' electoral calculation required sizeable Catholic inputs in 1931 and again in 1932. Even Ortega operatives who cynically played on religious sentiment had to honor electoral compromises or face a backlash. Consequently, Ortega's electoral slates contained many Catholic brokers. Three of thirty state congressmen and alternates were ex-cristeros.[38] Another, José Jesús Yáñez Maya, was a former sexton seen kneeling before the bishop. He drew strong Catholic support, including that of Valle de Santiago's Knights of Columbus. In office, Yáñez Maya reinstated government employees that Ortega had fired for fanaticism.[39] Bishop Valverde's ties to Martínez Vértiz and Yáñez Maya helped create an interlocking regional elite of Catholic notables and politicos. Ortega's congressmen and mayors in turn named ex-cristeros as *delegados municipales* (justices of the peace) in hamlets and on haciendas to harry agraristas.[40]

The alliance between Ortega's clique and Catholic brokers mitigated tensions over the religious question in 1932 and 1933. In October 1932, Ortega legally limited the number of priests to just thirty-nine but secretly met with Bishop Valverde and promised to apply the regulations "with benevolence."[41] When priests lost their licenses, Ortega permitted substitutions over federal officials' objections.[42] In October 1933, Ortega vowed to turn empty churches into schools, libraries, and museums as in Garrido Canabal's Tabasco. He then quietly let the matter drop.[43] Ortega's empty gestures masked his accommodation of Catholic interests.

During 1934, the arrival of a strident new SEP superintendent and the social strains caused by agrarian reform undermined the regional Church-state truce, as did growing grassroots Catholic militancy driven by national anxieties and Ortega's tepid anticlericalism. After Police Chief Pastor Ojeda's men attacked a peaceful UNPF demonstration against socialist education on April 21, 1934, in León, many Catholics accused Ortega of betrayal.[44] As momentum built toward Calles's Psychological Revolution, Ortega signed Decree #110 on June 28, 1934, to prohibit church bell ringing, ban the sale of religious items (even fireworks), and centralize all police forces in the state to beef up enforcement. Perhaps the law forestalled even stricter measures, but it inflamed Catholic opinion. In Moreleón, local authorities fined people who crossed themselves while passing in front of a church, and rumors flew that citizens were prosecuted for doffing their hats in front of churches.[45]

By the start of 1935, talk of the Tabascanization of Guanajuato did not seem so far-fetched. In September 1934, Ortega's administration closed churches in Celaya and sentenced Father Nicéforo Guerra to the harsh Islas Marías prison colony.[46] State employees who refused to march in an anticlerical parade on the Day of the Revolution (November 20) risked unemployment, as did state teachers who refused to adopt socialist education.[47] As of New Year's Day 1935, all religious education in Guanajuato was illegal. Yet Ortega still played a double game with Catholics; along with only ten licensed priests, Church sources estimated 290 unlicensed clergy still practiced in Guanajuato in late 1935—including many expelled from nearby states.[48] By tolerating such widespread evasion of the ley de cultos, Ortega hoped to convince Catholics that he was really their ally.

To appear radical on the religious question and thus reassure Calles, Ortega appointed a Yucatecan anticlerical and rational educator, Tiburcio Mena Alcocer, as state superintendent of education. Mena Alcocer sacked 150 teachers as "reactionary" in 1934 and early 1935.[49] Fired teachers often got their jobs back, while Mena eventually lost his.[50] In fact, Ortega and his Catholic allies used the state educational system to covertly oppose the SEP's socialist education. In 1932, the governor pressured the SEP to transfer Inspector Abel Ortega, an energetic advocate of the revolutionary project, out of the north.[51] Ortega's covert strategy of turning the population against federal education got an unintended boost when the SEP named the flamboyant and stridently anticlerical Tomás Cuervo federal superintendent in late 1934.

Born in Veracruz and educated at the national normal school, Cuervo was devoted to Tomás Garrido Canabal and the Communist Party. Because Cuervo made radical anticlericalism the central tenet of socialist education, he repeatedly clashed with "fanatical" state officials, Catholic parents—and many of his own teachers.[52] He told his maestros rurales that impoverished peasants would not turn to saints for succor once they understood the scientific causes of earthquakes and eclipses, nor would they drink once they practiced healthy pastimes like sports and theater. Although Cuervo instructed teachers to avoid offending religious beliefs, he also told them that "God does not exist: the saints do not exist, the believers are moral slaves of the exploiting class." Driving home his point, he handed out General Ignacio Ramírez's *Lucha contra el fanatismo* (Struggle against fanaticism) and *El martillo* (The hammer).[53]

His confrontational tactics sparked widespread attendance strikes in the fall of 1934; things only got worse for Cuervo in early 1935. He met with

Catholic Cacicazgos in Guanajuato

parents to explain that the new curriculum was not antireligious, but he lost his cool and denied the existence of God. Eventually, he could only visit schools with an escort of armed troops. His own teachers complained that Cuervo's provocations put their own lives at risk.[54]

Cuervo's brash words and blunt tactics seemingly confirmed Catholic fears that the SEP would Tabascanize society and thus strengthened Ortega's political position as Catholics' tacit protector. From January until June 1935, Ortega butted heads with Cuervo and his supporters in the Federación de Maestros Revolucionarios, who had been aggressively petitioning Mexico City to accelerate agrarian reform as well as punish the Church. After Cárdenas broke with Calles in June 1935, Cuervo denounced Ortega as the tool of fanatics, the rich, and Calles.[55] However, the religious question no longer had the same salience nationally. Ortega denied that Guanajuato had a religious problem at all, instead blaming attendance strikes and segunda violence on Cuervo and "Communist" agitation. In private, Ortega admitted that his own state educational system opposed Cardenismo.[56]

Ortega's point man in the covert fight against the revolutionary project was Atanasio Hernández Romo, who had once headed the SEP's cultural mission in León. Ortega funded Hernández's Centro Cultural and the León Alliance of Organized Labor. The groups mimicked the SEP's tactics of mass mobilization and corporatism but employed Catholic, anti-Communist rhetoric to convince parents to reject socialist education and peasants to reject ejidos. Once again, Catholicism drove a wedge between the revolutionary project and civil society. Hernández Romo coordinated his campaign with priests, lay leaders, and conservative local politicians. In the fall of 1935, the mayor of León signed proclamations supporting the SEP but at the same time told parents to keep students safely at home. Hernández Romo's Center and the Alliance forced out the SEP inspector in León, Roberto Oropeza, a champion of agrarian reform and anticlericalism, and convinced many federal teachers to reject the new curriculum.[57] When Cuervo tried to shut down priests' night schools for pulling students away from federal schools teaching socialist education in León, Governor Ortega thwarted him.[58] Catholic leaders collaborated with Ortega allies like Hernández Romo by drawing on conservative Catholic sentiment, suspicion of the national government, and hostility to leftist ideas to rally supporters against the revolutionary project. For them, Cuervo personified the evils of the revolutionary state that should be resisted. By the summer of 1935, Cuervo was transferred out, a victory for the Ortega-Catholic strategy of turning civil society against the SEP schools.[59]

Catholic leaders, organizations, and ideology kept the revolutionary project at bay. For his part, Bishop Valverde adopted a conciliatory public tone, forbidding priests from attending public demonstrations against the SEP.[60] Privately, Valverde collaborated with Ortega's operatives to oppose socialist education by encouraging Catholic parents' groups to start home schools to draw students away from federal schools. From the pulpit and in the confessional booth, priests condemned the revolutionary educational curriculum.[61] Valverde respected the letter of the law but surreptitiously directed lay mobilizations against SEP schools.

By implementing Rome's radial strategy, however, the diocese was not so much leading the laity as recognizing and attempting to control existing efforts. In June 1933, Celaya's Knights of Columbus had founded a supposedly secular parents' group to oppose SEP schools, anticipating by several months the national episcopal strategy.[62] During the Cristero War, the laity launched attendance strikes and set up underground schools on a massive scale. This successful rehearsal meant they would not necessarily need direction from above during the conflict in the mid-1930s. In a few instances, the clergy personally did direct some clandestine parochial schools.[63] Official lay groups ran eighty-five underground parochial schools. But parallel efforts by UNPF chapters and other semi-official or autonomous parents' groups ran many more, largely on their own.[64]

The successful, decentralized Catholic campaign to curtail federal school attendance forced Ortega to act. The state police raided ACM headquarters and dismantled official lay organizations.[65] This unintentionally freed some Catholics from Church supervision, and allowed them to resist violently on their own. Events justified violence in the eyes of many guanajuatense Catholics. When a lone knife-wielding admirer of Veracruz Jacobin Adalberto Tejeda murdered Father Martín Lawers as he was celebrating mass on February 19, 1933, in Irapuato, rumors flew that a cabal of Freemasons or Communists would kill more priests.[66]

Ortega's half-hearted crackdown on religious practice made it even more difficult for Valverde's priests to prevent violent resistance by the laity. The recristeros of the Segunda National Guard of Guanajuato criticized the diocese for trying to prevent illicit violence: "many priests submitted to the Ley Calles becoming his gendarmes... trying to impede armed action by Catholics." The pope, segunderos argued, would never prevent armed struggle as a last resort to defend religion.[67] The radial strategy allowed segunderos to burrow into largely autonomous clerical-laity task forces coordinating tru-

Catholic Cacicazgos in Guanajuato 167

ancy strikes; a Catholic advocate of armed struggle argued that antisocialist education demobilizations in León in 1934 prepared Catholics for the "greater struggle" against the revolutionary state.[68]

To gain support for insurrection from Catholic groups running home schools and organizing attendance strikes, segunderos pointed to the current persecution and recent history. Catholic paramilitary leaders could look back to the Cristiada-era experience of acting autonomously without clerical direction to justify ignoring Valverde's prohibition of violence. This time, however, Catholic insurgents had no centralized command structure, intelligence system, or logistical support—Bishop Valverde had seen to that. We know little about the Segunda in Guanajuato, but Guerra Manzo's fine study of recristeros in neighboring Michoacán suggests segunderos across the Bajío had complicated motives. They fought to thwart anticlericalism and socialist education, but they also took up arms again because of the difficulties of returning to civilian life after the first Cristero War. Some made political demands in return for laying down their arms—typically, amnesty and a share of local political power.[69] In Guanajuato, as in Michoacán, segunda bands never numbered more than ten or twenty and were generally too weak to systematically impose "war taxes" on landowners to fund the war. Consequently, they had to turn to kidnapping and banditry, or rely on patrons, be they politicos, landowners, or perhaps even federal military officers. Before his death in July 1936, segundero Fermín Sandoval accused Governor Enrique Fernández Martínez of giving him arms, money, and ammunition to kill agraristas aligned with political foes.[70]

Former cristeros, even if they did not take up arms against the government, could use coercion to influence local politics. Francisco Sánchez, son of the renowned cristero chieftain Fortuno Sánchez, slain in 1927, campaigned for Melchor Ortega for governor in 1931 in San Miguel Allende. His former *sanmiguelense* cristeros stoned the "masons" and "liberals."[71] In Pénjamo, at least two bands of recristeros intimidated agraristas throughout the 1930s.[72] In Moroleón, Dr. Baltasar López Serrato—a Knight of Columbus, ex-cristero, and the son of a man executed by federales for rebellion in 1927—headed a network of ex-combatants, priests, and lay leaders that violently opposed organized labor and a federal school. López's Society of Charros of the Bajío likely reconstituted an old cristero squadron.[73] In San Francisco Rincón, near the western town of León, José Orozco employed former cristeros as pistoleros to harry agraristas in the 1930s.[74] As in Guerrero, segunderos in Guanajuato often attacked ejidos with the support of local landowners; offensive segunda violence blurred into white terror aimed at halting agrarian reform.

In Guanajuato as in Guerrero, more than just religion drove the Segunda. Resentment of Governor Melchor Ortega's administration also fueled segunda violence in the state. In León, where the voto morado helped anoint Ortega governor in 1931, an opposition paper noted that even the flies stayed away from the polls in mid-1934 elections, testimony to the growing gap between the governor and Catholics.[75] Segunderos criticized Ortega's controversial alcohol monopoly (administered by his brother) and his reputed enrichment due to concessions to wealthy Spaniards. Teasing out the Segunda's diverse causes, however, requires looking at its local roots. In the north, it was linked to Salvador Azanza's consolidation of a strong Catholic cacicazgo with the help of Luis Martínez Vértiz.

Salvador Azanza's Catholic Cacicazgo

Wealthy and pious, with a bloodline stretching back to a colonial viceroy, the Azanza ranked among the greatest landowning dynasties in Guanajuato; their largest hacienda, Trancas, encompassed some twenty-six thousand hectares at its peak.[76] Although patriarch Manuel Azanza supported Catholic resistance to the revolutionary state, he kept the clan's patrimony largely intact by shrewdly playing revolutionary middle politics. Crescencio Aguilar, the Green state congressman, helped Don Manuel evade agrarian reform and keep Trancas's core intact by transferring landholdings to *prestanombres* (fictive owners).[77] In return, Manuel Azanza turned out clients to vote against a Red, pro-Calles, agrarista challenger to Aguilar in 1922.[78] Manuel Azanza seriously misstepped in 1923 by joining the ill-fated delahuertista rebellion with Father Margarito Medina at his side.[79] Defeated, Don Manuel briefly fled Dolores Hidalgo, with General Joaquín Amaro's troops hot on his heels. Remarkably, he came home in a few days, protected by former governor and leading Green Enrique Colunga.[80] The delahuertista revolt in northern Guanajuato would be the first in a series of insurgencies uniting hacendados and Catholics against the revolutionary state.

When the Cristero War erupted in 1926, the Azanza clan once again led Catholic rebels. This time, Salvador Azanza led the family, sheltering cristero warlord Fermín Sandoval and his two brothers, who operated out of Trancas. Azanza employees and clients joined, probably salaried and supplied by

Don Salvador. Several leading cristeros, however, questioned Salvador Azanza's devotion to the cause. He was almost certainly the "well-known hacendado of Dolores Hidalgo" whom the cristero commander of Guanajuato, Rodolfo Gallegos, entrusted with six hundred thousand pesos robbed from a federal train—only to have his accomplice pocket the funds. Salvador Azanza also clashed with other cristero leaders. Azanza's cristeros shot it out with cristeros loyal to his in-law, Dr. Donaciano Cano Sauto, killing two of them.[81] Still, federales considered Don Salvador dangerous enough to imprison him on the Islas Marías.

As the saying goes, sometimes when God shuts the door, the Devil opens a window. The Arreglos led to Azanza's parole, and he soon sat in Guanajuato's state congress. His remarkable rehabilitation resulted from the nature of Mexico's revolutionary democracy, Governor Melchor Ortega's political weakness, and the potency of Guanajuato's voto morado. Catholic electoral clout had long decided elections in Dolores Hidalgo. Greens practiced Catholic countercorporatism; a Catholic union organized by Isaac Espinosa, the proud father of a seminarian, helped elect a former Knight of Columbus mayor in 1925.[82] To rouse the north's voto morado in 1931 and 1932, candidate Ortega counted on Azanza and Luis Martínez Vértiz, a wealthy landowner, entrepreneur, and close confidante of the bishop. Aided by his mother, the president of San Luis de la Paz's Damas Católicas, Don Luis set up social Catholic organs across the state in the 1920s and helped direct the Cristiada in Guanajuato alongside General Rodolfo Gallegos. In the early 1930s, Martínez Vértiz served as Ortega's bridge to a range of Catholic groups—Damas, Knights, ACJMistas, and veterans of the Cristiada—and helped redeem Azanza after his less-than-honorable conduct in the Cristiada. It would be a mistake to discount Don Luis's faith, but he certainly enjoyed numerous political and economic advantages by serving as a prominent lay leader and cristero consigliere. Kinsman Mariano Vértiz was mayor of the southeastern city of Acámbaro, brother José was Dolores Hidalgo's mayor and Azanza's alternate in the state congress. Luis himself sat in the national congress in the 1932–34 session. Political clout helped shield Martínez Vértiz's considerable capital at a time of economic upheaval and political chaos. The family's economic portfolio diversified during the depression years, acquiring upscale retail stores in Mexico City and a radio station in San Luis de la Paz. Don Luis rubbed elbows with the bishop, played cards with Calles's congressional whip, Gonzalo Santos, and raised prize-winning fighting bulls, a source of immense cultural prestige in this horse-loving state (descendants helped build Mexico City's mammoth bull-fighting ring and rode for the Olympic equestrian team).[83] By helping Melchor Ortega move the voto morado from the Greens to the Reds, Martínez Vértiz advanced his own interests and those of the Church.

Beaten at their own game, the Greens played their only remaining card: they charged that Azanza and other Ortega allies campaigned with religious propaganda.[84] Ortega, immunized by his ties to Calles, seated Azanza in the state congress and sealed their political pact by going into business. Azanza, Ortega, and the governor's father-in-law sold firewood together, probably under the guise of a tax-exempt cooperative run from Azanza's Trancas and two other haciendas.[85] Secure in his Dolores Hidalgo base, Azanza controlled elections in his cacicazgo for the benefit of Ortega with patronage, with violence, and with appeals to Catholicism. Azanza's influence expanded beyond the north when, in May 1935, Ortega asked him to manage the gubernatorial campaign of his man, José Jesús Yáñez Maya.[86]

Governor Ortega's pact with Martínez Vértiz and Azanza enabled other northern hacendados to carve out Catholic cacicazgos.[87] Jorge Lámbarri of Ciudad González and José Hernández Alcocer in Ciudad Alvaro Obregón (San José Iturbide) won elective office, raised paramilitaries, and appointed former cristeros as comisarios to small rural communities. Comisarios licensed ex-cristeros to carry firearms and deputized them to serve in local paramilitary police forces (defensas sociales) that harried agraristas. Comisarios also protected roving priests from prosecution; the clergy soon began publicly condemning agraristas for receiving "stolen" land in ejidos and denouncing federal teachers for spreading immoral ideas. To make matters even worse for agraristas, Melchor Ortega convinced Mexico City to install new pro-landlord federal and state agrarian bureaucrats. By December 1932, the hard-won victories claimed by isolated agrarista communities and federal teachers in the north since the Arreglos had largely been reversed. Federal teachers, in fact, felt so threatened that many fled the countryside to take refuge in Dolores Hidalgo.[88]

By bringing Azanza and other ex-cristeros into his administration, Ortega discouraged some potential support for another cristero insurrection, at least in the short run. But their inclusion in regional politics gave former cristeros free rein to attack ejidos and SEP schools using the institutions of the postrevolutionary state. Moreover, some rebuffed Ortega's and Azanza's offers of amnesty and protection and plotted a second insurgency. As early as March 1932, Guanajuato's recristeros proclaimed another armed revolution. By 1933, small bands of insurgents operated around Manuel Ocampo and

Ciudad González municipios to the west of Dolores Hidalgo as well as in San Luis de la Paz in the far northeast. Soon they would roam the hills around Dolores Hidalgo and pop up from León in southwestern Guanajuato to the Sierra de los Agustinos in the southeast. Because General Genovevo Rivas's federal cavalry regiment was thinly stretched across the north, Governor Ortega reinforced it with paramilitaries raised by Red diputados Azanza and Jorge Lámbarri.[89] They recruited former cristeros into their paramilitary defensas sociales, licensing them to attack agraristas across the north.

Throughout the 1930s, Dolores Hidalgo was among the most dangerous segunda foci in Mexico. Small segundero squads regularly received intelligence and supplies from the sympathetic populace and apparently from Salvador Azanza as well. They targeted isolated ejidos and rural schoolhouses, then outran army pursuit. Ejidatarios and teachers could only flee. Agrarista communities eventually received arms, but the speed of recristero cavalry attacks meant that they rarely had enough time to mount an adequate defense. On September 1, 1936, segunderos cut down five agraristas not far from Dolores Hidalgo. Many agraristas, along with most federal teachers, spent much of 1936 holed up in town.[90] Federal troops scored occasional victories: they killed Fermín Sandoval and paraded his head on a stick in Ciudad González in July 1936; in 1937 they eliminated two other chieftains.[91] But victories were few and far between.

The subregion, however, was never a priority for the army, leaving Azanza's and other landowner-led defensas sociales the main check on segunderos. The revolutionary state was often ill-served by such unreliable allies. For instance, Azanza set out to convince segunderos to surrender and join his militia; Fermín Sandoval accepted, turned bandit, then revolted again. In February 1935, the amnestied cristeros in Azanza's posse failed to follow Don Salvador into battle against raiding segunderos. In response, Azanza armed peons of his estate, Trancas—then promptly rode straight into a rebel ambush. On July 8, 1935, Azanza broke his arm when his horse was shot out from under him, forcing him into semiretirement. He continued to sell horses to federal troops and to scout for them occasionally. Yet he also reportedly tipped off segunderos when government forces were closing in on them. As *Hombre Libre*'s local stringer fittingly put it, Azanza was a "political amphibian," walking with the revolutionaries but still swimming with the cristeros.[92] Azanza's military failures, in spite of his considerable local knowledge and ties to ex-insurgents, suggest that his loyalties were always divided. Dolores Hidalgo remained a hostile environment for agraristas and federal teachers while becoming fertile ground for segunderos.⁹³ Matthew Butler's fine-grained study of "liberal cristero" Ladislao Molina sketched a mestizo Catholic landowner remarkably similar to Azanza, one who collaborated with the state when it benefited him, but also used Catholicism as a "dissident ideology for resisting state encroachments on his sphere of influence." Like Molina, Azanza was particularly concerned with exterminating revolutionary agrarianism, and found coopting state institutions the best means to do so.⁹⁴

In spite of Azanza's ambiguous relationship with the federal government, General Rivas Guillén, the army commander in northern Guanajuato, protected Azanza from 1933 until the general's transfer out of Guanajuato on April 16, 1935. Guillén bestowed on Azanza the rank of colonel of irregulars and thus de facto legal impunity. Why did Rivas place his confidence in such a slippery ally? Rivas was a brave, unusually competent commander in both the Cristiada and the Segunda, and he proved his loyalty to Cárdenas by helping to push rebel warlord Cedillo from power in San Luis Potosí in 1938. Rivas was no closet Catholic, either; during the Cristero War he exhumed and exhibited skeletons that he claimed were aborted infants buried behind a convent in San Luis de la Paz. Azanza apparently provided Rivas with just enough information and assistance to appear loyal. Civilian collaborators like Azanza were potentially a force multiplier for hard-pressed federal garrison commanders, who chronically lacked enough men and resources. Furthermore, for generals, friendship with landowners could yield lucrative business opportunities. Grateful hacendados called Rivas a "guarantee of peace and order." Rivas's uneasy alliance with Azanza meant agraristas and federal teachers were left unprotected.⁹⁵

While no scourge of the segunderos, Azanza proved deadly against supporters of the revolutionary project. Azanza's own *medioderos* (middling farmers who rented and sharecropped his land), peons, and paroled cristeros that constituted his defensa social nursed old grievances with local agraristas. Thanks to Rivas and Azanza, they had good new guns and the legal authority to kill. With these, Azanza's paramilitary murdered agraristas and intimidated several ejidos across northern Guanajuato in the mid-1930s. His most telling blow against the revolutionary project in the north was his assassination of Ezequiel Aguilera on October 22, 1934. The brazen killing eliminated the main champion of land reform and the head of Cárdenas's presidential campaign in the subregion. Aguilera was an unlikely agrarista; he owned Dolores Hidalgo's trolley company and represented a foreign oil company. But he had exposed corruption in local government and had helped organize ejidos. Luis Martínez Vértiz had vetoed then-candidate Melchor Ortega's attempted alliance with Aguilera and then dispatched Azanza to eliminate Aguilera once and for all. A federal investigation revealed Azanza's guilt. He had tried to kill Aguilera a year earlier; the murder weapon was an army-issued gun, and his own mother implicated him. Nevertheless, General Rivas blocked his prosecution.[96]

The Azanza cacicazgo could be seen as yet another case of regional elites adeptly exploiting the contradictions in the revolutionary project for material ends. Yet Azanza could not have controlled politics in the north had Catholic organizations not constituted so much of civil society and had Church ideology not been so compelling to the population. To explain religiously informed politics in terms of either instrumentality or ideology is to accept a false choice. The Church's doctrine of civic action obliged Catholic voters to support sympathetic candidates at the ballot box. Church teachings and landowner prerogatives frequently coincided, as both supported a conservative social hierarchy and the near-sanctity of private property. Consider how two foes took the measure of Azanza. Superintendent Arnulfo Ochoa called his nemesis "the greatest cacique I have known," but he always held the deeply ingrained Catholicism of the north just as culpable for the violence against his SEP schools and ejidos.[97] Following Marxist economic determinism, Ochoa believed the Church was directed by landowners like Azanza, supported by the "eminently refractory" city women and the rural working people, "enemies of the current regime and completely fanaticized."[98] Another bitter enemy of Azanza, Cardenista teacher and agrarista organizer Alfredo Guerrero Tarquín, admitted that the cacique was genuinely popular in the subregion.[99] Azanza's Catholic cacicazgo in Dolores Hidalgo, then, reflected the region's distinctive social structure and religious character. Understanding the relationship between Azanza's political power and Catholicism requires a closer look both at socioeconomic arrangements and religious practices in this subregion.

Azanza's World: God and Man in Northern Guanajuato

In spite of the Revolution, Dolores Hidalgo remained the Azanza family's domain. Salvador Azanza represented himself as a defender of the Church, enhancing his family's formidable social capital. Like other northern magnates, he could call upon many clients distributed across different social strata. Tenants and ranchers were beholden to him for land and pasturage rights. Town merchants and artisans could not get by without his business. Peons depended on him for work, and losing his favor had serious consequences. Geographic isolation and the generally low yield of the soil meant rural laborers earned under thirty centavos for well over eight hours of daily work, mean pay even in the Bajío's abysmal labor market. Wages often had to be spent in the *tienda de raya* (the hacienda's company store). Penury reinforced codes of deference. Outsiders remarked not only on the north's poverty but also on its steep social hierarchy.[100] SEP inspector Rafael Villeda bemoaned "blind loyalty to the Boss."[101] In a 1935 election, Azanza personally brought one thousand employees and other clients to the polls, evidence, in the words of an awed federal electoral monitor, of the "Cristero General's" "great number of adherents."[102] Gonzalo Santos accused another northern grandee, León Peña, of literally enslaving peasants and maintaining a harem of fifteen campesinas.[103] Even architecture suggested feudalism to outsiders: the castlelike El Rosario hacienda (municipio Manuel Ocampo) shut its gates at night to lock in peons.[104]

Illiteracy reinforced strong patron-client relationships, further isolating the subregion. An estimated 95 percent of the population could not read in the 1930s, remarkably high given the very low number of speakers of indigenous languages.[105] Most sharecropping arrangements were oral agreements, denying tenants legal protections.[106] While the working poor, middling farmers, and artisans were segmented by vertical ties to *norteño* landowners, the hacendados themselves were exceptionally unified and homogeneous; the great clans rarely resided outside the north, spent a lot of time on their haciendas, and were horizontally linked by intermarriage, political alliances, shared economic interest, and strong support for Catholicism.[107]

The Azanza family was long associated with the Church. Likely a Knight of Columbus, Salvador Azanza sheltered the clergy in Dolores Hidalgo from anticlerical legislation using his office and political connections, one of the many means the clergy used to escape state control and maintain a strong influence over society. In early 1935, four priests furtively ministered in town, using their moral suasion to discourage the rural poor from signing agrarian reform petitions or supporting SEP schools.[108] When the clergy invoked values like the necessity of hierarchy, the sanctity of private property, and the natural right of the father to decide his children's education, peasants and peons listened respectfully. In San Diego de la Union, priests accused ejidatarios of "robbing the patron and selling [themselves] to the government." Agrarian reform, clergy explained, was like coveting thy neighbor's wealth.

Events in the 1920s on the vast Jaral de Berrio estate illustrate how Catholic belief and symbols could turn the rural poor against the revolutionary project and underscore owners' power over peons.[109]

Jaral de Berrio had long been contested ground; labor activists, agraristas, and federal teachers squared off against owners (sisters María de la Concepción, María de las Mercedes, and Rosa María Blanco y Pastor, scions of genuine Spanish nobility), trusted employees (many Spanish), and loyal peons. During the 1920s, federal labor inspectors and agraristas tried to enforce Guanajuato's labor code and found a CROM syndicate on the hacienda. Pro-owner Green officials insured that the police disarmed agraristas and permitted the state teacher to include the rosary and catechism in his curriculum. Priests visited frequently to counter the union. The three sisters who owned Jaral took a personal interest in rebuilding its chapel. They patronized the new cult of the Niño Dios in 1920 and personally performed "spiritual work" among campesino families on their hacienda and on surrounding ranchos. Anticlerical and labor organizers charged that the cult hardened peons' hearts against the Revolution and agrarian reform.[110]

In many other communities, religion insulated the rural poor against agents of revolutionary change and socially quarantined those peasants who accepted ejidal grants. In much of the north, ejidatarios were not allowed to tithe, confess, or even set foot in church.[111] Agraristas in Ocampo municipio complained that ex-cristero Father Ignacio Lara condemned all those associated with the government as "a plague of crows" who would be exterminated; those who asked for land, he said, were no better than thieves.[112] In response to such incidents, SEP Superintendent Tomás Cuervo tried to launch an intense defanaticization campaign from February through May 1935. However, popular resistance was so widespread and potentially volatile across the north that he dared not hold a quemasantos. Instead, he stuck close to the SEP's institutional strategy of re-training teachers, community outreach, and closing private schools. In response, clergy and lay Catholic leaders encouraged communities to boycott schools and shun teachers. Isolated acts of defensive segunda violence (stoning and attacks by mobs) erupted. When the SEP inspector in Dolores Hidalgo leaned on state authorities to close four parochial schools in March 1935, middle- and upper-class *catequistas* and priests visited villages in Dolores Hidalgo municipio and encouraged peasants to drive out the federal teachers (one fled fearing for his life). Cuervo blamed the emptied schools in ranchos Cabras and San Isidro on Father Miguel Godínez's fiery sermons.[113]

Reports from SEP often dwelt on obstinate priests; inspectors nagged reluctant state and local officials to expel clergy. The priest, after all, was highly visible in the pulpit and drew attention when he visited hamlets and haciendas. But ultimately, he was less an obstacle to federal schools than the lay groups embedded in civil society. It was to these organizations, not to the clergy, that the Church in northern Guanajuato owed its formidable capability to monitor and socially sanction foes, buck up waiverers, and mobilize followers. Northern Guanajuato's male lay organs seemed exceptionally robust; remnants of the Catholic National Party (or PCN) remained active, at least one Catholic labor union still met, and a Knights of Columbus chapter continued to function. But in the campaigns against SEP schools, it was Catholic women who outnumbered and outworked the men.[114]

Some operated as part of supposedly secular civic organizations, like the Charitable and Social Moralization Board. In the late 1920s, this organization ran Dolores Hidalgo's Red Cross, opened a soup kitchen, held clothing drives, and visited prisoners. But the board also kept a close eye on teachers' "moral conduct" through its Union of Parents of the Family.[115]

The mobilization against the SEP in Dolores Hidalgo and across the north predated the early 1930s polemics over socialist education and Rome's radial strategy. In 1922–23, Father Manuel Medina, Manuel Azanza's bellicose chaplain, closed the first SEP school in Dolores Hidalgo by calling for a boycott of "heretics." Worried state authorities armed thirty local liberals until federal troops could arrive to contain popular outrage. During the Cristiada, Damas Católicas all but stood in the federal schoolhouse's door, and attendance dropped from five hundred to just eighty. In early 1929, the SEP demanded that Guanajuato's state police protect Dolores Hidalgo's federal schools from cristeros in the hills and force parents to send their children to school.[116] By 1931, priests were once again convening attendance strikes across the north to undo Inspector Ochoa's work.[117]

The Cristiada in Dolores Hidalgo hardened local Catholic attitudes against the federal government. In February 1928, federal troops executed a priest in Dolores Hidalgo; a year earlier in León, they had shot another priest who was born in the municipio. When Gonzalo Santos's troops occupied the town, he had a priest whipped with an aluminum-tipped cane for preaching against agrarian reform. Federal soldiers jailed nuns, female teachers, and suspected cristero collaborators in military camps, denying them habeas corpus.[118] Memories of these events profoundly and negatively shaped Catholics' perceptions of the revolutionary project.

The Cristero War also shaped, or better put, warped, the process of land reform in Dolores Hidalgo. During the war, Santos, General Genovevo Rivas, and Alfredo Guerrero Tarquín, the leading Cardenista organizer in the north, all fruitlessly tried to raise peasant militias in Dolores Hidalgo municipio to fight cristeros in exchange for land.[119] After the Arreglos, when the SEP attempted to revive the revolutionary project, peasant communities across the subregion generally remained reticent to accept the overtures of the revolutionary state. El Llanito, just four kilometers outside the town of Dolores Hidalgo, offered the SEP one of the few prospects for realizing revolutionary change in the north. A closer look at the community, though, suggests the limits of the revolutionary project in the north and the subtle but decisive role of Catholicism in its failure.

The SEP assumed that smaller, poorer, more indigenous communities like El Llanito were structurally predisposed to welcome teachers and request ejidos. Although Guanajuato was among the most mestizo, monolingual Spanish states in Mexico, its peasant culture had African and indigenous substrates; El Llanito, while Hispanized, had Otomí roots. Its elders still sustained the cult of the Santa Cruz (Holy Cross) found across the Laja River valley where Otomí auxiliaries of the conquistadores settled. Once a small colonial Otomí settlement on a hacienda, it gained some land as the estate was slowly partitioned. The old chapel was still its symbolic heart. However, poverty forced some to leave to seek day labor on neighboring estates or to harvest firewood.[120] Their more Hispanized way of life distanced them from the more traditional farmers who still lived in El Llanito.

El Llanito seems exactly the sort of community that would welcome the SEP for land and a better future, and the more mestizo faction seemed more open to the revolutionary project. Jeffrey Gould has shown how some Nicaraguan indigenous communities, even after adopting the Spanish language and Western folkways, retain a collective identity as indigenous, one that in the right circumstances could serve as the basis for revolutionary struggle.[121] When General Amaro offered arms to those who would fight against Azanza in the delahuertista revolt, though, it was El Llanito's minority of more mestizo woodcutters, not its more Otomí sharecroppers, who accepted. As in Nahua villages in Guerrero, indigenous traditionalists linked to a syncretic Catholic mayordomía were reluctant to ally with agents of the revolutionary state. While the revolutionary project appealed to indigenous communities' desire for communal land, it also threatened their syncretic Catholic cultural core. The SEP's dilemma was that community membership was inseparable from the practice of "fanatical" syncretic Catholicism.

This perhaps explains why it was Hispanized woodsmen, not self-identified Otomí farmers, who helped apprehend a priest implicated in the Cristiada. In return, the revolutionary state promised them land.[122] By 1926, El Llanito's veteran militiamen had formed a campesino syndicate named after Miguel Hidalgo and affiliated with the CROM, thereby forging connections that encouraged militia veterans to self-consciously identify as working-class, anticlerical revolutionaries. Although they might well have still venerated the Santa Cruz, they described themselves as "one of the few groups of peasants outside of the control of religious fanaticism." Eusebio Mejía, El Llanito's controversial but long-serving agrarista leader, remained in power until the 1940s.[123] Fighting Cristeros in the mid-1920s crystallized this new identity for Mejía and his men: "we have fought with rifle in hand against traitors to the Revolution [delahuertistas], then against the Cristeros."[124] Military experience, political connections, and their new identity emboldened them to occupy hacienda land and challenge the institutional Church's presence in the village.[125]

Many in El Llanito did not embrace this new revolutionary identity, opening a rift. Mejía's foes branded him a cacique and rejected ejidal land as immorally acquired. Ejidal requests from El Llanito's core of agraristas, along with similar petitions filed by factions from Tierra Blanca, Joconoxtle, and La Trinidad, allowed the federal government to press ahead with twenty-six ejido grants in Dolores Hidalgo municipio in the later 1930s. Nevertheless, most peasants and nearly all peons refused to participate.[126]

Accelerating land reform ignited offensive segunda violence in Dolores Hidalgo; the proagrarian, progovernment stance of Mejía and the hostility of surrounding communities and hacendados toward the agraristas made El Llanito a central flashpoint. Agraristas were hunted "like rabbits" by bands linked to Azanza's cacicazgo; antiagrarian peasants resentful of Mejía probably abetted these segunderos. In 1932, intracommunal strife intensified when ejidatarios asked to nationalize the chapel and other Church buildings for their use. The struggle dragged on for seven years before the government finally said no, but in the meantime the intracommunal rift widened.[127] Ejidatarios recalled they were treated like "skunks or Communists. Excommunicated, they could not even set foot in chapel."[128] When the local priest visited, they complained, he delivered diatribes against socialist education and "our agrarian class."¹²⁹ The SEP hoped to ring recalcitrant, levitical towns like Dolores Hidalgo with prorevolutionary ejidos and schools. But even El Llanito, with something of an agrarian tradition, proved problematic. Things for the SEP were even worse in the county seat. The voto morado forced the state administration to repeatedly nullify local elections (1923, 1924, twice in 1928, and 1932).¹³⁰ Interventions only strengthened resentment against the postrevolutionary state, and Catholic parents' groups tapped these sentiments.

The UNPF's organizer in Dolores Hidalgo, J. Jesús Soto, was a veteran Catholic lay leader and probably a Knight of Columbus. By 1943, he was president of Dolores Hidalgo's Sinarquistas, the popular lay movement that claimed to be both apolitical and autonomous from existing Church organizations. Taking advantage of Cárdenas's relaxation of censorship, Soto published a small newspaper attacking socialist education.¹³¹ Thanks to the dense network of formal and informal Catholic groups, he had many collaborators. UNPF block captains in town and rural intermediaries (even in El Llanito) passed on episcopal orders to boycott SEP schools and set up underground parochial schools.¹³² The UNPF worked with older, official groups like the Damas to slip propaganda like Soto's newspaper episcopal pastorals, and official Church publications (*El Paroco*) under doors at night.¹³³ In 1929, Catholic activists in Dolores Hidalgo also distributed Bishop Manríquez y Zárate's incendiary pastoral letter, "Cosas de actualidad que todo buen Católico debe saber" (Current events that every good Catholic should know about). It read, in part, that "it is illicit for Catholics to serve in the ranks of tyranny. Catholic teachers cannot teach anything besides the truths of the Catholic religion without staining their consciences any more than they can serve as soldiers. . . . It is better to have a generation of poor but honorable and Christian ignoramuses, than a brood of bandits and murderers that offend God."¹³⁴

By accusing federal teachers of menacing religion and equating them with soldiers, Manríquez's pamphlet contradicted repeated episcopal counsel against violent resistance. By endorsing this discourse, local Catholic organizations skirted Church orders to resist socialist education licitly and instead legitimized violence.

Catholics in Dolores Hidalgo saw their struggle as patriotic as well as religious. Given Dolores Hidalgo's hallowed place in Mexican history as the cradle of independence, this narrative was especially compelling. Father Miguel Hidalgo rang Dolores Hidalgo's church bells in 1810 to begin Mexico's

War of Independence. Captured, he was defrocked and executed. Nineteenth-century Liberals claimed him (minus his clerical title) as the father of a secular nation; revolutionaries expanded his patriotic cult.[135] Catholics, on the other hand, generally followed the great nineteenth-century conservative intellectual (and native Guanajuatan) Lucas Alamán, who bitterly denounced Hidalgo as leading "a vandalistic revolution that would have destroyed the civilization of the country." For him, Agustín Iturbide was Mexico's real father, a view advanced by the national Knights of Columbus and Damas Católicas, as well as by Catholic textbooks.[136] In Salvatierra (southeastern Guanajuato) Catholics celebrated independence day 1926 with "*Our* Patriotic Celebration," contrasting Calles's anti-Catholic tyranny with Iturbide's Three Liberties of Religion, Union, and Independence.[137] When León's clergy and the ACM founded the Unión de Acción Cívico-Social to oppose socialist education, its hymn praised Iturbide.[138]

Neat generalizations about the secular leftist and Catholic rightist brands of nationalism, however, can gloss over important local variations and contradictions. In Dolores Hidalgo, at least, Catholics contested the revolutionaries' claim to Father Miguel Hidalgo. The faithful in Dolores Hidalgo shunned every SEP patriotic festival except the Grito, which reenacted Father Hidalgo's proclamation of independence.[139] By reclaiming Father Hidalgo's legacy, Catholics also criticized the revolutionary project. How, they asked, could anticlerical legislation prohibit church bells from pealing when Father Hidalgo rang them?[140]

The Catholic appropriation of Hidalgo figured in a larger narrative of defending the "true" Mexico against foreign (Soviet or Yankee or Masonic or Protestant) conspiracies.[141] Mario Vázquez's study of Dolores Hidalgo as symbolic space shows that the example of Father Hidalgo inspired cristeros and sinarquistas to "take up arms again to defend their right to conserve their beliefs, values, and culture" against secularization and political centralization.[142] The conservative, faith-based nationalism of Martínez Vértiz and Azanza referenced and reinforced the Catholic interpretation of Hidalgo. The two probably advised Melchor Ortega to campaign on a promise to bring back Hidalgo's remains, which had been transferred to Mexico City's Angel of Independence monument by President Calles in 1925.[143] Fittingly enough, Salvador Azanza's first act as a congressman was to preside over a celebration of Mexican independence.[144]

Salvador Azanza's political trajectory wove together several significant strands of Catholic resistance to the revolutionary project. He championed the Catholic hero cult of Hidalgo while holding public office in the revolutionary regime. Azanza's ambiguous relationship with cristeros allowed him to pose as a Catholic paladin waging a just war against atheistic teachers and agraristas while simultaneously scouting for and supplying the federal army. His battery of Ochoa, assassination of Ezequiel Aguilera, and complicity with some segunderos denied the postrevolutionary state a monopoly on violence in the north. This in turn facilitated the UNPF's truancy strikes and segunderos' attacks against ejidatarios. In short, Azanza's cacicazgo in northern Guanajuato depended upon Catholicism and enabled a variety of religiously informed responses to the revolutionary project. Although Salvador Azanza's Catholic cacicazgo aided Melchor Ortega, it delayed and debilitated key elements of the revolutionary project. This close examination of the Azanza cacicazgo, with all its complexity and contradictions, reveals the difficulty of explaining Catholic resistance to the revolutionary project without considering its political and socioeconomic context.

Even Azanza, untouchable for so long, was ultimately vulnerable to national political upheavals. Cárdenas removed General Rivas Guillén from the north in April 1935, and the new garrison commander disarmed Azanza's defensa social. On December 16, 1935, Cardenista senators ousted Red governor José Jesús Yáñez Maya in a national purge of Callistas.[145] Azanza flirted with armed revolt in favor of Ortega and Calles and against Cárdenas. But in the end, the plot fizzled, and friends in the federal military allowed him to keep his colonel's rank and legal impunity. Still, Azanza had to accept a transfer from Dolores Hidalgo to San Luis de la Paz in northeastern Guanajuato; agraristas blamed him for the murder of two peasants there in 1937. After backing a losing gubernatorial candidate that year, his influence waned. He was even jailed for Aguilera's murder but soon released. Azanza's power in Dolores Hidalgo certainly declined during his absence; a Cardenista, agrarista mayor of Dolores Hidalgo was elected for the 1937–38 term.[146] However, Salvador Azanza's political fall failed to calm the north.

Clash in Ciudad González and Cardenismo's Second Wind

Cárdenas's displacement of Calles atop the postrevolutionary state in June 1935 touched off a number of important regional changes. It restored the Greens (once Obregonista, now Cardenista) to power. After Red governor Yáñez Maya's removal, Green federal congressman Enrique Fernández Martínez was named to serve a short interim term. Fernández Martínez energized the state agrarian bureaucracy, raised pay for rural teachers, and pledged to realize Cárdenas's radical agenda. In the March 14, 1937 gubernatorial election, only one candidate ran: Luis I. Rodríguez, Cárdenas' personal secretary and veteran Guanajuatan Green.[147] Then, in May 1939, Rodríguez resigned to undertake a prestigious European diplomatic mission, and in yet another extraordinary election, Enrique Fernández was elected governor over a strong Red challenge.

The Greens' resurgence promised revolutionary change. Melchor Ortega's "aristocrats and reactionaries," in the words of a young Cardenista, were discredited.[148] But early attempts to accelerate land reform floundered. Catholic sentiment against the ejido still ran strong. Pragmatic peasants remained wary, fearing that accepting land grants would make them targets of reprisals in the future.[149] On embattled ejidos, former sharecroppers and peons faced economic embargos from hacendados and merchants who refused to sell seeds or rent tools and oxen to them. Agraristas who received land usually did not get guns, which left them vulnerable to retaliation.[150]

To protect the ejidos and schools from segunderos' depredations, in the fall of 1935 President Cárdenas personally ordered the army to organize agraristas as defensas rurales. As long as army officers were corruptible by hacendados, however, offensive segunda violence continued.[151] On March 18, 1936, Governor Fernández Martínez and the new army commander in the state, Ernesto Aguirre Colorado, promised to arm residents of thirty ejidos, which offered a degree of protection.[152] Nevertheless, the difficulties and high cost of creating ejidos meant agrarian reform proceeded slowly. For the moment at least, the president remained preoccupied with other pressing national matters, among them the Church-state conflict that still simmered.

On March 4, 1936, President Cárdenas explicitly ended Calles's Psychological Revolution, saying the entire revolutionary project's success could not hinge on the religious question.[153] Only a few days later, Cárdenas was forced to confront the religious question yet again when a bloody clash in Guanajuato threatened to inflame Catholic feelings across Mexico.

Professor Rolando C. Uribe's cultural mission #18 had been visiting communities across the state since April 1935.[154] Like other SEP cultural missions, Uribe's roving team of educators had been tasked with in-service training of teachers as well as reversing widespread popular opposition to agrarian reform and socialist education. In León, thanks to ex-maestro Hernández's cultural center and the opposition of state and local officials, the population turned its back on Uribe's secular missionaries.[155] In early March 1936, Uribe set up his temporary headquarters in Ciudad González's elementary school. Uribe and his staff worked closely with Juan C. Cruz's Agrarian Engineer Brigade #3 to convince peons, peasants, and sharecroppers to sign agrarian reform petitions.[156]

Uribe and Cruz had their work cut out for them. Attendance strikes hit SEP schools hard during the 1934–35 school year. Local officials offered little help, even allowing the traditional Holy Week celebrations to openly resume in 1935. Priests J. Refugio Méndez (licensed), Estanislao Velázquez, and J. Jesús García Escobar (both unlicensed) worked closely with the Daughters of Maria to thwart the SEP. The Daughters accused the mission of plotting to take their children to Communist Russia and sterilize them with vaccinations. Triumphs for maestros rurales were rare, but there were a few. On the hacienda la Herreria, they overcame peasants' and peons' "dogmas of faith" to set up an ejido. The new agraristas joined a few other established ejidos, veterans who battled cristeros and Escobaristas, pushing for an expansion of agrarian reform in the municipio.[157]

Cruz's agrarian brigade and Uribe's cultural missionaries blamed lack of overall progress on the institutional Church. With their month in Ciudad González coming to a close, Uribe and Cruz made one last effort to open hearts and minds. They scheduled a peaceful rally for March 28, 1936, in the public gardens directly in front of San Felipe the Apostle, a colonial church with a massive Porfirian tower that lent the town its former name, San Felipe de los Torres. Teachers went unarmed to demonstrate that they were neither Communists nor anticlericals. Cultural missionaries' speeches promised land for those who tilled it and schools for the children, offering material and mental liberation from the landlord and priest. Teachers, engineers, and agraristas sang corridos like "Canción de Fierro" (Song of iron), "El 30–30" (the favored rifle of the Revolution), and "Máquinista y Hombre" (Mechanic and man) to draw a crowd from the nearby public market.[158]

Only a few meters away, mass was ending. When the bells pealed and the faithful recessed, trouble began. At this point, progovernment and antigovernment accounts diverge widely. The former charged that Catholics swarmed out of the church's atrium, shouting slogans against socialist education, throwing rocks and swinging sticks; meanwhile, gunmen atop a nearby store, the atrium, and the bell tower opened fire. Armed agraristas from the local ejidos of Catarina and Santa Rosa escorting the teachers and engineers returned fire. Then soldiers tried to separate both sides. But, progovernment sources concluded, the Catholics continued to throw rocks and sticks, forcing federal soldiers to fire into the Catholic crowd in self-defense. When the shooting stopped, at least nineteen people lay dead and thirty were wounded. All of the dead and most of the wounded were Catholics, but official sources attributed these casualties to Catholic friendly fire. Teachers and agraristas suffered mostly minor wounds, although a machete blow to the head gravely injured Cruz.[159]

The opposition press and the Church's own official investigation, based on Catholic eyewitnesses, told an entirely different story. They put the number of wounded at around one hundred, virtually all from soldiers' and agraristas' bullets. The Church's account described "a natural venting of the people (*el pueblo*) whose most sacred beliefs were offended" by years of anticlericalism. It blamed Cruz for haranguing a group of Catholics milling about in front of a statue of Hidalgo. Finally, an old campesino snapped, picked up his machete, and split the agrarian engineer's skull. In retaliation, agraristas and soldiers opened fire: "The poor people who were going to be redeemed by agrarismo, by the cultural mission, and by the new ideas instead were killed and wounded." The Church's investigation concluded that the revolutionary state was fundamentally culpable because it ignored the "profoundly honest religious ideology of those masses."[160]

Pro-Church accounts cited several factors to fix blame on revolutionary officials. Uribe and Cruz brought a federal military escort and agrarista militiamen from two ejidos to cow civilians. The agraristas of Catarina ejido were spoiling for a fight, as the pro-landowner defensa social of Ciudad González had recently assassinated their ejidal secretary.[161] Dramatic dialogues performed at the rally, like "Una Sola Cobija" (presumably about rural poverty) and "La Explotación del Campesino" might have attacked the clergy. Certainly, the national opposition daily newspaper *La Prensa* and pro-Church sources accused orators at the rally of yelling and waving provocative posters at Catholics.[162] Some Catholics suggested that the exits from the front of the church were intentionally blocked to force them to listen to the rally.[163] From pro-Catholic perspectives, these all amounted to provocations.

Progovernment accounts, on the other hand, accused the clergy of scheduling a special event to assemble as many Catholics as possible at the same time and place as the rally.[164] In other words, this was no ordinary mass. Seen from this perspective, the clash was but the latest attack hatched by an underground network that coordinated attendance strikes and supported segunda bands in Ciudad González. Among the local politicos, lay activists, and clergy that doggedly opposed the revolutionary project in Ciudad González for years, three figures loomed large: Catholic cacique Jorge Lámbarri, lay organizer and ex-cristero Ireneo Salazar, and Catholic electoral broker Vicente Guzmán. No thread of evidence ties Lámbarri, Salazar, and Guzmán (or other Catholic leaders) directly to the violent conspiracy Cruz and Uribe charged with causing the bloodshed. Instead, it seems much more likely that a tragic combination of defensive segunda violence against one federal engineer and the lethal overreaction by the federal army and agrarian militia were to blame. State investigations of the clash did, however, document how Lámbarri, Salazar, and Guzmán used the radial strategy to support segundero violence, oversee truancy strikes, and capture local organs of the postrevolutionary state. This shadowy triumvirate emerged out of the local Red-Green rivalry and the rise of the voto morado in Ciudad González.

As leaders of the Green Party, the Hernández Álvarez brothers controlled Ciudad González's electoral politics during the 1920s. Dr. Enrique Hernández Álvarez served as a local (1920–28) and state (1928–32) congressman; as interim governor (1930–31) he renamed the city Ciudad Hernández. Cárdenas gave him the portfolio for public health in his cabinet, helping brothers Federico (state comptroller, congressman) and Jesús José (mayor and congressman) rule their home town.[165] Like most Greens, the Hernández Álvarez brothers harassed agraristas and labor unions to weaken the Reds.[166]

Their cacicazgo was backed by a string of key Catholic brokers linked to landowners and businessmen. Cipriano Espinosa, once commander of a Huertista white guard, later headed a four-hundred-strong Catholic syndicate that helped elect José Jesús Hernández Álvarez mayor and brother Enrique a federal congressman. Espinosa also supplied arms and information to cristero chieftain Fermín Sandoval.[167] Alberto Camacho was the acknowledged leader of Ciudad González's business community in addition to heading the local Knights of Columbus and social Catholic organizations. When Green officials closed churches during the Cristiada, they gave the keys to Camacho's Knights. When Camacho funneled aid to cristeros, they took no action. When under federal pressure the Hernández Álvarez acted against key cristero supporters like Camacho, they took half measures at best.[168] Securing the voto morado required exactly this kind of toleration and collusion.

The Red electoral tide in 1931–32 swept out the Hernández Álvarez, but left Catholic political power undiminished. New cacique (state congressman, mayor, Azanza's alternate for federal congress) Jorge Lámbarri was a landowner, reputed cristero, and colonel of irregulars who scouted for the army against segunderos. Enemies charged that Lámbarri terrorized agraristas and peons on the Lamadrid family's hacienda. They pointed to Jesús López, an amnestied ex-cristero chieftain from neighboring Jalisco, whom Lámbarri named to head his paramilitary. Like that other amphibian Azanza, Lámbarri was playing both sides of the conflict, providing aid and comfort to some segunderos active in the area even as he assisted General Rivas in catching others.[169] In other words, Lámbarri's Catholic cacicazgo, like Azanza's, rested on a combination of wealth, social capital, land, a large armed retinue, wartime opportunities, and the voto morado.

In the benign political atmosphere of the Hernández Álvarez Green and then Lámbarri Red cacicazgos, Catholic mobilizations against the revolutionary project flourished. In 1926, the first federal school opened; catechists immediately set up their own academy as an alternative, while the Knights of Columbus started an attendance strike. By late 1928, the apostolic SEP inspector, Arnulfo Ochoa, doubled attendance in the municipio, despite periodic cristero raids, by dispatching federal troops to close parochial schools and protect teachers. When the Arreglos ended the Cristiada the soldiers went home and a young priest, Patricio Arroyo, arrived. Charismatic, highly educated, and well versed in social Catholic doctrine and practice, the ardent cristero sympathizer evaded capture during the war by disguising himself. In 1930, he inaugurated the ACM and opened a new Catholic campaign against the SEP, setting up alternative schools even on the smallest rancho. By the time that he left in 1933, the SEP feared the priest had both the populace and its officials in his sway. He trained a new cadre of leaders to oppose the revolutionary project, including Vicente Guzmán, an ACJM member from a strongly pro-cristero family (his mother and brother were arrested for sedition during the war). By 1933, the voto morado elected Guzmán mayor, and Governor Ortega would make him a state congressman.[170] Arroyo's third key protégé, Ireneo Salazar, fled town to avoid arrest during the Cristero War and returned home to work for hacendados after the conflict. Father Arroyo hired him as his business agent, probably to collect tithes. Serving as the nexus between the clergy and Ciudad González landowners, Salazar was perfectly positioned to lead a successful campaign against socialist education and organize an underground Catholic school operated by nuns.[171] In the minds of the cultural missionaries, these were the men responsible for the violence of March 28.

Lámbarri's, Salazar's, and Guzmán's successes reveal how Catholic networks straddled the boundary between licit resistance (boycotts) and illicit violence; the three organized a paramilitary gang masquerading as a defensa social to carry out offensive segunda violence. Although they were apparently not responsible for the clash on March 28, defenders of the cultural mission felt vindicated by Cárdenas's response. On March 29, 1936, President Cárdenas issued a statement blaming fanatics, specifically the parish priests, for inciting a gullible mob to lynch SEP cultural missionaries. He then boarded the Presidential Olive Train for Ciudad González. Cárdenas dramatically strode into the church of San Felipe the Apostle. Speaking in front of the altar before the national press corps, he accused "priests and fanatical women" of goading Catholics into attacking. Cárdenas explained that religious sentiment was determined by socioeconomic structure; "fanaticism," he said, resulted from the economic stranglehold of "the señores, the exploiters and ranch-owners." Before taking on latifundia, he gave the city's four priests twenty-four hours to leave, closed the church, and banned services at San Felipe for at least nineteen months. The president reinforced the thinly stretched soldiers in the north with another cavalry regiment, ordering a harsh crackdown on segunderos in Ciudad González and two neighboring municipios.[172]

After taking these public punitive measures, Cárdenas quietly made a number of conciliatory gestures to the Church during his brief foray in Guanajuato. When the Olive Train left Ciudad González and pulled into San Miguel Allende, President Cárdenas gave the unlicensed priest, Father José Mercadillo, "verbal permission" to minister.[173] While national and state legal authorities expelled priests from Ciudad González, they never prosecuted them. Father J. Refugio Méndez, blamed by the SEP for the violence in Ciudad González, remained free to practice in León.[174] Significantly, Cárdenas did not lower the number of priests in the rest of the Guanajuato, nor did he prosecute Lámbarri and other lay activists in Ciudad González.

The problem, in the president's mind, was that "the Revolution has not been felt in the northern part of Guanajuato."[175] Solving the religious question required ejidos and schools, not defanaticization. Early results were promising. In April 1936, federal officials credibly claimed that agrarian reform was finally being carried out in Dolores Hidalgo and San Miguel Allende municipios.[176] Peasants in Dolores Hidalgo who had rejected ejidos in 1935 were now "elated" to receive land, according to reliable U.S. diplomatic sources in May 1936.[177] By July 1, 1936, state and federal agrarian officials had approved 123 new ejidos. San Miguel Allende, one of the few agrarista toeholds in the north, proved to be the key Cardenista fulcrum to move the subregion.[178]

Regional political support was crucial to carry out agrarian reform, but it was far from a given. Green Party governor Enrique Fernández Martínez (1935–37, 1939–43) blamed "latifundist and clergy" for the Ciudad González violence.[179] But he and Luis I. Rodríguez (governor 1937–39) both resumed the old Green Party line of collaboration with Catholic brokers and uneven support for ejidos. The leftist teachers and the key Cardenista agrarista organization in the north, Alfredo Guerrero Tarquín's Alianza de Acción Revolucionario (Alliance for Revolutionary Action), feared that the priests exiled from Ciudad González would fan the flames of antiagrarian violence across the north.[180] The moderation exercised by Cárdenas and the Greens on the religious question was not matched by a conciliatory attitude on the part of the Catholics, at least in the short run. Offensive segunda violence was spreading throughout the north in 1936; in March, attacks increased in San Miguel Allende and Dolores Hidalgo.[181] In May 1936, armed agraristas were so fearful they refused to accompany federals as scouts.[182] On August 20, 1936, Amado Sandoval's band raided la Cieneguita's ejido in San Miguel Allende municipio, killing and dismembering seven after its teacher complained about Ciudad González's priests. On February 27, 1937, segunderos assassinated the president of la Cienguita's ejido and three more agraristas.[183]

Even as Cárdenas sought to reassure the Church of his moderate intentions and as the federal educators dropped anticlerical elements from their curriculum, offensive segunda violence escalated. The gangs' motives, of course, are difficult to discern. Some were hard men forced by hard times to serve as pistoleros for hacendados seeking to halt land grants. In other cases, antigovernment propaganda seemed to be the catalyst. Anti-Cardenista newspapers like *Omega* and *La Prensa* and the pro-Segunda *Pro Patria* blamed the Ciudad González bloodshed on SEP irreligiosity.[184]

As long as segunderos roamed the countryside, the fledgling ejidos were vulnerable. Many hacendados still fielded white guards and supplied segunderos. Even after Cárdenas removed officers linked to Azanza and Lámbarri, the army performed poorly. In 1936, the colonel commanding the cavalry regiment garrisoned in San Miguel Allende collaborated with Green governor Enrique Fernández Martínez to install ex-cristero Francisco Rocha as mayor. The same officer refused to disarm a local paramilitary force linked to the municipal police and ran agraristas off a newly created ejido.[185] In

March 1936, Salvador Saenz, Martínez Vértiz's pistolero who enjoyed the protection of a high-ranking federal army officer, killed Guadalupe Olvera, a key agrarista organizer in northeastern Guanajuato.[186]

Olvera's murder convinced Cárdenas to smash offensive segunda violence in the subregion. The national government sent two thousand rifles to arm agraristas. Thanks to Cardenista organizer Alfredo Guerrero Tarquín, other agrarian leaders, and brave federal teachers, the number of ejidal grants in the north increased from just 10 percent of Guanajuato's total in 1930–34 to 60 percent during the Cárdenas sexenio (1935–40). For the first time, some peons began to accept land. Agrarista leaders walked with new swagger; on the run for years, they sported six shooters Tom Mix-style, along with high Huasteca sombreros, red kerchiefs, and leather jackets.[187]

However, geography, the federal bureaucracy, regional politics, and above all Catholic sentiment and associations dashed the agraristas' hopes. Agrarian reform hinged on a viable ejidal economy. Without a massive investment in irrigation, crops planted on new ejidos inaugurated between March and July 1936 withered when the rains failed.[188] Ranching, as opposed to farming, would have been a better use for northern land, yet the plans drafted in Mexico City created grants too small to support cattle.[189] In mid-1938, interim governor Rafael Rangel admitted that agrarian reform was in crisis in Guanajuato, especially in the north. Some 600 ejidos existed on paper, but there were only 112 in fact. Only 5,400 families had received land. Of course, Cárdenas had sped up the process and outpaced predecessors, but he preferred to channel scarce resources to his agrarian showcase, the cotton-growing Lagunera region straddling the Coahuila-Durango border. The federal government sent only thirteen federal engineers to Guanajuato and later reduced their number to ten. For its part, the state government focused on the more fertile Bajío in the south. By the middle of 1938, twenty northern ejidos were emptied after ejidatarios had gone back to their former livelihoods as peons or tenant farmers. Engineers in 1936 were so desperate to meet quotas set in Mexico City that they forged bogus agrarian petitions by taking names directly off census forms; two years later, they had to import agraristas from the neighboring states of Michoacán and Jalisco to populate deserted ejidos.[190] In February 1938, a SEP inspector complained that unqualified people had infiltrated Ciudad González's nine ejidos because local peasants refused them.[191] Anthropologist Manola Sepúlveda Garza argues that in the north, "the ejido was more an obligation than a right."[192]

In the last two years of the Cárdenas sexenio, federal officials stationed in the north were downright pessimistic. In March 1939, the SEP inspector of Dolores Hidalgo reported "the distribution of ejidal land has almost failed."[193] In 1940, only one out of five eligible peasants and peons had agreed to join ejidos in Dolores Hidalgo and San Miguel Allende municipios; most called themselves "campesinos libres" (free peasants) and despised ejidatarios.[194] While federal agrarian reform did eventually dismantle the great estates in Dolores Hidalgo and San Miguel Allende municipios, they survived largely intact in San Diego de la Unión, Ciudad González, and San Luis de la Paz.[195] Agraristas in Manuel Ocampo lamented that "since 1936 when the Revolution slowly entered this municipio" there were still "twenty-seven haciendas where the Revolution hasn't even shown its shadow" in 1941.[196]

Regional politics and the religious question played a significant role in the dismal failure of agrarian reform in the north. Azanza's ouster created a vacuum, and it was soon filled by a new Catholic cacique, León Peña, of San Diego de la Unión. Peña used the weapons of the strong: endless legal and bureaucratic appeals, fictitious division of his holdings among family and prestanombres, and the creation of fraudulent "ghost" ejidos. Not only did he exploit the revolutionary project's vulnerabilities, but he also invoked the Catholic ideology that working people in the north shared. Most peasants saw the federal state as an amoral oppressor, betraying traditional Christian values and depriving them of their God-given freedom. Peña shrewdly supported the new ejidatarios' genuine demands to divide the collective, federally controlled ejido into private plots (*parcelas*).[197] Peasants and Peña invoked Catholic symbolism to defy agrarian reform: antiagrarian peons on the Azanza's La Sauceda hacienda were nicknamed the Guadalupanas, and one of his ghost ejidos was christened Liberación.[198]

Peña's Catholic cacicazgo also prolonged offensive segunda violence in northern Guanajuato. Northern grandees like the Peña, the Azanza, the Gaviño, the Sauto, and the Obregón outfitted and salaried platoons of segunderos—though only at peon rates. León Peña provided them with barracks on his La Noria hacienda, and his political allies disarmed agraristas' defensa rural (paramilitaries raised on ejidos).[199] Just as in the latter stages of the Cristero War, these were part-time warriors. When timely intelligence from friends in the government, irregular forces, and federal military revealed that isolated SEP schools or ejidos were unprotected, small bands came together, struck, then dispersed. This offensive segunda violence amounted to white terror.[200] The strategy, however, was not without risk for landowners. In 1939, when Cardenista agrarian reform was clearly on its last legs, most landlords ended their support of the insurgency. One squadron of segunderos killed its former sponsors Amador and Luis Azanza, owners of La Sauceda hacienda, in retaliation.²⁰¹ Even after most segunderos were amnestied or eliminated, León Peña's squadron still terrorized agraristas across the north.²⁰²

While segunderos attacked, Catholic leaders took advantage of the relaxation of anticlerical regulations by openly organizing anti-SEP boycotts. When the number of priests openly operating went up in Guanajuato, campaigns against SEP schools actually increased. Eighteen priests in Dolores Hidalgo coordinated efforts by an ACJM brigade and Catholic *organizadoras* (female catechists) to convince peasants on the newly minted ejidos to boycott SEP schools. Activist women openly charged fees to run the dozens of parochial schools that sprang up in Dolores Hidalgo and San Miguel Allende. Task forces aimed to peacefully organize truancy strikes, but exhortations to wage "war without quarter" against the federal school and agrarismo were not always taken metaphorically. In Joconoxtle, an isolated agrarista stronghold in Dolores Hidalgo municipio, segunderos burned the federal school to the ground. Teachers elsewhere received anonymous death threats. By early 1939, only one out of eight families sent children to federal or state schools in San Miguel Allende. Ironically, the SEP closed many hacienda schools after their students' parents had received ejidal land and landowners were no longer obliged to pay their teachers. A Cardenista teacher called their loss "the Failure of the Revolution" and a victory for "capital and the reaction in this zone."²⁰³ In March 1939, some one hundred agrarista communities across Guanajuato fruitlessly requested federal schools—another stark reminder of the SEP's declining fortunes and Cárdenismo shortcomings.²⁰⁴

In northern Guanajuato as in Guerrero, the Catholic reconquest of the countryside filled the void left by the retreating SEP and reached into the few remaining pockets of prorevolutionary popular sentiment. In 1938, Catholics reopened the long-closed chapel in the agrarista bulwark of El Llanito; a priest soon visited to deliver angry jeremiads against the SEP and President Cárdenas.²⁰⁵ The SEP inspector for Dolores Hidalgo in 1939 complained that a priest alienated potential agraristas by calling the landowner "God's trustee."²⁰⁶ Clerical condemnation sapped popular support for agrarian reform in the late 1930s.

To what extent was Catholicism responsible for Cardenismo's failure in the subregion? Bungled central planning, chronic institutional corruption on all levels, and arid soil should not be discounted. Most importantly, however, revolutionary narratives of liberation and progress through secular schooling and collective land grants failed to erode the strong Catholic sentiment that equated SEP schools with immorality, ejidos with slavery, agrarian reform with theft, and the federal government with tyranny. Offensive segunda violence was subsidized by hacendados but was fundamentally an expression of popular Catholic hostility to the revolutionary project. The Catholic cacicazgos, carved out by northern barons like Azanza, Lámbarri, and Peña, both reflected and sharpened popular Catholic antagonism toward the revolutionary project.

Counterpoint: Southeastern Guanajuato, 1929–1940

In southeastern Guanajuato, Catholics contested the revolutionary project in different, ultimately less successful, ways. Red Party honcho David Ayala mobilized Catholic supporters; he then abandoned them at the peak of Calles's Psychological Revolution. In the later 1930s, Catholics in this subregion deployed a familiar combination of tactics ranging from truancy strikes and the voto morado to sporadic segunda violence. Their aggregate impact was not inconsequential, draining the SEP's energy and scuttling many ejidos. But by 1940, the revolutionary project had enjoyed modest success in two of the six southeastern municipios and had made some limited but solid gains in a third. To explain the split decision in the southeast, I will first examine Acámbaro municipio, then turn to surrounding, more rural municipalities: Salvatierra, Tarimoro, Jerécuaro, Tarandacuao, and Coroneo.

Subregional geography molded religious practices. The hills of the Sierra de Agustinos divided the southeast into fertile valleys; irrigation canals from the Rio Lerma watered fields. Porfirian development had made the area into a breadbasket and turned Acámbaro into its transportation and commercial hub. By 1930, the town's population had climbed to around 15,000. Politics here was long the domain of its respectable middle class, educators, businessmen, professionals, government employees, and a couple of hundred rail workers, the nobility of Acámbaro's labor.[207] Outside the city, land here was rarely concentrated into vast estates of over a thousand hectares. Still, many *apareceros* (tenant farmers) and *medieros* (sharecroppers) depended on wealthier owners of larger estates for access to land. Peons, salaried agricultural laborers, constituted the bottom rung of society in southeastern Guanajuato. In 1929, they earned barely thirty to forty cents a day. Peasant communities survived up in the hills, although decompression of land ownership meant rancherías had sprung up on lands once concentrated into a few large estates.[208] Generally speaking, the poor in the southeast were not quite as destitute as the poor in the north. But Acámbaro's large landowners were usually absentee, and so they lacked strong personal bonds with tenants and peons.

Catholicism was deeply woven into the fiber of daily life of southeastern Guanajuato. The numerous clergy enjoyed considerable social influence, political clout, and even (relatively speaking) economic resources. The ACM, however, did not recover from state persecution during the Maximato until the end of the 1930s. The Sierra de Agustinos' very name honored one of the missionary orders that Christianized indigenous people early in the colonial era. Their brother order, the Franciscans, made Acámbaro its provincial headquarters in 1535, initiating a "symbiotic relationship that endures to the present day."[209] The men in brown introduced wheat cultivation and baking (Acámbaro is still famed for its bread) and incorporated Otomí, Tarascan, and Chichimec peoples into the Hispanic colonial order. In the 1930s, the Terciarios (a lay order of the Franciscans) still had a strong presence.[210] The Porfirian renaissance of the Church in southeastern Guanajuato was built on a strong colonial foundation; venerable religious symbols and narratives still ordered and gave meaning to urban space and time in Acámbaro.[211] One hallowed street had fourteen chapels, one for each of the Stations of the Cross. In 1933, the city defied the ley de cultos to honor the Virgin of Guadalupe with bands and fireworks.[212] Statistics confirm Acámbaro's levitical nature; in 1940 only 5 percent of the population married outside the Church, and only 1 percent self-identified as non-Catholic.[213] Such enduring religious belief explains why rich landowners, tenants, lowly peons, and even many ejidatarios willingly offered tithes and first fruits to Terciarios and why the town council did not prevent the practice.[214]

Reports of an inspector from SEP, José Macías Padilla, confirm the subregion's levitical character. For Macías, neither the federalization of schools begun in 1922, nor the creation of some successful ejidos, nor even a modest workers' movement had erased "feudal morality." The inspector had all but given up on the pariahlike peons—deferential to the boss and ignored by the priest, they nevertheless clung to the hope of heavenly reward. Macías pinned his hopes on ejidatarios and rancheros, inspired by glimmers of grassroots anticlericalism. "It is admirable," he said, "to hear the priest spoken of with bloody rancor" in a few communities. Even after land was granted and federal schools were opened, most peasants were still "weighed down by religious prejudices and superstitions."[215] Macías blamed the omnipresent priestly influence that naturalized social hierarchy, sanctified private property, and stigmatized the Revolution.[216] Though reductionist and somewhat biased, Macías's frank appraisal captured just how thoroughly Catholic values permeated society and shaped politics.

For the inspector, change required that federal teachers root out "prejudices and superstitions." Some (male) rancheros and peasants already hated priests, but would they accept socialist education and the collective ejido? Building strong coalitions to unite mestizo ejidatarios, rancheros, and laborers behind teachers was no easy task. In Acámbaro proper, a small but dynamic minority of workers (above all in its large rail yard) and freethinking, middle-class intellectuals (especially Freemasons) could be allies. Yet even after the Revolution, Catholic corporatist guilds aligned with the commercial and landowning oligarchy were still Acámbaro's strongest political constituency. Their conservative message of individual hard work, piety, and traditional morality had been diffused across southeastern Guanajuato by the Church's network of convents, charities, and schools since Francisco Madero's day. The neighboring Diocese of Querétaro had pursued a similar strategy since the Revolution began; it distributed a quietist "Catechism for the Inferior Classes" and encouraged the cult of Saint Zita for servants.[217]

The Archdiocese of Morelia, headquartered in the neighboring state of Michoacán and metropolitan of the Diocese of León, administered this part of Guanajuato. Like Bishop Valverde of León, Morelia's archbishop, Leopoldo Ruiz y Flores (1912–41), was a long-serving, dedicated administrator whose Roman formation instilled a lasting ultramontane orientation and enthusiasm for social Catholic doctrine. Ruiz endured personal misfortunes and long exiles during the Revolution's armed phase and the Cristiada, yet he remained unfailingly moderate, temperate, and diplomatic—even after a third exile in 1932. He helped craft the Arreglos and suppressed the Cristiada revolt. Yet as Matthew Butler points out, Ruiz was a committed integralist, determined to reconsecrate society by reversing revolutionary secularization and refusing to compromise when it came to socialist education.[218]

To repel the SEP, Archbishop Ruiz energetically implemented Rome's radial strategy in southeastern Guanajuato. In fact, the prelate anticipated the strategy during the Cristiada, granting the laity some temporary sacerdotal authority during the conflict. He already appreciated laywomen's centrality; in the 1920s, Ruiz stated that they were the Church's only real leaders.

Not all of his flock in and around Acámbaro shared his faith in a pacific strategy. Recristeros especially resented Ruiz's insistence on exclusively licit resistance.[219]

Throughout the 1930s, the Guanajuato part of Ruiz's archdiocese had a much higher ratio of priests to parishioners than was the case in most of Mexico. Thanks to the deal cut with Melchor Ortega in 1932, about thirty priests (plus seminarians from Tarandacuao) ministered there. Even a few rancherías had resident priests. Renewed state repression between 1933 and 1935 disrupted routine archdiocesan administration, so priests enjoyed a high degree of autonomy during the mid-1930s. Lay organizations had even more freedom of action. In fact, the ACM's diocesan directorate rarely met in Morelia before the late 1930s; clandestine ACM centers in Salvatierra and Acámbaro received only sporadic direction from the archdiocese and were largely left on their own to manage dispersed, semiautonomous, underground parochial schools, roving catechists, and parents' groups. Although there was considerable overlap between official and informal groups (in 1940, the head of the UNPF in Acámbaro was also on the parish ACM committee), such double militancy did not always facilitate the control of informal groups. In fact, in the mid-1930s, formal lay organizations were at times infiltrated by radicals set on breaking Church prohibitions against violence. Veterans of Damas Católicas and Knights of Columbus, the venerable Franciscan Terciarios and Hijas de María, home school teachers, and catechist matrons formed the core of dozens of largely autonomous cells. These nuclei coordinated hundreds of catechists (from girls to matrons) and dozens of male sacristans and acolytes.[220] More than a few were recristeros; many more would likely have supported the first Cristero War.[221] Southeastern Guanajuato's profoundly Catholic civil society was energized by these networks to repel the revolutionary project.

A spectrum of institutions ranging from Ruiz's canon chapter to Catholic electoral brokers shaped Catholic political attitudes. The voto morado decided elections in much of the subregion, a fact local Greens could not ignore. During the 1920s, small cliques of Greens with narrow popular support but long political lifespans dominated town halls in the southeast—a triumvirate branded the Tres Mosqueteros (Three Musketeers) and the Vallejo family "dynasty"—ruled Salvatierra; in Acámbaro David Ayala and his clique held sway. These Green leaders sporadically harassed organized labor, agraristas, and the occasional anticlerical linked to the rival Red Party. To accommodate Catholics, they generally ignored the ley de culto.[222]

The Greens' monopoly of public office ended in 1931 when their veteran fixer, David Ayala (state congressman 1926–28, federal congressman 1928–32), abandoned his old party to help orchestrate Ortega's victory. As Ortega's agent in the southeast in the 1931 and 1932 gubernatorial elections, Ayala turned out the vote for the little-known candidate largely by appealing to his traditional constituency, the Catholics. Prominent leaders of the Terciarios even trucked voters to the polls.[223] Service as counsel and all-around electoral manager to Ortega was Ayala's ticket to the senate (1934–40). Once in the upper chamber, Ayala ingratiated himself with the emerging leftist Cardenista majority. Mastering the platitudes of Cardenista discourse, Senator Ayala positioned himself as an outsider fighting for workers and peasants against corrupt, reactionary Green politicians.[224]

Before his opportunistic embrace of Cardenismo in 1935, Ayala's remarkable political rise was predicated upon a series of alliances with key Catholic leaders. Membership in an elite, landowning family facilitated networking with prominent Catholics. Marriage linked Ayala to Mariano M. Vértiz, a close relative of Luis Martínez Vértiz.[225] His in-law Vértiz became his *mancuerno* (political alter ego), following Ayala up the electoral ladder as Acámbaro's mayor and then federal congressman. In spite of these social advantages, Ayala could represent himself as a proper plebeian. He worked for a spell on the railroads tending the locomotive, and ostentatiously gave away his share of the family hacienda, "Inchamácuaro," to peasants. At the same time, he continued to own a ranch-sized piece of it through prestanombres and terrorized nearby agraristas.[226] An early leader of Acámbaro's Greens, Ayala counted on electoral brokers like the officers of Catholic guilds and Knights of Columbus. During the Cristero War, state congressman Ayala held Catholic services in his own house and pulled his pistol to help the Knights of Columbus stop agraristas from occupying a nationalized church. While campaigning for Ortega in 1932, Ayala handed out "canonical" propaganda that blamed his former party, the Greens, for destroying the Cubilete monument to the Sacred Heart near Silao. Ayala also courted Catholic brokers with patronages: he privately promised to give back the job of jail warden to Terciarios potentate Pablo Domínguez in return for the voto morado.[227]

Ayala publicly posed as a defender of local Catholic values against revolutionary anticlericalism, but Catholic reliance on a slippery figure like Ayala came with considerable risks. When the national Church-state conflict reignited in 1931, Ayala denounced his former mentor, Luis Pato, and Acámbaro's town council for attending a dinner in honor of an aide of Archbishop

Ruiz.²²⁸ Ayala, now safe in the national congress, definitively jettisoned his Catholic supporters in late 1934. After wavering, he succumbed to pressure from national Callistas and began an anticlerical campaign in Acámbaro spearheaded by federal teachers and the city's masonic lodge, Essences.²²⁹

Masons had much to complain about. Largely due to Ayala, anticlerical laws were dead letters in Acámbaro. After the Arreglos, Archbishop Ruiz visited and circulated a blacklist of masons and other liberals, leading to their social isolation. Long-suffering Freemasons saw their first political opening in 1932, when an interim state administration armed and deputized thirteen brothers as law enforcement agents. They used their new authority to help a Freemason, Nemesio Galindo, win the mayoral election. Throughout 1933, masons barraged Governor Ortega with demands to prosecute many violations of the ley de cultos, but Ortega and even Mayor Galindo dragged their feet.²³⁰ By 1934, Calles's bellicosity on the religious question gave the lodge's calls for a crackdown political traction, and the brothers denounced Ayala's complicity with Catholics before Governor Ortega's Committee of Public Safety. Feeling the heat, Mayor Galindo fired Catholics from government posts. New police chief (and Freemason) Rafael Robles came down hard on the Virgin of Refugio's fiesta, banning fireworks, forbidding music, and refusing to open a sealed church. Another mason closed a popular, legally operating private school linked to Acámbaro's UNPF and allegedly staffed by nuns. More menacingly, the masonic police chief and mayor were implicated in two murders.²³¹ In the July 1934 ruling party mayoral primary, Ortega and Ayala disenfranchised "reactionaries" (their Catholic former supporters). This left only government employees, railroad workers, and agraristas (about 5 percent of the electorate) to choose between two candidates nominated in a kitchen caucus in Ayala's house.²³²

The clash between masons and Catholics was as much a struggle over spoils as it was a contest for consciences. One of the masons' alleged murder victims, a wealthy banker and Knight of Columbus, was killed to prevent him from collecting a gambling debt from a lodge brother. After another Freemason was named labor inspector, he reportedly pocketed bribes from landowners to not enforce the minimum wage law. So much for Acámbaro's revolutionary alliance against reaction.²³³ Acámbaro's lodge, like the Oaxacan lodges examined by Benjamin Smith, probably attracted many job seekers and the politically ambitious. Entangling alliances between lodges and revolutionary politicos only intensified this trend.²³⁴

During the Psychological Revolution, lodge membership proved particularly advantageous to politicos in levitical places like Acámbaro, protecting them from charges of petty corruption and helping overcome a lack of popular support. To demonstrate their ideological purity and support a SEP conference, Acámbaro's masonic town council organized a parade on October 29, 1934, in favor of socialist education.[235] Federal congressman Mariano M. Vértiz, who was desperately trying to avoid charges of fanaticism, publicized the rally in the ruling party's Mexico City daily, *El Nacional*. Vértiz boasted that three thousand agraristas and workers marched alongside teachers in a show of revolutionary solidarity. In fact, only a few dozen Freemasons, government employees, workers, and agraristas defied Church prohibitions against joining the parade; even Acámbaro's state congressman claimed he was too sick to participate. When the town council banned a Catholic counterdemonstration against the SEP, Acámbaro's UNPF members responded by infiltrating the prorevolutionary march, shouting "down with socialist education!" and "death to General Calles!" Knives were reportedly brandished.[236] In retaliation, Governor Ortega arrested Father Daniel Mireles, Acámbaro ACM's chaplain, for ringing church bells on Christmas Eve. Ortega refused to negotiate a resolution with Acámbaro's business community, and a few weeks later an entire family was arrested for reading a pastoral letter against socialist education.[237] The October 29 demonstration and subsequent crackdown fueled a sense of moral outrage among Catholics in Acámbaro.

The demonstration debacle revealed three serious obstacles to the revolutionary project. First, anticlericalism splintered the SEP's natural constituency in Acámbaro. Government employees and state teachers refused to march even when it might cost them their jobs. Against an effective campaign by Catholic organizers working inside agrarista communities and the rail workers' union, government organizers desperately offered marchers "pulque, pesos, and barbecue"—but found few takers.[238] Second, SEP teachers were now identified with unpopular local politicians linked to the masonic clique; some were pulled into Ayala's political orbit.[239] Third, Catholic opposition could no longer be contained by Ayala.

By the end of 1934, Acámbaro's Catholics felt besieged: unjust laws silenced church bells, perfidious politicians broke promises, a murderous masonic cabal ruled town hall, and federal teachers taught immorality. This powerful narrative of Catholic victimization inspired many to embrace the Church's call for licit civil disobedience. Others went further. Under the aegis of the Church's radial strategy, female teachers, catechists, and activists set up chapters of the UNPF and another, more radical Catholic parents' organization in neighborhoods and rural communities. Veterans of the pro-cristero LNDLR enlisted as well. Betrayed by Ortega and Ayala, Acámbaro's commercial elites lent the movement their economic and social capital.[240]

Catholic resistance took many forms, from refusal to rent public buildings to the SEP for Red Saturday cultural assemblies to appointing pro-Catholic antiagrarista comisarios and delegados municipales to govern villages and haciendas. The latter frustrated attempts to open schools and stymied teachers' attempts to draft petitions for land grants.[241] The Church's grassroots campaign against socialist education dovetailed with landowner resistance to ejidos.

José de Jesús Álvarez del Castillo had much to fear from agrarian reform: at nine thousand hectares, his hacienda Andocutín was by far the largest in Acámbaro. (It included two railroad stations.) In spite of his wealth, Don José was reportedly so cheap that he went to the barbershop to read the newspaper. He supported the delahuertista revolt and Green candidates to keep agraristas at bay during the 1920s. In the mid-1930s, he wanted to elect the head of his white guard, Melchor Velarde, mayor. At the same time, Álvarez del Castillo sponsored Parents of the Family chapters on his haciendas Jaripeo (the overseer's wife helped run it) and Andocutín to foil federal teachers.[242]

The contentious reception of the revolutionary project posed a number of thorny challenges for the SEP. In Acámbaro, teachers tried to build support by opening a night school for male workers as well as one that taught the domestic arts to young women.[243] Intentionally or not, these programs competed with the ACM for the same social sectors: young, working-class men and women. Urban areas, though, were always secondary to the campo. Educators presumed the unschooled hamlets in the Sierra de los Agustinos or large haciendas like Andocutín would welcome agrarian reform along with their schools. But the SEP faced, in Inspector Macías's words, "scorn and hostility from all quarters."[244] By the end of the 1933–34 school year, only six of the forty-odd schools in the district still functioned normally.[245]

Many factors hampered the SEP. One inspector admitted that most teachers lacked sufficient preparation. Some male teachers drank, he complained, and some female instructors were *liviana* (flighty or flirty, a term that says as much about institutionalized sexism in the SEP as it does about the women's performance). Many were chronically late; others eventually stopped coming to work. These were common problems for the SEP across Mexico, given its low salaries and the insufficient preparation of teachers for their demanding jobs.[246] Yet the SEP managed to eventually mitigate such shortcomings in many regions. In southeastern Guanajuato, however, Catholic resistance deeply embedded in society played a decisive role in hamstringing the SEP.

The revolutionary project did germinate in some places in the subregion. The most fertile soil was found in small agrarista communities like Chupícuaro (Jerécuaro municipio), Irámuco, and Chamácuaro (the latter two in Acámbaro municipio). A few villages, such as Irámuco, were still indigenous. Irámuco's ethnic identity, which survived acculturating pressures during the Liberal Reform and Porfiriato, unified the community during a long struggle (dating back to 1917) trying to recover communal land from hacienda Andocutín.[247]

But agrarista communities, whether mestizo or Indian, were few and far between. White terror and Catholic resistance in the 1920s halted some nascent agrarista movements sparked by the Revolution. In May 1926, federal troops prevented a shoot-out in the village of Chamácuaro between agraristas and a Catholic syndicate founded by Father José Guillén of Acámbaro (a Catholic gunman shouted "death to the agraristas" and "viva Cristo Rey!").[248] Under the guise of keeping the peace in the midst of the Cristiada, Ayala deputized antiagrarian pistoleros to terrorize prorevolutionary peasants. Acámbaro's *acordada* (constabulary) colluded with a feared cristero captain, Vicente "el Catorce" Hernández, to eliminate agraristas. One white guard killed and mutilated the president of Chupícuaro's ejido. Only the presence of federal troops restrained Ayala from killing an agrarista defensa rural leader from Cañadas de Tiro in Tarimoro municipio. With good reason, agraristas of Obrajuelos considered Ayala a blood enemy.[249]

Ayala's caciquismo, the clergy, and Cristeros together denied scattered agrarista communities security, divided them along religious lines, and isolated them from federal support. It is not surprising, then, that in the early 1930s few peasant communities followed the agrarista example of Obrajuelos, the federal government's model ejido. Once communal identity was solidified as agrarista or Catholic during the mid-1920s, political and cultural valency was firmly set. Such polarization helps explain why agrarista Obrajuelos founded an Anticlerical League at the prompting of a federal teacher in the thirties—and why only three other communities did the same. Once a peasant or peon community's Catholic identity hardened in Guanajuato, it rarely "flipped" to embrace the revolutionary project even after the Church-state conflict waned.

After suffering numerous setbacks during the 1933–34 academic year, the SEP regrouped, wagering that Calles's mandate and the newfound support of local politicos for socialist education would lead to breakthroughs in the fall of 1934. Inspectors and teachers lectured parents on the benefits of the new educational methods and reassured them about their intentions. At the same time, they hoped to use these meetings to subtly undermine "fanaticism" by explaining natural phenomena with science.[250] There were no recorded incidents of iconoclasm in the subregion, even at the height of the Psychological Revolution. Yet outside of a handful of communities, positive results were not forthcoming.

Like Catholics, teachers and inspectors fashioned narratives combining fact and presumption to rationalize failures and demonize foes. Gloomy SEP reports attest to the effectiveness of Catholic civil disobedience and blamed a global reactionary plot for duping parents. Why else would the ignorant parents "blindly" follow priestly orders to keep children home?[251]

Catholic parents' groups and activists intensified their work in the fall of 1934, distributing pastoral letters and occasionally penning anonymous manifestos brimming with incendiary charges and occasional threats. In response to teachers' resistance to socialist education, the SEP tried to force maestros to pledge to teach the new curriculum. Several female teachers refused and were dismissed from their posts.[252] During the 1935 calendar year, of the approximately forty federal rural schools in the subregion, boycotts forced the SEP to close seven by June and seven more by December. On at least one hacienda, Catholic parents' groups refused to let the federal school open at all.[253]

As the Catholic campaign grew, physical intimidation became a factor. During 1935, a potshot barely missed teacher Alfonso Durán, and a mob of women tried to stab maestro rural David Cano. Agrarista peasants saved both of them, as well as a third teacher, Miss María Guadalupe Álvarez. Her school was located on a ranch in Jaral del Progreso municipio, just east of Salvatierra. Faced by an effective truancy strike, the SEP inspector came to the community in March 1935. When inducements failed, she threatened parents with arrest and fines for breaking truancy laws. Peasant mothers retaliated by stoning the building, breaking down the door, and smashing desks, then beating the teacher. Community members barely managed to save the teacher's life. She soon fled to Acámbaro.[254]

This was defensive segunda violence (female perpetrators, often ritual nature, nonlethal outcome), but its connection to the Church remains murky. The cells of catechists and clergy coordinating attendance strikes probably primed peasant communities to take violent measures because their attacks on socialist education were laced with talk of bolshevik plots and even innuendo about child molestation. For instance, in Tacamballo hamlet (Jerécuaro municipio), the federal teacher received an anonymous letter under his door at the end of the 1933–34 school year, reading in part, "We do not want Protestant teachers here. If you don't want to happen to you what happened to those [teachers] of Puroagua then by August first either resign or we will wring your neck for teaching sensuality to the children." The SEP blamed a priest and catechists for spreading the rumors. True or not, the letter proves that peasants had knowledge of a wider campaign against the SEP thanks to the efforts of Catholic organizers.[255] Wild gossip, of course, could and did spread on its own, and Archbishop Ruiz condemned violence.[256] The dense Catholic network of catechists, priests, and parents' groups, combined with its anti-SEP discourse, explains why defensive segunda violence erupted here despite the absence of direct provocations like iconoclasm or recorded cases of sexual abuse.

The institutional Church's response to the revolutionary project certainly played a significant role in creating conditions that enabled segunda violence to erupt in southeastern Guanajuato. Cuervo's talk of Tabascanizing Guanajuato's schools in the spring of 1935 made matters worse. An inspector elsewhere in the Bajío criticized Cuervo's incendiary threats: "it would not be humane to spring a stupid or insincere 'Red Shirt' campaign on the teachers because they would be assassinated."[257] Countermeasures by SEP, such as forcing Catholic teachers to choose between their jobs and their religious beliefs and threatening parents with jail sentences, were counterproductive and antagonized ardent Catholics and moderates in the revolutionary camp alike.

Defensive violence in this subregion and elsewhere was not just a product of the conflicts over socialist education. Catholics here, like those in the north, viewed the Psychological Revolution and socialist education as the latest in a series of threats to communal religious unity. Long before the Psychological Revolution, Catholics had violently reacted against religious dissidence. In June 1922, a Catholic mob in Acámbaro ripped the doors off the Baptist mission and looted it.[258] On August 1, 1926, two federal employees driving past a closed church in the town were recognized and stoned. One of the engineers pulled his pistol and jumped out of the car but was enveloped by a mob that gathered quickly. Both federal officials died in the ensuing melee.[259] Given this history, some spontaneous defensive violence would probably have erupted against SEP schools when they opened with or without the Church's radial campaign, and institutional restraint was much more difficult because of this tradition of faith-based vigilantism.

The campaign against socialist education unintentionally encouraged offensive segunda violence as well, although attacks against teachers and agraristas perpetrated by well-armed, mounted, all-male commandos were less common in the southeast than in the rest of Guanajuato.[260] Segunderos' motives are always hard to pinpoint, given the scant historical record. Insurgents in southeastern Guanajuato probably fought for the same mix of reasons identified by Enrique Guerra in neighboring Michoacán's Segunda. There, ragtag bands with complex motives had neither widespread popular support nor many volunteers. Morale was low due to the opposition of the Archdiocese of Morelia's clergy to the Segunda. Consequently, they operated in small, autonomous, self-sustained groups. Some segunda chieftains fought for the faith. Others sought amnesty for previous violence or other political concessions. Still others were recristeros unable to reintegrate into civilian society after the Arreglos. Like their counterparts in Michoacán, segunderos in Acámbaro had to cut deals with hacendados or steal from the poor simply to survive.[261]

The connection to Catholicism was much weaker in offensive than defensive violence, although many who rode in segunda gangs undoubtedly felt that they were defending the faith. Furthermore, the role of hacendados was unquestionably greater in offensive violence. In some places, ties between hacendados and segunderos reactivated old bonds forged in the first Cristiada. One Acámbaro hacendado gave cristeros a stud bull in hopes that the fighters would keep agraristas at bay.[262] In the 1930s, as in the 1920s, white terror silenced federal teachers and agrarista leaders. That said, Acámbaro's landowners were much less willing to back segunderos than their more martial northern counterparts like the Azanza, perhaps because so many were absentee owners with weak ties to their employees.

The relatively pacific attitude of southeastern hacendados assisted the government's counterinsurgency campaign. Groups of segunderos who dared to operate for any length of time around Acámbaro ran a much greater risk of detection and elimination by the federal military than those in the north. As in the first Cristero War, agraristas served as scouts, spies, and auxiliaries for federal troops in the Sierra de los Agustinos.[263] Ramón Silva's small band of segunderos roamed around Acámbaro municipio, but in spring of 1936, federal forces chased Silva north to Celaya and soundly defeated him.[264]

By the end of 1937, sagging popular support and military reverses forced Acámbaro's segunderos to choose among four paths: become white guards, turn to banditry, give up the fight entirely, or temporarily go back to civilian life and reform their unit in the future. A few groups took this last option and continued to menace federal schools sporadically in remote upcountry settlements or on hacienda Puroagua in Jerécuaro.[265] One segunda cell dared to operate in the town of Acámbaro, killing a teacher the day before Christmas Eve in 1938 and almost assassinating SEP inspector and Communist organizer Genaro Hernández a few weeks later.[266] Before considering the eventual fate of the revolutionary project and its Catholic opponents in Acámbaro in the late 1930s, though, I want to turn to the peripheral municipios in the southeast.

Salvatierra was a typical Bajío town of about eight thousand souls. With a tiny liberal minority (CROMista bakery workers and a few other anticlericals so frightened that their denunciations of "fanatics" were invariably anonymous), the voto morado was virtually sovereign. The National Catholic Party candidates swept elections in 1912; after the Constitutionalists disbanded it, local party activists joined the Knights of Columbus. Salvatierra's Knights bitterly protested Obregón's religious policy in 1923. From his pulpit, a priest endorsed Angel Flores over "clerophobe" Calles in 1924. State authorities had to forcibly close Flores's campaign headquarters and nullify municipal elections that same year. During the Cristiada, Salvatierra's lay leaders (industrialists, hotel owners, and other businessmen) paralyzed local commerce; some broke Ruiz's strict orders against aiding the Cristiada and supported Rodolfo Gallegos, a local tenant farmer who became cristero commander of Guanajuato.[267]

As in Acámbaro, Salvatierra's Catholic leaders were used and then discarded by Ortega's local operative in 1931 and 1932. Red state congressman Rafael Patiño campaigned promising to defend religious liberties and clean up town hall. Once in office, he and his cronies skimmed from public works projects and exploited Ortega's hated alcohol and salt taxes. By 1934, Patiño was harshly (if unevenly) enforcing anticlerical laws, expelling three Capuchin nuns and mochos (presumably lay activists) and nationalizing a chapel. Even worse in the eyes of Catholics, Patiño patronized a masonic lodge that enlisted local workers and anti-Catholic pistoleros from Michoacán and tried to set up satellite lodges in nearby villages and rancherías, probably hoping to unite old CROMistas and veteran agraristas into a single revolutionary front.[268] Facing Catholic protests, Ortega and Patiño named a despised former tax collector as police chief to repress lay activists. In January 1935, the new chief jailed two "innocent damas" for passing out flyers against the SEP, and Patiño's masonic regime allegedly murdered a young carpenter.[269]

A trio of priests captained Salvatierra's faithful against their revolutionary oppressors. Saintly, poor, and much beloved, Father Rafael Lemus led nonviolent resistance to the government during the Cristiada. Father Miguel Lucatero was a former cristero chaplain run out of Michoacán by General Lázaro Cárdenas. His fiery homilies alleged federal schools taught Communist impiety and perverted children; he even blamed the drought on Patiño's masonic lodge. More ominously, Lucatero warned the faithful, "prepare yourselves, brothers, because the struggle will be terrible." Father José María Espinosa was a man cut from Patricio Arroyo's cloth, schooled in Ruiz's social Catholic doctrine and skilled at organizing. With the help of seminarians, Espinosa set up UNPF chapters to oversee attendance strikes in Salvatierra's surrounding villages and hamlets. The unusually high number of priests in the municipio (ten, reportedly) led anticlericals to call Salvatierra a veritable "monks' birdcage." The UNPF passed out fascist-leaning newspapers like *Acción Cívica* and alarming flyers—one charged that atheistic socialist education was "destroying the family by despoiling parents of their children [by teaching] acceptance of free love and taking advantage of so-called sexual education to corrupt the youth."[270]

The radial strategy blanketed peasant villages and peon communities across Salvatierra municipio with propaganda, Catholic parents' meetings, and priestly visits. One hacendado salaried catechists.[271] Salvatierra's venerable Damas Católicas, recruited mainly from the town's notable families, were the heart and soul of the underground ACM and its public front, a UNPF chapter. The Damas used home visits (including large-scale pamphleteering) to spur attendance strikes. They even filed complaints about chronically tardy teachers. Church propaganda, confessional advisories, and angry sermons convinced many female teachers in federal service to refuse to teach the new methods.[272]

Local authorities, in spite of diputado Patiño's conversion to anticlericalism, were notably unsympathetic to federal teachers. Salvatierra's town council and municipal employees rarely missed mass in 1935, and they appointed municipal delegates to rural communities that refused to support SEP schools without direct orders from Melchor Ortega. The orders never came.[273]

Initially, federal teachers were optimistic that local agraristas would second their efforts. Back in 1923, federal authorities created three ejidos in the municipio (Urireo and Cupareo villages, the peon community of hacienda San José del Carmen). But Governor Colunga and the Greens mercilessly harried agraristas during the 1920s, deputizing hacendado pistoleros to disarm them as bandits, blocking a CROM request for land and the hacienda's chapel, and busting a CROMista bakery workers syndicate in Salvatierra proper.[274] In 1931 and 1932, Ortega's administration, along with Patiño and the town council, used the pretense of electoral violence and a crime wave to form posses—technically acordadas or defensas sociales—to disarm agraristas who had fought against cristeros; they also jailed a peasant leader who had long tried to carve an ejido out of the Villagómez's hacienda. With the help of Governor Ortega and General Bonifacio Salinas, the federal army commander for the region, Father J. Jesús Arriaga set up a defensa social in Urireo village to suppress the agraristas' defensa rural.[275]

Social agitation over the religious question undid remarkable progress by SEP teachers in Salvatierra. In the early 1930s, maestros rurales overcame priestly condemnation of agrarian reform to help set up three new ejidos. The federal schools combined material improvements with what Inspector Arnulfo Ochoa called "spiritual betterment," which he believed to be the best way to defanaticize. The key was to convince peasants of the "voracity of priests." Didactic plays staged by teachers created a "new consciousness of spiritual liberty."[276] However, charges that socialist education posed a moral threat to the family halted the SEP's momentum. Women in hamlets and on haciendas once cheered for the agraristas against the jefe político and priest in plays performed in federal schools. Now, however, they heeded the warning of the Damas Católicas about the danger of sexual education and the Red Shirts. In 1935, the SEP worked with embattled agraristas to try to open new schools and petition for new ejidos, but the municipal delegates and UNPF chapters thwarted them. Three schools had to be closed at the end of the 1934–35 school year.[277]

Conservative local politicos and Catholic activists arrayed against the revolutionary teacher-worker-agrarista alliance had two advantages: a long tradition of educated laywomen and an unusually large rural middle class of tenants and sharecroppers due to the absence of latifundia in the municipio. On the first count, Salvatierra's female Catholic activists were the modern equivalent of the town's colonial Carmelite *beateria*, a community of literate laywomen who lived regulated, secluded, habited lives and ran a boarding school for girls. Patiño closed Salvatierra's Capuchin convent, but its nuns probably stayed close to home and helped run home schools.[278]

On the second count, only Salvatierra of the six southeastern counties had no large haciendas. This was ranchero country.[279] In another part of the Bajío, northwestern Michoacán, Purnell argues that similar ranchero communities like San José de Gracia and Cojumatlán were Hispanic and levitical. Priests, not the ayuntamiento, made important communal decisions. The trinity of a resurgent Church, upwardly mobile rancheros, and Porfirian railroads made ranchero Michoacán prosperous before the Revolution. For Catholic smallholders, the revolutionary state's anticlericalism and agrarianism attacked their most cherished notions: private property rights, orthodox Catholic culture, and the priests' authority.[280] A similar dynamic prevailed in Salvatierra, where ranchero piety (and willingness to tithe), along with priests and Catholic matrons, contained the spread of agrarian reform and socialist education. The efficacy of licit civil resistance and high density of priests explains why there was little segunda violence in Salvatierra, even though some landowners led armed bands to support the delahuertistas and extinguish agrarian "bandits."[281]

In rural Tarandacuao municipio, the archdiocesan seminary gave the institutional Church considerable influence. Throughout the 1930s, dozens of young seminarians cooperated with landowners José Morelos and Victor Campos to organize opposition to SEP schools and ejidos. Both answered to José Martínez, president of the parochial ACM, head of the dominant political clique from 1935 on, and Almazán's campaign chief in 1939–40. Tarandacuao's Catholics grew stronger during the Cardenista sexenio: in 1938, the mayor received mass dressed as a Tereciario; the wife of a former federal teacher directed a successful boycott of SEP schools. In 1940, federal teachers lamented that "reaction is totally secure" in Tarandacuao.[282]

In Tarimoro municipio, Catholics never strayed from the Church's strategy of apolitical, licit resistance. Politicians long catered to Catholic brokers here; in the heated 1931 gubernatorial election, Greens promised to return Tarimoro's church.[283] No surprise, then, that the SEP made little headway. In mid-1933, priests denounced peasants who sent children to federal schools as heretics. Attendance quickly plummeted. Catholic parents' groups monitored schools for any hint of socialist education, reminded parents of Church teachings, and opened home schools. The SEP was soon forced to close schools and transfer some teachers out of Tarimoro to more promising municipios. By the fall of 1935, the SEP superintendent complained that many classrooms were vacant, while teachers feared for their lives. When the SEP's roving cultural mission arrived, pro-Catholic propaganda claimed it insulted the family by teaching prostitution. When federal teachers staged civic fiestas in schools to honor national heroes and celebrate student athletic events, priests' homilies kept parishioners at home. In Llano Grande ranchería, Catholics burned school books and demanded the return of the syllabary of San Miguel used in Porfirian classrooms. Its school, like many others in Tarimoro, was soon empty and then closed.[284] Land reform, teachers hoped, would turn the tide, but when ejidos were granted in late 1935, the archdiocese insured that catechists visited communities to counsel against signing agrarian petitions.[285]

More than anything else, the teachers lacked reliable local collaborators in Tarimoro. The Church's influence had not always been hegemonic. In the 1920s, agraristas took up arms to fight white terror at the hands of pro-landowner rural guards. To break an economic boycott, agraristas raided haciendas for seeds and animals. The cycle of violence allowed landowners to brand agraristas as criminals.[286] Proclaiming that law and order had to be restored, Green governor Enrique Colunga and Congressman David Ayala named local landowner Felipe Montoyo to raise a home guard, which disarmed and selectively murdered agraristas between 1924 and 1927.[287] Terror smothered Tarimoro's nascent agrarista movement. In the 1930s, catechists and Catholic parents' organizations successfully isolated federal schools from any social support. Federal teachers simply arrived too late in Tarimoro.

In Jerécuaro municipio, the revolutionary project experienced its greatest success in the southeast. Here agrarista allies helped revolutionary teachers wear down a strong coalition of landowners, Catholic activists, and sharecroppers. Their name, Aparecerios Libres (free tenant farmers), underscored their appeal to rugged ranchero individualism against agrarista collectivism. Jerécuaro's clergy tried to quarantine agrarian sentiment, which had had sympathizers since the 1920s. In April 1935 on hacienda Petemoro, Father Carlos Rios tried to get peasants to resign from the agrarian committee and join the ACM.[288] The municipio's socioeconomic inequality favored the revolutionary coalition; seven large haciendas monopolized most arable land (other southeastern municipios had three or fewer), making peasants more land hungry.[289] Intriguingly, Jerécuaro is the only municipio in Guanajuato outside the Sierra Gorda where at least one indigenous language is still spoken today; indigenous identity must have been even stronger in the 1930s, a cultural trait that could have facilitated bottom-up, prorevolutionary mobilizations. Since the Revolution's armed phase, the agraristas of Chupícuaro (a sizeable village) not only had demanded land, but also had attacked the Church. Since the 1920s, Jerécuaro's Green boss, Mariano Martínez, patronized and helped arm residents of the San Lucas ejido. By 1936, Cardenista officials had granted land and arms to agraristas of Santa Isabel and Paso de Oveja.[290] Even the election of pro-Catholic, antiagrarian town councils throughout the 1930s could not roll back the revolutionary project in Jerécuaro.

Still, the SEP found it hard to expand beyond the preexisting pockets of agrarista sentiment in the municipio. On hacienda Puroagua, a vast estate founded in the late sixteenth century, a formidable coalition of landowners, clergy, and Catholics prevailed over the federal schools. When the SEP tried to open a school for peons on the hacienda grounds in the fall of 1934, the hacendado patronized a large, clandestine parochial school and subsidized catechists from Acámbaro to visit and aid the resident priest in organizing a boycott. The standoff dragged on for months, then years. The SEP refused to close its school, but most peons refused to send their children to class. After the teacher received death threats, Inspector Macías expelled Father Perea in retaliation; however, opposition to SEP schooling only deepened. As late as 1939, a band of segunderos, probably supported by the hacendado, were still menacing agraristas on Puroagua. In 1940, the SEP finally closed its school there.[291] Still, in Jerécuaro municipio as a whole, agraristas and federal teachers held their own against segunderos and catechists. Chupícuaro and two nearby ejidos were rare agrarian strongholds in the Bajío; their existence allowed the revolutionary project to claim a measure of success in the subregion.[292]

In Coroneo, the SEP made more modest but still substantial gains. In this small (population five thousand), mountainous municipio wedged between Jerécuaro and the state of Querétaro, a revolutionary coalition of agraristas and teachers gained the upper hand after a long struggle. Their chief opponent, Father Antonio Romero López, operated in spite of numerous legal charges lodged against him. He and his allies helped to elect Catholics to the town hall; his sister ran the local state school. Father Romero gave Coroneo's Catholics a stark message: "to be an agrarista . . . is to be an enemy of religion." In Coroneo, it was also to risk your life. Segunderos were underwritten by prominent merchants in town, and the Segunda in Coroneo followed a larger, statewide trend and evolved into white terror aimed at stymieing land reform. In 1937, segunderos attacked houses of peasants who signed an agrarian petition. Yet teachers persevered, ejidos survived, and the SEP concluded in 1940 that the municipio was "one of the few places we have conquered." Why did the revolutionary coalition prevail? Perhaps teachers were more skilled and determined. Some rural communities self-identified as indigenous, which may have facilitated land reform by overcoming divisions. Local leadership also attracted strong patrons. The Green federal congressman and governor, Enrique Fernández Martínez, took an unusually strong interest in Coroneo's ejidos. Agrarista leader Juventino Mondragón sent the ruling party's National Peasant Confederation (CNC) frequent complaints.[293] Although the revolutionary project gained a measure of success in the smaller communities of the municipio, Jesús Pérez Tinajero, a wealthy merchant who backed the Segunda, went on to be elected mayor of the town at least three times.[294]

Heedless of the chronic conflicts roiling southeastern Guanajuato due largely to the religious question, the federal agrarian bureaucracy ground slowly ahead in processing petitions for ejidal grants in the southeast. By the end of the 1930s, the rate of agrarian reform was accelerating. In 1938, only 10 percent of the land designated for transfer in Acámbaro was in the hands of ejidatarios. By 1940, virtually all of it was. On paper, Cárdenas could claim a resounding success here: haciendas shrank into small holdings (*pequeñas propiedades*) and many ejidos were on the map. But owners were allowed to keep irrigated land, meaning that most new grants, especially those made to peons, were of dry, infertile land. Many medium farmers still had to lease or sharecrop.[295] Corruption made matters even worse. By 1939, some Ejidal Bank officials were in cahoots with Bajío grain merchants close to Governor Fernández Martínez to sell ejidatarios short and even pilfer their parcels of land.[296]

The other pillar of the revolutionary project, federal schools, was just as shaky in southeastern Guanajuato by 1940. The ebbing of conflicts around the religious question meant the Church slowly relaxed the attendance strikes, but cultural resistance to schooling girls remained. In rural areas of the Rosary Belt, coeducation was seen as a slippery slope leading to immorality. The illiterate father or husband thought his literate daughter or wife might deceive him.[297] New problems emerged. To survive, sharecroppers and ejidatarios had to send children to work, not to school. Legally, once hacendados were transformed into smallholders due to the loss of much of their land, they no longer had to legally pay teachers. So while in 1929 every ejido had its own SEP school, many of those created during the push at the end of the Cardenista sexenio did not.[298] For all these reasons, only 29 percent of boys and 22 percent of girls went to federal schools in Acámbaro in 1938.[299] Francisco Javier Meyer Cosío concluded that even after agrarian reform's completion, Acámbaro was still "almost exclusively Catholic, young, and illiterate."[300]

The Cardenista agrarian reform failed to transform local politics. Green governors Enrique Fernández Martínez and Luis I. Rodríguez preferred to come to terms with established local cliques rather than reach out to agrarista-teacher coalitions, another consequence of the enduring electoral power of Catholics. In Acámbaro, a clique of veteran Red politicos controlling voting blocs of railroad workers and ejidatarios claimed town hall, but these politicos did little to aid struggling ejidos and had no stomach to take on a resurgent Church. In Salvatierra, a faction with little backing among the ejidatarios and conservative views on the religious question was ascendant by the late 1930s. It was headed by an unlikely troika: Ignacio Ortíz, a former state congressman and one of the "Three Musketeers" who ran Salvatierra's politics in the 1920s; Miguel Chimes, an up-and-coming Lebanese Mexican entrepreneur looking to turn a business fortune into real estate by buying up chunks of ejidos; and Rafael Murillo Moreno, state congressman and former mayor who was close to Governor Enrique Fernández and federal bureaucrats. In Tarandacuao, Cardenista governor Luis I. Rodríguez backed the antiagrarian triumvirate that represented Catholic and hacendado interests. In Jerécuaro, Cardenista governors of the late 1930s backed the return to power of another veteran Green, Mariano Martínez. The former seminarian protected the collection of tithes when anticlerical agraristas in Chupícuaro tried to end them.[301]

In this political climate, the ACM and other formal Catholic organizations operated with a great deal more liberty across the subregion. The arrival of a SEP cultural mission at the start of the 1936 school year was greeted with an angry sermon by the ACM delivered via loudspeaker in Acámbaro. By 1937, Acámbaro's ACM had a fully functioning parish committee with four branches separated by gender and age and an impressive twenty subcommittees in rural hamlets and haciendas.[302] Sinarquismo grew even faster. In Acámbaro proper, Arturo Vallejo, a pharmacist, headed a large chapter with the support of at least one hacendado.[303] By 1943, the Sinarchists in Acámbaro municipio had fifty subcommittees with 2,200 male and 1,200 female members.[304] Its rapid growth reflected not only the persistence of Catholic values, but also the troubled history of agrarian reform.

To suppress the growing Sinarquista movement and end scattered segunda violence, the army dispatched Colonel Roberto Calvo Ramírez and his Eighteenth Infantry Battalion to Acámbaro in late 1939. The colonel armed and organized scattered agrarista militias into a reserve army battalion. An ardent Communist, Calvo proved incorruptible by landowners. Following his orders, soldiers and agrarian militia suppressed white guards and surviving segunda bands in Puroagua, Jerécuaro, and a few other foci of white terror. Calvo's men also broke up the sinarquistas and campaign committees organized by opposition presidential candidate Juan Andreu Almazán in late 1939 and early 1940. Eventually, popular repudiation of Calvo's tactics forced his removal; some agrarian militia members reportedly murdered, raped, and even castrated their foes. By arming and deputizing agrarian leaders like Ignacio Sánchez, Calvo rendered the landowners powerless to violently intimidate ejidos; when agraristas took revenge for years of repression, Catholics believed that the federal government was fomenting atheistic anarchy.[305]

By 1940, the SEP could claim few successes in changing the deeply rooted religious practices and beliefs in southeastern Guanajuato. Years of teaching scientific explanations of nature had, noted one federal educator, "persuaded [peasants] of the practical necessity of using science to better their standard of living," but they were still just as attached to the Church and as suspicious of the federal government.[306] Agents of the revolutionary project always believed changing the socioeconomic structure would alter religious beliefs. Did new ejidatarios reject the old faith? When federal authorities set up ejidos in Acámbaro municipio in late 1934, Terciarios soon came to collect tithes and first fruits.[307] Most apparently paid. By the time the reform wound down in 1940, most ejidatarios self-identified as Catholic.[308]

A few levitical communities in southeastern Guanajuato did become pro-revolutionary, accepting federal schools and ejidos. The question remains: why did a few "flip"? Few microhistories of peasant communities in the guanajuatense Bajío exist to identify the factors explaining revolutionary transformation. Chris Boyer, Matthew Butler, and Jenny Purnell, however, all examined local conflicts between cristeros and agraristas in another Bajío state, Michoacán, during the Cristiada. Their works show that in the space of a few years, pro-Church peasant communities could be persuaded to support the revolutionary project—given the right conditions. Boyer found that in the

Catholic Cacicazgos in Guanajuato 213

largely indigenous community of Chichimequillas, for example, Governor Francisco Múgica's land reform in the early 1920s "uncorked popular radicalism," although a substantial number of peasants still clung to the Church.[309]

For his part, Matthew Butler focused on the struggle between priests and revolutionaries (Protestants, agraristas, and some teachers) in Michoacán in the 1920s and came to four conclusions quite relevant for southeastern Guanajuato in the 1930s. First, many mestizo ranchero communities that "flipped" revolutionary were only superficially Catholic to begin with, due largely to their historical origins in the nineteenth-century Liberal Reform. Second, lack of priests and a declining economic base debilitated the Church presence in many communities before the Revolution; if a degree of pro-revolutionary sentiment ruptured Catholic hegemony and destigmatized agrarianism, the Church's influence over public life declined even more. This decline, in turn, increased the likelihood of a far-reaching realignment. Third, some indigenous (Otomí, Mazahua) communities accepted Protestantism and agrarianism even as they continued to observe some elements of syncretic Catholic worship, suggesting that indigenous communities were more receptive than mestizo ones to the revolutionary project. Fourth, exemplary priests (men like Arroyo in Ciudad González and Espinosa in Salvatierra) with abundant "charismatic energy" could help keep wavering communities from embracing the revolutionary project. Priestly sponsorship of strong lay organizations (Nocturnal Vigil, Union of Catholic Workers and Farmers) seems to have been especially important.[310] Underdeveloped Catholic institutions, the desacralization of local life, indigenous culture's openness to agrarianismo, and the absence of energetic priests disposed communities to accept the revolutionary project. But such communities were relatively uncommon.

In southeastern Guanajuato, communities possessing these characteristics were even more rare than in Michoacán. Ironically, the absence of a large, self-identified indigenous population was largely the work of the nineteenth-century Liberal Reform, which privatized Tarascan, Otomí, and Chichimec pueblos' ejidos. Indians Hispanicized when they became peon haciendas or urban house servants.[311] In Acámbaro municipio, the village of Irámuco could still look back to its indigenous past in the sixteenth century, although Red Party agrarista leader Romulo Morales renamed his Agrarian Indigenous Committee in Acámbaro a "peasant organization" in 1926, suggesting that indigenous identity had limited political value and tenuous historical roots.[312]

The fact that the rural poor predominantly identified as mestizo facilitated the institutional Church's attempts to standardize and Hispanicize religious practice to supplant syncretic ritual. The patron-client connections between wealthy white patrons and servant and peon clients created cross-class linkages used by lay activists and clergy to convince peasants to boycott schools and reject land reform. As we have seen in Campeche, Guerrero, and Hidalgo, the revolutionary project "took" best where effective teachers found preexisting peasant support for revolutionary change, and where teachers found ethnic and class divisions that they could leverage. The SEP was much more likely to succeed where its teachers allied with poor peons and peasants against wealthier townsfolk and landowners. In some predominantly indigenous communities, class lines paralleled ethnic divisions. But there were only a small number of places in southeastern Guanajuato where this strategy could work. Catholic values complicated attempts to forge teacher-agrarista coalitions in the southeast. The Church's defense of private property as a natural right helped divide agrarian communities. In agrarista Obrajuelos (and likely elsewhere), many peasants rejected land reform as not *decente* (roughly, moral).[313] In Jerécuaro and Coroneo, the survival of indigenous self-identity in some communities might well have helped to neutralize Catholic condemnations of land reform.

Conclusion

Strong Catholic cacicazgos headed by Azanza, Lámbarri, and Peña in the north and Ayala's weaker one in the southeast frustrated the revolutionary project—even as they helped sustain some aspects of the postrevolutionary regime including basic governance. Catholic cacicazgos empowered the voto morado, facilitated the Segunda, and protected cells boycotting federal schools. At times their impact was subtle. For instance, when faced with widespread resistance of Ciudad González's civil society sustained by Lámbarri's Catholic cacicazgo, the cultural mission and military overreacted. The resulting bloody conflict further delegitimized the revolutionary state in Guanajuato, and pushed Cárdenas to more quickly abandon defanaticization and to accelerate land reform. Cárdenas believed that ending the Psychological Revolution, combined with intensified agrarian reform, would create a structural transformation that would open the minds of the rural poor to a new, modern mentality free of "fanaticism." In spite of episcopal moderation, the Church in Guanajuato was slow to warm to such overtures.

Bishop Valverde warned of "the great danger of the socialist school" in April 1938.[314] During the 1940s, Bishop Valverde skillfully countered the revolutionary project. For instance, he parried SEP attempts to appropriate Mother's Day by organizing special masses for the same. By attending Catholic services instead of teachers' celebrations, women and children would not, in his words, "become enveloped in the cultural current of paganization."[315]

Catholicism alone cannot explain the failure of the revolutionary project in Guanajuato; the debacle of agrarian reform also played a role. Sociologist Nathaniel Whetten's exhaustive statistical analysis paints a bleak picture for the state. Wages actually fell in Guanajuato from 0.92 to 0.79 pesos a day from 1935 to 1940 while they rose modestly from 0.94 pesos to 1.09 pesos nationally.[316] Almost half of Guanajuato's population still went barefoot or wore sandals in 1940.[317] The illiteracy rate was 64.5 percent, far above the national rate of 51.6 percent.[318] Peasants responded not only by migrating, but also by supporting the Sinarquista movement.[319] By 1941, even unions of the CTM, the corporatist labor wing of the ruling party, were not immune from capture by Catholics.[320] Mario Armando Vázquez Soriano provocatively argues that the struggle to defend their faith from the revolutionary project begun in Guanajuato by cristeros and continued by sinarquistas culminated in the election of guanajuatense Vicente Fox as president in July 2000.[321]

Such sweeping claims must be carefully weighed against historical evidence but on the whole ring true. To start with, millions of Mexicans outside the Rosary Belt cast votes for Fox. Returning to the 1930s, some Catholics were drawn into the revolutionary political sphere by Catholic caciques such as those of Azanza and Ayala—men who claimed to defend the Church's moral order. During the 1930s, links between Catholic brokers and the postrevolutionary state made another Cristiada less likely and legitimized the fragile revolutionary state; local Callistas and Cardenistas alike needed the voto morado to claim electoral mandates. Yet these electoral bargains allowed Catholic middlemen to demand important concessions and claim local and regional offices. This dynamic doomed socialist education and disrupted agrarian reform in the short run. Over the long run, it allowed an opposition party that claimed to defend the Catholic moral order and relied heavily on Catholic lay leadership and Catholic ideology to take power democratically in 2000.[322]

Since its foundation in 1939, the Party of National Action (PAN, for Partido de Acción Nacional) was closely identified with the Church. While conservative business interests as well as secular intellectuals headed by the party's first president, Manuel Gómez Morin, played important roles, "militant Catholics such as [Efraín] González Luna clearly controlled the new party."[323] In the 1940 presidential campaign, a strong majority of delegates to its first convention favored endorsing Juan Andreu Almazán; reluctant leaders agreed to support him as long as Almazán upheld the party's generally Catholic principles.[324] Local histories of the PAN and Catholicism have demonstrated just how deeply connected the two were. Rossana Almada's history of the PAN in Zamora, Michoacán, shows its first cohort of leaders ran both the local chapter of the ACM and Zamora's Chamber of Commerce; their political baptism was the 1939 opposition presidential campaign of Juan Andreu Almazán. The PAN's strength, she argues, consistently lay where the "Catholic moral order" (low divorces, deference to the paterfamilias) prevailed.[325] David Shirk's perceptive study of the PAN recognizes important regional and local variations in the party's origins and trajectory and does not deny the historical tension between Catholic and more secular factions of the party. Still, Shirk concludes that in many locales Catholicism strongly influenced the PAN. Moreover, Catholic organizations like UNEC (Unión Nacional de Estudiantes Católicos, or National Union of Catholic Students) and the Sinarchistas served as "feeder organizations whose militants were channeled directly into the PAN."[326] Seen in this light, Catholic resistance to the postrevolutionary state not only frustrated agrarian reform and revolutionary schooling; it also politically mobilized a cohort of Catholic leaders. This cadre helped found and lead a largely Catholic opposition party that would take power democratically six decades later.

CONCLUSION

The End of the Religious Question

In the early 1930s, the Callista revolutionary project used SEP schools and anticlerical legislation to defanaticize, provoking widespread Catholic resistance. Clerical guidance, Catholic discourse, and the Church's organizational matrix enabled school boycotts to undermine federal schooling and in the process to imperil other, key aspects of the revolutionary project as well. Informal networks motivated by Catholic values, sanctioned by Rome's radial strategy, and loosely centered on hubs of clergy and lay activists extended into much of civil society, filling the gap between the weakened institutional Church and the fragile revolutionary state even in less levitical areas.

Instead of marginalizing Catholics politically, the renewed anticlerical campaign of the early 1930s antagonized and ultimately empowered them. Catholic electoral brokers drew on formal and informal Church organizations, ideology, and symbols to influence balloting. Ironically, governors closely identified with Calles such as Guevara and Ortega owed their elections to the voto morado.[1] Remarkably, the Catholic presence in revolutionary politics actually grew from the Arreglos to the end of the Maximato in mid-1935 as a dense but fragile web of alliances linked nominally to revolutionary officials and Catholic mediators in middle politics. Such clandestine pacts failed to decisively dull revolutionary defanaticization because regional politicos remained vulnerable to pressure from Mexico City and could not restrain determined anticlericals like Superintendent Tomás Cuervo and General Francisco Múgica who had federal authority. In this environment, some moderate revolutionary officials like Inspector Ruben Rodríguez Lozano became radicalized.

While regional and local alliances with politicos allowed the Church to weather the worst of Callista anticlericalism, they enmeshed Catholic leaders (including more than a few clergy) in electoral politics. This clearly compromised the episcopal policy of strict nonpartisanship. Even official lay organizations could be divided by factionalism. For instance, in 1939 the National Union of Catholic Students (UNEC, Unión Nacional de Estudiantes Católicos) was polarized into pro-Almazán and pro-Ávila Camacho camps.[2] For good reason, the institutional Church feared its local activists and clergy would pursue their own political ambitions as they defended the faith. Such *liderismo*, however, was an unavoidable consequence of the radial strategy of decentralized grassroots mobilizations. So too was the complicity of some Catholic leaders in segunda violence.

After breaking with Calles in mid-1935, Cárdenas restrained direct attacks on Catholics' beliefs to calm the conflicts stirred by the religious question. Events in the four states considered here corroborate Bantjes's contention that Catholic mass resistance pushed Cárdenas in a more conciliatory direction.[3] Chronic segunda violence and the bloody clash in Ciudad González also spurred Cárdenas to relax anticlerical regulation and drop defanaticization from the SEP curriculum.

In light of the broad range and cumulative impact of Catholic responses to the revolutionary project in Campeche, Hidalgo, Guerrero, and Guanajuato, recent interpretations of Cardenismo which posit that federal schooling and other culturally sensitive programs consolidated the postrevolutionary state by generating a widespread popular consensus seem less than convincing. The simple existence of negotiations and compromises between state actors and Catholic brokers does not indicate successful state formation; the outcomes of such negotiations and compromises must be carefully considered. More often than not, the postrevolutionary state failed to persuade most Mexicans to enthusiastically support secularization via federal schools or the state's agrarian reform in spite of concessions on the religious question.

Moreover, claims that Cárdenas successfully resolved the religious question by accommodating Catholic demands also misreads the Church's ultimate intent. The Church never directly challenged the postrevolutionary state. Instead, it deepened its presence in civil society to undermine key aspects of the revolutionary project and sap its legitimacy over the long run. The subtle but pervasive influence of the Church over Mexican society reflected the fact that it was far from a monolithic, timeless institution. Catholics' attitudes, just like those of the institutional Church, evolved substantially between 1929 and 1940. Kristina Boylan's perceptive study of annulment petitions during this period reveals that Catholics invoked notions of personal happiness and defined marriage as a companionate relationship, not just a sacrament.[4] Devout Catholics were not unaffected by the spread of individualism and a less patriarchal definition of the family after the Revolution. Such changes, however, were largely due to spreading market forces and the mass media (which reflected U.S. influence and growing consumerism). These trends, in addition, were only tenuously linked to the revolutionary project and likely would have taken place even without the Revolution—albeit at a slower pace.[5]

Cárdenas's concessions on the religious question in the face of this Catholic resistance did have some significant effects. The second Cristero revolt ultimately fizzled, in part because the president's cautious relaxation of anticlerical regulations discouraged support for another insurgency. Eventually, offensive segunda violence petered out in many areas. In Durgano, one important national focus of the Segunda, Cardenista agrarian reform and populism helped convince all but the most determined segunderos to lay down their arms.[6] In many regions, however, Catholic networks continued to use moral suasion to prevent peasants from joining ejidos after the Cardenista thaw in Church-state relations. Many clergy and lay leaders continued to resolutely oppose federal schooling as irreligious, even after overt anticlericalism was removed from the SEP curriculum.[7] Cárdenas's conciliation on the religious question was often not reciprocated by Catholics when it came to agrarian reform and federal schooling.

This was especially apparent in regional and local politics. In state after state, Catholics took advantage of electoral openings during the Cárdenas sexenio to extract even more concessions and isolate and marginalize local supporters of the revolutionary project. In Chiapas, Alberto Pineda (a conservative, regionalist politico) took Ciudad las Casas's town hall thanks to the voto morado. Fulfilling an electoral pact, Pineda gave Catholics keys to padlocked sanctuaries. On July 9, 1937, the city's "economic and social elite and its underground Catholic hierarchy" raised supporters who drove off federal soldiers to forcibly reopen churches. Pro-Pineda landowners also sponsored offensive segunda violence against federal teachers as well as the attempted assassination of Chiapas's principal Cardenista organizer, Erasto Urbina.[8]

The voto morado's power grew in much of Mexico during Cárdenas's presidency. Toppling Callista political machines on the state level required

Cardenistas to cobble together heterogeneous coalitions that often relied on Catholics as a crucial constituency. After mid-1935, pragmatic politicians tied to the president could court Catholic electoral brokers without fear of retribution. The inclusion of Catholics in governing coalitions pushed many state administrations farther right, and not just on the religious question. In Sonora, middle- and upper-class Catholics provided a significant base of support for Roman Yocupicio in his successful 1937 gubernatorial run—much to the dismay of organized labor and agraristas, who suffered during his administration.[9] In the 1936 election in Puebla, key Cárdenas ally Maximino Ávila Camacho received the support of right-wing Catholic civic organizations; his ally, Senator Gonzalo Bautista, had sheltered ex-cristeros since 1929.[10] Of course, the voto morado was not invincible during the Cárdenas sexenio; it could be neutralized by fraud or wasted on a weak candidate. In Sinaloa "pro-clerical and reactionary" elements and "fanatical women directed by the clergy" backed Ramón Iturbe, but he ultimately lost.[11] When and where such candidates did prevail, Catholic voters helped nudge governors and mayors away from socialist education and agrarian reform.

Undoubtedly, this dynamic implicated many Catholic intermediaries in the process of postrevolutionary state formation and so prevented the emergence of a clearly defined alternative Catholic polity and undermined a second Catholic insurgency. After all, Azanza ultimately betrayed Guanajuatan recristeros because of his understandings with Governor Ortega and General Rivas Guillén. But the price of his tepid loyalty was high, and its cost was paid by Cardenista agraristas and federal teachers. Moreover, many Catholic brokers proved to be quite capable of negotiating with the state actors even as they resisted the revolutionary project. Such resistance was sometimes violent.

The institutional Church partnered with the postrevolutionary state at crucial historical moments, but its ultimate goal was to preserve domestic peace, restore its own authority, and encourage a democratic opening that could eventually allow for a bloodless victory at the ballot box through civic action. If Catholics aided Cárdenas to displace Calles and to nationalize Mexico's oil, they also repeatedly countered crucial elements of the Cardenista revolutionary project such as agrarian reform and indigenism. In all likelihood, the institutional Church and many Catholics envisioned engagement with the postrevolutionary state as a *hudnah*, or strategic pause, rather than an act of legitimization. Consider the Church's response to Cárdenas's most important agrarian initiatives: the creation of hundreds of ejidos carved out of the cotton haciendas of the Laguna region (southwestern Coahuila and northeast Durango). Initially, Lagunera landowners received little help from the Church, apart from a few homilies, in trying to frustrate Cárdenas's plan.[12] However, after the Cardenista agrarian reforms were carried out, the Church moved to extend its influence over the newly created ejidos. In the Laguna, it sent in Jesuits to set up Congregaciones Marianas, open schools, and build chapels on twenty-two ejidos. In 1938, the bishop crowned the Virgin of Guadalupe the Queen of Torreón and the Laguna.[13]

Seen from this perspective, the postrevolutionary state at the dawning of the PRI's golden age in 1940 was much feebler, and its social support was much shallower, than the current scholarly consensus represents. Rather than deepening grassroots support, the numerous ties between state actors and Catholic brokers ultimately unsettled the postrevolutionary state. The failure of the Segunda and lack of widespread Catholic support for Cedillo's uprising does not indicate a comprehensive Catholic reconciliation with the postrevolutionary order. Rather, it reflects popular aversion to widespread civil strife, coupled with the institutional Church's desire to avoid another futile military struggle.

The 1940 election is remembered as a monumental watershed: the end of the religious question and the beginning of the Pax PRIista. Yet in much of rural Mexico, the endemic segunda violence that smoldered throughout the 1930s refused to burn out in the 1940s.[14] In the regions examined here, the postrevolutionary regime's hold on power at the end of the Cárdenas presidency resembled the condition Gramsci calls dominance without hegemony.[15] As a new generation of historians examines the 1940s and 1950s, the absence of widespread popular consent for PRI rule and the state's reliance on coercion becomes more and more apparent.[16] Catholic activists forged in the crucible of the religious struggle of the 1930s continued to mobilize popular support, which leached away the PRI's legitimacy well into the 1950s. In Oaxaca, for instance, Austreberto Aragón Maldonado, an ACM leader in the late 1930s, organized market women into a potent opposition force that consistently hindered the ruling party well into the postwar period.[17]

At least in the four regions studied here, state formation during the 1930s had an equivocal impact on the lives of most Mexicans. Peasant congresses, civic assemblies, and ceremonies marking agrarian grants allowed teachers and politicos to claim victory. But self-congratulatory federal reports, portentous presidential pronouncements, and hollow revolutionary ritual obscured the widespread popular apathy and antagonism toward the postrevolutionary state. The latter was often grounded in and expressed through Catholicism. Of course, a number of other factors besides the religious conflict undermined postrevolutionary state formation. Bureaucratic incompetence, Calles's aversion to Keynesian remedies to the Great Depression, Cárdenas's expensive romance with oil, Mexico's rugged topography, lingering postcolonial social deficits, and the indirect influence of the United States all took their toll. However, the religious question was the single most decisive factor in much of rural Mexico—even far from the Rosary Belt.

Neither Calles's Psychological Revolution nor Cárdenas's popular touch could realize the promise of revolutionary transformation in Campeche, Hidalgo, Guerrero, and Guanajuato. True, the postrevolutionary state eventually opened (or federalized) an impressive number of schools, redistributed thousands of hectares of land, and dispersed bands of segunderos. Yet the key missionaries of the postrevolutionary state, SEP inspectors and teachers, failed to convince many peasants to accept land and schools in return for their allegiance. The outcomes in these four states suggest that we need to look closely at claims that Cárdenas created a lasting reservoir of popular support for the postrevolutionary state by accelerating agrarian reform and quietly dropping anticlerical regulations.

Ultimately, national authorities could do only so much. In the end, the failures and frustrations of the revolutionary project were due not to Rome but to hundreds of local Catholic leaders, men and women largely lost to posterity. These pivotal actors who decided the religious question largely in the Church's favor were unlikely protagonists, people who seemed more like bit players than the heels of the historia patria or the heroes of Catholic counternarratives. Cumulatively, however, their prosaic forms of political practice frustrated the revolutionary project and sapped the authority of the postrevolutionary state. Calkiní's wily cacique Ignacio Reyes Ortega exemplifies these largely overlooked figures. By fusing his syncretic gremio with the local chapter of Campeche's Socialist Party, he bested Garridista maestros and *cooperativista* peasants. In Hidalgo, priests like the bellicose Mateo Ochoa and the resolute Luis Marín revived old lay groups like the Vela Perpetua and marshaled the Hijas de María to stymie indigenista teachers. In Guerrero, beatas brought Nahua voters to the polls to support pro-Church Ranchero politicos, while Father Roman Salgado used Catholic corporatism to counter Zapatista agraristas in Iguala. Outside these levitical islands, gangs of segunderos gunned down agraristas, a kind of white terror often blessed by militant *curas* like David Salgado. In Guanajuato, Salvador Azana and León Peña cannily collaborated with segunderos and catechists and politicos alike to carve out lasting cacicazgos that blocked Cárdenas's agrarian aspirations. In just these four states, thousands of Catholic female activists opened home schools, campaigned for pro-Church candidates, and turned Mexicans from all social strata against the revolutionary project.

The fate of the revolutionary project during the crucial middle years of the 1930s hinged on the outcome of hundreds of isolated confrontations and compromises between this cadre of Catholic leaders and agents of the revolutionary state. In much of the countryside, the SEP's secular apostles, agrarian engineers, revolutionary *militares*, and their local collaborators (agraristas, Zapatista veterans, Garridistas, Communists, the odd spiritists) could not overcome these heterogeneous coalitions that owed their ideological appeal and organizational strength largely to Catholicism. In the end, religious symbols and sociability often proved much more adaptable to local conditions and more capable of carrying out popular mobilizations than did their revolutionary rivals' alternatives. The institutional Church's radial strategy in effect made a virtue out of necessity, encouraging and legitimizing a wide range of networks headed by autonomous lay and clerical leaders who waged a successful struggle against an anticlerical revolutionary project in a largely Catholic nation.

Faced with deserted schools and ejidos without ejidatarios, many revolutionary elites blamed their rural failures on campesinos' fanaticism. Consequently, the appeal of urbanization and industrialization only grew in the eyes of the PRI elite. The state slowly abandoned its commitment to transform the countryside outside a few flagship agrarian projects. The process began with its tacit recognition of defeat on the religious question.[18] Developmentalism, demographics, economic nationalism, and World War II all played a role in the retreat from the campo. But the unsettled outcome of Mexico's religious problem remained the single greatest obstacle to the dream of a secular, modernized rural Mexico that Calles and Cárdenas shared.

Notes

Introduction

1. Founded as the Partido Nacional Revolucionario (PNR, or National Revolutionary Party) in 1928, it changed its name to the Partido Revolucionario Mexicano (PRM, or Revolutionary Mexican Party) in 1938 and then became the PRI in 1946.
2. Some students of hegemony seem to relish indeterminacy and fragmentation, at times making their arguments seem opaque to the uninitiated. See Alan Knight, "Subalterns, Signifiers, and Statistics: Perspectives on Mexican Historiography," *Latin American Research Review* 37, no. 2 (2002): 136–58, 148–52. For my purposes, civil society is "the arena of the politically active citizen" that is "distinct from the state and with forms and principles of its own." Antonio Gramsci, whose ideas have influenced notions of postrevolutionary state formation, considered it the "sphere of 'cultural politics' . . . the church, schools, trade unions, and other organizations through which the ruling class exercises 'hegemony' over society. The hegemony is vulnerable to contestation in this same realm." William Outhwaite and Tom Bottomore, eds., *The Blackwell Dictionary of Twentieth-Century Social Thought* (Cambridge: Blackwell, 1993), 75–76.
3. See the seminal essays in Gilbert M. Joseph and Daniel Nugent, eds., *Everyday Forms of State Formation: Revolution and the Negotiation of Rule in Modern Mexico* (Durham, NC: Duke University Press, 1994); Florencia Mallon, *Peasant and Nation: The Making of Postcolonial Mexico and Peru* (Berkeley: University of California Press, 1995); Anne Rubenstein, *Bad Language, Naked Ladies, and Other Threats to the Nation: A Political History of Comic Books in Mexico* (Durham, NC: Duke University Press, 1998); and Mary Kay Vaughan, *Cultural Politics in Revolution: Teachers, Peasants, and Schools in Mexico, 1930–1940* (Tucson: University of Arizona, 1997). Knight has left his mark on the historiography of postrevolutionary Mexico, writing extensively on what is often termed cultural politics. While he contributed to *Everyday Forms* and has criticized structural determinism, he has

not adopted many of the theoretical perspectives that characterize the New Cultural History. For an overview of some of the debate over the New Cultural History's impact, see *Hispanic American Historical Review* 79, no. 2 (May 1999), and Alan Knight, "Subalterns, Signifiers, and Statistics: Perspectives on Mexican Historiography," *Latin American Research Review* 37, no. 2 (2002): 136–58.

4 Jocelyn Olcott's study of women's struggle for citizenship in the 1930s was particularly well received because of its uncommon combination of theoretical richness and careful archival work in three regions. See her *Revolutionary Women in Postrevolutionary Mexico* (Durham, NC: Duke University Press, 2005).

5 Revisionists generally considered Catholics as counterrevolutionary defenders of the upper class—if they considered them at all. Most recent regional monographs of postrevolutionary Mexico ignore the Church, mine included. (See my *Cárdenas Compromised: The Failure of Reform in Yucatán* [Durham, NC: Duke University Press, 2001].) Marjorie Becker was among the few scholars of state formation in the 1990s to take Catholicism seriously. See *Setting the Virgin on Fire: Lázaro Cárdenas, Michoacán Peasants, and the Redemption of the Mexican Revolution* (Berkeley: University of California Press, 1995). See also Adrian Bantjes's work, in particular, "Idolatry and Iconoclasm in Revolutionary Mexico: The De-Christianization Campaigns, 1929–1940," *Mexican Studies/Estudios Mexicanos* 13:1 (Winter 1997): 87–120.

6 Roberto Blancarte, ed., *El Pensamiento social de los católicos mexicanos* (Mexico City: Fondo de Cultura Económica, 1996); Manuel Ceballos Ramírez, *El catolicismo social: Un tercero en discordia. Rerum Novarum, la "cuestión social" y la movilización de los católicos mexicanos (1891–1911)* (Mexico City: El Colegio de México, 1991); Bernardo Barranco V., "Posiciones Políticas en la Historia de la Acción Católica Mexicana," in *El pensamiento social de los católicos mexicanos*, ed. Roberto Blancarte (Mexico City: Fondo de Cultura Económica, 1996), 39–70; Randall Hanson, "Day of Ideals: Catholic Social Action in the Age of the Mexican Revolution, 1867–1929" (PhD diss., Indiana University, 1994).

7 Agrarian reform, often seen as the most important measure of revolutionary change, was plagued by chronic economic and social problems. See Eyler N. Simpson, *The Ejido: Mexico's Way Out* (Chapel Hill: University of North Carolina, 1937). U.S. pressure also played a role. See Friedrich Schuler, *Mexico between Hitler and Roosevelt: Mexican Foreign Relations in the Age of Lázaro Cárdenas, 1934–1940* (Albuquerque: University of New Mexico Press, 1998), 63–112; and John Dwyer, *The Agrarian Dispute: The Expropriation of American-Owned Rural Land in Postrevolutionary Mexico* (Durham, NC: Duke University Press, 2008).

8 Ben Smith notes that the notion of hegemony as used in postrevolutionary Mexico at times downplays "coercion and violence," overestimates "the state's coherency and strength," often misses "spaces, improvisations, and contradictions," and assumes that at certain key moments "national domination became irrevers-

ible." See his *Pistoleros and Popular Movements: The Politics of State Formation in Postrevolutionary Oaxaca* (Lincoln: University of Nebraska, 2009), 7–8.

9   On the Church's history in Mexico, see Roberto Blancarte, *Historia de la iglesia católica en México* (Mexico City: Colegio Mexiquense y Fondo de Cultura Económica, 1992). The scholarly literature on religious change in the Catholic Church during 1929–40 is far too vast to be summarized here. Important recent works published in English include Matthew Butler, *Popular Piety and Political Identity in Mexico's Cristero Rebellion: Michoacán, 1927–29*, British Academy Postdoctoral Fellowship Monograph (Oxford: Oxford University Press, 2004); Matthew Butler, ed., *Faith and Impiety in Revolutionary Mexico* (London: Institute for the Study of the Americas, 2007); Martin Austin Nesvig, ed., *Religious Culture in Modern Mexico* (Lanham, MD: Rowman & Littlefield, 2007); Jennifer Scheper-Hughes, *Biography of a Mexican Crucifix: Lived Religion and Local Faith from the Conquest to the Present* (New York: Oxford University Press, 2009); and Edward Wright-Rios, *Revolutions in Mexican Catholicism: Reform and Revelation in Oaxaca, 1887–1934* (Durham, NC: Duke University Press, 2009).

10 James W. Wilkie, "Statistical Indicators of the Impact of National Revolution on the Catholic Church in Mexico, 1910–1967," *Journal of Church and State* 12, no. 1 (1970): 92.

11 Archivo Histórico Plutarco Elías Calles (hereafter AHPEC) 58 52 4240 1, Alfonso Ortíz S. et al. to Soledad González, October 17, 1927; Archivo General de la Nación (hereafter AGN), Dirección General de Gobierno (hereafter DGG) 2.384 caja 15 exp. 2; AHAM Archivo Pascual Díaz (hereafter APD) caja 1 AG 192 exp. Orozco, Francisco Orozco Jiménez to Pascual Díaz, August 21, 1930.

12 AHAM, APD, Archbishop of Mexico to Filiberto Gómez, May 5, 1934; Archbishop Díaz to Leopoldo Ruiz, May 27, 1932; Alfonso Sánchez García, *El Círculo Rojinegro* (Mexico City: Universidad Autónoma del Estado de México, 1984), 12–23.

13 AHAM, APD, caja 3 exp. 33, Archbishop Díaz to Ruiz, March 22, 1933.

14 Gilbert M. Joseph and Daniel Nugent, "Popular Culture and State Formation in Revolutionary Mexico," in *Everyday Forms of State Formation*, 14.

15 William Beezley, Cheryl English Martin, and William French, eds., *Rituals of Rule, Rituals of Resistance: Public Celebrations and Popular Culture in Mexico* (Wilmington, DE: Scholarly Resources, 1994).

16 Joseph and Nugent, eds., *Everyday Forms of State Formation*; Vaughan, *Cultural Politics in Revolution*.

17 Here I answer Florencia Mallon's call to address "abstract categories" in the New Cultural History of Mexico. Florencia Mallon, "Time on the Wheel: Cycles of Historical Revisionism and the 'New Cultural History,'" *Hispanic American Historical Review* 79:2, 20, no. 2 (May 1999): 331–51, esp. 337, 340.

18 Guillermo Guzmán Flores used the term *morados* (purples) to refer to the pro-Catholic, conservative faction in Nieves, Zacatecas. See his "El Cardenismo y la

Nueva Democracia," in *Historia de la cuestión agraria mexicana, estado de Zacatecas*, ed. Ramón Vera Salvo, vol. 2, *1940* (Mexico City: Juan Pablos Editor, S.A., 1992), 256–63.

19 Michael Erwin, "The 1930 Agrarian Census in Mexico: Agronomists, Middle Politics, and the Negotiation of Nationalism," *Hispanic American Historical Review* 87, no. 3 (August 2007): 539–72.

20 David LaFrance, *Revolution in Mexico's Heartland: Politics, War, and State Building in Puebla, 1913–1920* (Wilmington, DE: Scholarly Resources, 2003), xx.

21 Chris Boyer, *Becoming Campesinos: Politics, Identity, and Agrarian Struggle in Postrevolutionary Michoacán, 1920–1935* (Stanford, CA: Stanford University Press, 2003), 124–25.

22 Quetzil Casteñeda, "'We Are Not Indigenous!' An Introduction to the Maya Identity of Yucatán," *Journal of Latin American Anthropology* 9, no. 1 (Spring 2004): 36–63, esp. 51.

23 Vaughan, *Cultural Politics in Revolution*, 57–59, 87–94, 122, 179.

24 Kristina Boylan, "Mexican Catholic Women's Activism, 1929–1940" (PhD diss., Oxford University, 2000).

25 David Raby, *Educación y revolución social en México (1921–1940)*, trans. Roberto Gómez Ciriza (Mexico City: Sep-Setentas, 1974).

26 Emilia Viotti da Costa warns of the danger in rejecting economic reductionism only to embrace cultural reductionism. Emilia Viotti da Costa, "New Publics, New Politics, New Histories: From Economic Reductionism to Cultural Reductionism—in Search of Dialectics," in *Reclaiming the Political in Latin American History*, ed. Gilbert Joseph (Durham, NC: Duke University Press, 2001), 10. Of late, other scholars have criticized this trend. Tanalís Padilla wants to rescue "historical process" from "cultural or linguistic reductionism." See her *Rural Resistance in the Land of Zapata: The Jaramillista Movement and the Myth of the Pax-Priísta, 1940–1962* (Durham, NC: Duke University Press, 2008), 16.

27 Kathryn Burns, *Colonial Habits: Convents and the Spiritual Economy of Cuzco, Peru* (Durham, NC: Duke University Press, 1999), 4, 146–49.

28 William H. Sewell Jr., "Towards a Post-materialist Rhetoric for Labor History," in *Rethinking Labor History*, ed. Lenard R. Berlangstein (Champagne: University of Illinois Press, 1993). By imperialistic, Sewell means not colonial but paradigms that claim to explain economic, cultural, and political processes to the exclusion of other approaches. Along those lines, one promising approach is Claudio Lomnitz-Adler's notion of regional culture, which considers the subtle interaction of symbolic systems and political economy. Rather than returning to the economic determinism of the revisionist historiography of modern Mexico, he suggests reconciling material and symbolic forces. Claudio Lomnitz-Adler, *Exits from the Labyrinth: Culture and Ideology in the Mexican National Space* (Berkeley: University of California Press, 1992).

29 Julio Tresierra, "Mexico: Indigenous Peoples and the Nation-State," in Donna Lee

Van Cott, *Indigenous Peoples and Democracy in Latin America* (New York: St. Martin's Press, 1994), 187–210, esp. 190.

30 AGN DGG 2.347 caja 3 bis exp. 18, Manuel Acevedo to sub-SG, July 28, 1934.

31 Following Pablo Serrano Álvarez, I use the term *segundero* to refer to antigovernment insurgents in the Segunda, just as *cristero* refers to rebels in the first Cristero War. Pablo Serrano Álvarez, *La batalla del espíritu: El movimiento sinarquista en el Bajío*, 2 vols. (1932–1951) (Mexico City: Consejo Nacional Para la Cultura y las Artes, 1992), 1:100, 102.

32 Records of the Department of State Related to the Internal Affairs of Mexico (hereafter RDSRIAM), 1930–39 reel 2, Clark to SOS, September 6, 1932. Another consul noted the barrage of rumors that consuls had to sort through: "Something is always about to happen, so-and-so is always just about to be ousted, or named for a high post in Mexico or abroad, somebody's land is about to be taken away, or somebody is about to do away with somebody else either politically or actually, and they frequently do." RDSRIAM 1930–39, reel 17, Shaw to SOS, January 31, 1932.

33 Jean Meyer, "La cuestión religiosa en las revoluciones francesa y mexicana," in *México y Francia: dos perspectivas revolucionarias*, ed. Carlos Martínez Assad, Carmen Castañeda García, Jean Meyer, Ricardo Ávila Palafox (Guadalajara, México: Editorial Universidad de Guadalajara, 1992), 79; Albert Michaels, "The Modification of the Anti-Clerical Nationalism of the Mexican Revolution by General Lázaro Cárdenas and Its Relationship to the Church-State Detente in Mexico," *Americas* 26, no. 1 (July 1969): 36–53, esp. 48–49.

34 Becker, *Setting the Virgin on Fire*.

35 Vaughan, *Cultural Politics in Revolution*.

36 Peter Reich, *Mexico's Hidden Revolution: The Catholic Church in Law and Politics since 1929* (Notre Dame, IN: University of Notre Dame Press, 1995).

37 Bantjes, "Idolatry and Iconoclasm," 99, 103, 109–11, 118–120. See also Adrian Bantjes, "Burning Saints, Molding Minds: Iconoclasm, Civic Ritual, and the Failed Cultural Revolution," in *Rituals of Rule, Rituals of Resistance: Public Celebrations and Popular Culture in Mexico*, ed. William Beezley, Cheryl English Martin, and William E. French (Wilmington, DE: Scholarly Resources, 1994), 261–284.

38 Terry Rugeley, *Of Wonders and Wise Men: Religion and Popular Culture in Southeast Mexico, 1800–1876* (Austin: University of Texas Press, 2001); Paul Vanderwood, "Religion: Official, Popular and Otherwise," *Mexican Studies/Estudios Mexicanos* 16, no. 2 (Summer 2000): 411–41.

39 Jennie Purnell, *Popular Movements and State Formation in Revolutionary Mexico: The Agraristas and Cristeros of Michoacán* (Durham, NC: Duke University Press, 1999).

40 Butler, *Popular Piety and Political Identity in Mexico's Cristero Rebellion*.

41 Boyer, *Becoming Campesinos*.

Chapter 1: The Church and the Religious Question

1 Jean Meyer's magisterial work on the Cristiada is far from state-centric. See his *La Cristiada*, 2nd ed., 3 vols. (Mexico City: Siglo XXI, 1970–76).
2 Austen Iverleigh, "The Politics of Religion in an Age of Revival," in *The Politics of Religion in an Age of Revival: Studies in Nineteenth-Century Europe and Latin America*, ed. Austen Iverleigh (London: Institute of Latin American Studies, 2000), 1–21.
3 John Lynch, "The Catholic Church in Latin America, 1830–1930," in *Cambridge History of Latin America*, ed. Leslie Bethell (Cambridge: Cambridge University Press, 1986), 4:527–95.
4 Christopher Clark, "The New Catholicism and the European Culture Wars," in *Culture Wars: Secular-Catholic Conflict in Nineteenth-Century Europe*, ed. Christopher Clark and Wolfram Kaiser (New York: Cambridge University Press, 2003), 11–46, esp. 44–45; Julio de la Cueva, "Spain: The Assault on the City of Levites," in *Culture Wars*, 181–201; Enrique Dussel, *A History of the Church in Latin America: Colonialism to Liberation (1492–1979)*, rev. ed., trans. Alan Neely (Grand Rapids, MI: William B. Eerdmans, 1981); Franco Savarino Rogerro, *Pueblos y nacionalismo: Del régimen oligárquico a la sociedad de masas en Yucatán, 1894–1925* (Mexico City: Instituto Nacional de Estudios Históricos de la Revolución Mexicana, 1997).
5 Ivan Vallier, *Catholicism, Social Control, and Modernization in Latin America* (Englewood Cliffs, NJ: Prentice-Hall, 1970), esp. 9.
6 Anthony Gill, *Rendering unto Caesar: The Catholic Church and the State in Latin America* (Chicago: University of Chicago Press, 1998), 32–34.
7 Rome vetoed the creation of a Catholic party in Mexico during the Porfiriato and again in the 1920s. Jean Meyer, *El sinarquismo, el cardenismo y la iglesia (1937–1941)* (Mexico City: Tiempo de memoria TusQuets, 2003), 19. The Partido Católico Nacional (PCN, or National Catholic Party), formed during the brief presidency of Francisco Madero, apparently represents an exception to Rome's larger strategy.
8 Vallier, *Catholicism, Social Control, and Modernization in Latin America*, 6–10.
9 Mark Overmyer-Velázquez, *Visions of the Emerald City: Modernity, Tradition, and the Formation of Porfirian Oaxaca* (Durham, NC: Duke University Press, 2006), 70–97.
10 Hernán Menéndez Rodríguez, *Iglesia y Poder: Proyectos sociales, alianzas políticas y económicas en Yucatán (1857–1917)* (Merida, Mexico: Editorial Nuestra America y Consejo Nacional para la Cultura y las Artes, 1995).
11 See Salvador Camacho Sandoval, *Controversia educativa entre la ideología y la fe. La educación socialista en la historia de Aguascalientes, 1876–1940* (Mexico City: Consejo Nacional para la Cultura y las Artes, 1991), 58–59.
12 Matthew Butler, "La coronación del Sagrado Corazón de Jesús en la Arquidiócesis de México, 1914," in *Revolución, cultura, y religión: ensayos de historia regional*, ed.

Yolanda Padilla Rangel, Javier Delgado, and Luciano Ramírez (Aguascalientes, Mexico: Universidad Autónoma de Aguascalientes, 2012), 24–68. John Lynch, "The Catholic Church in Latin America, 1830–1930." *Cambridge History of Latin America*, 12 vols. (New York: Cambridge University Press, 1986), 4: 527–95, esp. 552–53. The cult of the Sacred Heart Symbolized resistance to liberal influences and promoted "observance, private piety, and individual morality."

13 Matthew Butler, *Popular Piety and Political Identity in Mexico's Cristero Rebellion: Michoacán, 1927–29* (Oxford: Oxford University Press, 2004), esp. chap. 4.

14 Peter Reich, *Mexico's Hidden Revolution: The Catholic Church in Law and Politics since 1929* (Notre Dame, IN: University of Notre Dame Press, 1995), 22–23.

15 Daniela Spenser, *The Impossible Triangle: Mexico, Soviet Russia, and the United States in the 1920s* (Durham, NC: Duke University Press, 1999), 189; *Hombre Libre*, January 17, 1930.

16 *Hombre Libre*, January 17, 1930.

17 Reich, *Mexico's Hidden Revolution*, 41–44.

18 AHSMM, DECP 14–15; Pascual Díaz, *Segunda Carta Pastoral del Ilmo. y Ruvo. Sr. Arzobispado de Mexico* (Mexico City, 1930).

19 Roberto Blancarte, *Historia de la Iglesia Católica en México* (Mexico City: Colegio Mexiquense y Fondo de Cultura Económica, 1992), 54.

20 Charles MacFarland, *Chaos in Mexico: The Conflict of Church and State* (New York: Harper and Brothers, 1935), 149.

21 Bernardo Barranco V., "Posiciones políticas en la historia de la Acción Católica Mexicana," in *El Pensamiento Social de los Católicos Mexicanos*, ed. Roberto Blancarte (Mexico City: Fondo de Cultura Económica, 1996), 39–70, esp. 62; AHAM caja Conflicto Religiosa Correspondencia A-B 1928–35 leg. Apeitia Palomar, Manuel, Obispo de Tepic, Apeitia to Manriquez y Zárate, October 15, 1928.

22 Barranco, "Posiciones políticas en la historia de la Acción Católica Mexicana," 62.

23 AHAM, Caja Subcomité Episcopal 1926–28 Sección B. leg. "Subcomité episcopal," Contestación a unos sacerdotes que se abstengan de política, August 18, 1928.

24 AGN DGG 2.340 caja 19 exp. 8, Circular #38, September 10, 1929; *Hombre Libre*, September 14, 1929; Alberto A. Rodríguez, *El Proceso de la Religion en Mexico* (Jalapa, Mexico: Talleres del Gobierno del Estado, 1930), 313–14; RDSRIAM 1930–39 reel 11, Vice Consul Bonnet to SOS, August 12, 1931; AHSEP caja 1535 exp. 7, Aureliano Esquivel to SEP, January 28, 1932; Beatriz Cervantes, "La educación y el conflicto iglesia-estado," in *IV Jornadas de Historia de Occidente* (Jiquilpan, Mexico: Centro de Estudios de la Revolución Mexicana Lázaro Cárdenas, A.C., 1981), 79–100, esp. 82.

25 J. Lloyd Mecham, *Church and State in Latin America: A History of Politico-Ecclesiastical Relations* (Chapel Hill: University of North Carolina Press, 1966), 404; Alfonso Taracena, *La verdadera revolucion mexicana. Decimaséptima etapa (1931): La Familia Revolucionaria I* (Mexico City: Editorial Jus, 1965), 223–27; Gonzalo N. Santos, *Memorias*. 2 vols. (Mexico City: Grijalbo, 1986), 468–73.

26 RDSRIAM 1930–39 reel 4, Josephus Daniels to Secretary of State, April 2, 1935.
27 Nathaniel Weyl and Sylvia Weyl, *The Reconquest of Mexico. The Years of Lázaro Cárdenas* (New York: Oxford University Press, 1939), 149–52; Rafael Vera Sánchez, *Matías Rodríguez, Vidas Exactas* (Mexico City: Herrero Hermanos, 1931), 233; Javier Moctezuma Barragán, ed., *Francisco J. Múgica: Un romántico rebelde* (Mexico City: FCE, 2001), 285; Archivo Histórico Secretariado Social Mexicano (hereafter AHSSM), Conflictos Religiosos por Diócesis (hereafter CRD), J. Banon Martínez, Bishop of Queretaro, "ACONTECIMIENTOS . . . EN EL MES DE OCTUBRE DE 1935"; RDSRIAM reel 43, Josephus Daniels, "Memorandum of Conversation with acting SRE Ceniceros," November 21, 1935; Charles MacFarland, *Chaos in Mexico: The Conflict of Church and State* (New York: Harper and Brothers, 1935), 51–53; AHSSM CRD, Cgo. José D. Cuevas "Respuestas . . . ," July 20, 1935.
28 José Gutiérrez Casillas, *Jesuitas en Mexico durante el siglo XX* (Mexico City: Editorial Porrúa, 1981), 91, 199; For an overview of the Church-state conflict, see Lorenzo Meyer, *Historia de la revolución mexicana: Periódo 1928–1934*, vol. 12 (Mexico City: El Colegio de Mexico, 1978), 181.
29 RDSRIAM 1930–39 reel 42, Consul George Shaw to SOS, March 15, 1935.
30 Ibid., reel 11, Vice Consul Bonnet to SOS, August 12, 1931.
31 Mary Kay Vaughan, *Cultural Politics in Revolution: Teachers, Peasants, and Schools in Mexico, 1930–1940* (Tucson: University of Arizona, 1997), 33, 65.
32 Marcela Tostado Gutiérrez, *El intento de liberar a un pueblo: Educación y magisterio tabasqueño con Garrido Canabal: 1924–1935* (Mexico City: INAH, 1991), 83.
33 Vaughan, *Cultural*, 90, 122.
34 *Hombre Libre*, September 28, 1934, October 8, 1935, *La Prensa*, November 27, 1934.
35 *Hombre Libre*, June 7, 1935.
36 AHSEP caja 1337 exp. 10, Antonio R. García report; AHSEP caja 1337 exp. 3, Ruben Rodríguez Lozano report, March 31, 1935; AHSEP caja 1337, exp. 4, Alfonso Hernández to Superintendent, June 10, 1935.
37 David Raby, *Educación y revolución social en México (1921–1940)*, trans. Roberto Gómez Ciriza (Mexico City: Sep-Setentas, 1974), 147, 190–91.
38 Pablo Serrano Álvarez, *La batalla del espíritu: El movimiento sinarquista en el Bajío (1932–1951)*, 2 vols. (Mexico City: Consejo Nacional Para la Cultura y las Artes, 1992), 1:91–103.
39 Pablo Serrano Álvarez, *La batalla del espíritu: El movimiento sinarquista en el Bajío (1932–1951)* 2 vols. (Mexico City: Consejo Nacional Para la Cultura y las Artes, 1992) 1:101; Jean Meyer, *La Cristiada*, 8th ed. (Mexico City: Siglo XXI, 1983), 1:363.
40 Antonio Avitia Hernández, *El caudillo sagrado: Historia de las rebeliones cristeras en el estado de Durango* (Mexico City: Impresos Castellanos, 2000), 217–370; John W. F. Dulles, *Yesterday in Mexico: A Chronicle of the Revolution, 1919–1936* (Austin: University of Texas Press, 1961), 531–32; Randall Hanson, "Day of Ideals: Catholic Social Action in the Age of the Mexican Revolution, 1867–1929" (PhD diss., Indiana University, 1994), 536–41; Moisés González Navarro, *Cristeros y Agraristas en*

Jalisco, 5 vols. (Mexico City: Colegio de México, 2000), 1:104–55; Raquel Sosa Elízaga, *Los códigos ocultos del cardenismo: Un estudio de la violencia política, el cambio social y la continuidad institucional* (Mexico City: Universidad Nacional Autónoma de México and Plaza y Valdés, 1996), 100–102; Meyer, *La Cristiada*, 1:369–74; Camacho Sandoval, *Controversia educativa entre la ideología y la fe*, 67–68, 110, 112, 162–65, 218–19, 274.

41 Timothy Clarke Hanley, "Civilian Leadership of the Cristero Movement: The Liga Nacional Defensora de la Libertad Religiosa and the Church-State Conflict in Mexico, 1924–1938" (PhD diss., Columbia University, 1977), 473–79.

42 *La Prensa*, December 1, 1935.

43 Hanley, "Civilian Leadership of the Cristero Movement," 488–89.

44 *La Prensa*, November 10, 1934; Hanley, "Civilian Leadership of the Cristero Movement," 475; Servando Ortoll, "Catholic Organizations in Mexico's National Politics and International Diplomacy (1926–1942)" (PhD diss., Columbia University, 1986), 103–58, 198.

45 Pope Pius XI, "No es muy Conocida" on the "religious situation in Mexico," March 28, 1937, http://www.vatican.va/holy_father/pius_xi/encyclicals/documents/hf_p-xi_enc_28031937, p. 5 (accessed November 17, 2006). See also Blancarte, *Historia de la Iglesia Católica en México*, 56.

46 RDSRIAM 1930–1939 reel 44, "First Pastoral Letter Addressed by the Most Excellent and Most Reverend Dr. José Garibi Rivera to the Clergy and Faithful of the Archdiocese of Guadalajara on the Subject, Present Problems of the Church in this Archdiocese and Means Adopted to their Solution," April 12, 1936.

47 AHSSM, DEHM, Pascual Díaz, *Instrucción Pastoral que dirige en forma confidencial a sus Párrocos y demás Sacerdotes el Excmo. y Rmo. Sr. Arzobispo de México* (Mexico City, 1934).

48 AHSSM, DECP, "Carta Pastoral Colectiva," January 1936; AHAM PD caja 5 AG 192 exp. 59, Díaz to Ruiz, July 5, 1935, September 16, 1935; Blancarte, *Historia de la Iglesia Católica en México*, 45.

49 Lyle C. Brown, "Mexican Church-State Relations, 1933–1940," *A Journal of Church and State* 6, no. 2 (Spring 1964), 202–22, 213–14.

50 Blancarte, *Historia de la Iglesia Católica en* México, 41; Brown, "Mexican Church-State Relations, 1933–1940," 214; William Townsend, *Lazaro Cardenas Mexican Democrat* (Ann Arbor, MI: George Wahr, 1952), 95, 97, 133–35.

51 AGN DGG 2.340 caja 25 exp. 1; RDSRIAM 1930–39 reel 43, Division of Mexican Affairs Memorandum to Mr. Welles, March 14, 1936; RDSRIAM reel 43, Josephus Daniels to SOS, March 28, 1936; AGN LC 543.1/16, anonymous memorandum, January 30, 1937.

52 RDSRIAM 1930–39 reel 22, Charles Taliaferro to SOS, January 30, 1937.

53 Cf. Marjorie Becker, *Setting the Virgin on Fire: Lázaro Cárdenas, Michoacán Peasants, and the Redemption of the Mexican Revolution* (Berkeley: University of Cal-

ifornia Press, 1995). Also see Adrian Bantjes, "Idolatry and Iconoclasm in Revolutionary Mexico: The De-Christianization Campaigns, 1929–1940," *Mexican Studies/Estudios Mexicanos* 13:1 (Winter 1997): 87–120; page 118 emphasizes Catholic resistance, while Reich, *Hidden*, stresses the off-stage pacts between governors and bishops.

54 AGN LC 574.4/100.
55 RDSRIAM 1930–39 reel 43, Josephus Daniels to SOS, March 6, 1936.
56 RDSRIAM 1930–39, Charles Taliaferro to SOS, November 30, 1938, and Stephen C. Worster to SOS, January 1, 1939; MS, Martin Palmira L. to Paul Murray, June 2, 1936; *Diario de Yucatán*, November 29, 1936; Brown, "Mexican Church-State Relations, 1933–1940," 215–18.
57 Valentina Torres Septién, *La Educación Privada en México (1903–1976)* (Mexico City: El Colegio de México and Universidad Iberoamericana, 1997), 135, 144.
58 AGN DGG 2.340 caja 44 exp. 2, Timoteo Gutiérrez et al., July 25, 1936.
59 RDSRIAM 1930–39 reel 44, NCWC (National Catholic Welfare Conference) News Service, May 25, 1936. The quotation is from RDSRIAM 1930–39 reel 44, *Excelsior*, April 18, 1937.
60 Reich, *Hidden*, 57–67; Brown, "Mexican Church-State Relations," 219.
61 Chris Boyer, *Becoming Campesinos: Politics, Identity, and Agrarian Struggle in Postrevolutionary Michoacán, 1920–1935* (Stanford, CA: Stanford University Press, 2003), 230–31.
62 Luis González González, *San José de Gracia: Mexican Village in Transition*, trans. John Upton (Austin: University of Texas Press, 1974), 204–5.
63 Scholarly biographies of priests and bishops are few and far between. Examples include Carlos Martínez Assad, ed., *A Dios lo que es de Dios* (Mexico City: Aguilar, Nuevo Siglo, 1994), and Félix Báez-Jorge, *Olor de Santidad. San Rafael Guízar y Valencia: Articulaciones históricas, políticas y simbólicas de una devoción popular* (Xalapa, Mexico: Universidad Veracruzana, 2006).
64 Lynch, "The Catholic Church in Latin America, 1830–1930," 543.
65 Báez-Jorge, *Olor de Santidad. San Rafael Guízar y Valencia*, 65–75.
66 J. Ignacio Rubio Mañé, *El Excmo: Dr. D. Martín Tritschler y Córdova Primer Arzobispo de Yucatán* (Mexico City: SAG, S. de R.L., 1941).
67 Hanson, "Day of Ideals," 492–93.
68 Archivo del Instituto Nacional de la Antropología y Historia (hereafter AINAH) CR reel 33, Juan García H. to Comité Directiva of LNDL (Liga Nacional para la Defensa de la Libertad).
69 Brown, "Mexican Church-State Relations, 1933–1940," 209–10; Hanson, "Day of Ideals," 492–96, 495n11; AINAH CR reel 38, Presidente [LNDL] to Pascual Díaz, December 24, 1935.
70 Báez-Jorge, *Olor de Santidad*, 283, 299, 308–10.
71 RDSRIAM 1930–39 reel 5, Josephus Daniels to SOS, July 15, 1936.
72 Antonio Avitia Hernández, *El Caudillo sagrado: Historia de las rebeliones cristeras*

en el estado de Durango (Mexico City: Impresos Castellanos, 2000), 180–82; Moisés González Navarro, *Cristeros y agraristas en Jalisco* (Mexico City: Colegio de Mexico, 2000), 4:150, 157.

73 Craig Harline and Eddy Put, *A Bishop's Tale: Mathias Hovius among His Flock in Seventeenth-Century Flanders* (New Haven, CT: Yale University Press, 2000).

74 Lynch, "The Catholic Church in Latin America, 1830–1930," 532–37.

75 Mario Ramírez Rancaño, *El patriarca Pérez. La Iglesia católica apostólica mexicana* (Mexico City: Universidad Nacional Autónoma de México, Instituto de Investigaciones Sociales, 2006), 55.

76 Matthew Butler promises to rectify this in his forthcoming book, "Father Perez's Revolution: Or, Making Catholicism 'Mexican' in 20th-Century Mexico" (Albuquerque: University of New Mexico Press, forthcoming).

77 USSD RDSRIAM 1910–29 reel 146, "The Religious Crisis in Mexico," September 18, 1926.

78 José Gutiérrez Casillas, *Jesuitas en Mexico durante el siglo XX* (Mexico City: Editorial Porrua, 1981), 195.

79 AGN DGG 2.347 caja 3 bis exp. 24, 33; José Mario Contreras Valdez, *Reparto de Tierras en Nayarit, 1916–1940: Un proceso de ruptura y continuidad* (Mexico City: Instituto Nacional de Estudios Históricos de la Revolución Mexicana and Universidad Autónoma de Nayarit, 2001), 113.

80 Richard Weiner, *Race, Nation, and Market: Economic Culture in Porfirian Mexico* (Tucson: University of Arizona Press, 2004), 70–84.

81 Ernest Gruening, *Mexico and Its Heritage* (New York: Century, 1928), 221–26.

82 Robert Conger, "Porfirio Díaz and the Church Hierarchy, 1876–1911" (PhD diss., University of New Mexico, 1985), 109.

83 Hernán Menéndez Rodríguez with Ben Fallaw, "The Resurgence of the Church in Yucatán: The Olegario Molina-Crescencio Carrillo Alliance, 1867–1901," in Edward Terry, Ben Fallaw, Gilbert Joseph, and Edward Moseley, eds., *Peripheral Visions: Politics, Society, and the Challenges of Modernity in Yucatan* (Tuscaloosa: University of Alabama Press, 2010), 213–26, esp. 219–22.

84 José Roberto Juárez, *Reclaiming Church Wealth: The Recovery of Church Property after Expropriation in the Archdiocese of Guadalajara, 1860–1911* (Albuquerque: University of New Mexico Press, 2004), esp. 50, 163; Benjamin Smith, "'The Priest's Party': Local Catholicism and Panismo in Huajuapam de León," in *Faith and Impiety in Revolutionary Mexico*, ed. Matthew Butler (London: Institute for the Study of the America, 2007), 261–77, esp. 263.

85 RDSRIAM 1910–29 reel 143, R. H. Tierney to SOS, October 17, 1914, Document "A"; Gabino Chávez, *Novísimo catecismo de los diezmos: Su naturaleza y origen, su obligación y legislación, su sanción y práctica* (Mexico City: Talleres J. de Elizalde, 1901).

86 *Instrucciones de los ilmos. y rvmos. prelados de la provincia mexicana a los señores vicarios foráneos y sus respectivas diócesis sobre los puntos que deben informar anualmente* (Mexico City: Escuela Tipografica Salesiana, 1924), 6.

87 Blancarte, *Historia de la Iglesia Católica en México*, 39; James W. Wilkie, "Statistical Indicators of the Impact of National Revolution on the Catholic Church in Mexico, 1910–1967," *A Journal of Church and State* 12, no. 1 (1970): 89–110, esp. 98; Mariano Cuevas, *Historia de la Iglesia en México*, vol. 5, *1700–1800*, 5th ed. (Mexico City: Editorial Patria, 1947), 460; RDSRIAM 1930–39 reel 41, Josephus Daniels to SOS, December 18, 1934.

88 Silvia Arrom, *The Women of Mexico City, 1790–1857* (Stanford, CA: Stanford University Press, 1985), 261–69; Lynch, "The Catholic Church in Latin America, 1830–1930," 550–52.

89 Butler, *Popular Piety and Political Identity in Mexico's Cristero Rebellion*, 123.

90 Kristina A. Boylan, "The Feminine 'Apostolate in Society' versus the Secular State: The Unión Femenina Católica Mexicana, 1929–1940," 169–182; Paola Bacchetta and Margaret Power, eds., *Right Wing Women: From Conservatives to Extremists around the World* (London: Routledge, 2002); Patience Schell, "Of the Sublime Mission of Mothers of Families: The Union of Mexican Catholic Ladies in Revolutionary Mexico," in *The Women's Revolution in Mexico, 1910–1953* (Boulder, CO.: Rowman & Littlefield, 2007), 99–123.

91 David Espinosa, "Jesuit Higher Education in Post-revolutionary Mexico: The Iberoamerican University, 1943–1971" (PhD diss., University of California–Santa Barbara, 1998), 122–27.

92 María Luisa Aspe Armella, *La formación social y política de los católicos mexicanos: La Acción Católica Mexicana y la Unión Nacional de Estudiantes Católicos, 1929–1958* (Mexico City: Universidad Iberoamericana, 2008), esp. 156–73. See also Hanson, "Day of Ideals."

93 AINAH CR reel 34, Palomar to Ing. León, October 31, 1932.

94 Elwood Gotshall, "Catholicism and Catholic Action in Mexico, 1929–1941: A Church's Response to a Revolutionary Society and the Politics of the Modern Age," (PhD diss., University of Pittsburgh, 1970), 24, 58–59, 65.

95 ASSOCIATION DE SCOUTS DE MEXICO (July 22, 1946) exp. Confederados, Informe que rinde la asociación de Scouts de Mexico a la ACM, es su calidad de confederara.

96 AHAM LMM caja 5 carpeta 75 Sociedad EVC, Secretariado Social exp. Secretariado Social Mexican, "Seis años de Actividades del Secretariado Social Mexicano 1925–1931," 2.

97 RDSRIAM 1910–29 reel 146, "The Religious Crisis in Mexico," February 18, 1927.

98 AHAM Luis María Martínez, caja 3 (anterior gaveta número 197) exp. ACM 197 72, Luis Vargas to Comité Central, July 22, 1931.

99 *Pax*, año 2 #5 (August 1933), 8, 11, A.N. (Adolfo Nieto).

100 AHAM LMM caja 5 carpeta 75 Sociedad EVC, Secretariado Social exp. Secretariado Social Mexicano, "Seis años de Actividades del Secretariado," 2; Archivo Acción Católica (hereafter AAC), exp. 2.10.1 Informes 1930–33, Elena L. de Silo to Pascual Díaz, October 18, 1930.

101 AHAM APD caja 1 AG 192 exp. ACM, Luis Bustos to Pascual Díaz, April 11, 1935.
102 ACC 7.1 Caballeros de Colon, 1930–34.
103 AHAM, LMM, carpeta 32 Episcopado 1920–39 exp., M, Pascual Díaz to Luis Martínez, September 10, 1934.
104 AAC exp. 2.10.1 Informes de visitas a diócesis 1938–42, Informe sobre la visita a la H. Junta Diocesana de Morelia (December 26–29, 1938).
105 *Pax*, November 1935, 15, P.B. "UCM"; *Gaceta Oficial del Arzobispado de Mexico*, January 1935, Circular 3 (January 5, 1935).
106 AHAM APD caja 1 AG 192 exp. ACM, Luis Bustos to Pascual Díaz, April 11, 1935.
107 *Pax*, 2:1, 2 (April–May 1933), p. 8, 16 J.V. "ACJM: JUVENTUD CAMPESINA."
108 AHAM LMM caja 3 (anterior gaveta número 197) exp. Acción Católica 195, Luis Bustos to Martínez, December 21, 1930.
109 AHAM LMM caja 5 carpeta 75 Sociedad EVC, Secretariado Social 5–7, "Informe de gestión del Secretariado Social Mexicano . . . desde 1931 hasta 1937."
110 ACC 2.10 Junta Diocesana, Eusebio Cervantes T. to Mariano Alcocer, February 3, 1940.
111 *Pax*, año 2 #5 (August 1933), 8.
112 AAC exp. 2.10.1 Informes 1930–33, Elena L. de Silo to Pascual Díaz, October 18, 1930.
113 Boylan, "The Feminine 'Apostolate in Society' versus the Secular State, 1940," 169.
114 AHAM, LMM, carpeta 32 Episcopado 1920–1939 exp. M., Pascual Díaz, August 1934; AHSSM, DEHM, Pascual Díaz, *Instrucción Pastoral que dirige en forma confidencial a sus Párrocos y demás Sacerdotes el Excmo. y Rmo. Sr. Arzobispo de México* (Mexico City, 1934).
115 "No es muy Conocida," March 28, 1937, 5, http://www.vatican.va/holy_father/pius_xi/encyclicals/documents/hf_p-xi_enc_28031937 (accessed November 17, 2006).
116 Richard Samuels, *Machiavelli's Children: Leaders and Their Legacies in Italy and Japan* (Ithaca, NY: Cornell University Press, 2003), 25.
117 Camacho Sandoval, *Controversia educativa entre la ideología y la fe*, 91; Wilfrid Parsons, *Mexican Martyrdom*, 2nd ed. (Rockford, IL: Tan Books and Publishers 1987), 250–51.
118 AHAM LMM caja 5 carpeta 75 Sociedad EVC, Secretariado Social exp. Secretariado Social Mexican, "Seis años de Actividades del Secretariado Social Mexicano 1925–1931," 5; Torres Septién, *La Educación Privada en México (1903–1976)*, 107, 118–123.
119 Torres Septién, *La Educación Privada en México (1903–1976)*, 119.
120 Ramón Sánchez Medal, *En defensa del derecho de los padres de familia* (Mexico City: Editorial Jus, 1964), 55–74.
121 Torres Septién, *La Educación Privada en México (1903–1976)*, 134.
122 AINAH CR reel 36, *¡Un Hecho, un secreto, un peligro!* (Mexico?: n.p. 1934); Elvia Montes de Oca, *La educación socialista en el Estado de México 1934–1940. Una Historia olvidada* (Zinacantepec, Mexico: El Colegio Mexiquense, 1998), 184–86.

123 Montes de Oca, *La Educación socialista*, 191–95.
124 Ibid., 193.
125 AAC 7.7 Union Nacional de Padres de Familia, 1931–36, C. B. Salgado to Luis G. Bustos, June 26, 1933; Blancarte, *Historia de la Iglesia Católica en México*, 33.
126 AINAH CR reel 34, Aurelio Díaz [December 1932]; AINAH CR reel 36, ANPLE *Boletín*, año 11 no. 4 (September 1934).
127 Blancarte, *Historia de la Iglesia Católica en México*, 33; ACC 2.10 JD, Eusebio Cervantes T. to Mariano Alcocer, February 3, 1940.
128 Blancarte, *Historia de la Iglesia Católica en México*, 94.
129 *Hombre Libre*, October 21, 1935, 2, letter to editor from Agapito Martínez et al., October 9, 1935.
130 Pablo Serrano Álvarez, *La batalla del espíritu: El movimiento sinarquista en el Bajío (1932–1951)*, 2 vols. (Mexico City: Consejo Nacional Para la Cultura y las Artes, 1992).
131 Jean Meyer, *The Cristero Rebellion: The Mexican People between Church and State*, trans. Richard Southern (Cambridge: Cambridge University Press, 1976), 25.
132 Antonio Rius Facius, *De don Porfirio a Plutarco: Historia de la A.C.J.M* (Mexico City: Editorial Jus, 1958), 177.
133 Alan Knight, "Popular Culture and the Revolutionary State in Mexico, 1910–1940," *Hispanic American Historical Review* 74, no. 3 (1994): 393–444. esp., 432–35.
134 De la Cueva, "Spain: The Assault," in *Culture Wars*, 181–201, esp. 182–83; Butler, *Popular Piety*, 9–10.
135 Blancarte, *Historia de la Iglesia Católica en México*, 33, 67.
136 AHAM LMM Caja Comite Episcopal exp. "F y G," J. M. Maya to Luis M. Martínez, December 16, 1944.
137 On the June 22, 1891, bull, see M. Rodolfo Escobedo, *La diócesis de Saltillo: Notas históricas* (Saltillo, Mexico: Gobierno Eclesiástico del Obispado de Saltillo, 1989), 26.
138 Moisés de la Peña, *Zacatecas económico* (Mexico City: Revista de Economía, 1948), 52.

Chapter 2: Catholic-Socialists against Anti-Priests in Campeche

1 For different accounts of the event, see AHSSM, "Conflictos Religiosos por Diócesis" (hereafter CRD), "Puntos concretos sobre la persecución religiosa en el edo. De Yucatán desde el año de 1926 a julio 13 de 1935" (hereafter "Puntos concretos"); AGN DGG 2.340 caja 24 exp. 12, Bishop Luis Guízar B. to Secretaría de Gobernación (hereafter SG), August 18, 1934; Carlos J. Sierra, *Diccionario Biográfico de Campeche* (Mexico City: La Muralla, 1997), 16; and Alicia Gómez Montejo, *Las H. Juntas Municipales del Estado de Campeche: Una breve descripción* (Campeche, Mexico: Congreso del Estado de Campeche, 2002), 50–51.

2 Ben Fallaw, "Rethinking Mayan Resistance: Changing Relations between Federal Teachers and Mayan Communities in Eastern Yucatán, 1929–1935," *Journal of Latin American Anthropology* 9, no. 1 (Spring 2004): 151–78, esp. 155.
3 AHSEP Campeche (hereafter CAM) caja 21 exp. 5960, Claudio Cortés report, April 30, 1934.
4 AAC exp. 2.10.1 Informes de visitas a Diócesis 1939–47, Luis G. Bustos, "Informe de Visita a Dióceses de Campeche y Tabasco" (hereafter "Informe de Visita"), April 6, 1941; Moisés T. de la Peña, *Campeche Económico*, 2 vols. (Campeche, Mexico: Gobierno Constitucional del Estado de Campeche, 1942), 1:1–42.
5 The Partido Socialista Agrarista pro-Campeche, later known as the Partido Socialista Agrarista del Sureste, was recognized in 1929 by the PNR as its sole official Campeche affiliate. Mario Aranda González, *El Municipio de Calkiní* (Campeche, Mexico, 1981), 48, 65–66; José Alberto Abud Flores, *Campeche: Revolución y Movimiento Social (1911–1923)* (Campeche, Mexico: INEHRM, Secretaría de Gobernación, Universidad Autónoma de Campeche, 1992), 52.
6 My division of Campeche into north and south reflects very different geographic, political, and social characteristics but not an implicit sense of subregional loyalty. In Van Young's terminology, this division expresses subregionality, but not subregionalism. Eric Van Young, "Are Regions Good to Think?" in *Mexico's Regions: Comparative History and Development*, ed. Eric Van Young (San Diego: Center for U.S.-Mexican Studies, University of California–San Diego, 1992), 2.
7 AHSEP CAM caja 1802 exp. 8, Inspector 20 zone report, August 2, 1933.
8 *Hombre Libre*, September 26, 1934.
9 Terry Rugeley, *Rebellion Now and Forever: Mayas, Hispanics, and Caste War Violence in Yucatán, 1800–1880* (Stanford, CA: Stanford University Press, 2009), 219–24, 277–84.
10 "Puntos concretos"; AGN DGG 2.340 caja 24 exp. 12; Sierra, *Diccionario Biográfico de Campeche*, 16.
11 Archivo Personal de Tomás Garrido Canabal (hereafter APTGC) caja 133 exp. 12, Garrido Canabal to Angli Lara, December 19, 1933.
12 Mary Kay Vaughan, *Cultural Politics in Revolution: Teachers, Peasants, and Schools in Mexico, 1930–1940* (Tucson: University of Arizona, 1997), 25–46.
13 AHSEP Dirección General de Misiones Culturales (hereafter DGMC) caja 22, Claudio Cortés to Inspectors, January 24, 1933.
14 Andrae Marak, "Federalization of Education in Chihuahua," *Paedagógica Histórica*, 41, no. 3 (June 2005), 357–75, 369–70.
15 George Isidore Sánchez, *Mexico: A Revolution by Education* (New York: Viking Press, 1936), 90–91, 118–20.
16 Andrés Uc Dzib, "La escuela rural, una nueva escuela de la época de oro de la educación en México," in *Los maestros y la cultura nacional, 1920–1952*, ed. Engracia Loyo, Cecilia Greaves, and Valentina Torres (Mexico City: SEP, 1987), 5:17–

25, 17–18; AHSEP Campeche (hereafter CAM) caja 20, Superintendent report, July (1933) and 1933 year; AHSEP DGMC 5963/18, Director ENR-H July 1932; Sierra, *Diccionario Biográfico de Campeche*, 19.

17 Román Piña Chán, *Enciclopedia histórica de Campeche. De la revolución a la época moderna, 1911–1961* (Mexico City: Porrúa and Gobierno de Campeche, 2003), 4:79, 87–88.

18 APTGC caja 85 exp. 9, Luis Álvarez Barret to Garrido Canabal, January 29, 1935.

19 Rodolfo López Sosa, *Tarjeta presidencial* (Mérida, Mexico: Guerra, 1952), 9; APTGC caja 87 exp. 33, Claudio Cortés to Tomás Garrido Canabal, June 6, 1935; APTGC caja 87 exp. 35, Claudio Cortés to Tomás Garrido Canabal, March 14, 1935.

20 APTGC caja 133 exp. 12, caja 85 and exp. 9, various cor.

21 [Luis] Amendolla, *La revolución comienza a los cuarenta* (Mexico, n.d.), 98; Amado Alfonso Caparroso V., *Tal cual fue Tomás Garrido Canabal* (Mexico City: Editorial Libros de México, 1985), 357.

22 Mario Aranda González, *Hecelchakán: Historia, geografía, cultura* (Campeche, Mexico: CONACULTA, INAH, 2003), 134; Marío Aranda González, *Masonería en el estado de Campeche* (Campeche, Mexico: Instituto Campechano, 1990), 31–34. SEP educators across Mexico fashioned revolutionary ideology from remarkably diverse sources. One Michoacán teacher combined Rosicrucian, Communist, and Masonic symbols with the hero cult of Bartolomé de las Casas. Jesús Tapia Santamaría, *Campo religioso y evolución política en el Bajío zamorano* (Morelia, Mexico: Colegio de Michoacán and Gobierno del estado de Michoacán, 1986), 221.

23 AHSEP caja 21 exp. 5960, Claudio Cortés report, April 30, 1934.

24 Carlos Martínez Assad, *El laboratorio de la revolución: El tabasco garridista* (Mexico City: Siglo XXI, 1979), 129–55.

25 AGN Colección Lázaro Cárdenas (hereafter LC) 521.7/110, Governor Benjamín Romero E. to Francisco Avalos; AHSEP CAM caja 21 exp. 68, Samuel Pérez, January 15, 1934; AHSEP CAM caja 1802 exp. 2, Acto of Fundación de Cooperativa de consumo, "Abastecedora de viveres y medicinas de la Región de Los Chenes"; AHSEP CAM caja 1802 exp. 8, Rubén Rodríguez Lozano report, January 4, 1934; López Sosa, *Tarjeta presidencial*, 10; Wolfgang Gabbert, *Becoming Maya: Ethnicity and Social Inequality in Yucatán since 1500* (Tucson: University of Arizona, 2004), 130–32.

26 AHSEP caja 21 exp. 5960, Claudio Cortés, April 30, 1934; AHSEP CAM caja 21 exp. 91, Gustavo Jarquín to Manuel Mesa, December 29, 1934; AHSEP CAM caja 47 exp. 20, Claudio Cortés report, 1931–32.

27 Benjamin Smith, "Anticlericalism, Politics, and Freemasonry in Mexico," *The Americas* 65, no. 4 (April 2009): 559–88, 567.

28 Paul Vanderwood, "Religion: Official, Popular and Otherwise," *Mexican Studies/Estudios Mexicanos* 16, no. 2 (Summer 2000): 411–41, esp. 434.

29 Fallaw, "Varieties of Mexican Revolutionary Anticlericalism," *The Americas* 65, no. 4 (April 2009): 477–505.

30 AHSEP CAM caja 1802 exp. 8, Francisco Ovalle report, November 9, 1934.
31 AHSEP CAM caja 20 exp. 5, Luis Álvarez Barret report, March 10, 1935.
32 AHSEP CAM caja 1802 exp. 5, Luis Espinosa Morales report, April 19, 1934.
33 On revolutionary attempts to restore Christianity to its primitive purity, see Matthew Butler, "Sotanas Rojinegras: Catholic Anticlericalism and Mexico's Revolutionary Schism," *The Americas* 65, no. 4 (April 2009): 535–58.
34 Robert Quirk, *The Mexican Revolution and the Catholic Church, 1910–1929* (Bloomington: Indiana University Press, 1973), 90.
35 AHSEP CAM caja 21 exp. 5960, Claudio Cortés report, April 30, 1934; AGN DGG 2.340 caja 24 exp. 12, Luis Guízar B., August 18, 1934. On Espinosa's religious ideas, see in particular AHSEP CAM caja 1802 exp. 5, Luis Espinosa Morales report, February 4, 1935.
36 AHSEP DGMC exp. 1, Claudio Cortés report, 1927.
37 AHSEP CAM caja 47 exp. 20; AHSEP DGMC 22, Claudio Cortés, "Nueva Orientación," January 18, 1933; Uc Dzib, "La escuela rural, una nueva escuela de la época de oro de la educación en México," 5:18, 24–25; de la Peña, *Campeche económica*, 1:45.
38 Patience Schell, *Church and State Education in Revolutionary Mexico* (Tucson: University of Arizona Press, 2003), 27–35.
39 Adrian Bantjes, "Saints, Sinners and State Formation," in *The Eagle and the Virgin: Nation and Cultural Revolution in Mexico, 1920–1940*, ed. Stephen E. Lewis and Mary Kay Vaughn (Durham, NC: Duke University Press, 2006), 146.
40 Baltazar Pinto Ávila, "Carretero historiador y crítico," http: www.calkini.net/ (accessed September 9, 2006).
41 AHSEP CAM caja 47 exp. 20, Claudio Cortés report, July 1932.
42 AHSEP CAM caja 21 exp. 68, Samuel Pérez, January 15, 1934.
43 Ramón Berzunza Pinto, *Una chispa en el sureste (Pasado y futuro de los indios mayas)* (Mexico City: Talleres de la Cooperativa, 1942), 42.
44 Julio Tresierra, "Mexico: Indigenous Peoples and the Nation-State," in *Indigenous Peoples and Democracy in Latin America*, ed. Donna Lee Van Cott (New York: St. Martin's Press, 1994), 187–210, esp. 190.
45 AHSEP CAM caja 21 exp. 49, Claudio Cortés, December 24, 1934; AGN AR 011/11, Múgica to President (hereafter PR), June 29, 1934; AGN DGG 2.340 caja 24 exp. 12, Luis Guízar to SG, August 18, 1934; AHSEP CAM caja 20, Claudio Cortés report, December 12, 1934; AHSEP CAM caja 20 exp. 70, Luis Álvarez Barret to Ignacio García Téllez, March 8, 1935.
46 AHSEP CAM caja 1802 exp. 5, Luis Espinosa Morales report, April 19, 1934.
47 AHSSM CRD, Martín, Archbishop of Yucatán, "Arquiodiócesis de Yucatán. Contestación al cuestionario," No. 2, 9, September 1935.
48 Carlos Sierra, *Acción gubernamental en Campeche 1857–1960* (Mexico City: Talleres de Impresión de Estampillas y Valores, 1972), 84–85; Abud Flores, *Campeche*,

104; AGN DGG 2.345 caja 1A exp. 1, Castillo Lanz to SG, February 15, 1926; AGN DGG 2.340 caja 15 exp. 6, Castillo Lanz to SG, August 16, 1926; AGN DGG 2.340 caja 24, Ulises Sansores to SG, August 27, 1928.

49 AHSEP CAM caja 20 exp. 70, Luis Álvarez Barret to Ignacio García Téllez, March 8, 1935.

50 *Desdeldiez: Boletín del Centro de Estudios de la Revolución Mexicana "Lázaro Cárdenas,"* AC, September 1984, "Península de Yucatán," 87–99. On President Abelardo Rodríguez's pressure on state governments to pass anticlerical legislation, see AHSSM CR, J. Bañon Martínez, "Acontecimientos verificados en Querétaro en el mes de octubre de 1935, en relación con la iglesia católica"; Records of the Department of State Relating to the Internal Affairs of Mexico (hereafter RDSRIAM) reel 43, Josephus Daniels, "Memorandum of Conversation with Acting SRE Ceniceros," November 13, 1935; Lorenzo Meyer, *Historia de la Revolución Mexicana: Período 1928–1934*, vol. 12 (Mexico City: El Colegio de México, 1978), 178–80.

51 AGN DGG 2.340 caja 25 exp. 1., Benjamín Romero to Abelardo Rodríguez, September 23, 1934; Archivo Histórico Arzobispado de México (hereafter AHAM), Archivo Pascual Díaz (hereafter APD) caja 3 AG exp. 33; AGN AR 514.3/3; AGN DGG 2.340 caja 24 exp. 12; *Ley reglamentaria de cultos del estado de Campeche* (Campeche, Mexico: Gobierno del Estado, 1934); AGN DGG 2.340 caja 25 exp. 1; Murray Survey (hereafter MS), Martín Palmira L. to Paul Murray, June 2, 1936.

52 RDSRIAM 1930–39 reel 43, Charles H. Taliaferro to Secretary of State (hereafter SOS), December 5, 1934; RDSRIAM 1930–39 reel 22, Waldo E Bailey to SOS, November 30, 1934.

53 AGN DGG 2.340 caja 24 exp. 12 and caja 25 exps. 1, 25; AGN DGG 2.340 caja 25 exp. 1, Subsrio SG to Bishop, October 3, 1934; AGN DGG 2.347(2) caja 1 bis exp. 7, Esteban García to SG, September 25, 1934; AHSEP CAM caja 1802 exp. 8, FO report, November 9, 1934; RDSRIAM 1930–39 reel 22, Waldo E. Bailey to SOS, November 30, 1934; AGN LC 521.7/47; RDSRIAM 1930–39 reel 43, Charles H. Taliaferro to SOS, December 5, 1935.

54 Alan Knight, "Popular Culture and the Revolutionary State in Mexico, 1910–1940," *Hispanic American Historical Review* 74, no. 3 (1994): 393–444, esp. 438.

55 AHSEP CAM caja 1802 exp. 8, F. Ovalle report, November 9, 1934; Mario H. Aranda González, *Apuntaciones históricas y literarias del municipo de Hopelchen, Campeche* (Mérida, Mexico: Maldonado, 1985) 188.

56 AHSEP CAM caja 1802 exp. 8, F. Ovalle report, November 9, 1934; AHSEP CAM caja 21 exp. 49, Claudio Cortés report, December 24, 1934; AHSEP CAM caja 20 exp. 70, Claudio Cortés report, December 12, 1934; AHSEP CAM caja 20 exp. 5, Luis Álvarez Barret, "Informe General Sintético," March 10, 1935.

57 AHSEP CAM caja 1802 exp. 8, F. Ovalle report, November 9, 1934.

58 AHSEP CAM caja 21 exp. 5960, Claudio Cortés report, April 9, 1934.

59 AGN DGG 2.340 caja 25 exp. 1, Josefa de la Cebada de Azcue to SG, December 14, 1934.
60 I thank Terry Rugeley for pointing out the historical influence of the old Camino Real in northern Campeche.
61 de la Peña, *Campeche económica*, 1:18–29.
62 Fideicomiso Archivo Plutarco Elías Calles y Fernando Torreblanco (hereafter FAPECYFT), Archivo Plutarco Elías Calles, Fondo Plutarco Elías Calles (hereafter APEC) GAV. 33 FLORES, Ramón Félix exp. 24 inv. 2115 leg. 1, Ramón Félix Flores to Calles, February 12, 1923; AGN DGG 2.74 caja 7 exp. 2, J. Certucha to SG, June 29, 1922, July 1, 1922; Juan Bolívar, *Compendio de historia de ciudad de Carmen, Campeche* (Carmen, Mexico: Ediciones Contraste, 1989), 85–86.
63 Enrique Canudas, *Trópico rojo: Historia política y social de Tabasco, Los años garridistas 1919/1934*. 3 vols. (Villahermosa, Mexico: Gobierno del estado de Tabasco and Instituto de Cultura de Tabasco, 1982), 2:72.
64 APTGC caja 133 exp. 9, Manuel Barrera L. to Tomás Garrido Canabal, August 5, 1930, and reply, August 25, 1930.
65 AHSEP CAM caja 20 exp. 76, Celso Flores Jefe DER/SEP to Banco Nacional de Crédito Agrícola, February 19, 1935; AHSEP CAM caja 20 exp. 70, Luis Álvarez Barret to Ignacio García Téllez, March 8, 1935; López Sosa, *Tarjeta presidencial*, 10.
66 AHSEP CAM caja 21 exp. 68, Samuel Pérez, January 15, 1934.
67 John Coatsworth, "Obstacles to Economic Growth in Nineteenth-Century Mexico," *American Historical Review*. 83, no. 1 (February 1978), 80–100.
68 AHSEP CAM caja 20 exp. 75, Claudio Cortés report, December 12, 1934; AHSEP CAM caja 20 exp. 70, Luis Álvarez Barret to Ignacio García Téllez, March 8, 1935. On señoritismo, see AHSEP CAM caja 1802 exp. 5, Luis Espinosa Morales, April 19, 1934.
69 AHSEP CAM caja 20 exp. 70, "Muera el Burgués" (Death to the bourgeosie), in *Álbum de cantos revolucionarios. Colaboración de los profesores de música Fco. Amezquita de la Misión Cultural #17 y Angel Cu L. de la DEF. Obsequio de la Dirección de Educación Federal en el Edo. y de la Misión Cultural de la Zona 17 a los maestros de la República* (Campeche, Mexico: n.p., 1935).
70 David Raby, *Educación y revolución social en México (1921–1940)*, trans. Roberto Gómez Ciriza (Mexico City: Sep-Setentas, 1974), 220.
71 AGN DGG 2.311 DS (2) 2 vols. 138, Agente Confidencial #2 SG to SG, July 28, 1928; Sierra, *Diccionario Biográfico de Campeche*, 19; Amendolla, *La revolución comienza a los cuarenta*, 98.
72 Amendolla, *La revolución comienza a los cuarenta*, 87–88.
73 AGN LC 544.3/3, Góngora Gala to PR 7, August 1940; AGN DGG 2.311G caja 226; AGN DGG 2.311 G (6–3) 1 exp. "Informe de elecciones," June 28, 1927.
74 Silvia Molina, *Imagen de Héctor* (Mexico City: Cal y Arena, 1990), 125; Sierra, *Diccionario Biográfico de Campeche*, 250; AGN 543.11/7, Alfonso Ramírez Altamirano et al. to PR, January 14, 1937.

75 AGN LC 543.1/16, Anonymous memorandum, January 30, 1937.
76 AHSEP CAM caja 20 exp. 71, Juan Pacheco Torres to Gral. Múgica, February 20, 1935, February 22, 1935; AHSEP CAM caja 20 exp. 70; AHSEP CAM caja 20 exp. 5, Luis Álvarez Barrer report, March 10, 1935; AHSEP CAM caja 20 exp. 75, Luis Espinosa Morales report, April 27, 1935; AHSEP Campeche caja 20 exp. 71, Luis Espinosa Morales, February 1935; AGN DGG 2.347(2) caja 1 bis exp. 9, Rita Monroy to Luis I. Rodríguez, November 12, 1936; AGN LC 534.6/1112, Francisco Múgica to Lázaro Cárdenas, January 20, 1936; AHSEP MC 5963/18, Juan Pacheco Torres ENR-H, March 1932; Manuel Herrera P., *Apuntes para la historia de Calkiní* (Calkiní, Mexico, 1966), 70, 111–13, 118, 138, 189–91.
77 AGN LC 544.2/3, Angli Lara to PR, March 24, 1935; AHSEP CAM caja 20 exp.20 Luis Álvarez Barret to Ignacio García Téllez, March 8, 1935.
78 AGN Colección Obregón y Calles (hereafter OyC) 104-L-23 annex #3, Manuel J. Mex, March 2, 1926.
79 Mex was state congressman in 1939 and *regidor* of the city of Campeche in 1921. Manuel Alcocer Bernes, *Historia del Ayuntamiento de Campeche, 1540–1991* (Campeche, Mexico: Ayuntamiento de Campeche, 1991), 295; AHSEP CAM caja 20 exp. 70, Luis Álvarez Barret to PR, February 7, 1935; ACC 2.10 Comité Diocesano, 30–46, Justina Rebollado to Luis Bustos, January 17, 1939. Bernabé Euán was *suplente* for the Hecelchakán district for the 1927–29 period. Emilio Rodríguez Herrera, *Legislaturas Campechanas: Compendio Histórico (1861–1998)* (Campeche, Mexico: Congreso del Estado de Campeche, 1999), 140; Aranda González, *Hecelchakán*, 146.
80 Juan Barbosa's family occupied a string of local offices from tax collector to justice of the peace; at the time, Barbosa was a (state) congressman elect. AHSEP CAM caja 21 exp. 53, CC, "Informe . . . respecto a los sucesos de Hecelchakán," June 9, 1934; AGN DGG 2.340 caja 25 exp. 1, petition from Hecelchakán, October 30, 1934, attached to Luis Guízar B to SG, October 20, 1934; AHSEP CAM caja 20 exp. 70, Luis Álvarez Barret to Ignacio García Téllez, March 8, 1935; AGN LC 544.4/484, Pedro Velázquez et al., October 23, 1935; AGN LC 544.2/3, Nicolás Tamayo et al. to President, March 20, 1935; ANSEP CAM caja 20 exp. 71, CC, "Síntesis" [February 23, 1935].
81 Jeffrey Pilcher, *¡Que vivan los Tamales!* (Wilmington, DE: Scholarly Resources, 1998), 108; AHSEP CAM caja 20 exp. 71, CC, "Síntesis"; AGN LC 521.7/47, Herculano Farfán, December 24, 1934; AGN LC 521.7/47, Matilde Chí to PR, August 24, 1936.
82 AHSEP CAM caja 21 exp. 91, Gustavo Jarquín to Manuel Mesa A., December 29, 1934.
83 Paul Eiss, "Hunting for the Virgin: Meat, Money and Memory in Tetiz, Yucatán," *Cultural Anthropology* 17, no. 3 (August 2002), 291–30, 298, 317.
84 Alejandro Negrín Muñoz, *Campeche: Una historia compartida* (Mexico City: Gobierno del Estado de Campeche and Instituto de Investigaciones, Dr. José María Luis Mora, 1991), 90.
85 RDSRIAM 1930–39 reel 43, Charles H. Taliaferro to SOS, December 5, 1935.

86 AHAM APD, caja 1 (A.G. 196) exp. 16, Archbishop Pascual Díaz to Bishop Luis Guízar, April 25, 1933.
87 Piña Chán, *Enciclopedia histórica*, 3:367–68.
88 Alberto Marcilla López, *Resumen histórico del Obispado de Campeche* (Mérida, Mexico: Colegio San José de Artes y Oficios, 1908), 43–75; Bravo 37, http://orbita.starmedia.com/diocesis_de_campeche/Obispos1.htm (accessed August 22, 2006).
89 Bravo 37; AHAM APD caja 1 (A.G. 196) exp. 16, Luis Obispo to Archbishop Díaz, July 10, 1933.
90 AHAM APD, exp. González Fco Obispo de Campeche, Francisco Obispo de Campeche to Archbishop, October 20, 1927.
91 AHAM, APD caja 1 (A.G. 196) exp. 16, various cor.
92 AGN DGG.340 caja 24 exp. 8, Interim gov. to SG, January 21, 1930; Marcilla, *Resumen histórico*, 75.
93 AHSEP CAM caja 1802 exp. 8, Inspector 20 zone, August 2, 1933.
94 de la Peña, *Campeche económica*, 1:41–42.
95 AGN DGG 2.340 caja 24 exp. 8, Interim governor to SG, January 21, 1930; AGN DGG 2.347(2) caja 1 bis exp. 9.
96 AHSEP CAM caja 20 exp. 71, Juan Pacheco to Múgica, February 22, 1935; AGN DGG 2.340 caja 25 exp. 1, Raúl G. Domínguez to SG, January 2, 1936.
97 AGN 2.347(2) caja 1 bis exp. 6, Oficina de Migración to SG, September 24, 1931.
98 AHAM LLM Caja Comité Episcopal exp. "T," José del Valle, February 18, 1945.
99 Across Mexico, state persecution restricted the regular sacramental life directed by the clergy, but lay-led forms contributed to a spiritual "effervescence" that awaits investigation. See Matthew Butler, "A Revolution in Spirit? Mexico, 1910–1940," in *Faith and Impiety in Revolutionary Mexico*, ed. Matthew Butler (New York: Palgrave Macmillan, 2007), 1–20, esp. 11–16.
100 Terry Rugeley, *Of Wonders and Wisemen: Religion and Popular Cultures in Southeast Mexico, 1800–1876* (Austin: University of Texas Press, 2001), 81–82; Rugeley, *Rebellion Now and Forever*, 312–13.
101 Ron Loewe, "Marching with San Miguel: Festivity, Obligation, and Hierarchy in a Mexican Town," *Journal of Anthropological Research* 59, no. 4 (Winter 2003): 463–86; Denise Fay Brown, "Yucatec Maya Settling, Settlement and Spatiality" (PhD diss., University of California–Riverside, 1993), 210–12; Franco Savarino Rogerro, *Pueblos y nacionalismo: Del régimen oligárquico a la sociedad de masas en Yucatán, 1894–1925* (Mexico City: Instituto Nacional de Estudios Históricos de la Revolución Mexicana, 1997), 205. See also Francisco Fernández Repetto and Genny Negroe Sierra, "Caminando y 'paseando' con la Virgen: Prácticas de la religión popular e identidades sociales en el noroccidente de Yucatán," in *Identidades Sociales en Yucatán*, ed. María Cecilia Lara Cebada (Mérida, Mexico: Facultad de Ciencias Antropológicas, 1997), 99–132.
102 Stuart Voss, *Latin America in the Middle Period, 1750–1929* (Wilmington, DE: Scholarly Resources, 2002), 167.

103 Rugeley, *Wonders*, 82.
104 Francisco Fernández Repetto and Genny Negroe Sierra, "Resistencia cultural a través de la religión popular. Los gremios y las fiestas de Yucatán," in *Persistencia cultural entre los Mayas frente al cambio y la modernidad*, ed. Ramón Arzápalo Marín and Ruth Gubler (Mérida, Mexico: Universidad Autónoma de Yucatán, 1997), 1–12, esp. 6–7.
105 de la Peña, *Campeche económico*, 1:41–42; Robert Redfield, *The Folk Culture of Yucatán* (Chicago: University of Chicago Press, 1941), 274–301.
106 Brown, "Yucatec Maya Settling," 210–12; Ella Quintal Avilés, " 'Según su fe de cada uno': Patronos poderosos y control cultural en el oriente de Yucatán," in *Religión popular: de la reconstrucción histórica al análisis antropológico (aproximaciones casuísticas)*, ed. Genny Negroe Sierra and Fernández Repetto Francisco (Mérida, Mexico: Universidad Autónoma de Yucatán, 2000), 231–59, esp. 237–39.
107 de la Peña, *Campeche Económico*, 41–42. Edward Wright-Rios reminds us that supposedly traditional lay organizations are often of more recent origin. See his *Revolution in Mexican Catholicism: Reform and Revelation in Oaxaca, 1887–1934* (Durham, NC: Duke University Press, 2009).
108 AGN DGG 2.340 caja 25 exp. 1.
109 MS, Father Martín Palmira L. to Paul Murray, June 2, 1936.
110 AGN AR 514.3/3, Sub SG to Ramón Uc, July 20, 1934, and Manuel Andrés to Ignacio Quijano et al., November 5, 1934.
111 AGN DGG 2.340 caja 25 exp. 1.
112 AHAM APD, caja 1 (A.G. 196) exp. 16, Bishop Campeche to Archbishop, April 16, 1933; AHAM APD, caja 3 AG exp. 33.
113 AGN LC 544.2/3, Fernando Enrique Angli to President, March 24, 1935, and Manuel Ferrer Vega to President, March 22, 1935.
114 Various AGN DGG 2.340 caja 25 exp. 1 and 2.347(2) caja 1 bis exp. 8; RDSRIAM 1930–39 reel 43, Charles H. Taliaferro, December 5, 1935.
115 RDSRIAM 1930–39 reel 22, various correspondence; MS, Martin Palmira L. to Paul Murray, June 2, 1936; *Diario de Yucatán*, November 26, 1936.
116 AGN LC 2.347(2) caja 1 bis exp. 9, Rita Monroy to Luis R. Rodríguez, November 12, 1936; AGN LC 543.1/16, anonymous memorandum, January 30, 1937; AGN DGG 2.340 caja 24 exp. 10; Raby, *Educación y revolución social en México (1921–1940)*, 217–36.
117 Ute Schuren, "La revolución tardía: Reforma agraria y cambio político en Campeche (1910–1940)," in *Yucatán a través de los siglos*, ed. Ruth Gubler and Patricia Maskel (Mérida, Mexico: Universidad Autónoma de Yucatán, 2001), 285–318; Raby, *Educación y revolución social en México (1921–1940)*, 224, 228–34.
118 AGN LC 544.61/33; AGN LC 544.5/615; AGN DGG 2.311 G-6-(2.)-6 caja 194 exp. 3; Salvador López Espínola, *Nuestras huellas recientes: Las sucesiones gubernamentales en Campeche de 1939 a 1991* (Mexico City: Editorial Cumbres, 1999), 29–30; Claudio Vadillo López, *Campeche: Sociedad, economía, política y cultural* (Mexico City: Universidad Nacional Autónoma de México, 2000), esp. 43; Molina, *Imagen*

de Héctor, esp. 124–25; AGG DGG 2.311G (2–5)(2–6) caja 191, E. López to PR, March 5, 1943.
119 López Sosa, *Tarjeta presidencial*.
120 AHAM APD, caja 1 A.G. 196 exp. 16, Bishop Campeche to Archbishop, April 16, 1933.
121 AHSEP CAM caja 21 exp. 5960, Claudio Cortés report, April 30, 1934.
122 ACC 2.10 Comité Diocesano 30–46, Francisco M. Barahona P. to Luis G. Bustos, June 5, 1938, and Justina Rebollado to Luis G. Bustos, January 17, 1939.
123 ACC exp. 2.10.1, Informes de visitas a Diócesis 1939–47, Luís G. Bustos, "Informe de Visita a Dioceses de Campeche y Tabasco," April 6, 1941.
124 AHAM LMM Caja Comité Episcopal exp. "F y G," J. M. Maya et al. to Archbishop Luis M. Martínez, December 16, 1944.
125 For a different view, see Marjorie Becker, "Torching La Purísima, Dancing at the Altar: The Construction of Revolutionary Hegemony in Michoacán, 1934–40," in *Everyday Forms of State Formation: Revolution and the Negotiation of Rule in Modern Mexico*, ed. Gilbert M. Joseph and Daniel Nugent (Durham, NC: Duke University Press, 1994), 247–64, esp. 260.

Chapter 3: The Bishop, the SEP, and the Emancipation of the Indian in Hidalgo

1 Peter Reich, *Mexico's Hidden Revolution: The Catholic Church in Law and Politics since 1929* (Notre Dame, IN: University of Notre Dame Press, 1995), 44; Jean Meyer, *La Cristiada*, 8th ed., 3 vols. (Mexico City: Siglo XXI, 1983), 1:360, 2:255–56.
2 Teodomiro Manzano, *Anales del estado de Hidalgo: Desde los tiempos mas remotos hasta nuestros días* (Pachuca, Mexico: Gobierno del estado de Hidalgo, 1927), 2:347.
3 Rocío Ruiz de Barrera, *Breve historia de Hidalgo* (Mexico City: El Colegio de México, Fideicomiso Historia de las Américas and Fondo de Cultura Económica, 2000), 145; Timothy Clarke Hanley, "Civilian Leadership of the Cristero Movement: The Liga Nacional Defensora de la Libertad Religiosa and the Church-State Conflict in Mexico, 1924–1938" (PhD diss., Columbia University, 1977), 321, 526, 551; Alberto María Carreño, *Páginas de Historia Mexicana* (Mexico City: Ediciones Victoria, 1936), 3:101; AINAH reel 34, Pedro Benavides to Andrés Barquín y Ruiz, October 21, 1932; Luis Álvarez Flores et al., *J. de Jesús Manríquez y Zárate, Gran Defensor de la Iglesia* (Mexico City: Editorial Rex-Mex, 1952), 346. On the nickname Hombre Obispo, see AINAH CR reel 34, Jefe Celaya to JOM, October 26, 1934.
4 Strictly speaking, highland semitropical valleys drained by the Panuco River make up the Huasteca. Administratively, it is divided among the states of Hidalgo, Puebla, Querétaro, San Luis Potosí, and Veracruz. Hidalgo's Huasteca roughly corresponds to the district of Huejutla, including the municipalities of Huejutla, Orizatlán, Jaltocan, Altapexco, Tlanchinol, Huazalingo, Yahualica, Xochiatipan,

and Huatla. Religious, social, and political ties long linked the highland valleys of the Huasteca proper to the Sierra (highland) districts of Molango (Molango, Calnali, Lolotla, Tepehuacán, Tlahuiltepa, Xochicoatlán municipalities) and Zacaultipan. See Frans Schryer, *Ethnicity and Class Conflict in Rural Mexico* (Princeton, NJ: Princeton University Press, 1990), 50–55. Geographically, the upstate encompasses four distinct ecological zones: the mountainous Sierra Gorda; the Sierra Baja, or foothills; the Sierra Alta, or high mountains; and the Hidalgan Huasteca proper. My division of Hidalgo into upstate (Sierra and Huasteca proper) and downstate (the rest) reflects environmental, historical, ethnic, and political differences. Upstaters called themselves serranos (highlanders) and huastecos. On the upstate "indio Huasteco," see AHSEP HGO caja 5800 exp. 12, Superintendant Leobardo Parra y Marquina report, 1935. In Eric Van Young's terminology, the upstate possesses both subregionality and a degree of subregionalism. Eric Van Young, "Are Regions Good to Think?" in *Mexico's Regions: Comparative History and Development*, ed. Eric Van Young (San Diego: Center for U.S.-Mexican Studies, University of California–San Diego, 1992), 2. Subregionalism stimulated nineteenth-century separatism. Michael Ducey, *A Nation of Villages: Riot and Rebellion in the Mexican Huasteca, 1750–1850* (Tucson: University of Arizona Press, 2004), 13, 15.

5 Ruiz de Barrera, *Breve historia de Hidalgo*, 16–17, 108–9; José de Jesús Montoya Briones, *Etnografía de la dominación en México. Cien años de violencia en la Huasteca* (Mexico City: Instituto Nacional de Antropología e Historia, 1996), 34–36; Efrain Buenrostro, *Geografía Económica del Estado de Hidalgo* (Mexico City: Secretaria de la Economia Nacional, 1939), esp. 38–39; Irma Eugenia Gutiérrez, *Hidalgo: Sociedad, economía, política y cultura* (Mexico City: UNAM, 1990), 18; Jesus Angeles Contreras, *Monografía del municipio de Molango* (Pachuca, Mexico: Gobierno del Estado de Hidalgo, Instituto Hidalguense de la Cultura, 1993), 42–43, 57–58; Alfonso Fabila, *Valle del mezquital* (Mexico City: Ediciones Culturales, 1938), 147; William Millsap, "An Otomí Village in the Mezquital Valley: A Study of History and Cultural Adaptation in México" (PhD diss., University of Missouri, 1976).

6 Angeles Contreras, *Monografía del municipio de Molango*, 42–45; AGN DGG 2.72 caja 2 exp. 10, Antonio Chávez et al., March 17, 1920; AGN DGG 2.72 caja 2 exp. 70, Father Jesús Herrera, August 26, 1920.

7 Gutiérrez, *Hidalgo*, esp. 57; Angeles Contreras, *Monografía*, esp. 44–45; Juan Manuel Menes Llaguno, *Pachuca diez décadas de su historia* (Itzmiquilpan, Mexico: Presidencia Municipal de Pachuca, 1999), esp. 52, 66–67; Alexander Dawson, *Indian and Nation in Revolutionary Mexico* (Tucson: University of Arizona Press, 2004), 127–33. Information on Tulancingo's bishops was gleaned from http://www.catholic-hierarchy.org/diocese.html (accessed December 11, 2007).

8 AGN DGG 2.347 caja 5 exp. 3; Manzano, *Anales*, 2:319–21; AGN DGG 2.72 caja 5 exp. 33, Sub-SG to Presidente Municipal Arenal, March 24, 1923; AGN DGG 2.72 caja 8

exp. 2, Governor Azuara to SG, July 4, 1924; AGN DGG 2.345 caja 1A exp. 1, Vicente Gómez, September 21, 1925.

9 AGN DGG 2.74 caja 12 exp. 8, José S. Bravo to Sub-SG, July 2, 1924.
10 Arturo Herrera Cabañas, "Poder y familia en el mezquital," in *Nos queda la esperanza. El valle del mezquital*, ed. Carlos Martínez Assad and Sergio Sarmiento (Mexico City: Consejo Nacional para la Cultura y las Artes, 1991), 135–47; Schryer, *Ethnicity and Class Conflict in Rural Mexico*, 122; AHSEP HGO caja 822 exp. 16, Rafael Pérez de León to SEP, January 10, 1930; FAPECYFT *Plutarco Elías Calles* GAV. 52 MEDINA ESTRADA, Narciso (Gral.) exp. 13 inv. 3587; Ernest Gruening, *Mexico and Its Heritage* (New York: Century, 1928), 389.
11 Montoya Briones, *Etnografía de la dominación en México*, 73.
12 Schryer, *Ethnicity and Class Conflict in Rural Mexico*, 121–22.
13 AHSEP HGO caja 807 exp. 1, superintendent report, 1929.
14 Rafael Vera Sánchez, *Matías Rodríguez, Vidas Exactas* (Mexico City: Herrero Hermanos, 1931), 233; Ruiz de Barrera, *Breve historia de Hidalgo*, 145.
15 AGN DGG 2.347 caja 26 exps. 53, 55; AGN DGG 2.340 caja 43 exp. 33; AGN DGG 2.347 caja 26 exps. 41, 42; Montoya Briones, *Etnografía de la dominación en México*, 162.
16 Adriaan Van Oss, "La Iglesia en Hidalgo hacia 1930," *Historia Mexicana* 29, no. 2 (October–December 1970): 301–24, esp. 311–14.
17 AGN DGG 2.347 caja 26 exp. 49, gov. to SG, August 2, 1926; Schryer, *Ethnicity and Class Conflict in Rural Mexico*, 123.
18 AGN DGG 2.347 caja 26 exp. 45, gov. to SG, February 20, 1928.
19 AGN DGG 2.347 caja 26 exp. 50, gov. to SG, April 14, 1928.
20 AGN DGG 2.347 caja 26 exps. 46, 49, 56.
21 María Teresa Rodríguez López and Pablo Valderrama Rouy, "The Gulf Coast Nahua," in *Native Peoples of the Gulf Coast of Mexico*, ed. Alan R. Sandstrom and E. Hugo García Valencia (Tucson: University of Arizona Press, 2006), 158–86.
22 Called the dioceses of the Mixtecas in 1903, the next year it became Huajuapam de León. See Benjamin Smith, "The Politics of Anticlericalism and Resistance: The Diocese of Huajuapam de León 1930–1940," *Journal of Latin American Studies* 37, no. 3 (August 2005), 469–509, and Benjamin Smith, "'The Priest's Party': Local Catholicism and Panismo in Huajuapam de León," in *Faith and Impiety in Revolutionary Mexico*, ed. Matthew Butler (New York: Palgrave Macmillan, 2007), 263.
23 The Church's weakness in the Huasteca of Hidalgo in the Porfiriato seems remarkably similar to its institutional debility in Papantla in northern Veracruz. See Emilio Kouri, *Business, Property, and Community in Papantla, Mexico* (Stanford, CA: Stanford University Press, 2004), 57.
24 Lauro López Beltrán, *Manríquez y Zárate, Primero obispo de Huejutla. Sublimador de Juan Diego. Heroico defensor de la fe* (Mexico City: Editorial Tradición, 1974), 230–36.

25 Ibid., esp. 14–24, 230–37.
26 Frans Schryer, *The Rancheros of Pisaflores: History of a Peasant Bourgeoisie in Twentieth-century Mexico* (Toronto: University of Toronto Press, 1980), 69–84; Schryer, *Ethnicity and Class Conflict in Rural Mexico*, 27–72.
27 Hernán Menéndez Rodríguez, *Iglesia y poder. Proyectos sociales, alianzas políticas y económicas en Yucatán (1857–1917)* (Mexico City: Editorial Nuestra América and Consejo Nacional para la Cultura y las Artes, 1995), 280–85. Even earlier, during the U.S. invasion of Mexico, a so-called Caste War erupted in the Huasteca region. Even though the rebels did not identify as indigenous, the Mexican press described the insurgency as an ethnic conflict. See Ducey, *A Nation of Villages*, 142–70.
28 López Beltrán, *Manríquez y Zárate, Primero obispo de Huejutla*, 14–18, 21–23, 207–8, 230–37.
29 Smith, "The Politics of Anticlericalism and Resistance," 476–77; Frans Schryer, personal communication to the author, April 4, 2008.
30 Frans Schryer, "Discussion and Conclusions: Agrarian Conflict and Pilgrimage," in *Pilgrimage in Latin America*, ed. N. Ross Crumrine and Alan Morinis (New York: Greenwood, 1991), 357–68, esp. 360.
31 Nathaniel Whetten, *Rural Mexico* (Chicago: University of Chicago Press, 1948), 376.
32 Claudio Lomnitz-Adler, *Exits from the Labyrinth: Culture and Ideology in the Mexican National Space* (Berkeley: University of California Press, 1992), 165–68.
33 López Beltrán, *Manríquez y Zárate, Primero obispo de Huejutla*, 207.
34 AHSEP HGO caja 1337 exp. 9, Anatolio G. Bautista to SG, April 24, 1935; AHSEP HGO caja 5800 exp. 7, J. Jesús Vite Mercado to PR, January 16, 1936.
35 Smith, "The Politics of Anticlericalism and Resistance," 475.
36 Sergio Edmundo Carrera Quezada, *A son de campana: La fragua de Xochiatipan* (Mexico City: CIEAS, Colegio de San Luis, Universidad Autónoma del Estado de Hidalgo, 2007), 162–63.
37 Rodríguez López and Valderrama Rouy, "The Gulf Coast Nahua," 176–83; Schryer, *Ethnicity and Class Conflict in Rural Mexico*, 123.
38 Rodríguez López and Valderrama Rouy, "The Gulf Coast Nahua," 172.
39 Alan Sandstrom, *Corn Is Our Blood: Culture and Ethnic Identity in a Contemporary Aztec Indian Village* (Norman: University of Oklahoma Press, 1991), 317.
40 Schryer, "Discussion and Conclusions," in *Pilgrimage*, 357–68, esp. 363–66.
41 AHSEP HGO caja 940 exp. 33, Felipe Sierra to SG, June 16, 1934; López Beltrán, *Manríquez*, 238. On the *besamano*, see AHSEP HGO caja 874 exp. 12, Francisco Moreno to SEP, February 5, 1932. On ethnic inequality, see Schryer, *Ethnicity and Class Conflict in Rural Mexico*, 62–63. On the clergy's and the bishop's economic activities, see AGN DGG.347 caja 26 exp. 60; AHSEP HGO caja 1060 exp. 36, Rubén Rodríguez Lozano to SEP, November 30, 1934.
42 Carrera Quezada, *A son de campana*, 162–63.
43 López Beltrán, *Manríquez y Zárate, Primero obispo de Huejutla*, 238; Gonzalo

Aquiles Serna Alcántara, "La escuela normal libre de Huejutla (1925–1935): Una historia para preservar," at http://www.comie.org.mx/congreso/memoria/v9/ponencias/ato9/PRE1177698825.pdf (accessed March 27, 2008); Rubén Rodríguez Lozano, *Maestros revolucionarios* (Mexico City: Instituto Nacional de Juventud Mexicana, 1963), 108.

44 AGN DGG 2.311M caja 9 exp. 11, Esteban Reyes to SG, January 13, 1933.
45 AGN DGG 2.311 DL caja 30 exp. 1, G. González to PR, January 29, 1933.
46 AGN DGG 2.340 caja 43 exp. 45, Tomas Zuñiga Lima et al. to gov., October 19, 1933. See also AGN DGG 2.347 caja 26 exp. 60; AGN DGG 2.347 caja 5 exp. 6; AHSEP HGO caja 874 exp. 12.
47 Schryer, *Ethnicity and Class Conflict in Rural Mexico*, 123; Montoya Briones, *Etnografía de la dominación en México. Cien años de violencia en la Huasteca*, 162–63.
48 There are local exceptions. In Huazalingo, mestizos and Nahua peasants alike had an obligation to perform unpaid labor, and sharecroppers of both ethnicities were expected to provide from two to three days of uncompensated labor a week. See Schryer, *Ethnicity and Class Conflict in Rural Mexico*, 104, 124.
49 Frans J. Schryer, "Peasants and the Law: A History of Land Tenure and the Conflict in the Huastecas," *Journal of Latin American Studies* 18, no. 2 (November 1986), 293.
50 *Hombre Libre*, July 19, 1937, letter to editor by Florencio F. Rodríguez.
51 Antonio Escobar Ohmstede and Frans Schryer, "Las sociedades agrarias en el norte de Hidalgo, 1856–1900," *Mexican Studies/Estudios Mexicanos* 8 no. 1 (winter 1992), 19.
52 Schryer, *Ethnicity and Class Conflict in Rural Mexico*, 122.
53 Augusto Santiago Sierra, *Las misiones culturales (1923–1973)* (Mexico City: SepSetentas, 1973), 16, 23, 37.
54 AHSEP HGO caja 1660 exp. 20, Jenaro G. Rodríguez to JDER/SEP, October 6, 1927; AHSEP HGO caja 1060 exp. 36, Rubén Rodríguez Lozano to SEP, November 20, 1934; Lomnitz-Adler, *Exits from the Labyrinth*, 153–68.
55 Secretaria de Educacion Pública, *Las misiones culturales en 1927: Las escuelas normales rurales* (Mexico City: SEP, 1928), 140.
56 AHSEP HGO caja 1060 exp. 20, Jenaro G. Rodríguez to JDER/SEP, October 6, 1927.
57 AGN DGG 2.382 caja 20 exp. 4, Manuel Almariza to SG, June 18, 1937; Albino Ahumada Medina, *Organización campesina y lucha agraria en el estado de Hidalgo, 1917–1940* (Pachuca, Mexico: Universidad Autónoma del Estado de Hidalgo, 2000), 90–91.
58 George Isidore Sánchez, *Mexico: A Revolution by Education* (New York: Viking Press, 1936), 90–92.
59 Steve Lewis, "A Window into the Recent Past in Chiapas: Federal Education and Indigenismo in the Highlands, 1921–1940," *Journal of Latin American Anthropology* 6, no. 1 (2001), 63–65; http://www.seycc.gob.mx/galeriaspec/federicocorozo.html (accessed December 3, 2007).

60 AHSEP caja 1337 exp. 10; AHSEP caja 1337 exp. 3, Rubén Rodríguez Lozano, March 31, 1935; AHSEP caja 1337 exp. 4, Alfonso Hernández to SEP, June 10, 1935.
61 Rodríguez Lozano, *Maestros revolucionarios*, 1–105, 128–49; Rubén Rodríguez Lozano, *San Luis Potosí en su lucha por la libertad* (Mexico City: Artes Gráficas del Estado, 1938); Gustavo Díaz Ordaz and Rubén Rodríguez Lozano, *Los gobiernos de la revolución contra la ignorancia* (Mexico City: Instituto Nacional de la Juventud Mexicana, 1965).
62 Dawson, *Indian and Nation in Revolutionary Mexico*, 120–21.
63 AHSEP CAMP caja 1802 exp. 8, Rubén Rodríguez Lozano, August 2, 1933; Rodríguez Lozano, *Maestros revolucionarios*, 106.
64 AHSEP HGO caja 1060 exp. 36, Rubén Rodríguez Lozano to SEP, May 31, 1934.
65 Ibid.
66 Rodríguez Lozano, *Maestros revolucionarios*, 107–13.
67 Schryer, *Ethnicity and Class Conflict in Rural Mexico*, 117–26.
68 Sandstrom, *Corn Is Our Blood*, 348.
69 Susan Kellogg, *Law and the Transformation of Aztec Culture, 1500–1700* (Norman: University of Oklahoma Press, 1995), 227; Schryer, *Ethnicity and Class Conflict in Rural Mexico*, 63; AHSEP HGO caja 1060 exp. 36, Rubén Rodríguez Lozano report, May 31, 1934, and caja 1660 exp. 20, Jenaro G. Rodríguez to JDER/SEP, October 6, 1927.
70 Schryer, *Ethnicity and Class Conflict in Rural Mexico*, 114–15.
71 AHSEP HGO caja 1660 exp. 20, Jenaro G. Rodríguez to JDER/SEP, October 6, 1927.
72 AHSEP HGO 1368 exp. 2, Francisco Zárate González to Superintendent, March 20, 1935; AHSEP caja 1337 exp. 9, Anatolio G. Bautista to SG, April 24, 1935.
73 AHSEP HGO caja 1060 exp. 36, Rubén Rodríguez Lozano to SEP, November 30, 1934.
74 Wendy Waters, "Revolutionizing Childhood: Schools, Roads, and the Revolutionary Generation Gap in Tepoztlán, Mexico, 1928–1944," *Journal of Family History* 23, no. 3 (July 1998), 302–4.
75 Schryer, *Ethnicity and Class Conflict in Rural Mexico*, 125–26.
76 On forcible application of "pants laws" against the Mam of Chiapas, see R. Aída Hernández Castillo, *Histories and Stories from Chiapas: Border Identities in Southern Mexico*, trans. Martha Poulos (Austin: University of Texas Press, 2001), 21–26.
77 AHSEP HGO caja 1060 exp. 36, Rubén Rodríguez Lozano report, May 31, 1934.
78 AHSEP HGO caja 1337 exp. 9, Adolfo Espinosa, July 31, 1935; Mary Kay Vaughan, *Cultural Politics in Revolution: Teachers, Peasants, and Schools in Mexico, 1930–1940* (Tucson: University of Arizona, 1997), 15–16, 59–60, 75–76.
79 AHSEP HGO caja 1060 exp. 36, Rubén Rodríguez Lozano to SEP, June 16, 1934.
80 Dawson, *Indian and Nation in Revolutionary Mexico*, 192n101.
81 AGN IPS caja 305 exp. 345 (4.6)-12, Javier Rojo G. to President Partido Socialista del Estado de Hidalgo, August 8, 1934.
82 AHSEP HGO caja 883 exp. 1, Francisco Zárate González to Superintendent, Sep-

tember 18, 1935; AHSSM CR, José de Jesús [Manríquez] Obispo de Huejutla, "Informe"; AGN DGG 2.095 caja 1 exp. 38, Margarita Amador to SG, February 24, 1932; López Beltrán, *Manríquez*, 36, 214, 259.

83 AHSEP HGO caja 1060 exp. 36, Rubén Rodríguez Lozano report, May 31, 1934.
84 Álvarez Flores et al., *J. de Jesús Manríquez*, 10–11.
85 AHSEP HGO caja 1060 exp. 36, Rubén Rodríguez Lozano report, May 31, 1934.
86 AHSEP HGO caja 940 exp. 6, Francisco Zárate González to Superintendent, May 30, 1934.
87 AHSEP HGO caja 1060 exp. 36, Rubén Rodríguez Lozano report, November 30, 1934.
88 Luis Quintanilla, *The Other Side of the Mexican Church Question* (Washington, DC: Luis Quintanilla, 1935), 17.
89 Álvarez Flores et al., *J. de Jesús Manríquez*, 10–11.
90 Fabila, *Valle del mezquital*, 248.
91 Schryer, *Ethnicity and Class Conflict in Rural Mexico*, 125; AHSEP HGO caja 1060 exp. 36, Rubén Rodríguez Lozano report, November 20, 1934.
92 AHSEP HGO caja 940 exp. 36, Federico A. Corzo report, December 20, 1934; AHSEP HGO caja 940 exp. 6, Francisco Zárate González to SEP, December 20, 1934.
93 George Isidore Sánchez, *Mexico: A Revolution by Education* (New York: Viking Press, 1936), 90, 120.
94 AHSSM CR, José de Jesús Obispo de Huejutla, "Informe"; Fabila, *Valle del mezquital*, 23–24.
95 AHSEP HGO caja 1060 exp. 36, Rubén Rodríguez Lozano report, November 30, 1934.
96 Jean Meyer, "El anticlerical revolucionario, 1910–1940: Un ensayo de empatía histórica," in *Las formas y las políticas del dominio agrario: Homenaje a François Chevalier*, ed. Ricardo Ávila Palafox, Carlos Martínez Assad, and Jean Meyer (Guadalajara, Mexico: Editorial Universidad de Guadalajara, 1992), 284–304, esp. 286–287.
97 AGN DGG 2.340 caja 43 exp. 30, governor to SG, August 10, 1928.
98 María Trinidad Torres Vera, *Mujeres y utopía: Tabasco garridista* (Tabasco, Mexico: Universidad Juárez Autónoma de Tabasco, 2001), 38.
99 AGN DGG 2.311 DL caja 30 exp. 1, G. González Flores to PR, January 29, 1933.
100 AHSEP HGO caja 874 exp. 12, Francisco Moreno to SEP, February 5, 1932.
101 AGN DGG 2.347 caja 26 exp. 60; AHSSM CR, José de Jesús, "Informe"; Schryer, *Ethnicity and Class Conflict in Rural Mexico*, 122–23.
102 AGN DGG 2.340 caja 44 exp. 2.
103 AHSEP HGO caja 1060 exp. 36, Rubén Rodríguez Lozano report, October 1, 1934.
104 AHSEP HGO caja 1060 exp. 36, Rubén Rodríguez Lozano report, November 30, 1934.
105 AGN DGG 2.340 caja 44 exp. 2; AGN DGG 2.340 caja 43 exp. 33, "Lista . . . ," January 24, 1934; RDSRIAM 1930–39 reel 44, NCWC News Service, May 25, 1936; AHSEP HGO

caja 1337 exp. 8; AHSEP HGO caja 940 exp. 36, Federico A. Corzo report, December 20, 1934; RDSRIAM 1930–39 reel 41, Josephus Daniels to SOS, November 6, 1934; *La Prensa*, November 18, 1934; Fabila, *Valle del mezquital*.

106 AHSEP HGO caja 940 exp. 36 and 38; Sierra, *Las misiones culturales (1923–1973)*, 41–42.

107 AHSEP HGO caja 5328 exp. 27, Ernesto Ublado Jr. Report, November 30, 1935; AHSEP HGO caja 1367 exp. 3, Leobardo Parra y Marquina to gov., November 6, 1935; AGN DGG 2.347 caja 5 exp. 2, Nahum Martínez R. to SG, February 23, 1935.

108 *Hombre Libre*, February 27, 1935; Charles MacFarland, *Chaos in Mexico: The Conflict of Church and State* (New York: Harper and Brothers, 1935), 100–102.

109 AHSEP HGO caja 1367 exp. 0, Rafael Villeda to JDER/SEP, June 27, 1935.

110 Rodríguez Lozano, *Maestros revolucionarios*, 113.

111 AHSEP HGO caja 1060 exp. 36, Rubén Rodríguez Lozano report, October 12, 1934.

112 AHSEP HGO caja 1060 exp. 36, Rubén Rodríguez Lozano report, November 30, 1934.

113 Adrian Bantjes, "The War against Idols: The Meanings of Iconoclasm in Revolutionary Mexico, 1910–1940," in *Negating the Image: Case Studies in Iconoclasm*, ed. Anne McClanan and Jeff Johnson (Burlington, VT: Ashgate, 2005), 41–66, esp. 56.

114 AHSEP HGO caja 1060 exp. 36, Rubén Rodríguez Lozano report, November 30, 1934.

115 AHSEP HGO caja 940 exp. 6, Francisco Zárate González report, December 20, 1934.

116 Frans J. Schryer, "Discussion and Conclusions," in *Pilgrimage*, 364.

117 Sandstrom, *Corn Is Our Blood*, 257. See also Roberto González, *Zapotec Science: Farming and Food in the Northern Sierra of Oaxaca* (Austin: University of Texas Press, 2001), esp. 95.

118 Sandstrom, *Corn Is Our Blood*, 231–32.

119 AHSEP HGO caja 1060 exp. 36, Rubén Rodríguez Lozano report, November 30, 1934.

120 Ibid.

121 José Castillo Torre, *A la luz de relámpago. Ensayo de biografía subjetiva de Felipe Carrillo Torre* (Mexico City: Ediciones Botas, 1934), 105–6; José de la Luz Mena, *La Escuela Socialista* (Mexico City: A. Sola, 1941), esp. 279–81, 302; AGN IPS caja 172 cont. exp. 9, Agente #7, September 9, 1925.

122 AHSEP HGO caja 5328 exp. "Francisco Zárate González," Francisco Zárate González, Plan de Trabajo, March 1, 1936.

123 AHSEP HGO caja 5328 exp. "Francisco Zárate González," Francisco Zárate González, report, January 2, 1936.

124 AHSEP HGO caja 5328 exp. "Francisco Zárate González," Francisco Zárate González, Plan de Trabajo, March 1, 1936.

125 Ibid.

126 AGN IPS caja 305 exp. 345 (4.6)-12.

127 AGN IPS caja 305 exp. 345 (4.6)-12, Javier Rojo G. to President Partido Socialista

del Estado de Hidalgo, August 8, 1934; AHSEP HGO caja 940 exps. 6 and 33, Felipe Sierra to SG, June 16, 1934; Montoya Briones, *Etnografía de la dominación en México. Cien años de violencia en la Huasteca* (Mexico City: INAH, 1996), 77n70.

128 AHSEP HGO caja 940 exp. 33.

129 Montoya Briones, *Etnografía de la dominación en México*, 164.

130 AGN IPS caja 305 exp. 345 (4.6)-12, Agent Y-136 report, August 17, 1934. On the San Marcos fiesta, see http://www.e-local.gob.mx/work/templates/enciclo/hidalgo/municipios /13014a.htm 25–27 iv 08 (accessed March 27, 2008).

131 AHSEP HGO caja 5328 exp. "Francisco Zárate González," Francisco Zárate González, Plan de Trabajo, March 1, 1936.

132 AGN IPS caja 305 exp. 345 (4.6)-12, Agent Y-136 report, August 17, 1934; AHSEP HGO caja 940 exp. 33.

133 Claudio Favier Orendáin, *Ruinas de utopia. San Juan de Tlayacapan. Espacio y tiempo en el encuentro de dos culturas* (Mexico City: Gobierno del Estado de Morelos, Instituto de Investigaciones Estéticas, Universidad Nacional Autónoma de México, and Fondo de Cultura Económica, 1989).

134 AGN IPS caja 305 exp. 345 (4.6)-12, Javier Rojo G. to President Partido Socialista del Estado de Hidalgo, August 8, 1934; AGN 2.382 caja 21 exp. 5642, Felipe Sierra to SG, October 1, 1935.

135 AHSEP caja 1337 exp. 9, Anatolio Bautista report, March 31, 1935.

136 AHSEP HGO caja 1337 exp. 9, Anatolio Bautista report, March 31, 1935; AHSEP HGO caja 5800 exp. 7, J. Jesús Vite Mercado to PR, January 16, 1936.

137 AHSEP HGO caja 1368 exp. 2, Francisco Zárate González to superintendent, March 20, 1935.

138 AHSEP HGO caja 5328 exp. "Francisco Zárate González," Francisco Zárate González report, January 2, 1936.

139 Schryer, *Ethnicity and Class Conflict in Rural Mexico*, 123, 126; AHSEP HGO caja 1060 exp. 36, Rubén Rodríguez Lozano report, November 30, 1934; AHSEP HGO caja 883 exp. 1; AGN DGG 2.311M caja 365 exp. 40, Leonardo Bustos to SG, October 4, 1935; AHSEP HGO caja 1368 exp. 21, Tomás Campoy to PR, October 5, 1935; AGN DGG 2.311M caja 365 exp. 40, I-65 report, December 12, 1935; http://www.hidalguia.com.mx/xochiatipan/politica.htm (accessed March 28, 2008).

140 AHSEP caja 1337 exp. 9; AGN DGG 2.347 caja 5 exp. 9.

141 AHSEP HGO caja 883 exp. 1, Francisco Zárate González to Manuel Medina, December 6, 1935.

142 AHSEP HGO caja 883 exp. 11; Aquiles Serna Alcántara, "La escuela normal," 8; AHSSM CR, José de Jesús [Manríquez] Obispo de Huejutla, "Informe."

143 AHSEP HGO caja 5800 exp. 12, Leobardo Parra y Marquina report, 1935; AHSEP HGO caja 1367 exp. 0, Rafael Villada to JDER/SEP, June 27, 1935; AHSEP HGO 1368 exp. 21, Tomás Campoy to PR, October 5, 1935.

144 Fabila, *Valle del mezquital*, 243.

145 AHSEP HGO 2.382 caja 20 exp. 4180, Sub secretary Agriculture to SG, July 22, 1935;

AHSEP HGO caja 883 exp. 1, Leobardo Parra y Marquina to Ponciano Rivera, December 6, 1935; http://sistemas.e-hidalgo.gob.mx:8585/DirEscuelas/dir_escuela.jsp?municipio=SAN+FELIPE+ORIZATLAN&nivel=Preescolar+General (accessed May 30, 2008); AHSEP HGO caja 1060 exp. 36, Rubén Rodríguez Lozano report, November 30, 1934.

146 Rodríguez Lozano and Pablo Valderrama, "The Gulf Coast Nahua,"172.
147 AHSSM CR, José de Jesús Obispo, "Informe."
148 AHSEP HGO 1368 exp. 21, Tomás Campoy to PR, October 5, 1935; AHSEP HGO caja 883 exp. 1, Francisco Zárate González to Lázaro Cárdenas, June 3, 1935.
149 AHSEP HGO caja 883 exp. 1, Francisco Zárate González to Lázaro Cárdenas, June 3, 1935.
150 AGN IPS caja 305 exp. 345 (4.6)-12, Javier Rojo G to President Partido Socialista del Estado de Hidalgo (P.S.E.H.), August 8, 1934; AHSEP HGO caja 1367 exp. 0, Rafael Villada to JDER/SEP, June 27, 1935; AHSEP HGO 1368 exp. 21, Tomás Campoy to PR, October 5, 1935; *Hombre Libre*, June 7, 1935, August 23, 1935.
151 AHSEP HGO caja 5328 exp. "Francisco Zárate González," Francisco Zárate González Plan de Trabajo, March 1, 1936.
152 Ibid. Some educators advocated the whitening of Mexico's indigenous peoples; in 1934, the state superintendent of education in Chiapas, Angel M. Corzo, called for indigenous women to "procreate with ladino or white men" to promote "a slow but firm progress of our race." See Rosilva Aída Hernández Castillo, *Histories and Stories from Chiapas: Border Identities in Southern Mexico*, trans. Martha Poulos (Austin: University of Texas Press, 2001), 28–29.
153 *La Revista de Yucatán*, January 1, 1919.
154 http://www.sec sonora.gob.mx/peditorial/publicaciones/ENLACE/90.pdf (accessed October 5, 2010).
155 AHSEP HGO caja 883 exp. 1, Rafael Villeda to Zárate, August 9, 1935; AHSEP HGO caja 1367 exp. 0, Rafael Villada to JDER/SEP, June 27, 1935.
156 *Hombre Libre*, June 7, 1935, "Un Profesor fué Consignado por Abuso de una Joven en Hidalgo."
157 Ibid.
158 AHSEP HGO caja 1337 exp. 3, Rubén Rodríguez Lozano report, March 31, 1935, and exp. 4, Alfonso Hernández to superintendent, June 10, 1935. On the role of Mother's Day in teacher-community negotiation, see Mary Kay Vaughan, "The Construction of the Patriotic Festival in Tecamachalco," in *Rituals of Rule, Rituals of Resistance: Public Celebrations and Popular Culture in Mexico*, ed. William Beezley, Cheryl English Martin, and William E. French (Wilmington, DE: Scholarly Resources, 1994), 213–46.
159 For instance, in February 1936, a SEP inspector was accused of the *rapto* of an indigenous girl in Puebla. *La Prensa*, February 26, 1935.
160 AHSEP DGMC caja 57 exp. 14, Jefe Misión Cultural Malinalco to Rafael Ramírez, December 5, 1927.

161 AGEY PE 824 SG, Mayor Cuncunul to governor, May 14, 1926, and reply on May 17, 1926; Robert Redfield, *A Village that Chose Progress: Chan Kom Revisited* (Chicago: University of Chicago Press, 1957), 12–13.
162 AHSEP DEF-Chihuahua (CHIH) caja 1465 exp. 23, Galileo Castillo to Rafael Ramírez, July 2, 1931; *La Prensa*, February 26, 1935.
163 Katherine Bliss, *Compromised Positions: Prostitution, Public Health, and Gender Politics in Revolutionary Mexico City* (University Park: Penn State University Press, 2001), 128.
164 RDSRIAM reel 43, Josephus Daniels to SOS, June 17, 1935 (extract).
165 AHSEP HGO caja 883 exp. 1, Francisco Zárate González to Wenceslao Martínez, June 21, 1935.
166 AHSEP caja 5800 exp. 12, Leobardo Parra y Marquina report, 1935.
167 AHSEP caja 1337 exp. 9, Anatolio G. Bautista, March 31, 1935; AHSEP HGO caja 940 exp. 36, Federico A. Corzo report, December 20, 1934.
168 AHSEP HGO caja 5800 exp. 12, Leobardo Parra y Marquina report, 1935.
169 AHSEP HGO caja 5328 exp. 30, Rubén Rodríguez Lozano report, March 24, 1936.
170 Dawson, *Indian and Nation in Revolutionary Mexico*, 192n101.
171 Schryer, "Peasants and the Law," 293.
172 From http://www.catholic-hierarchy.org/diocese/dtulo.html (accessed December 11, 2007).
173 ACC 2.10, Junta Diocesana de Tulancingo, 30–40.
174 Ibid., Bishop Luis M. Altamirano to Luis G. Bustos, February 26, 1936.
175 AGN DGG 2.347 caja 26 exp. 42, October 31, 1926, Padres de Familia of Pachuca to SG, October 31, 1926; *Hombre Libre*, August 21, 1935.
176 AHSEP HGO caja 1367 exp. 0, Rafael Villeda to Rafael Ramírez, June 27, 1935, and caja 5328 exp. 27, Ernesto Ublado Jr. report, November 30, 1935.
177 AGN DGG 2.347 caja 5 exp. 4.
178 AHSEP HGO caja 807 exp. 1, superintendent report, February 7, 1930; AGN DGG 2.340 caja 44 exp. 9 and 10; AHSEP HGO caja 5328 exp. 27, Ernesto Ublado Jr. reports, November 30, 1935, December 7, 1935.
179 AGN DGG 2.340 caja 43 exp. 22, Pedro Yañez to SG, December 6, 1926; Teodomiro Manzano, *Anales del estado de Hidalgo: Desde los tiempos mas remotos hasta nuestros dias* (Pachuca, Mexico: Gobierno del estado de Hidalgo, 1927), 2:333–35. On the ICAM, see Matthew Butler, "God's Campesinos?: Mexico's Revolutionary Church in the Countryside," *Bulletin of Latin American Research* 28, no. 2 (April 2009), 172–78.
180 James Dow, "Saints and Survival: The Functions of Religion in a Central Mexican Indian Society" (PhD diss., Brandeis University, 1973), 159; AGN DGG 2.347 caja 5, David Ruesga to PR, May 14, 1936.
181 AGN DGG 2.340 caja 44 exp. 2, Timoteo Gutiérrez et al. to PR, July 25, 1936.
182 AGN DGG 2.382 caja 20 exp. 30, Confederación Campesina Mexicana to SG, November 19, 1934; AGN DGG 2.384 caja 51 exp. 6536; AGN DGG 2.311G caja 247 exp. 36G, vol. 1, Confederación Campesina Mexicana to SG, April 18, 1936.

183 AGN DGG 2.347 caja 5 exp. 16.
184 AGN DGG 2.347 caja 5 exp. 15, Artemio Serna to PR, October 17, 1935.
185 Fabila, *Valle del mezquital*, 248.
186 Rodríguez Lozano, *Maestros revolucionarios*, 118–19; AHSEP caja 1337 exp. 3, Rubén Rodríguez Lozano report, March 31, 1935.
187 Vaughan, *Cultural Politics*, 189–201.
188 AGN DGG 2.347 caja 5 exp. 18, anonymous to SG, November 8, 1931; AGN DGG 2.340 caja 43 exp. 37, Domingo Villiva to SG, September 22, 1931; AGN DGG 2.347 caja 5 exp. 2, Tiburcio Medina to SG, March 28, 1931; AGN DGG 2.347 caja 5 exp. 10; AHSEP HGO caja 1368 exp. 1.
189 AGN DGG 2.340 caja 43 exp. 35; AGN DGG 2.347 caja 26 exp. 59; AGN DGG 2.347 caja 5 exp. 6, SG to gov., April 15, 1932.
190 Vega Sánchez, 178; AGN DGG 2.311 DL caja 30 exp. 1, G. González to PR, January 29, 1933; AGN DGG 2.311G caja 29G vol. 1, Victoriano López Bello to PR, December 10, 1928.
191 AGN DGG 2.311 DL caja 30 exp. 1, G. González to PR, January 29, 1933.
192 AGN DGG 2.347 caja 5 exp. 14, Alberto Ramírez Bautista to SG, May 16, 1935.
193 AHSEP HGO caja 1367 exp. 3, superintendent to gov., November 6, 1935.
194 AGN DGG 2.311G caja 248. Technically, the election was a primary to select the ruling party nominee.
195 *La Verdad*, 1, no. 8 (January 12, 1928); Javier Hurtado, *Familia, política y parentesco: Jalisco 1919–1981* (Mexico City: Fondo de Cultura Económica and Universidad de Guadalajara, 1993), 34–35; Esteban David Rodríguez, *Derecho de sangre: Historias familiares de herencia del poder público en México* (Mexico City: Grijalbo, 2005), 204; Ruiz de Barrera, *Breve historia de Hidalgo*, 143–44; AGN DGG 2.311G caja 248 exp. 36G, vol. 4; Baltasar Dromundo, *Rojo Gómez: Bosquejo de un hombre* (Mexico City: Federación de Escritores de México, 1946); Juan M. Menes Llaguno, *Javier Rojo Gómez (Apuntes biográficos)* (Mexico City: Editorial Penelope, 1980).
196 *Hombre Libre*, July 19, 1937, letter to editor by Florencio F. Rodríguez; Ruiz de Barrera, *Breve historia de Hidalgo*.
197 AHSEP HGO caja 5328 exp. 30; Rodríguez Lozano, *Maestros revolucionarios*,118; Rodríguez Lozano, *San Luis Potosí en su lucha por la libertad*,182–84.
198 AGN DGG 2.311G caja 248 exp. 36G, vols. 1, 2.
199 AGN DGG 2.311G caja 249, vol. 7, Gerónimo Uribe, Memorandum, November 24, 1936.
200 AGN DGG 2.311M caja 10 exp. 21, 46, 52, 56.
201 Federico Besserer, Victoria Novelo, and Juan Luis Sariego, *El sindicalismo minero en México, 1900–1952* (Mexico City: Ediciones Era, 1983), 39, 39n15; AGN DGG 2.311G caja 41G, Roque Espinosa report, January 15, 1941.
202 AGN DGG 2.311G caja 248 exp. 36G, Memorando, "Sus Aspectos Sociales, Políticos y el Aspecto Legal"; AGN DGG 2.311 DL caja 30 exp. 35; *La Prensa*, December 24,

1935; AGN DGG 2.311M caja 9 exp. 25, caja 10 exp.30; AGN DGG 2.311 DL caja 30 exp. 10, Cándido Cornejo to SG, November 1936; Vega Sánchez, 103; Schryer, *Ethnicity and Class Conflict in Rural Mexico*, 127–30; Schryer, "Peasants and the Law," 294n28.

203 AGN DGG 2.311G caja 247 exp. 36G, vol. 1, Francisco Maldonado et al. to PR, August 22, 1936; AGN DGG 2.311G caja 248 exp. 36G, vol. 4, Leopoldo Hernández to PR, November 18, 1936; Montoya Briones, *Etnografía de la dominación en México*, esp. 74–77.

204 Montoya Briones, *Etnografía de la dominación en México*, 79, 164.

205 On the Austrias, see ibid., 162. Fabila, *Valle del mezquital*, 228, 248.

206 AHSEP HGO caja 5800 exp. 12, Leobardo Parra y Marquina report, 1935.

207 On Porfirio Rubio's conflict with SEP teachers and Nahua campesinos, see AGN DGG 2.340 caja 44 exp. 2, and Schryer, *Rancheros*, 85–100.

208 Schryer, *Ethnicity and Class Conflict in Rural Mexico*, 177–256; Gutiérrez, *Hidalgo*, 45.

209 AHSEP HGO caja 5328 exp. 36, Fernando Castellanos report, March 8, 1936; AHSEP HGO caja 5328 exp. 21, Ernesto Porte Petit report, March 13, 1936; AHSEP HGO caja 5328 exp. 22, Froylan Fuentes report, December 15, 1936; AHSEP HGO caja 5491 exp. 15, Francisco Marquez report, March 20, 1937; AHSEP HGO caja 5328 exp. 27, Alfonso Hernández report, 1936.

210 AHSEP HGO caja 5328 exp. 30, Rubén Rodríguez Lozano report, March 24, 1936; AHSEP HGO caja 5328 exp. 29, Bartolomé Gómez report, December 24, 1936; AHSEP HGO caja 5328 exp. 33, Antonio H. García report, March 21, 1936.

211 AHSEP HGO caja 5491 exp. 60.

212 Buenrostro, *Geografía Económica del Estado de Hidalgo*, 70–71.

213 AHSEP HGO caja 5800 exp. 4, Manuel R. Martínez to Sub-SEP, September 21, 1937; AGN DGG 2.347 caja 5 exp. 20, Gilberto González Vargas to SG, June 4, 1937.

214 AGN DGG 2.340 caja 44 exp. 2; RDSRIAM 1930–39 reel 6, James B. Stewart to SOS, February 8, 1938.

215 RDSRIAM 1930–39 reel 5, Josephus Daniels to SOS, November 18, 1936.

216 AHAM LMM caja Comité Episcopal exp. "F y G," J. M. Maya et al. to Luís M. Martínez, December 16, 1944; Alfredo Galindo Mendoza, *Apuntes geográficos y estadísticos de la iglesia católica en México* (Mexico City: La Cruz, 1954), 22, 25.

217 Schryer, *Rancheros*, 93; AHAM LMM caja Comité Episcopal exp. "F y G," J. M. Maya et al. to Luís M. Martínez, December 16, 1944.

218 ACC 2.10 JD de Tulancingo, 30–40.

219 AHAM LMM caja Comité Episcopal exp. "F y G," J. M. Maya et al. to Luís M. Martínez, December 16, 1944; Galindo Mendoza, *Apuntes geográficos y estadísticos de la iglesia católica en México*, 22, 25.

220 *Pro-Patria*, July 20, 1935, letter to editor from Bishop Manríquez, July 2, 1935.

221 José de Jesús Manríquez y Zarate, *El Socialismo* (Mexico City: PAGF, 1936), 158–59, 171.

222 Jorge López Guzmán, "La Cuestión Educativa en Guanajuato. Proceso de Modernización y Cambio Político 1915–1939" (master's thesis, Universidad Iberoamericana, 2004), 201–2.
223 Meyer, *La Cristiada*, 2:255–56; Ruiz de Barrera, *Breve historia de Hidalgo*, 145; Schryer, *Ethnicity and Class Conflict in Rural Mexico*, 122–23; López Beltrán, *Manríquez y Zárate, Primer obispo de Huejutla*, 19–20; Hanley, "Civilian Leadership of the Cristero Movement," 526–27, 551.
224 AHSSM, CR, José de Jesús Obispo de Huejutla, "Informe."
225 Alan Knight, "The Mentality and Modus Operandi of Revolutionary Anticlericalism," in *Faith and Impiety in Revolutionary Mexico*, ed. Matthew Butler (London: Institute for the Study of the Americas, 2007), 34.
226 AHSEP GTO caja 1834 exp. 42, Arnulfo Ochoa report, January 12, 1929.
227 AINAH reel 34, Jefe Celaya to Jefe de Operaciones Militares, October 26, 1932.
228 López Guzmán, "La Cuestión Educativa en Guanajuato," 201–2.
229 Nahua shepherd Juan Diego saw the apparition of the Virgin of Guadalupe. David Brading, *Mexican Phoenix, Our Lady of Guadalupe: Image and Tradition across Five Centuries* (Cambridge: Cambridge University Press, 2001), 311–12.

Chapter 4: Beatas, Ballots, and Bullets in Guerrero

1 Technically a PNR *plebecito* (primary election); victors, however, rarely lost in general elections.
2 AGN DGG 2.311G(9) caja 242 exp. Plebiscitos; AGN DGG 2.311G(9)2 caja 240 exp. 1932; AGN DGG 2.347 caja 4 exp. 8.
3 Arturo Figueroa Uriza, *Andrés Figueroa. Biografía* (Mexico City, 2000), 73; FAPECYFT Archivo Personal Joaquín Amaro (hereafter APJA) exp. Andrés Figueroa leg. 14/18, Amaro to Andrés Figueroa, June 14, 1928; Ian Jacobs, *Ranchero Revolt: The Mexican Revolution in Guerrero* (Austin: University of Texas, 1982), 108; Tomás Bustamante Álvarez, "Periodo 1934–1940," in *Historia de la Cuestión Agrario Mexicana: Estado de Guerrero, 1867–1940*, ed. Jaime Salazar Adame, Renato Rabelo Lecuona, Daniel Molina Álvarez, and Tomás Bustamante Álvarez (Mexico City: Gobierno del Estado de Guerrero, Universidad Autónoma de Guerrero, Centro de Estudios Historicos del Agrarismo en Mexico, 1987), 337–534, 380–81; Daniel Molina Álvarez, "Periodo 1920–1934," in *Historia de la Cuestión Agraria Mexicana: Estado de Guerrero, 1867–1940*, ed. Jaime Salazar Adame, Renato Ravelo Lecona, Daniel Molina Álvarez, and Tomás Bustamante Álvarez (Mexico City: Gobierno del Estado de Guerrero, Universidad Autónoma de Guerrero, Centro de Estudios Históricos del Agrarismo en México, 1987), 223–33.
4 Armando Bartra, *Guerrero Bronco: Campesinos, ciudadanos y guerrilleros en la Costa Grande* (Mexico City: Ediciones Sinfiltro, 1996); Paul Gillingham, "Ambig-

uous Missionaries: Rural Teachers and State Facades in Guerrero, 1930–1950," *Mexican Studies/Estudios Mexicanos* 22, no. 2 (summer 2006), 331–60.

5 Molina Álvarez, "Período 1920–1934," 300–301; Bustamante Álvarez, "Período 1934–1940," 303, 360–61, 380–81; Jacobs, *Ranchero Revolt*, 108; José C. Tapia Gómez, *Feliciano Radilla, un líder natural costeño* (Guerrero, Mexico: Universidad Autónoma de Guerrero and Centro de Estudios Históricos de Agrarismo en México, 1992), 49; Febronio Díaz Figueroa, "Lo dulce y amargo de la tierra," in *Historia de las ligas de comunidades agrarias y sindicatos campesinos: primer concurso estatal*, Vol. 3: *Centro Sur*, ed. Bertha Beatriz Martínez G. (Mexico City: Confederación Nacional Campesina, 1988), 261–340, esp. 309; FAPECYFT PEC GAV. 38 GUEVARA, Gabriel R. (Gral.) exp. 107 inv. 2559 leg. 4/4, Gabriel R. Guevara to Calles, April 18, 1933; AGN DGG 2.311 caja 3b, Samuel Escobar to PR, October 18, 1935.

6 Alba Teresa Estrada Castañón, *Guerrero: Sociedad, economía, política y cultura* (Mexico City: Universidad Autónoma de México, 1994); Moisés T. de la Peña, *Guerrero económico*, 2 vols. (Mexico City: Gobierno del Estado de Guerrero, 1949), esp. 1:299–334; Díaz Figueroa, "Lo dulce y amargo de la tierra," 3:271–72.

7 These divisions reflect both subregionality (geographic, historical, social) and a degree of subregionalism (sentimental attachment). Eric Van Young, "Are Regions Good to Think?" in *Mexico's Regions: Comparative History and Development*, ed. Eric Van Young (San Diego: Center for U.S.-Mexican Studies, University of California–San Diego, 1992). Geographic divisions are contested. I follow Gillingham in referring to four, while others recognize up to seven; see Estrada Castañón, *Guerrero*, 25, and Gillingham, "Ambiguous Missionaries," 337.

8 Estrada Castañón, *Guerrero*, 12.

9 On the Twin Coasts, see ibid., 8; Bustamante Álvarez, "Período 1934–1940," 376–77; and Díaz Figueroa, "Lo dulce y amargo de la tierra," 3:272. On the Costa Chica, see María de los Angeles Manzano A., *Cuajinicuilapa, Guerrero: Historia oral (1900–1940)* ([Mexico City]: Artesa, 1991).

10 Jacobs, *Ranchero Revolt*, 36–37.

11 Estrada Castañón, *Guerrero*, 17.

12 Gillingham, "Ambiguous Missionaries," 340, 359.

13 Manzano, *Cuajinicuilapa, Guerrero*, 78–79, 91–93.

14 Jacobs, *Ranchero Revolt*, esp. 78–109.

15 Alan Knight, *The Mexican Revolution*. 2 vols. (Lincoln: University of Nebraska Press, 1986), 1:100–101.

16 Tapia Gómez, *Feliciano Radilla, un líder natural costeño*, 33, 41; Molina Álvarez, "Período 1920–1934"; Jacobs, *Ranchero Revolt*, 123–27.

17 AGN DGG 2.72 caja 5 exp. 60 and DGG 2.311 DL caja 88 exp. 1, P. Sierra Guevara to SG, February 18, 1927; Román Juan Guadarrama Gómez, *Notas eclesiásticas del estado de Guerrero* (Mexico City, 1992), 319.

18 AHSSM CRD, Obispo de Chilapa to Dario Miranda, March 21, 1936.

19   AGN DGG 2.311 DS caja 154 exp. 1.
20   AGN DGG 2.311 DL caja 88 exp.1, Agente #7 report, March 5, 1927.
21   AGN DGG 2.311 DL caja 88 exp.1, Andrés Galeana to PR, January 30, 1927.
22   AGN DGG 2.311 DS caja 154 exp. 1, Miguel Andreu Almazán to SG, June 30, 1926.
23   Jean Meyer, *Historia de la Revolución Mexicana*, vol. 11, *Período 1928–1934: Estado y Sociedad con Calles* (Mexico City: el Colegio de México, 1977), 66–67, 69–70; RDSRIAM 1910–29 reel 92, Harry Pangburn to SOS, February 4, 1928; AHPEC PEC Gav. 90 EL PROBLEMA RELIGIOSO EN MEXICO, INFORME DE 10-b exp. 11 inv. 1504; Bartra, *Guerrero Bronco*, 66–67.
24   RDSRIAM reel 1910–29 reel 92, Harry Pangburn to SOS, February 4, 1928; AGN DGG 2.311 DL caja 88 exp. 1, Agent #7 report, March 5, 1927; Molina Álvarez, "Período 1920–1934," 292–93; "Emilio Portes Gil: ¿Quién los mando matar?: No se sabe," in *La sombra de Serrano: De la matanza de Huitzilac a la expulsión de Calles por Cárdenas*, ed. Federico Campbell (Mexico City: Proceso, 1981), 39–42, esp. 41.
25   RDSRIAM 1910–29 reel 92, Harry Pangburn to SOS, February 4, 1928; Díaz Figueroa, "Lo dulce y amargo de la tierra," 316–17; Molina Álvarez, "Período 1920–1934," 292–95; Desiderio Borja, *Perfil Suriano* (Mexico, ca. 1929), 158–62; Jacobs, *Ranchero Revolt*, 109.
26   Bartra, *Guerrero Bronco*, 71; Jacobs, *Ranchero Revolt*, 129.
27   Borja, *Perfil Suriano*, 158–62; Jacobs, *Ranchero Revolt*, 109, 128–29; Bartra, *Guerrero Bronco*, 60–66, 71–73; Díaz Figueroa, "Lo dulce y amargo de la tierra," 316–17; Molina Álvarez, "Período 1920–1934," 294–95, 337–34, esp. 302; Tapia Gómez, *Feliciano Radilla, un líder natural costeño*, 41–42; Tomás Bustamante Álvarez, "Período 1934–1940."
28   Gillingham, "Ambiguous Missionaries," 338; *Hombre Libre*, August 2, 1935; AHSEP GRO caja 1365 exp. 18, Guillermo Bonilla S. report, 1934–35.
29   Guadarrama Gómez, *Notas eclesiásticas del estado de Guerrero*, 275–77; Catalina Pastrana, *Remembranzas históricas de Iguala y apuntes de su tradición* (Chilpacingo, Mexico: Ayuntamiento municipal constitucional de Iguala, 1990), 124.
30   AGN DGG 2.340 caja 41 exp. 29.
31   AGN DGG 2.340 caja 41 exp. 25, 34; AGN DGG 2.347 caja 4 exp. 6; AGN DGG 2.311M caja 6B exp. 72, 77.
32   Aaron Oosterhout and Benjamin T. Smith, "The Limits of Catholic Science and the Mexican Revolution," *Endeavor* 34, no. 2 (June 2010): 55–60.
33   Octaviano Márquez, *Monseñor Ibarra. Biografía del Excmo. Sr. Dr. y Maestro D. Ramón Ibarra y González, cuarto obispo de Chilapa, ultimo Obispo y primer Arzobispo de Puebla* (Mexico City: Editorial Jus, 1962), esp. 69–71, 85, 94; *Octava carta pastoral que el Ilmo. Sr. Dr. D. Ramón Ibarra y González dirige al clero y fieles de la diócesis de Chilapa dando a conocer las letras apostólicas del santo padre y el nuevo Instituto de misioneros Guadalupanos* (Puebla, Mexico: Colegio Pio de Artes y Oficios, 1895).
34   Mark Overmyer-Velázquez, *Visions of the Emerald City: Modernity, Tradition,*

and the Formation of Porfirian Oaxaca, Mexico* (Durham, NC: Duke University Press, 2006), 70–97.

35 de la Peña, *Guerrero económico*, 1:139.
36 Ibid., 1:150–54.
37 Overmyer-Velázquez, *Visions*, 77–78, 84–94.
38 Márquez, *Monseñor Ibarra*, 128, 154, 172–173; Guadarrama Gómez, *Notas eclesiásticas del estado de Guerrero*, 212–13.
39 AGN DGG 2.340 caja 42 exp. 6, Emilio González Adame to PR, April 16, 1935.
40 Guadarrama Gómez, *Notas eclesiásticas del estado de Guerrero*, 220–27; Bustamante, "Período 1934–1940," 405; José Tapia Gómez, "Episodio Almazanista en Tlapa: Elecciones presidenciales, 1939–1940," in *Tlapa: Origen y memoria histórica*, ed. Mario O. Martínez (Chilpancingo, Mexico: Universidad Autónoma de Guerrero and Ayuntamiento Municipal de Tlapa de Comonfort, 2000), 224; AGN DGG 2.340 caja 41 exp. 34, Marciano Talavera to SG, February 15, 1932; RDSRIAM 1930–39 reel 41, Josephus Daniels to SOS, October 29, 1934.
41 Márquez, *Monseñor Ibarra*, 78; AGN DGG 2.340 caja 14 exp. 7, "Relación que manifiesta . . . los sacerdotes o ministerios existentes"; AGN DGG 2.340 caja 41 exp. 28; RDSRIAM 1930–39 reel 43, R. Henry Norweb to SOS.
42 AGN DGG 2.347 caja 4 exp. 11, SG estado (hereafter edo.) to SG, December 4, 1932.
43 de la Peña, *Guerrero económico*, 1:323–24.
44 Ibid.; Paul Gillingham, "Force and Consent in Mexican Provincial Politics: Guerrero and Veracruz, 1945–1953" (PhD. diss., Oxford University 2005), 32–33.
45 Pastrana, *Remembranzas históricas de Iguala y apuntes de su tradición*, 124.
46 ACC 2.10 Junta Diocesano Chilapa, Armando Salmerón Jr. to Carlos Rovalo, January 3, 1941.
47 http://www.wandea.org.pl/carmona-rivera.html (accessed December 14, 2006).
48 *Restauración*, May 1, 1928.
49 Elwood Gotshall, "Catholicism and Catholic Action in Mexico, 1929–1941: A Church's Response to a Revolutionary Society and the Politics of the Modern Age" (PhD diss., University of Pittsburgh, 1970), 24, 58–59, 63, 65.
50 Jesús Guzmán Urióstegui, *Evila Franco Nájera, a pesar del olvido* (Mexico City: INEHRM and Secretaría de Gobernación, 1995), 64.
51 Guadarrama Gómez, *Notas eclesiásticas del estado de Guerrero*, 199–202; de la Peña, *Guerrero económico*, 1:357; AHSEP GRO caja 1081 exp. 13, Inspector Zone II report, October 1, 1933.
52 Bustamante, "Período 1934–1940," 414.
53 AGN DGG 2.347 caja 4 exp. 1, gov. to SG, June 7, 1932.
54 de la Peña, *Guerrero económico*, 1:356; AGN DGG 2.347 caja 26 exp. 9, "Carta Abierta. . . ."
55 de la Peña, *Guerrero económico*, 1:356–57.
56 AAC exp. 2.10.1, varios, AAC 2.10.2 Directorios 1939–1942; ACM caja 3 (A.G. 197) exp. ACM 195 (60), "Comites Diocesanos of UCM"; AAC exp. 2.10.1 Informes 1930–

33; AAC directorate 1937–39; ACC 2.10 Junta Diocesano Chilapa, Armando Salmerón Jr. to Carlos Rovalo, January 3, 1941.

57 Edward Wright-Rios, *Revolutions in Mexican Catholicism: Reform and Revelation in Oaxaca, 1887–1934* (Durham, NC: Duke University Press, 2009), 57–58, 104–6.

58 AAC exp. 2.10.1 Informes de visitas a diócesis 1939–47, Francisco Hernández, "Informe del estado . . ." and "Informe de la visita . . . ," January 17, 1941.

59 AGN DGG 2.347 caja 4 exp. 1, gov. to SG, June 7, 1932.

60 AAC 7.7 Unión Nacional de Padres de Familia, 1931–36, UNPF organizadores, February 12, 1932; AAC 2.10.2 Directorios 1939–42.

61 Gillingham, "Ambiguous Missionaries," 338–41.

62 Kristina Boylan, "The Feminine 'Apostolate in Society' versus the Secular State: The Unión Femenina Católica Mexicana, 1929–1940," in *Right Wing Women: From Conservatives to Extremists Around the World*, ed. Paola Bacchetta and Margaret Power (London: Routledge, 2002), 169–82, esp. 169.

63 de la Peña, *Guerrero económico*, 1:356–57.

64 AGN DGG 2.347 caja 4 exp. 25.

65 AGN DGG 2.340 caja 42 exp. 17.

66 AGN DGG 2.347 caja 26 exp. 1; AGN DGG 2.347 caja 26 exp. 29.

67 AAC exp. 2.10.1 Informes de visitas a diócesis 1939–47, Francisco Hernández, "Informe de la visita."

68 Michael Smith, "The Strategic Provinces," in *Aztec Imperial Strategies*, ed. Frances Berdan et al. (Washington, DC: Dumbarton Oaks Research Library and Collection, 1996), 137–79, esp. 141.

69 de la Peña, *Guerrero económico*, 1:301–8.

70 Beatriz Canabal Cristiani and José Joaquin Flores Félix, *Montañeros: Actores sociales en la montaña del estado de Guerrero* (Mexico City: Universidad Autónoma Metropolitana, Universidad Autónoma Chapingo, El Atajo Ediciones, 2004), 37; Danièle Dehouve, "The 'Money of the Saint': Ceremonial Organization and Monetary Capital in Tlapa, Guerrero, Mexico," in *Manipulating the Saints: Religious Brotherhoods and Social Integration in Postconquest Latin America*, ed. Albert Meyers and Diane Elizabeth Hopkins (Hamburg, Germany: Wayasbah, 1988), 149–74, esp. 151–53.

71 Wright-Rios, *Revolutions*, 104–5.

72 Estrada Castañon, *Guerrero*, 89–90; Nathaniel Whetten, *Rural Mexico* (Chicago: University of Chicago Press, 1948), 376; de la Peña, *Guerrero económico*, 1:324–27; Dehouve, "The 'Money of the Saint'"; Pastrana, *Remembranzas históricas de Iguala y apuntes de su tradición*, 118.

73 AGN DGG 2.347 caja 4 exp. 16.

74 AGN DGG 2.347 caja 4 exp. 9.

75 AHSEP DEF GRO 1090 exp. 46, Leopoldo Caranca Cardoso report, September 25, 1930; AHSEP GRO caja 1336, Francisco Torres report, September 1, 1934.

76 Norberto Valdez, *Ethnicity, Class and the Indigenous Struggle for Land in Guerrero, Mexico* (New York: Garland, 1998), 49–50.
77 Valle Basilio, Sabas, Salvador Rebolledo Orbe, and Filimón Vázquez Moreno. *Tlapa de Comonfort: primer centenario, 1890–1990* (Chilpancingo, Mexico: Gobierno del Estado de Guerrero, 1990), 72.
78 AGN DGG 2.73 caja 15 exp. 2; AGN DGG 2.72 caja 8 exp. 9; AGN DGG 2.347 caja 26 exp. 14; AGN DGG 2.382 caja 15 exp. 18; de la Peña, *Guerrero económico*, 1:135, 142; http://www.e-local.gob.mx/work/templates/enciclo/guerrero/municipios/12026a.htm (accessed May 11, 2004).
79 AHSEP GRO caja 939 exp. 1, Rafael Molina report, December 16, 1932.
80 On varied indigenous reactions to leftist mobilizations, see Jeffrey Gould and Aldo Lauria-Santiago, *To Rise in Darkness: Revolution, Repression, and Memory in El Salvador* (Durham, NC: Duke University Press, 2008), 99–131.
81 Although Zapatista veterans often supported the revolutionary project, federal teachers largely failed to spread the posthumous hero cult of Zapata among other groups in the 1930s. Samuel Brunk notes that the postrevolutionary state's cultural project during this pivotal decade never penetrated deeply into society despite the official observance of Zapata's "martyrdom" (April 10) by the revolutionary civic calendar. See his *The Posthumous Career of Emiliano Zapata: Myth, Memory, and Mexico's Twentieth Century* (Austin: University of Texas Press, 2008), 91–93. For claims that Cárdenas "built the hegemonic postrevolutionary state" on the foundation of the "symbolism of Zapata," see Florencia Mallon, *Peasant and Nation: The Making of Postcolonial Mexico and Peru* (Berkeley: University of California Press, 1995), 310–11.
82 AGN DGG 2.311G(9)2 caja 240 exp. 1932; AGN DGG 2.340 caja 41 exp. 39.
83 AGN DGG 2.311 caja 3b exp. 17 and caja 5-B exp. 74.
84 Román Juan Guadarrama Gómez, *Reseña Histórica del Templo Parroquial de San Francisco de Asís. Iguala, Guerrero* (Iguala, Mexico: Grupo Cultural de Promotores del Arte y de la História de Iguala, 1988), 23–42.
85 http://igualaonline.com/nuestra-historia/informacion-general/cronologia-dehechos-historicos/los-cristeros (accessed June 5, 2007); Guadarrama Gómez, *Reseña Histórica del Templo Parroquial de San Francisco de Asís*, 35–36, 39–40.
86 Guadarrama Gómez, *Reseña Histórica del Templo Parroquial de San Francisco de Asís*, 23–42; Pastrana, *Remembranzas históricas de Iguala y apuntes de su tradición*, 124; AGN DGG 2.72 caja 4 exp. 39; AGN DGG 2.347 caja 26 exp. 9; AGN DGG 2.73 caja 15 exp. 38; AGN DGG 2.340 caja 41 exp. 42.
87 Pastrana, *Remembranzas históricas de Iguala y apuntes de su tradición*, 118; Díaz Figueroa, "Lo dulce y amargo de la tierra," 336.
88 Moisés González Navarro, *Masones y Cristeros en Jalisco* (Mexico City: Colegio de México, 2000), 1:90.
89 *La Prensa*, November 24, 1934; RDSRIAM 1930–39 reel 41, Josephus Daniels to SOS, October 29, 1934; AGN DGG 2.340 caja 43 exp. 33 and caja 41 exp. 38.

90 Guadarrama Gómez, *Reseña Histórica del Templo Parroquial de San Francisco de Asís*, 227; RDSRIAM 1930–39 reel 41, Josephus Daniel to SOS, October 29, 1934; AHSEP GRO caja 1668 exp. 1, superintendent to gov., December 24, 1934; AHSEP GRO 1668 exp. 26, Primitivo Alcocer report, May–June 1934.
91 AHSEP GRO caja 987 exp. 9, Leopoldo Carranca Cardoso report, October 16, 1932.
92 Gillingham, "Ambiguous Missionaries," 344.
93 de la Peña, *Guerrero económico*, 1:306–33.
94 Ibid., 1:395; AHSEP GRO caja 488 exp. Educación Indígena.
95 AHSEP GRO caja 1336 exp. 8, Francisco Torres report, September 1, 1935.
96 AGN DGG 2.340 caja 41 exp. 40.
97 AGN DGG 2.347 caja 4 exp. 22.
98 Adrian Bantjes, *As If Jesus Walked on Earth: Cardenismo, Sonora and the Mexican Revolution* (Wilmington, DE: Scholarly Resources, 1998), 10.
99 AHSEP GRO 1668 exp. 2, Isidro Rivera report, September–October 1935; AHSEP GRO caja 1081 exp. 13, Isidro Rivera reports, July 2, 1933, September 1, 1933, October 31, 1933.
100 AHSEP GRO caja 1336 exp. 8, Guillermo Bonilla S. to gov., November 9, 1935.
101 AHSEP GRO caja 1336 exp. 8, Francisco Torres report, March–April 1935.
102 AGN DGG 2.347 caja 4 exp. 17, superintendent to SG, September 25, 1936; AGN DGG 2.340 caja 42 exp. 17; AHSEP GRO caja 987 exp. 13, Luis Bobadilla to SEP, July 31, 1936.
103 AINAH CR reel 37, EPL Manifesto, January 1935.
104 On the Cristiada in Guerrero, see Guadarrama Gómez, *Notas eclesiásticas del estado de Guerrero*, 219–23, and Valle Basilio, *Tlapa*, 152. On rumors of recristeros in Chilapa, see AGN DGG 2.340 caja 42 exp. 17.
105 AINAH CR reel 37, EPL Manifesto, January 1935.
106 AINAH CR reel 37, various; AINAH reel 39, J. González report, April 1, 1937.
107 David Raby, *Educación y revolución social en México (1921–1940)*, trans. Roberto Gómez Ciriza (Mexico City: Sep-Setentas, 1974), 178.
108 This distinction between offensive and defensive violence can be made across Mexico. On the former, see Raby, *Educación*, 125, 241; Belinda Arteaga, *A gritos y sombrerazos. Historia de los debates sobre educación sexual en México, 1906–1946* (Mexico City: Universidad Pedagógica Nacional and Miguel Angel Porrúa, 2002), 158–59. On the latter, see *La Prensa*, December 16, 1934, December 19, 1934; Salvador Camacho Sandoval, *Controversia Educativa entre la Ideologia y la Fe: La educación socialista en la historia de Aguascalientes, 1876–1940* (Mexico City: Consejo Nacional para la Cultura y las Artes, 1991), 155.
109 AGN DGG 2.384 caja 50 exp. 37 and caja 51 exp. 3919; Bustamante, "Período 1934–1940," 418; Díaz Figueroa, "Lo dulce y amargo de la tierra," 313; Bartra, *Guerrero Bronco*, 67; Tapia Gómez, *Feliciano Radilla, un líder natural costeño*, 40. On politicized gang violence, see Michael Schroeder, "From Horse Thieves to Rebels to Dogs: Political Gang Violence and the State in the Western Segovias, Nicaragua, in

the Time of Sandino, 1926–1934," *Journal of Latin American Studies* 28, no. 2 (May 1996): 383–434.
110 Jennie Purnell, *Popular Movements and State Formation in Revolutionary Mexico: The Agraristas and Cristeros of Michoacán* (Durham, NC: Duke University Press, 1999), 77.
111 William Taylor, *Drinking, Homicide, and Rebellion in Colonial Mexican Villages* (Stanford, CA: Stanford University Press, 1979), 113–51, esp. 116.
112 de la Peña, *Guerrero económico*, 1:356.
113 AHSEP GRO caja 1365 exp. 9, Salvador Gutiérrez report, February 18, 1935.
114 AGN DGG 2.347 caja 3 bis exp. 13, Rafael M. Campos report, July 4, 1932.
115 AHSEP GRO caja 1336 exp. 8, Francisco Torres report, November–December 1934.
116 Valdez, *Ethnicity, Class and the Indigenous Struggle for Land in Guerrero, Mexico*, esp. 87–91.
117 AHSEP GRO caja 1336 exp. 8, Francisco Torres report, September 1, 1934; AHSEP GRO caja 1081 exp. 24, Guillermo Bonilla S. to Rafael Ramírez, August 25, 1933; Valdez, *Ethnicity, Class and the Indigenous Struggle for Land in Guerrero, Mexico*, 42–47, 66–67, 74–75; Jesús Guzmán Urióstegui, *Evila Franco Nájera, a pesar del olvido* (Mexico City: INEHRM and Secretaría de Gobernación, 1995), 63. In 1929, while federal superintendent of neighboring Oaxaca, Bonilla backed Daniel Martínez, a controversial cacique, because Martínez supported federal schools and staged an anticlerical play. Benjamin Smith, "Inventing Tradition at Gunpoint: Culture, Caciquismo and State Formation in the Región Mixe, Oaxaca (1930–1959)," *Bulletin of Latin American Research* 27, no. 2 (April 2008): 215–34, esp. 217.
118 AHSEP GRO caja 1336 exp. 8, Francisco Torres report, September, 1, 1934.
119 Ibid.
120 Ibid.
121 AHSEP GRO caja 1336 exp. 8, various.
122 AHSEP GRO caja 1336 exp. 8, Francisco Torres report, September–October 1934, Francisco Torres to SEP, October 22, 1934.
123 AHSEP GRO caja 1336 exp. 8, Francisco Torres report, March–April 1935.
124 Ibid.
125 AHSEP GRO caja 1081 exp. 24, Guillermo Bonilla S. to Rafael Ramírez, April 25, 1933; de la Peña, *Guerrero económico*, 1:86, 313, 319.
126 Mary Kay Vaughan, *Cultural Politics in Revolution: Teachers, Peasants, and Schools in Mexico, 1930–1940* (Tucson: University of Arizona, 1997), 42, 57–59.
127 AGN DGG 2.347 caja 4 exp. 29, 39.
128 Rossana Almada, *El vestido azul de la sultana: La construcción del PAN en Zamora 1940–1995* (Zamora, Mexico: Colegio de Michoacán, 2001), 94.
129 Valdez, *Ethnicity, Class and the Indigenous Struggle for Land in Guerrero, Mexico*, 42–47.
130 In Zilacayotitlán in la Montaña, nonindigenous merchants and ranchers who bought cattle from indigenous communities and controlled municipal govern-

ment were known as the *padrinos* (godparents). Danièle Dehouve, *Cuando los banqueros eran santos: Historia económia y social de la provincia de Tlapa, Guerrero*, trans. Bertha Chavelas Vázquez (Mexico City: Universidad Autónoma de Guerrero and Centro Francés de Estudio Mexicanos y Centroamericanos, 2002), 307.

131 Guadarrama Gómez, *Notas eclesiásticas del estado de Guerrero*, 215; Epigmenio López Barroso, *Diccionario Geográfico, Histórico y Estadístico del Distrito de Abasolo, del Estado de Guerrero* (Mexico City: Ediciones Botas, 1967), 67–68; AGN DGG 2.347 caja 4 exp. 11.

132 Guadarrama Gómez, *Notas eclesiásticas del estado de Guerrero*, 215; López Barroso, *Diccionario*, 67–68; AHSEP GRO caja 939 exp. 1, Superintendent report, December 16, 1932; AHSEP GRO 1336 exp. 8, Francisco Torres reports, March–April 1935, October 22, 1935.

133 AHSEP GRO caja 1336 exp. 8, Francisco Torres reports, October 22, 1934, November–December 1934.

134 AGN DGG 2.382 caja 17 vol. 2, José León, May 2, 1938; Bustamante, "Período 1934–1940," 416; Francisco Gomezjara, *Bonapartismo y lucha campesina en la Costa Grande de Guerrero* (Mexico City: Posada, 1979), 127; Efraín Flores Maldonado and Carlos Klimek Salgado, *Gobernadores del estado de Guerrero*, 4th ed. (Mexico City, 2005), 161.

135 AHSEP GRO caja 1336 exp. 8, Francisco Torres report, January–February 1935.

136 AGN DGG 2.347 caja 26 exp. 4, gov. to SG, November 12, 1926.

137 Miguel Angel Gutiérrez Ávila, *Nabor Ojeda, el batallador del sur* (Mexico City: CEHAM and CNC 1991), 14.

138 AHSEP GRO caja 1668 exp. 11; AHSEP GRO caja 1365 exp. 19, Guillermo Bonilla S. report, April 20, 1935.

139 *Hombre Libre*, January 28, 1935.

140 AGN DGG 2.347 caja 4 exp. 28.

141 Molina Álvarez, "Período 1920–1934," 233–36; AGN DGG 2.311M caja 397 exp. 1 and caja 3-B exp. 43; AGN DGG 2.382 caja 16, vol. 1; AGN DGG 2.345 caja 3 exp. 40516.

142 AGN DGG 2.347 caja 26 exp. 27, 30, 31.

143 AHSEP GRO caja 1336 exp. 8 and 14, Salvador Gutiérrez and Francisco Torres, various reports.

144 AGN DGG 2.347 caja 4 exp. 12.

145 *Hombre Libre*, August 2, 1935, 2; AHSEP GRO caja 1090 exp. 53, Primitivo Álvarez report, September 1930; AHSEP GRO caja 1668 exp. 7, Salvador Gutiérrez report, December 2, 1934; AHSEP GRO caja 1365 exp. 9, Salvador Gutiérrez to superintendent, February 18, 1935; AHSEP GRO caja 1336 exp. 14, Salvador Gutiérrez report, May 6, 1935, July 28, 1935.

146 Jesús Guzmán Urióstegui, *Evila Franco Nájera, a pesar del olvido* (Mexico City: INEHRM and Secretaría de Gobernación, 1995), 64–65.

147 Bustamante Álvarez, "Período 1934–1940," 379. On priests' involvement in agrar-

ian conflicts in a northern municipio, see Laura Espejel López and Salvador Rueda Smithers, *Reconstrucción histórica de una comunidad del norte de Guerrero: Ichcateopan* (Mexico City: INAH, 1979), 39.

148 AGN 2.340 caja 42 exp. 5; AHSEP GRO caja 1365 exp. 9, Inspector Zone II report 1, April 1936.
149 AGN DGG 2.340 caja 42 exp. 5, Ma. de Jesús Fernández et al. to PR, April 15, 1935, and Governor Lugo to SG, December 17, 1935; AHSEP GRO caja 1365 exp. 9, Inspector Zone II report, April 1, 1936.
150 AHSEP GRO caja 1668 exp. 3, Sebastian Peniche López report, October 31, 1935.
151 AGN DGG 2.347 caja 4 exp. 24, José Valle B et al. to PR, November 30, 1935.
152 AGN DGG 2.340 caja 42 exp. 5, 17; AHSEP GRO caja 1365 exp. 9, Inspector Zone II report, April 1, 1936; AGN DGG 2.347 caja 4 exp. 24.
153 AGN DGG 2.340 caja 42 exp. 17.
154 AGN DGG 2.382 caja 15 exp. 12.
155 AGN DGG 2.347 caja 4 exp. 8.
156 AGN DGG 2.347 caja 4 exp. 24.
157 AGN DGG 2.340 caja 42 exp. 5, Ma. de Jesús Fernández et al. to PR, April 15, 1935.
158 AGN DGG 2.340 caja 41 exp. 42, Act of Formation, January 25, 1935.
159 AGN DGG 2.311 caja 3b exp. 9; AGN DGG 2.340 caja 42 exp. 6; AGN DGG 2.340 caja 41 exp.41.
160 AGN DGG 2.340 caja 42 exp. 6.
161 *El Universal*, March 4, 1936, 1:1.
162 AGN DGG 2.347 caja 4 exp. 10, sub-SG to gov., October 27, 1936.
163 AGN DGG 2.347 caja 4 exp. 14; AGN DGG 2.311 caja 6 exp. 8, Francisco Rios M. to SG, July 31, 1940.
164 AGN DGG 2.347 caja 4 exps. 14, 10, 19, 31.
165 AHSEP GRO caja 1668 exp. 26, Primitivo Alcocer report, May–June 1934; AGN DGG 2.340 caja 41 exp. 38; AGN DGG 2.347 caja 4 exp. 21.
166 de la Peña, *Guerrero económico*, 1:357; Guadarrama Gómez, *Notas eclesiásticas del estado de Guerrero*, 227–29; AGN DGG 2.340 caja 41 exp. 12; AGN DGG 2.347 caja 4 exp. 21.
167 Guadarrama Gómez, *Notas eclesiásticas del estado de Guerrero*, 219; AGN DGG 2.347 caja 26 exp. 6, caja 4 exp. 9.
168 AHSEP GRO caja 1336 exp. 8, Miguel S. Hidalgo reports, May–June, September–October 1935; AGN DGG 2.347 caja 4 exp. 9, Arnulfo Pérez Zagal to SG, December 21, 1935; AHSEP GRO caja 1365 exp. 18, Guillermo Bonilla S. reports, August 3, 1935, 1934–35; AHSEP GRO caja 1336 exp. 8, Guillermo Bonilla S. to gov., November 9, 1935; AGN DGG 2.340 caja 41 exp. 38; AGN DGG 2.347 caja 4 exps. 9, 21, 23, caja 26 exp. 6.
169 AGN DGG 2.347 caja 4 exp. 21, 23; AGN DGG 2.340 caja 42 exp. 17; AHSEP GRO caja 1336 exp. 8, Guillermo Bonilla S. to gov., November 9, 1935.
170 AGN DGG 2.311M caja 397 exp. 29701.

171 AHSEP GRO caja 1336 exp. 11, Alberto González Valles to PR, March 31, 1935.
172 AHSEP GRO caja 987 exp. 9, Leopoldo Carranca Cardoso report, October 16, 1932; AHSEP GRO caja 1336 exp. 8, Manuel S. Hidalgo report, May–June 1935.
173 AHSEP GRO caja 1336 exp. 11, Alberto González Valles report, March 31, 1935.
174 Bartra, *Guerrero Bronco*.
175 Guadarrama Gómez, *Notas eclesiásticas del estado de Guerrero*, 319, 324.
176 de la Peña, *Guerrero económico*, 1:457–58; Guadarrama Gómez, *Notas eclesiásticas del estado de Guerrero*, 319, 324; AGN DGG 2.311M caja 6B exp. 28, Herminio Huato to SG, October 8, 1928; AGN DGG 2.311M caja 6B exp. 28, Herminio Huato to SG, January 3, 1929; AGN DGG 2.382 caja 15 exp. 27; AHSEP GRO caja 1753 exp. Estab. Escuelas, Oficinas y Bibliotecas, Manuel Urbina Castro to SEP, September 28, 1929; AGN DGG 2.340 caja 41 exp. 2, gov. to SG, July 31, 1929; AGN DGG 2.347 caja 26 exp. 37; AGN DGG 2.382 caja 15 exp. 27; AHSEP GRO caja 1365 exp. 19, Guillermo Bonilla to SEP, April 19, 1935; AHSEP GRO caja 987 exp. 9, Leopoldo Carranca Cardoso report, October 16, 1932; AHSEP GRO caja 939 exp. Establecimiento, DEF Guillermo Bonilla S. to SEP, January 27, 1933; AGN DGG 2.382 caja 16 vol. 1, Salustino Meza to SG, August 7, 1937.
177 AGN DGG 2.382 caja 15 exp. 27.
178 AGN DGG 2.382 caja 15 exp. 27; AHSEP GRO caja 939 exp. 1, Rafael Molina B. report, December 16, 1932.
179 AGN DGG 2.347 caja 26 exp. 4, gov. to SG, November 12, 1926; AHSEP GRO caja 1365 exp. 19, Guillermo Bonilla S. to SEP, April 19, 1935.
180 AHSEP GRO caja 1365 exp. 19, Guillermo Bonilla S. report, April 20, 1935.
181 Molina Álvarez, "Período 1920–1934," 238; Nélida Flores Arellano and América Wences Román, *Doña María de la O. Una mujer ejemplar* (Mexico City: Universidad Autónoma de Guerrero, Centro de Estudios Históricos del Agrarismo en México, 1992), 23.
182 AGN DGG 2.311 DS caja 154 exp. 1, Agent #22 to SG, June 19, 1926.
183 On López's ideology, see Jacobs, *Ranchero Revolt*, 129; AGN DGG 2.331 caja 25A exp. 4, gov. to SG, November 27, 1926; and AGN DGG 2.347 caja 26 exp. 22.
184 José Sánchez, *Anticlericalism: A Brief History* (Notre Dame, IN: University of Notre Dame, 1972), 109–10.
185 AGN DGG 2.311M caja 390 exp. 4, Francisco B. García to PR, January 2, 1927. On revolutionary politics and freemasonry, see Benjamin Smith, "Anticlericalism, Politics, and Freemasonry in Mexico, 1920–1940," *The Americas* 65, no. 4 (2009): 559–88.
186 ADN DGG 2.382 caja 16 vol. 1, Salustino Meza to PR, August 7, 1937.
187 ADN DGG 2.340 caja 41 exp. 25; *Hombre Libre*, August 13, 1931; ADN DGG 2.382 caja 16 vol. 1, Salustino Meza to PR, August 7, 1937; Díaz Figueroa, "Lo dulce y amargo de la tierra," 328.
188 Bustamante Álvarez, "Período 1934–1940," 364–65; Tapia Gómez, *Feliciano*

Radilla, un líder natural costeño, 45–54; Gomezjara, *Bonapartismo y lucha campesina en la Costa Grande de Guerrero*, 125.

189 AHSEP GRO caja 939 exp. 1, Rafael Molina B. report, December 16, 1932.
190 AINAH reel 55, *Acción: Organo del UNPF Jalisco*, February 10, 1935.
191 *Hombre Libre*, January 28, 1935, May 1, 1935, May 29, 1935.
192 Blanca M. Jiménez and Samuel Villela, *Los Salmerón: Un siglo de fotografía en Guerrero* (Mexico City: INAH, 1998), 35, 102, 149–56, 194.
193 Guillermo Zermeño and Roger Aguilar, *Hacia una reinterpretación del sinarquismo actual. Notas y materiales para su estudio* (Mexico City: Universidad Iberoamericana, 1988), 19–23, 49–50.
194 Molina Álvarez, "Período 1920–1934," 308; *Hombre Libre*, August 5, 1935.
195 Jacobs, *Ranchero Revolt*, 131–32; Bustamante Álvarez, "Período 1934–1940," 54–55, 363–64, 416; Bartra, *Guerrero Bronco*, 76–79; Gutiérrez Ávila, *Nabor Ojeda, el batallador del sur*, 38, 43–49; Tapia Gómez, *Feliciano Radilla, un líder natural costeño*, 54–55; de la Peña, *Guerrero económico*, 1:457–58.
196 Reich, *Mexico's Hidden Revolution*, 81; AHSSM CRD, Bishop Díaz to Dario Miranda, March 21, 1936; RDSRIAM reel 43, Josephus Daniels to SOS, March 28, 1936; Guadarrama Gómez, *Notas eclesiásticas del estado de Guerrero*, 227.
197 Sabas Valle Basilio, ed., *Tlapa de Comonfort. Primer Centenario: 1890–1990* (Mexico City, 1990), 155.
198 Adrian Bantjes, "Politics, Class, and Culture" (PhD diss., University of Texas, 1991), 275.
199 AGN DGG 2.311G caja 243 exp. 15458.
200 Bustamante, "Período 1934–1940," 416; Bartra, *Guerrero Bronco*, 79; Tapia Gómez, *Feliciano Radilla, un líder natural costeño*, 54–55.
201 Jacobs, *Ranchero Revolt*, 133–34; http://cronica.diputados.gob.mx/DDebates/36/1er/Ord/19340824.html (accessed August 8, 2008).
202 Bartra, *Guerrero Bronco*, 79–84; Gomezjara, *Bonapartismo y lucha campesina en la Costa Grande de Guerrero*, 125; Gutiérrez Ávila, *Nabor Ojeda, el batallador del sur*, 54–59; Tapia Gómez, *Feliciano Radilla, un líder natural costeño*, 56.
203 Archivo Personal de Tomás Garrido Canabal (hereafter APTGC) caja 133 exp. 12, Tomás Garrido Canabal to Alfredo F. Berber, December 28, 1933; APTGC caja 86 exp. 22, Alfredo F. Berber to Tomás Garrido Canabal, May 2, 1935.
204 AGN DGG 2.347 caja 4 exp. 13.
205 Bustamante, "Período 1934–1940," 405.
206 AGN DGG 2.347 caja 4 exp. 37.
207 ACM, Informe Diocesano Chilpancingo, June 10, 1936; AAC exp. 2.10.2 Directorios 1939–42, Chilpancingo, March 25, 1936; AAC exp. 2.10.1 Informes de visitas a Diócesis 1939–47, Francisco Hernández, "Informe del Estado," January 17, 1941, and "Informe de la Visita," August [1942].
208 Bustamante, "Período 1934–1940," 405.

209 de la Peña, *Guerrero económico*, 1: 369–71, 457–64; Bustamante, "Período 1934–1940," 429.
210 AGN DGG 2.340 caja 42 exp. 17.
211 AGN DGG 2.347 caja 4 exp. 9, 30, 36; AGN DGG 2.340 caja 42 exp. 17.
212 AGN DGG 2.347 caja 4 exp. 21, 23; AGN DGG 2.340 caja 42 exp. 17.
213 AGN DGG 2.340 caja 42 exp. 17.
214 AGN DGG 2.347 caja 4 exp. 6.
215 Francisca Tejeda de León, *Chilapa: Tierra de novela y ensoñación poética* (Mexico City: Costa-Amic Editores, 1999), 26–27; AGN DGG 2.311G(9), caja 244 exp. 40970, Cesar Pérez Almada, January 14, 1941.
216 AGN DGG 2.347 caja 4 exp. 13, 35; AGN DGG 2.340 caja 42 exp. 17.
217 AGN DGG 2.347 caja 4 exp. 35.
218 AGN DGG [sic] caja 5491 exp. 15, Prof. Luis F. Rodríguez report, August 1936.
219 AGN DGG 2.331 caja 24a exp. 3210, Felipe Medel to PR, October 1, 1938.
220 AGN DGG 2.345 caja 3 exp. 40516; AGN DGG 2.347 caja 4 exp. 8, 18.
221 AGN DGG 2.340 caja 43 exp. 8; Guadarrama Gómez, *Notas eclesiásticas del estado de Guerrero*, 229.
222 AHSEP GRO caja 1336 exp. 13, Leopoldo Caro report, April 30, 1935; AGN DGG 2.340 caja 42 exp. 41; AGN DGG 2.340 caja 42 exp. 17; Bartra, *Guerrero Bronco*, 79–84; Gomezjara, *Bonapartismo y lucha campesina en la Costa Grande de Guerrero*, 125; Gutiérrez Ávila, *Nabor Ojeda, el batallador del sur*, 59; Tapia Gómez, *Feliciano Radilla, un líder natural costeño*, 56; AGN LC 541/2300.
223 John W. F. Dulles, *Yesterday in Mexico: A Chronicle of the Revolution, 1919–1936* (Austin: University of Texas Press, 1961), 310; AGN LC 559.1/6, Matias Ramos S. to Lázaro Cárdenas, January 16, 1940.
224 RDSRIAM 1930–39 reel 7, Josephus Daniels to SOS, June 20, 1939.
225 José C. Tapia Gómez, "Episodio almazanista en Tlapa," in *Tlapa: origen y memoria histórica*, ed. Mario O. Martínez Rescalvo (Chilpancingo, Mexico: Universidad Autónoma de Guerrero and Ayuntamiento Municipal de Tlapa de Comonfort, 2000), 224; AGN DGG 2.311 caja 6 exp. 8; RDSRIAM 1930–39 reel 7, Raleigh A. Gibson, Memorandum of Conversation with Salvador Chávez, September 4, 1939.
226 *Time*, November 11, 1940, at http://www.time.com/time/magazine/article/0,9171,849338,00.html (accessed August 2, 2010).
227 On Ojeda and Radilla, see Gutiérrez Ávila, *Nabor Ojeda, el batallador del sur*, 60; Tapia Gómez, *Feliciano Radilla, un líder natural costeño*, 58.
228 Gillingham, "Ambiguous Missionaries," 338–41.
229 AGN DGG 2.347 caja 4 exp. 21, federal tax agent Taxco to SG, May 16, 1939.
230 AGN DGG 2.345 caja 2 exp. 4; Chris Boyer, *Becoming Campesinos: Politics, Identity, and Agrarian Struggle in Postrevolutionary Michoacán, 1920–1935* (Stanford, CA: Stanford University Press, 2003), 230–31.

Chapter 5: Catholic Cacicazgos in Guanajuato

1 Nathan Clarke, "Modernizing the Countryside: Agrarian Education, the Mexican Revolution and the Hacienda de Roque, Celaya, Guanajuato" (Master's thesis, University of California–San Diego, 2001), 78.

2 AHSEP GTO caja 1563 exp. 1, Eduardo Zarza report, December 31, 1932, and caja 897 exp. 3, var. corr.

3 The cacique needs no introduction to students of Mexico: local bosses who rule local fiefdoms or cacicazgos through a mix of violence and charisma. Recently, Alan Knight argued that caciques are inseparable from local factional violence, listing conservative versus progressive as one of four common divisions driving caciquismo. See Alan Knight, "Caciquismo in Twentieth Century Mexico," in *Caciquismo in Twentieth-Century Mexico*, ed. Alan Knight and Wil Pansters (London: Institute for the Study of the Americas, 2005), 3–48, esp. 33–38. I would add that Catholicism often serves to define conservativism by providing an institutional matrix and ideological impulse.

4 AGN IPS 156 exp. 3.

5 Carlos Monsivais, *El Estado laico y sus malquerientes (crónica/antología)* (Mexico City: UNAM, 2008), 135–36.

6 On the Cristiada and Segunda in Guanajuato, see Luis Miguel Rionda Ramírez, *Primer acercamiento a una historia política contemporánea de Guanajuato siglo XX* (Guanajuato, Mexico: Centro de Investigación en Ciencias Sociales de la Universidad de Guanajuato, 1997), 10–15; Raquel Sosa Elízaga, *Los códigos ocultos del cardenismo: Un estudio de la violencia política, el cambio social y la continuidad institucional* (Mexico City: Universidad Nacional Autónoma de México and Plaza y Valdés, 1996) 100–102; and Pablo Serrano Álvarez, *La batalla del espíritu: El movimiento sinarquista en el Bajío (1932–1951)*, 2 vols. (Mexico City: Consejo Nacional Para la Cultura y las Artes, 1992), esp. 1:13.

7 In Van Young's schema, these terms express subregionality, but not subregionalism. Eric Van Young, "Are Regions Good to Think?" in *Mexico's Regions: Comparative History and Development*, ed. Eric Van Young (San Diego: Center for U.S.-Mexican Studies, University of California–San Diego, 1992), 2.

8 David Brading, *Haciendas and Ranchos in the Mexican Bajío: León 1700–1860* (Cambridge: Cambridge University Press, 1978), esp. 216; Luis Miguel Rionda Ramírez, *El conservadurismo popular guanajuatense y el movimiento sinarquista* (Guanajuato, Mexico: Universidad de Guanajuato, Centro de Investigación en Ciencias Sociales, 1997), 15; Patricia Arias, *Irapuato: El bajío profundo* (Guanajuato, Mexico: Archivo General del Gobierno del Estado de Guanajuato, 1994).

9 Guadalupe Valencia García, *Guanajuato: Sociedad, economía, política y cultura* (Mexico City: UNAM, 1998); AHSEP GTO caja 3956 exp. 18, Rafael Rosas R. report, February 1940; Manuel Moreno, *Guanajuato: Cien años de historia (1867–1967)* (Guanajuato, Mexico: Gobierno del Estado de Guanajuato, 1989), 10–11.

10 José Gutiérrez Casillas, *Jesuitas en México durante el siglo XX* (Mexico City: Editorial Porrúa, 1981), 183; Rionda Ramírez, *El conservadurismo popular guanajuatense y el movimiento sinarquista*, 4.

11 AHSSM CRD, "Apuntes generales del movimiento social católica en la Diócesis de León desde el año de 1908 hasta la fecha," September 1935 (hereafter "Apuntes"); Rionda Ramírez, *El conservadurismo popular guanajuatense y el movimiento sinarquista*, esp. 7; Manuel Rangel Camacho, *D. Emeterio Valverde Téllez. obispo de León y asistente al sacro solio pontificio: Algo sobre su vida y su obra* (León, Mexico, 1950); Valencia García, *Guanajuato*, 150, 167–68; Lauro López Beltrán, *Manríquez y Zárate, Primero obispo de Huejutla. Sublimador de Juan Diego. Heroico defensor de la fe* (Mexico City: Editorial Tradición, 1974), 242.

12 Jean Meyer, *La cristiada*, 8th ed. (Mexico City: Siglo XXI, 1983), 1:141–42, 234–39, 265–68; Rionda Ramírez, *El conservadurismo popular guanajuatense y el movimiento sinarquista*, 10–11; Alfonso Sánchez Díaz, *La guerra cristera en Guanajuato. Apuntes para la historia regional* (Mexico City: La Rana, 2005).

13 In Colima, cristeros turned in old firearms and hid the good ones, likely a widely followed practice. John Adrian Foley, "Colima, Mexico and the Cristero Rebellion" (PhD diss., University of Chicago, 1979), 197, 360–62.

14 Rionda Ramírez, *El conservadurismo popular guanajuatense y el movimiento sinarquista*; Antonio Rius Facius, *Méjico Cristero: Historia de la ACJM 1925 a 1931* (Mexico City: Editorial Patria, 1960), 124–26.

15 Alfredo Guerrero Tarquín, *Memorias de un agrarista: Pasajes de la vida de un hombre y de toda una región del estado de Guanajuato (1913–1938)*, 2 vols. (Mexico City: INAH, 1987), 1:256.

16 FON FEC GAV. 90 Confederacion Regional De Obreros Católicos exp. 9 inv. 1502, B-10 Report, September 3, 1926; AGN DGG 2.347 caja 25 exp. 69, "Apuntes"; Rius Facius, *Méjico Cristero: Historia de la ACJM 1925 a 1931*, 165; Rangel Camacho, *D. Emeterio Valverde Téllez*, 202; AHAM, LMM, carpetas 78, 79, A. García de León, January 15, 1930; Randall Hanson, "Day of Ideals. Catholic Social Action in the Age of the Mexican Revolution, 1867–1929" (PhD diss., Indiana University, 1994), 544.

17 AGN DGG 2.347 caja 25 exp. 78–79, 86; AHSSM CRD, Luis Cabrera, "Respuesta al Cuestionario Número 2," León, May 7, 1935; Rangel Camacho, *D. Emeterio Valverde Téllez*, 183–89.

18 Juan José Prado and Manuel Leal, *Leyendas y tradiciones guanajatenses en prosa* (Guanajuato, Mexico: Prado Hermanos, 1955), 29; AGN DGG 2.331 caja 59a exp. 47.

19 AGN DGG 2.347 caja 25 exps. 68, 69, 72.

20 See, for example, AGN DGG 2.347(2) caja 25 exps. 7, 31, 69; AGN DGG 2.340 caja 38 exps. 33, 38.

21 José D. Pérez, *León Cristero, 1926–1929. Ave César! Moritori te salutant* (León, Mexico: 1969), 124.

22 Rangel Camacho, *D. Emeterio Valverde Téllez, 301*; ACC exp. 2.10.1 Informes 1930–33; Hanson, "Day of Ideals," 606–13.

23 Luis Miguel Rionda Ramírez notes that the state's historiography largely ends with Independence, leaving "an astonishing ignorance" of postcolonial Guanajuato. Rionda Ramírez, *Origen y evolución de los partidos políticos en el estado de Guanajuato* (Guanajuato, Mexico: Instituto Electoral del Estado de Guanajuato, 1998). On the armed phase, see Mónica Blanco, *Revolución y contienda política en Guanajuato: 1908–1913* (Mexico City: El Colegio de México, Universidad Nacional Autónoma de México, 1995). For an overview of high politics and agrarian reform in Guanajuato in the 1920s and 1930s, see the following works of Luis Miguel Rionda Ramírez: *Primer acercamiento a una historia política contemporánea de Guanajuato siglo XX*; *Movimientos populares y lucha de la izquierda en Guanajuato 1900–1994* (Guanajuato, Mexico: Centro de Investigación en Ciencias Sociales de la Universidad de Guanajuato, 2001); and *El conservadurismo popular guanajuatense y el movimiento sinarquista*.

24 AGN DGG 2.73 caja 21 exp. 21, José Narvaez et al. to PR Calles, December 29, 1924.

25 AGN DGG 2.311 DS caja 144 exp. 1, Pedro Suárez to PR, June 13, 1926; AGN DGG 2.347(2) caja 25 exps. 20, 48; Guerrero Tarquín, *Memorias de un agrarista*, 2:122–24, 202–5; *Hombre Libre*, July 23, 1931.

26 AGN DGG 2.347 caja 25 exp. 66.

27 Rius Facius, *Méjico Cristero*, 163; Fernando González, *Matar y morir por Cristo Rey: Aspectos de la cristiada* (Mexico City: Instituto de Investigaciones Sociales, Universidad Autónoma de México, 2001), 205–6, 206n325.

28 AGN DGG 2.340 caja 38 exp. 10; AGN DGG 2.347 caja 25 exp. 63; AGN DGG 2.347(2) caja 25 exp. 46; AGN IPS caja 156 exp. 3, José Rodríguez to Enrique Hernández Álvarez, March 21, 1932.

29 AGN DGG 2.73 caja 10 exp. 15 and caja 15 exp. 18.

30 Guerrero Tarquín, *Memorias de un agrarista*, 2:88–92; FAPECYFT PEC GAV.4 AMARO, Joaquín (Gral) exp. 19 inv. 245 leg. 1/4, Amaro to Calles, December 23, 1923; *Guanajuato en la voz de sus gobernadores. Compilación de informes de gobierno, 1917–1991*, 5 vols. (Guanajuato, Mexico: Gobierno de Estado de Guanajuato, 1991), 1:340–41.

31 AGN LC 544.2/10, Celestino Gasca, "La Situation en Estado de Guanajuato," June 8, 1935.

32 AHSEP GTO 1954 exp.1, Eduardo Zarza to SEP, March, 3, 1929.

33 AGN DGG 2.311G(8) 2–3 exp. 1, David Ayala to PNR, July 13, 1932; AGN DGG 2.384 caja 9 exp. 3, Arturo Gómez S. to PR, June 24, 1936; AGN DGG 2.311 DL caja 87 exp. 6, Cayetano Andrade to SG, April 30, 1932.

34 AGN DGG 2.311G(8) 23 exp. 2, Manuel Balderas, April 20, 1931; Jeffrey Weldon, "El congreso, las maquinarias políticas locales y el 'Maximato': Las reformas noreeleccionistas de 1933," in *El legislador a examen: El debate sobre la reelección legislativa en México*, ed. Fernando E. Dworak (Mexico City: Cámara de Diputados, FCE, 2003), 33–53, esp. 47–48; AHSEP DEF GTO caja 897 exp. 3, Arnulfo Ochoa report, November 4, 1932.

35 FAPECYFT PEC GAV. 57 ORTEGA Melchor (Corl. Y Dip) exp. 4 inv. 4192 leg 1/5; AGN

DGG 2.311 DL caja 87 exp. 6; AGN DGG 2.311S caja 155 exps. 5, 8; FAPECYFT PEC GAV. 12 CARDENAS, Lázaro (Gral) exp. 206 inv. 820 leg. 5/9, Cárdenas to Calles, May 17, 1932; RDSRIAM 1930–39 reel 1, Clark to SOS, June 17, 1932.

36. AGN DGG 2.311S caja 156 exp. 3, Ramón Orozco Ávila to PR, July, 21, 1934.
37. AGN DGG 2.347 caja 3 bis exp. 31.
38. AGN DGG 2.311 DL caja 87 exp. 6, Cayetano Andrade et al. to PR, April 30, 1932.
39. AGN DGG 2.384 caja 9 exp. 3 vol. 1, Lucas Barragán to Lázaro Cárdenas, June, 15, 1935.
40. AHSEP GTO caja 897 exp. 3, A. Ochao reports, June 8, 1932, July 1932, September 18, 1932.
41. Peter Reich, *Mexico's Hidden Revolution: The Catholic Church in Law and Politics since 1929* (Notre Dame, IN: University of Notre Dame Press, 1995), 79; John B. Williman, *La iglesia y el estado en Veracruz, 1840–1940* (Mexico City: Sep-Setentas, 1976), 160; Serrano Álvarez, *La batalla del espíritu*, 1:82; Pérez, *León Cristero*, 124.
42. AGN DGG 2.347 caja 3 bis exp. 6.
43. AGN DGG 2.340 caja 38 exp. 58.
44. Juan Ignacio Padilla, *Sinarquismo: Contrarevolución* (Mexico City: Editorial Polis, 1948), 81–82.
45. Jorge López Guzmán, "La cuestión educativa en Guanajuato. Proceso de modernización y cambio político 1915–1939" (Master's thesis, Universidad Iberoamericana, 2004), 130; *Hombre Libre*, July 2, 1934; RDSRIAM 1930–39 reel 17, Consul San Luis Potosí to SOS, April 1, 1934; AGN DGG 2.347 caja 3 bis exp. 22.
46. *Hombre Libre*, September 28, 1934.
47. Ibid., November 28, 1934; Luis Miguel Rionda Ramírez, "Enrique Fernández Martínez: Un gobernador de la vorágine. El Cardenismo y la ruptura generacional revolucionaria," www.cicsug.ugto.mx/Publico/Libros/Luis/FdezMrtz.pdf (accessed 6 February 6, 2006), 38.
48. RDSRIAM 1930–39 reel 43, Edmund Montgomery to SOS, December 18, 1935; AHSEP GTO caja 1364 exp. 1, Roland Uribe to SEP, April 1935; López Guzmán, "La cuestión educative," 117, 124–27, 151–52, 228–29.
49. López Guzmán, "La cuestión educativa," 185, 124–33; Luis Miguel Rionda Ramírez, *Primer acercamiento a una historia política contemporánea de Guanajuato siglo XX*, 50.
50. López Guzmán, "La cuestión educativa," 228–29.
51. AHSEP DEF GTO, caja 1563 exp. 10, Eduardo Zarza report, December 31, 1932.
52. Tomás Cuervo, *El Poema de los niños* (Mexico City, 1964); Dept. de Escuelas Rurales, Serie Personal (Maestros) caja 12 exp. 3; SEP, *Las misiones culturales en 1927: Las escuelas normales rurales* (Mexico City: SEP, 1928), 140–41; AHSEP SDER Campeche caja 20 exp. 5, Luis Álvarez Barret, March 10, 1935; AHSEP CAM caja 47 exp. 20, Claudio Cortés report, July 1932; *Hombre Libre*, August 2, 1935, 2; http://cronica.diputados.gob.mx/DDebates/35/2do/CPerma/19340517.html (accessed

July 31, 2007); Archivo Personal Tomás Garrido Canabal (hereafter APTGC) caja 141 exp. 2, Garrido Canabal to Armando Rovirosa, October 29, 1932.
53 AHSEP GTO caja 1363 exp. 7 and caja 1401 exp. 1, various cor.; AGN LC 534.6/67.
54 AHSEP GTO caja 1363 exp. 7, anon. teachers to SEP, June 1935.
55 AHSEP GTO caja 1363 exp. 7, Tomás Cuervo to gov., May 30, 1935; AGN LC 534.6/67.
56 RDSRIAM 1930–39 reel 43, Josephus Daniels to SOS, November 12, 1935.
57 AHSEP GTO caja 1154 exp. asuntos adm.; AHSEP GTO caja 1401 exp. 3, Francisco Torres to SEP, November 9, 1935; AGN DGG 2.347 caja 3 bis exp. 24, Ramón Gutiérrez to PR, December 15, 1935; http://www.leongto.com.mx/secciones/historia/historia_hechosimportantes.htm (accessed February 2, 2005); AHSEP DEF GTO caja 1401 exp. 5, Roberto Oropeza Najera report, October 21, 1935.
58 AHSEP GTO caja 1363 exp. 7, Tomás Cuervo to gov., February 23, 1935.
59 López Guzmán, "La cuestión educative en Guanajuato," 138.
60 Juan Ignacio Padilla, *Sinarquismo: Contrarrevolución* (Mexico City: Editorial Polis, 1948), 81–83.
61 AHSEP GTO DEF 1705 exp. Quejas Varias, José Meraz to SEP, June 7, 1934; AGN DGG 2.340 caja 38 exp. 50; AHSEP GTO caja 1684 exp. 7, José Macías Padilla report, October 30, 1934.
62 AAC 7.7 Union Nacional de Padres de Familia, 1931–36, C. B. Salgado to Luis G. Bustos, June 26, 1933.
63 AGN DGG 2.347 caja 25 exp. 69; AHSEP GTO caja 1363 exp. 7, TC to gov., February 23, 1935.
64 Rangel Camacho, *D. Emeterio Valverde Téllez*, 202.
65 *Hombre Libre*, December 31, 1934; RDSRIAM 1930–39 reel 41, Josephus Daniels to SOS, December 26, 1934; AGN DGG 2.347 caja 3 bis exp. 21, Alfonso Francisco Ramírez to SG, December 18, 1934.
66 *Siglo de Torreón*, February 28, 1933; RDSRIAM 1930–39 reel 17, Consul San Luis Potosi to SOS, February 28, 1933, March 31, 1933; José Mercadillo Miranda, *Anecdotas sin importancia* (San Miguel Allende, Mexico: Impresa San Miguel, 1960), 13, 19n1.
67 AGN DGG 2.347 caja 3 bis exp. 2.
68 Manuel Romo de Alba (Alonso Quijano Jr.), *El gobernador de las estrellas* (Guadalajara: Autorretrato, 1962) 264.
69 Ernesto Guerra Manzo, "El fuego sagrado. La segunda cristiada y el caso de Michoacán (1961–38)," *Historia Mexicana* 40, no. 2 (2005), 513–75, esp. 551–70.
70 RDSRIAM 1930–39 reel 17, Vice Consul Unversagt to SOS, July 1, 1936.
71 AGN DGG 2.311S caja 156 exp. 13, Francisco Rocha to SG, April 4, 1932.
72 AGN DGG 2.382 caja 13 exp. 16834, Comité Agrarista Cerritos Blanco to PR, March 11, 1936.
73 AGN DGG 2.331 caja 24a exp. 20889; AGN DGG 2.384 caja 48 exp. 24.
74 AGN DGG 2.311S caja 155 exp. 2, "Campesinos de los Sombres de Palma," to PR.
75 *Hombre Libre*, July 9, 1934.

76 http://reference.allrefer.com/encyclopedia/A/Azanza-M.html (accessed July 26, 2005).
77 AGN DGG 2.71 caja 3 exp. 3, Miguel González Caballero to SG, November 3, 1921; "A Brief History of Haciendas," at http://www.pmexc.com/pmexcold/pmc/tours/fieldtrp/fthcdas/fthcdhis.htm (accessed January 31, 2005).
78 AGN DGG 2.74 caja 7 exp. 7, José A. Aguilera to Calles, June 20, 1921.
79 AGN DGG 2.72 caja 5 exp. 3, Antonio Madrazo to SG, January 23, 1923; AGN DGG 2.71 caja 17 exp. 13, SEP to Calles, April 20, 1923.
80 FAPECYFT PEC GAV.14 COLUNGA, Enrique (Lic.) exp. 53 inv. 909, José A. Aguilera to Calles, February 8, 1924.
81 AINAH CR reel 38, V. C. Farril Elcoro, January 20, 1936; Guerrero Tarquín, *Memorias de un agrarista*, 2:53–57; *Hombre Libre*, July 6, 1934; Jean Meyer, *La Cristiada* 2:180.
82 AGN DGG 2.340 caja 38 exp. 10. On countercorporatism, see Adrian Bantjes, "Politics, Class and Culture in Post-Revolutionary Mexico: Cardenismo and Sonora, 1929–1940" (PhD diss., University of Texas, 1991), 275.
83 Beatriz Cervantes, Ana María Crespo, Luz María Flores, and Alfredo Guerrero Tarquín, *La Vida Airada: imágenes del agrarismo en Guanajuato* (Guanajuato, Mexico: Gobierno del Estado de Guanajuato, 1989), 35; Gonzalo Santos, *Memorias* (Mexico City: Grijalbo, 1986), 384–87; AGN DGG 2.311S caja 156 exp. 14, José Martínez Vértiz to SG, March 10, 1932; Guerrero Tarquín, *Memorias de un agrarista*, 2:253; AGN DGG 2.311M caja 395, Lázaro Maldonado to PNR, October 19, 1935; AGN DGG 2.347 caja 3 bis exp. 2; http://www.tvazteca.com/deportes/toros/2003/09/345811.shtml, http://www.sanluisdelapaz.com/cmsdreamer2/index.php?categoryid=15, http://www.gobernacion.gob.mx/transparencia/documentos/PERMISOS%20CABALLOS.pdf; and http://www.hipico.com.mx/hipico/canales/epicurea_ecuestre/olimpicos/equitacion_en_la_ciudad_de_mexico (all accessed August 5, 2005).
84 FAPECYFT PEC GAV.57 ORTEGA Melchor (Corl. Y Dip) exp. 4 inv. 4192 leg. 1/5, Ortega to Calles; AGN DGG 2.347 caja 3 bis exp. 9, Sub-SG to Sec. War, March 21, 1932.
85 AGN DGG 2.311S caja 156 exp. 10, Y-45 report, October 30, 1934; *Hombre Libre*, July 20, 1934.
86 AGN IPS caja 157 exp. 10, I-25 report, May 6, 1935.
87 AGN DGG 2.311S caja 156 exp. 13, Francisco Rocha to SG, April 4, 1932; AGN DGG 2.347 caja 3 bis exp. 2.
88 AGN DGG 2.311S caja 156 exp. 8, gov. to SG, March 8, 1932; AHSEP DEF GTO caja 897 exp. 3, AO various reports; AHSEP GTO caja 3956 exp. 12, Amado M. Piñon report, July 1, 1937.
89 *Guanajuato en la voz de sus gobernadores*, 2:422.
90 AGN DGG 2.311S caja 156 exp. 8, gov. to SG, March 8, 1932; AGN DGG 2.311S caja 156 exp. 14; RDSRIAM 1930–39 reel 17, Consul San Luis Potosí to SOS, May 29, 1936,

October 1, 1936; RDSRIAM 1930–39 reel 6, William Blocker Resumé of Conditions, July 1937; *Guanajuato en la voz de sus gobernadores*, 1:422.

91 RDSRIAM 1930–39 reel 17, Consul San Luis Potosí to SOS, August 2, 1937; "Heads on Parade," *Time*, June 8, 1936.

92 *Hombre Libre*, July 6, 1934.

93 *Guanajuato en la voz de sus gobernadores*, 1:422; FAPECYFT PEC GAV.57 ORTEGA Melchor (Corl. Y Dip) exp. 4 inv. 4192 leg 1/5, gov. to Calles, March 11, 1932; AGN DGG 2.347 caja 3 bis.; AINAH CR reel 38, V. C. Farril Elcoro, January 20, 1936; Guerrero Tarquín, *Memorias de un agrarista*, 2:57; AGN DGG 2.380 caja 11 exp. 4752, Antonio González to SG, August 18, 1935; *Movimiento Popular Libertador Boletín* #3, March 1, 1935; AINAH CR reel 37; *Reconquista*, July 16, 1935.

94 Matthew Butler, "The 'Liberal' Cristero: Ladislao Molina and the Cristero Rebellion in Michoacan, 1927–9," *Journal of Latin American Studies* 31, no. 3 (October 1999): 641–72, esp. 649.

95 FAPECYFT PEC GAV.72 SOTO, Everardo exp. 97 inv. 5508, Everardo Soto et al. to Calles, February 1, 1933; AGN LC 543.1/32, Benigno Arredondo Rivera to Luis I. Rodríguez, December 28, 1934; *Hombre Libre*, July 26, 1934; Guerrero Tarquín, *Memorias de un agrarista*, 2:141; Cristobal Rodríguez, *La influencia del clero en la América Latina* (Mexico City: Talleres Gráficos de la Nación, 1931), 163.

96 AGN DGG 2.380 caja 11 exp. 4752; AHSEP GTO caja 897 exp. 3, AO report, October 1932; AGN DGG 2.311S caja 156 exp. 10, Inspector Y-45 report, October 30, 1934; Guerrero Tarquín, *Memorias de un agrarista*, 2:195–98; AGN DGG 2.311 DL caja 87 exp. 5, F-5 report, July 4, 1935.

97 AHSEP GTO caja 1788 exp. 7, AO to superintendent, December 14, 1928.

98 Ibid.

99 Guerrero Tarquín, *Memorias de un agrarista*, 2:28.

100 AHSEP GTO caja 1788 exp. 7, AO to superintendent, December 14, 1928; AHSEP GTO DEF 1954 exp. 1, Eduardo Zarza report, March 3, 1929; RDSRIAM 1930–39 reel 17, Consul San Luís Potosí to SOS, May 4, 1936; AHSEP GRO caja 987 exp. 13, Gabino Vazquez to Gonzalo Vázquez Vela, June 9, 1935.

101 AHSEP GTO caja 1788, Villeda to SEP, January 16, 1929.

102 AGN IPS caja 157 exp. 10, I-25, May 6, 1935.

103 Santos, *Memorias*, 384.

104 AHSEP GTO caja 1335, José González report, May 2, 1935.

105 Eliseo Rodríguez Ramírez, "El agrarismo en Guanajuato," in *Historia de las ligas de comunidades agrarias y sindicatos campesinos: primer concurso estatal. Vol. 2: Centro,* ed. Julián Rodríguez Sesma (Mexico City: Confederación Nacional Campesina, 1988), 73–149, 107–108; AHSEP GTO caja 3956 exp. 18, Rafael Rosas report, February 1940; AHSEP GRO caja 987 exp. 13, Gabino Vázquez to Gonzalo Vázquez Vela, June 9, 1935.

106 Phyllis McFarland Correa, "Changing Patterns of Sharecropping Arrangements

in the Municipio of Allende, State of Guanajuato" (PhD diss., State University of New York–Stony Brook, 1991), 171.

107 Manola Sepúlveda Garza, *Políticas agrarias y luchas sociales: San Diego de la Unión, Guanajuato, 1900–2000* (Mexico City: Procuraduría Agraria and INAH, 2000), 35.

108 AHSEP GTO 1335 exp. 13, Rafael Rosas report, March 7, 1935.

109 AGN DGG 2.347(2) caja 25 exp. 2, 17; AGN DGG 2.384 caja 47 exp. 4.

110 Jesús Ibarra Grande, *Jaral de Berrio y su marquesado. Monografía Histórica* (León, Mexico, 1973), 168, 170, 179; AGN DGG 2.71 caja 25 exp. 69.

111 Sepúlveda Garza, *Políticas agrarias y luchas sociales*, 54.

112 AGN DGG 2.382 caja 13 exp. 58.

113 AHSEP GTO DEF 1335 exp. 13, Rafael Rosas, March 7, 1935; AHSEP GTO caja 1335 exp. 9, José González report, May 1935.

114 AGN DGG 2.72 caja 5 exp. 3; AGN DGG 2.340 caja 38 exp. 10; AGN DGG 2.331 caja 59a exp. 47, Clotilde L. de Carrillo et al. to PR, August 30, 1928; AHSEP GTO caja 1834 exp. 42, AO to Director de Educación (hereafter DEF), December 14, 1928; AHSEP GTO caja 1788 exp. 7, AO annual report, 1928; AGN DGG 2.347(2) caja 25 exp. 7; AGN DGG 2.347 caja 25 exp. 69; AHSEP GTO caja 1420 exp. 3, Efrén Ramírez to SEP, March 19, 1927; Rangel Camacho, *D. Emeterio Valverde Tellez*, 301; AAC exp. 2.10.1 Informes, 1930–33; AHSSM CRD, "Apuntos"; AHSEP GTO caja 1363 exp. 7, Tomás Cuervo to gov., May 31, 1935; AHSEP GTO caja 1335 exp. 9, José González report, May 19, 1935; Blanco, *Revolución y contienda política en Guanajuato*, 105; Rionda Ramírez, *El conservadurismo popular guanajuatense y el movimiento sinarquista*, 7; FAPECYFT GAV. 90 CONFEDERACION REGIONAL DE OBREROS CATOLICOS, exp. 9 inv 1502, B-10 report, September 3, 1926.

115 AGN DGG 2.331 caja 59a exp. 47, Clotilde L. De Carrillo et al. to PR, August 30, 1928.

116 AGN DGG 2.72 caja 5 exp. 3.

117 AHSEP GTO caja 1732 exp. 18, J. J. Campos report, June 11, 1930; AGN DGG 2.347 caja 3 bis exp. 2.

118 AGN DGG 2.340 caja 38 exp. 30; Pérez, *León Cristero*, 158; Santos, *Memorias*, 386; http://www.clavet.org.mx/sola.html (accessed August 5, 2009).

119 A. Guerrero Tarquín, *Memorias de un agrarista*, 2 vols.; Cervantes et al., *La Vida airada*, 49; Santos, *Memorias*, 384–87; AGN DGG 2.347(2) caja 25 exp. 47, Eusebio Mejo to PR, October 2, 1926.

120 Manola Sepúlveda Garza, "Paradojas de la historia ejidal: El Llanito, Dolores Hidalgo, Guanajuato, 1930–1960," *Cuicuilco* 11, no. 31 (May–August 2004): 1–21, esp. 4–6, 18.

121 Jeffrey Gould, *To Die in This Way: Nicaraguan Indians and the Myth of Mestizaje, 1880–1965* (Durham, NC: Duke University Press, 1998), 102–33.

122 Guerrero Tarquín, *Memorias de un agrarista*, 2:88–91; FAPECYFT PEC GAV. 4 AMARO, Joaquín (Gral) exp. 19 inv 245 leg. 1/4, Amaro to Calles, December 23, 1923.

123 AGN DGG 2.347(2) caja 25 exp. 47; AGN DGG 2.380 caja 10 exp. 20; Sepúlveda Garza, "Paradojas de la historia ejidal," 9, 15.
124 Rafael Perales et al. to governor, September 20, 1836, cited in Sepúlveda Garza, "Paradojas de la historia ejidal," 5.
125 AGN DGG 2.382 caja 14 vol. 2, Asociación Agrícola Regional de Productores de Maíz to SG, February 21, 1936.
126 Sepúlveda Garza, "Paradojas de la historia ejidal," 3–5.
127 Ibid., 5–8.
128 Ibid., 8.
129 AGN DGG 2.340 caja 40 exp. 7.
130 *Guanajuato en la voz de sus gobernadores*, 1:257–58, 340, 418–19; Rionda Ramírez, *Primer acercamiento a una historia política contemporánea de Guanajuato siglo XX*, 41; AGN DGG 2.347 caja 25 exp. 79.
131 AGN DGG 2.340 caja 40 exp. 9.
132 AAC exp. 2.10.1 Informes 1930–33, Junta Diocesana de ACM, León, April 7, 1930.
133 AHSEP GTO caja 1335 exp. 9, José González var. reports.
134 AHSEP GTO caja 1834 exp. 42, A. Ochoa report, January 21, 1929.
135 William Beezley and David Lorey, eds., *Viva México! Viva Independencia!: Celebrations of September 16* (Wilmington, DE: Scholarly Resources, 2001), esp. Isabel Fernández Trejo and Carmen Nava Nava, "Images of Independence in the Nineteenth Century: The Grito de Dolores, History and Myth," 1–42; Javier Rodríguez Piña, "Conservatives Contest the Meaning of Independence, 1846–1855," 101–30, esp. 101–2; and Nora Pérez-Rayón E., "The Capital Commemorates Independence at the Turn of the Century," 141–63. For a penetrating discussion of the conflicts over Mexico's founding fathers, see Christon I. Archer, "Death's Patriots: Celebration, Denunciation, and Memories of Mexico's Independence Heroes: Miguel Hidalgo, José María Morelos, and Agustín de Iturbide," in *Body Politics: Death, Dismemberment, and Memory in Latin America*, ed. Lyman L. Johnson (Albuquerque: University of New Mexico Press, 2004), 63–104. David Brading argues that Hidalgo never really fit into the secular nationalist pantheon, in part because of his Guadalupanism. See his *The First America: The Spanish Monarchy, Creole Patriots, and the Liberal State 1492–1867* (New York: Cambridge University Press, 1991), 572, 645–46, 659, 662.
136 Archer, "Death's Patriots"; Valentina Torres Septién, *La educación privada en México (1903–1976)* (Mexico City: Colegio de México and Universidad Iberoamericana, 1997), 255–59.
137 AGN DGG 2.347(2) caja 25 exp. 19.
138 López Guzmán, "La cuestión educativa," 165.
139 AHSEP GTO caja 3956 exp. 18, Rafael Rosas report, February 1940.
140 AGN DGG 2.340 caja 38 exp. 38.
141 On an analogous situation in Europe, see Christopher Clark, "The New Catholicism and the European Culture Wars," in *Culture Wars: Secular-Catholic Conflict*

     in *Nineteenth-Century Europe*, ed. Christopher Clark and Wolfram Kaiser (New York: Cambridge University Press, 2003), 11–46, 42.
142 Mario Armando Vázquez Soriano, *Signos de identidad: Los espacios simbólicos de Dolores Hidalgo* (Mexico City: Instituto Mora, 1999), 76, 160–61; Miguel Angel Granados Chapas, *Fox y Co.: Biografía no autorizada* (Mexico City: Grijalbo, 2000), 17–19.
143 "Don Melchor Ortega," *Hombre Libre*, October 18, 1933.
144 *Guanajuato en la voz de sus gobernadores*, 1:409–17.
145 Rionda Ramírez, *Primer acercamiento a una historia política contemporánea de Guanajuato siglo XX*, 51–52.
146 AGN DGG, 2.380 caja 11 exp. 4752; AGN DGG 2.347 caja 3 bis exp. 38; *Hombre Libre*, September 16, 1935.
147 Rionda Ramírez, *Primer acercamiento a una historia política contemporánea de Guanajuato siglo XX*, 52–56.
148 AGN LC 544.2/10 leg. 1, Adalberto Rincón Jaime to Luis I. Rodríguez, December 26, 1934.
149 Phyllis McFarland Correa, "Changing Patterns of Sharecropping Arrangements in the Municipio of Allende, State of Guanajuato" (PhD diss., State University of New York–Stony Brook, 1991), 41.
150 AHSEP GTO caja 987 exp. 13, Gabino Vázquez to Gonzalo Vázquez Vela, June 9, 1935.
151 AGN LC 544.2/10 leg. 2, PR to Commander Zona Militar Gto., September 4, 1935.
152 RDSRIAM 1930–39 reel 17, Consul Montgomery to SOS, March 31, 1936.
153 Roberto Blancarte, *Historia de la Iglesia Católica en México* (Mexico City: Colegio Mexiquense y Fondo de Cultura Económica, 1992), 41; Lyle C. Brown, "Mexican Church-State Relations, 1933–1940," *Journal of Church and State* 6, no. 2 (Spring 1964), 214.
154 López Guzmán, "La cuestión educativa," 148–49.
155 Ibid., 148–50, 210.
156 Ibid., 150–51, 210–11.
157 AGN DGG 2.384 caja 47 exp. 4; AGN DGG 2.347 caja 3 bis exp. 19; AGN DGG 2.311G(8) caja 234 vol. 3, Octavio Mendoza to SG, April 12, 1935; AHSEP GTO caja 1335 exp. 9, José González reports, May 2 1935, May 19 1935, June 19, 1935, September 30, 1935; AHSEP GTO caja 987 exp. 13, Gabino Vázquez to Gonzalo Vázquez Vela, June 9, 1935; María del Carmen Sandoval, interviewed in 1998, cited in López Guzmán, "La cuestión educativa," 168, 211.
158 AGN DGG 2.347 caja 3 bis exp. 38.
159 AHSSM CRD, Informe Mensual de León, LA VERDAD DE LOS SANGRIENTOS SUCESOS DE CD, Manuel González, GTO; AGN DGG 2.347 caja 3 bis exp. 38; RDSRIAM 1930–39 reel 17, Consul Montgomery to SOS, March 31, 1936; Guerrero Tarquín, *Memorias de un agrarista*, 2:162; AGN LC 547.1/19, Gabriel Mella Solórzano to PR, April 8, 1936; López Guzmán, "La cuestión educativa," 211–12.

160 AHSSM CRD, Informe Mensual de León, "LA VERDAD . . . de un Testigo. . . . que tomó parte principal en los acontecimientos"; RDSRIAM 1930–39 reel 17, Consul Montgomery to SOS, March 31, 1936.

161 Mercadillo Miranda, *Anecdotas sin importancia*, 167–68; AGN DGG 2.382 caja 13 exp. 433, Benito Aguilar to PR, May 2, 1935.

162 AHSSM CRD, Informe Mensual de León, "LA VERDAD . . . de un Testigo. . . . que tomó parte principal en los acontecimientos"; AGN DGG 2.347 caja 3 bis exp. 38; RDSRIAM 1930–39 reel 17, Consul Montgomery to SOS, March 31, 1936; Guerrero Tarquín, *Memorias de un agrarista*, 2:162; *La Prensa*, April 29, 1936, quoted in AGN LC 547.1/19; Gabriel Mella Solórzano to PR, April 8, 1936; *Omega*, April 16, 1936, quoted in Victoria Lerner, *La educación socialista. Historia de la Revolución Mexicana, 1934–1940*, vol. 17 (Mexico City: Colegio de Mexico, 1979), 36; *El Centro*, April 1, 1936, quoted in López Guzmán, "La cuestión educativa," 213.

163 AGN DGG 2.347 caja 3 bis exp. 38.

164 AGN DGG 2.347 caja 3 bis exp. 38; David Raby, *Educación y revolución social en México (1921–1940)*, trans. Roberto Gómez Ciriza (Mexico City: Sep-Setentas, 1974), 160.

165 AGN DGG 2.347(2) caja 25 exp. 54.

166 AGN IPS 156 exp. 3, José Rodríguez to Enrique Hernández Álvarez, March 21, 1931; FAPECYFT PEC GAV. 66 RODRÍGUEZ, Higinio exp. 176 inv. 4998, various; FAPECYFT PEC GAV. 67 ROMERO, Ramón exp. 38 inv. 5098; AGN LC 544.2/10, Asociación Agrarista Guanajuatense to PR, December 15, 1923; AGN DGG 2.311S caja 155 exp. 5, Froylán Manjárrez to SG, May 30, 1932; RDSRIAM 1930–39 reel 17, Consul Shaw to SOS, July 20, 1930, January 31, 1932.

167 AGN DGG 2.347(2) caja 25 exp. 43; RDSRIAM 1930–39 reel 17.

168 RDSRIAM 1930–39 reel 17, Vice Consul Unversagt to SOS, July 1, 1936; AGN DGG 2.347(2) caja 25 exp. 7, 20, 54, 63; AGN DGG 2.340 caja 38 exp. 38; AHSSM CRD, "Apuntos"; AGN DGG 2.340 caja 38 exp. 31.

169 AGN DGG 2.382 caja 13 exp. 433; AGN DGG 2.347 caja 3 bis exp. 2, 38; AGN DGG 2.331 caja 24a exp. 4284.

170 AGN DGG 2.347(2) caja 25 exp. 20; AHSEP GTO caja 1788 exp. 7, A. Ochoa report, 1928; AHSEP GTO caja 1834 exp. 42, A. Ochoa report; AHSEP GTO caja 1732 exp. 24, A. Ochoa report, February 10, 1930; AGN DGG 2.347 caja 3 bis exp. 2; RDSRIAM 1930–39 reel 17, Consul San Luis Potosí to SOS, May 4, 1936.

171 AGN DGG 2.347 caja 3 bis exp. 2; AGN LC 547.1/19, Oficina de Bienes Nationales to Tax Official San Miguel Allende, May 7, 1936.

172 *El Nacional*, March 31, 1936, cited in Lerner, *La educación*, 36; Mercadillo Miranda, *Anecdotas sin importancia*, 168; RDSRIAM 1930–39 reel 17, Consul San Luis Potosí to SOS, May 4, 1936; Cervantes et al., *La vida airada*, 62–63; Guerrero Tarquín, *Memorias de un agrarista*, 2:162; RDSRIAM reel 5, Josephus Daniels to SOS, April 15, 1936.

173 Mercadillo Miranda, *Anecdotas sin importancia*, 45, 168–80.

174 RDSRIAM 1930–39 reel 17, Consul San Luis Potosí to SOS, May 4, 1936; AGN DGG 2.340 caja 39 exp. 7.

175 AHSEP GTO caja 3956 exp. 12, Amado M. Piño report, July 1, 1937.
176 Sepúlveda Garza, *Políticas agrarias y luchas sociales*, 50.
177 RDSRIAM 1930–39 reel 17, Consul San Luis Potosí to SOS, May 4, 1936.
178 AGN DGG 2.382 caja 14, Salvador Teufler to SG, July 1, 1936.
179 AGN LC 547.1/19, gov. to PR, April 3, 1936.
180 AGN DGG 2.347 caja 3 bis exp. 39.
181 AGN DGG 2.347 caja 3 bis exp. 24.
182 RDSRIAM 1930–39 reel 17, Consul San Luis Potosí to SOS, May 29, 1936.
183 Cervantes et al., *La vida airada*, 62–63; AGN DGG 2.347 caja 3 bis exp. 38.
184 *La Prensa*, April 29, 1936, quoted in AGN LC 547.1/19; Gabriel Mella Solórzano to PR, April 8, 1936; *Pro-Patria*, August 13, 1936.
185 AGN DGG 2.382 caja 14, vol. 2, Manuel Ortiz to SG, June 26, 1936; AGN DGG 2.384 caja 49 exp. 7342, José López L. to PR, March 19, 1936; AGN DGG 2.384 caja 49 exp. 6334, anon. to SG, July 23, 1936.
186 AHSEP GTO caja 3956 exp. 12, Amado M. Piño report, July 1, 1937; Cervantes et al., *La vida airada*, 61.
187 Guerrero Tarquín, *Memorias de un agrarista*, 2:223–99; Rodríguez Ramírez, "El agrarismo en Guanajuato," 140; Cervantes et al., *La vida airada*, 26, 70–74.
188 RDSRIAM 1930–39 reel 17, Consul San Luis Potosí to SOS, August 31, 1936.
189 AHSEP GTO caja 3956 exp. 18, Rafael Rosas report, February 1940.
190 AGN LC 404.1/1965, Rafael Rangel memorandum, July 18, 1938; Sepúlveda Garza, *Políticas agrarias y luchas sociales*, 58.
191 AHSEP GTO caja 8193 exp. 13, Rafael Rosas report, February 1, 1938.
192 Sepúlveda Garza, "Paradojas de la historia ejidal," 1–21, esp. 3.
193 AHSEP GTO caja 8193 exp. 14, José Macías Padilla, March 12, 1939.
194 AHSEP GTO caja 3956 exp. 18, Rafael Rosas report, February 1940.
195 Sepúlveda Garza, *Políticas agrarias y luchas sociales*, 50–51.
196 AGN DGG 2.384 caja 9 exp. 1720, Ejidal Commission Santa Barbara to PR, December 8, 1941.
197 Sepúlveda Garza, *Políticas agrarias y luchas sociales*, 50–51.
198 Ibid., 74–80.
199 Ibid., 55–57.
200 AINAH CR reel 38, *Reconquista*, April 1, 1936, *Boletín de guerra*; AGN LC 404.1/1965, Rafael Rangel memorandum, July 18, 1938; RDSRIAM 1930–39 reel 8, Montgomery to SOS, September 21, 1939; Guerrero Tarquín, *Memorias de un agrarista*, 2:291; Sosa Elízaga, *Los códigos ocultos del Cardenismo*, 493.
201 Sepúlveda Garza, *Políticas agrarias y luchas sociales*, 57.
202 AGN DGG 2.384 caja 9 exp. 1720, Luis González to PR, August 20, 1941; Sepúlveda Garza, *Políticas agrarias y luchas sociales*; Guerrero Tarquín, *Memorias de un agrarista*, 2:180.
203 AHSEP GTO caja 3956 exp. 12, Amado M. Piñon, July 1, 1937; AHSEP GTO caja 8193 exp. 14, José Macias Padilla, March 12, 1939.

204　AHSEP GTO caja 8193 exp. 14, Ceferino Cano report, March 30, 1939.
205　AGN DGG 2.340 caja 40 exp. 7.
206　AHSEP GTO caja 8193 exp. 14, José Macías Padilla report, March 12, 1939.
207　Emma Yáñez Rizo, *Vida y muerte de Fidelita, la novia de Acámbaro: Una historia social de la tecnología en los años cuarenta: El caso de los Ferrocarriles Nacionales de México* (Mexico City: Consejo Nacional para la Cultura y las Artes, 1991), 105.
208　Moreno, *Guanajuato*, 63–80.
209　Francisco Javier Meyer Cosío, *Tradición y progreso: La reforma agraria en Acámbaro, Guanajuato (1915–1941)* (Mexico City: INEHRM, Secretaría de Gobernacíon, 1992).
210　Alan Knight, *Mexico: The Colonial Era* (Cambridge: Cambridge University Press, 2002); David Brading, *Church and State in Bourbon Mexico: The Diocese of Michoacán 1749–1810* (New York: Cambridge University Press, 1994), 138; Shirley Gorenstein, ed., *Acambaro: Frontier Settlement on the Tarascan-Aztec Border*, Vanderbilt University Publication in Anthropology No. 32 (Nashville, TN: Vanderbilt University Press, 1985); Pedro Rojas, *Acámbaro colonial: Estudio histórico, artístico e iconográfico* (Mexico City: Universidad Nacional Autónoma de México, 1967).
211　Daniel Newcomer, *Reconciling Modernity: Urban State Formation in 1940s León, Mexico* (Lincoln: University of Nebraska Press, 2004), 29–30.
212　José Guadalupe Romero, *La historia y la estadística del obsipado de Michoacán* (Mexico City: Vicente García Torres, 1862), 231; AGN DGG 2.347 caja 3 bis exp. 17.
213　Meyer Cosío, *Tradición y progreso*, 192.
214　AGN DGG 2.347 caja 3 bis exp. 17. On colonial tithing, see María Isabel Sánchez Maldonado, *Diezmos y crédito eclesiástico. El diezmatorio de Acámbaro 1724–1771* (Morelia, Mexico: El Colegio de Michoacán, 1994).
215　AHSEP GTO caja 1788 exp. 12, José Macías Padilla reports, December 10, 1928, July 2, 1929; Meyer Cosío, *Tradición y progreso*, 73.
216　Meyer Cosío, *Tradición y progreso*, 82.
217　Ramón del Llano Ibáñez, *El partido católico y el primer gobernador de la Revolución en Querétaro* (Querétaro, Mexico: Universidad Autónoma de Querétaro, 2005), 53–55.
218　Matthew Butler, *Popular Piety and Political Identity in Mexico's Cristero Rebellion: Michoacán, 1927–29* (Oxford: Oxford University Press 2004), 147–53, 159, 179; RDSRIAM 1910–29 reel 146, "The Religious Crisis in Mexico," February 18, 1927.
219　RDSRIAM 1910–29 reel 146, "The Religious Crisis in Mexico," February 18, 1927; Butler, *Popular Piety and Political Identity in Mexico's Cristero Rebellion*, 159–60.
220　ACC 2.10 JD de Morelia, Mich., exp. 1932–36, various; AHSSM CRD, Juan Buitrón, "Informe de la Diócesis Morelia," February 1936; ACM, "Grupos Parroquiales," caja 3 (A.G. 197) exp. Acción Católica; AGN DGG 2.347 caja 3 bis exp. 28; AAC exp. 2.10.1, exp. 7.3, Fidel Sánchez, "Informe 1939–47."
221　AGN DGG 2.347 caja 3 bis exp. 18.
222　AGN DGG 2.73 caja 21 exp. 21.
223　*Hombre Libre*, October 1, 1934, November 16, 1934; AGN DGG 2.311S caja 156 exp. 12,

Benjamín Herrera to Partido Nacional Revolucionario (hereafter PNR), March 20, 1932; AGN DGG 2.347 caja 3 bis exp. 18, 28; AGN DGG 2.73 caja 21 exp. 21.

224 AGN DGG 2.311 G(8) 2–3 exp. 1, David Ayala to PNR, July 13, 1932; AGN DGG 2.384 caja 9 exp. 3, Arturo Gómez S. to PR, June 24, 1936; AGN DGG 2.311 DL caja 87 exp. 6, Cayetano Andrade to SG, April, 30, 1932; AGN DGG 2.311S caja 154 exp. 3; RDSRIAM 1930–39 reel 4, Norweb to SOS, May 21, 1935, June 7, 1935, and reel 17, Edmund Montgomery to SOS, March 3, 1938, July 5, 1939; AGN IPS caja 762 exp. 4, PS-12, February 27, 1939; AGN LC 544.2/10, "Caso Electoral," August 9, 1939.

225 AGN DGG 2.73 caja 21 exp. 21; Guerrero Tarquín, *Memorias de un agrarista*, 2:249–53.

226 Meyer Cosío, *Tradición y progreso*, 86, 132; *Hombre Libre*, July 21, 1931; AGN DGG 2.382 caja 13 exp. 8, Calles to SG, January 21, 1927.

227 AGN DGG 2.347 caja 3 bis exp. 9; AGN DGG 2.311 DL caja 86 exp. 1, "Elecciones," September 20, 1926; AGN DGG 2.311S caja 154 exp. 2, "Un Alerta a los Verdaderos Revolucionarios"; AGN DGG 2.347(2) caja 25 exp. 51, Rómulo Morales, August 12, 1926; AGN DGG 2.384 caja 9 exp. 2, J. Medina Ortega to PR, January 28, 1928; AGN DGG 2.384 caja 9 exp. 3, Arturo Gómez to PR, January 24, 1936; *Hombre Libre*, November 16, 1934.

228 *Hombre Libre*, July 21, 1931.

229 Ibid., August 31, 1934.

230 AGN DGG 2.347 caja 3 bis exp. 9, 17.

231 *Hombre Libre*, July 12, 1934, July 23, 1934, August 20, 1934, August 31, 1934.

232 Ibid., July 12, 1934, August 20, 1934.

233 Ibid., July 23, 1934, September 26, 1934.

234 Benjamin Smith, "Anticlericalism, Politics, and Freemasonry in Mexico," *The Americas* 65, no. 4 (April 2009): 559–88.

235 AGN DGG 2.347 caja 3 bis exps. 9, 17; *Hombre Libre*, November 16, 1934.

236 AHSEP GTO caja 1684 exp. 7, José Macías Padilla report, October 30, 1934; *Hombre Libre*, November 5, 1934, November 14, 1934, November 16, 1934.

237 *Hombre Libre*, December 26, 1934; RDSRIAM 1930–39 reel 41, Josephus Daniel to SOS, December 26, 1934.

238 *Hombre Libre*, November 5, 1934; ibid., October 29, 1934.

239 AHSEP GTO DEF 1684 exp. 8, José Macías Padilla, August 1, 1934.

240 AHSEP GTO caja 8193 exp. 1, Clemente J. Nápoles, June 28, 1938; AHSEP GTO caja 1684 exp. 7, José Macías Padilla report, October 30, 1934.

241 AHSEP GTO caja 1335 exp. 7, Francisco Gutiérrez, September 19, 1935.

242 AHSEP GTO caja 1335 exp. 7, Francisco Gutiérrez, October 2, 1935, December 31, 1935; AGN DGG 2.331 caja 24a exp. 3981; Enrique Plascencia de la Parra, "Adolfo de la Huerta en el Exilio," *Boletín del Fideicomiso Archivos Plutarco Elías Calles y Fernando Torreblanca* 41 (September–December 2002): 1–32, esp. 10.

243 Meyer Cosío, *Tradición y progreso*, esp. 80–82, 99–102; AHSEP GTO caja 1684 exp. 8, José Macías Padilla to DEF August 1, 1934; AGN DGG 2.311S caja 156 exp. 10, Confederación Campesina Mexican to SG, November 20, 1934.

244   AHSEP GTO caja 1684 exp. 8, José Macías Padilla, August 1, 1934.
245   AHSEP GTO DEF caja 1335 exp. 4, various cor., and caja 1420, José Macías Padilla, September 30, 1933; AHSEP GTO DEF caja 1684 exp. 8, José Macías Padilla to superintendent, August 1, 1934; AHSEP GTO DEF caja 1335 exp. 7, Francisco Gutiérrez report, September 19, 1935.
246   AHSEP GTO caja 1684 exp. 8, José Macías Padilla to DEF, August 1, 1934. The translation of *liviana* comes from Real Academia Española, *Diccionario Manual e ilustrado de la Lengua Española* (Madrid: Espasa-Calpe, 1927), 1194.
247   Meyer Cosío, *Tradición y progreso*, 80–82, 99–100.
248   AGN DGG 2.347 caja 25 exp. 76.
249   AGN DGG 2.73 caja 21 exp. 21; *Hombre Libre*, July 21, 1931; AGN DGG 2.347(2) caja 25 exp. 51, Rómulo Morales, August 12, 1926; AGN DGG 2.382 caja 13 exps. 2, 13, 16.
250   AHSEP GTO caja 1335 exp. 7, Francisco Gutiérrez report, October 28, 1935.
251   *Hombre Libre*, February 20, 1935; AHSEP GTO caja 1335 exp. 7, Francisco Gutíerrez report, March 23, 1935.
252   AHSEP GTO caja 1684 exp. 7, José Macías Padilla report, October 30, 1934; AHSEP GTO caja 1684 exp. 15, A. Ochoa to Rafael Ramirez JDER, December 3, 1934.
253   AHSEP GTO caja 1335 exp. 7.
254   AHSEP GTO caja 1335 exp. 7, Francisco Gutiérrez, December 31, 1935; *Hombre Libre*, April 5, 1935.
255   AGN DGG 2.347 caja 3 bis exp. 18.
256   AHSEP GTO caja 1335 exp. 11, Jesús Mújica Martínez report, November 19, 1935.
257   Ibid.
258   AGN DGG 2.72 caja 4 exp. 49, Moisés Arevato, June 8, 1922.
259   AGN DGG 2.347(2) caja 25 exp. 29, 75.
260   AHSEP GTO caja 1363 exp. 1, A. Ochoa, November 29, 1935.
261   Guerra Manzo, "El fuego sagrado," 551–70, esp. 557.
262   Meyer Cosío, *Tradición y progreso*, 167.
263   *Hombre Libre*, November 16, 1934.
264   RDSRIAM 1930–39 reel 5, Josephus Daniels to SOS, May 13, 1936.
265   AHSEP GTO caja 8193 exp. 13, Clemente J. Nápoles report, June 28, 1938.
266   Raby, *Educación*, 174–76.
267   AGN DGG 2.73 caja 15 exp. 18; AGN DGG 2.347(2) caja 25 exp. 19; AGN DGG 2.74 caja 12 exp. 4; AGN DGG 2.347(2) caja 25 exps. 38, 58; AGN DGG 2.380 caja 10 exp. 15; AGN DGG 2.384 caja 47 exp. 2; Patricia Campos Rodríguez, "Salvatierra en el tiempo y en el espacio," in *Ciudades guanajuatense a la orilla del milenio*, ed. Patricia Campos Rodríguez (Guanajuato, Mexico: Universidad de Guanajuato y Ayuntamiento de Allende, 1996), 11–24, esp. 21; RDSRIAM 1930–39 reel 144, George Summerlin to SOS, January 25, 1923; Blanco, *Revolución y contienda política en Guanajuato*, 105; *Guanajuato en la voz de sus gobernadores*, 1:257–58, 319.
268   *Hombre Libre*, October 1, 1934.
269   Ibid., February 20, 1935.

270 López Guzmán, "La cuestión educativa," 163.
271 AGN DGG 2.347 caja 3 bis exp. 18; AHSEP GTO DEF 1705 exp. Quejas Varias, José Meraz, June 7, 1934; López Guzmán, "La cuestión educativa," 161–63; AHSEP GTO caja 1335 exp. 7, Francisco Gutiérrez report, November 20, 1935.
272 AHSEP GTO DEF 1684 exp. 15, A. Ochoa, June 20, 1934.
273 AGN DGG 2.347 caja 3 bis exp. 28; AHSEP GTO caja 1335 exp. 7, Francisco Gutiérrez, October 28, 1935.
274 AGN DGG 2.382 caja 13 exp. 3; FAPECYFT PEC GAV. 57 ORTEGA Melchor Corl. Y Dip exp. 4 inv. 4192 leg. 1/9, Ortega to Calles, October 25, 1933; Rodríguez Ramírez, "El agrarismo en Guanajuato," 10; AGN DGG 2.384 caja 47 exp. 2; AGN DGG 2.347(2) caja 25 exp. 19; AGN DGG 2.380 caja 10 exp. 24.
275 AGN DGG 2.347 caja 3 bis exps. 18, 37; AGN DGG 2.311G(8) 23 exp. 2; AGN DGG 2.382 caja 13 exp. 50; *Guanajuato en la voz de sus gobernadores*, 1:418–19.
276 AHSEP GTO DEF caja 1420 exp. 8, A. Ochoa reports, November 4, 1933, and December 19, 1933; AHSEP DEF GTO 897 exp. 5, Rafael Rosas report, May 3, 1932.
277 AHSEP GTO DEF caja 1335 exp. 7.
278 David Brading, *Church and State in Bourbon Mexico: The Diocese of Michoacán 1749–1810* (New York: Cambridge University Press, 1994), 92–100.
279 AHSEP JDER caja 8193 exp. "Relaciones y Constancias Art. 123 escuelas," March 9, 1938.
280 Jennie Purnell, *Popular Movements and State Formation in Revolutionary Mexico: The Agraristas and Cristeros of Michoacán* (Durham, NC: Duke University Press, 1999), 163–75.
281 AGN DGG 2.74 caja 12 exp. 4.
282 AGN DGG 2.311M caja 396 exp. 29813, J. Cruz Albarran, January 2, 1938; AGN DGG 2.384 caja 47 exp. 1, José Campos Rios, October 2, 1940; AHSEP GTO caja 1335 exp. 4, J. Jesús Rivera, October 19, 1935; AGN DGG 2.347 caja 3 bis exp. 18, Manuel Acevedo to SG, July 28, 1934; AAC exp. 2.10.1, "Informe 1939–47"; AHSEP GTO caja 3956 exp. 30, Angel Pineda García, August 31, 1940; Romero, *La historia y la estadística del obispado de Michoacán*, 233.
283 AGN DGG 2.311G(8) 23 exp. 2., Manuel Balderas, April 20, 1931; *Hombre Libre*, July 21, 1931.
284 AHSEP GTO caja 1335 exp. 4, var. corr., and caja 1420, José Macías Padilla, September 30, 1933.
285 AHSEP GTO DEF 1335 exp. 4, J. Jesús Rivera, November 19, 1935; AHSSM CRD, Juan Buitron, "Informe," March 3, 1936.
286 AGN DGG 2.382 caja 13 exp. 11.
287 AGN DGG 2.382 caja 13 exps. 2, 11.
288 AGN DGG 2.347 caja 3 bis exp. 4.
289 AHSEP JDER caja 8193 exp. "Relaciones y Constancias Art. 123 escuelas," March 9, 1938.
290 AGN DGG 2.347 caja 25 exp. 72; AGN DGG 2.384 caja 48 exp. 38; AGN DGG 2.384 caja 48 exp. 36.

291   AGN DGG 2.347 caja 3 bis exp. 18; AHSEP GTO caja 1335 exp. 4, J. Jesús Rivera, November 19, 1935; ACC 2.10 Junta Diocesana de Morelia, Mich. 1932–36, Miguel Alvarado, April 8, 1935; AHSEP GTO caja 3956 exp. 30, Angel Pineda García, August 31, 1940; AHSEP GTO caja 8193 exp. 13, Clemente J. Nápoles, June 28, 1938; AHSEP JDER caja 8193 exp. "Relaciones y Constancias Art. 123 escuelas," March 9, 1938; AHSEP GTO caja 1684 exp. 7, José Macías Padilla, October 4, 1934; AGN IPS caja 762 exp. 4, PS-6 29, September 1939.

292   AHSEP GTO caja 3956 exp. 18, Clemente Nápoles, February 16, 1940; AGN IPS caja 762 exp. 4, Ejido of Chupícuaro et al. to PR, April 5, 1935.

293   Rionda Ramírez, *Enrique Fernández Martínez: Un gobernador de la vorágine. El Cardenismo y la ruptura generacional revolucionaria,* http://www.cicug.ngto..mx/Public/Libros/Lug/FderMrtz.pdf (accessed February 6, 2006), 37–38; AGN DGG 2.311S caja 156 exp. 10; AGN DGG 2.347 caja 3 bis exp. 34; AGN DGG 2.382 caja 14, vol. 2; AGN IPS caja 762 exp. 4, PS-6, April 15, 1939; AHSEP GTO caja 3956 exp. 30, Angel Pineda García, August 31, 1940.

294   http://www.e-local.gob.mx/wb2/ELOCAL/EMM_guanajuato (accessed July 14, 2009).

295   AHSEP GTO caja 8193 exp. 13, Clemente J. Nápoles report, June 28, 1938; Meyer Cosío, *Tradición y progreso,* 192.

296   AGN LC 544.2/10, Frente Socialista Guanajuatense, July 27, 1939.

297   AHSEP GTO caja 1834 exp. 49, José Macías Padilla report, July 1929.

298   AHSEP caja 1684 exp. 7, José Macías Padilla to SEP, August 25, 1934; AHSEP GTO caja 1732 exp. 32, José Macías Padilla, December 20, 1930; AHSEP GTO DEF caja 1834 exp. 49, José Macías Padilla, July 2, 1929.

299   AHSEP GTO caja 8193 exp. 13, Clemente J. Nápoles, June 28, 1938.

300   Meyer Cosío, *Tradición y progreso,* 192.

301   AGN IPS caja 762 exp. 4, Ejido of Chupícuaro et al., April 5, 1935; AGN DGG 2.384 caja 48 exp. 38, Adolfo Maldonado to PR, October 9, 1939; AGN DGG 2.311 DL caja 87 exp. 6; AGN DGG 2.347 caja 25 exp. 72; AGN DGG 2.347 caja 3 bis exp. 18.

302   AGN DGG 2.347 caja 3 bis exp. 9; ACC 2.10 JD de Morelia, Mich. 1932–36, Miguel Alvarado G., August report, August 17, 1937.

303   Mario Gill (Mario Velasco Gil), *Sinarquismo. Su Origen, Su Esencia, Su Misión,* 2nd ed. (Mexico City: Comité de Defensa de la Revolución, 1944), 163, 172, 330.

304   AGN IPS caja 775 exp. 1 vol. 1, Informe de Comites Regionales Sinarquistas, March 1943.

305   RDSRIAM 1930–39 reel 17, Consul San Luis Potosí to SOS, January 3, 1940; AGN IPS caja 762 exp. 4, PS-6, September 29, 1939, and caja 760 exp. 7, various; AGN DGG 2.380 caja 10 exp. 22518; AGN DGG 2.384 caja 9 exp. 30448.

306   AHSEP GTO caja 3956 exp. 18, Clemente J. Nápoles report, February 16, 1940.

307   AGN DGG 2.347 caja 3 bis exp. 17.

308   Meyer Cosío, *Tradición y progreso,* 192.

309   Chris Boyer, *Becoming Campesinos: Politics, Identity, and Agrarian Struggle in Postrevolutionary Michoacán, 1920–1935* (Stanford, CA: Stanford University Press, 2003), 97–98.

310 Butler, *Popular Piety and Political Identity in Mexico's Cristero Rebellion*, 71, 130–34, 139–43.
311 Rojas, *Acámbaro colonial*; AGN DGG 2.347 caja 3 bis exp. 28.
312 Meyer Cosío, *Tradición y progreso*, 99; AGN DGG 2.311 DS caja 144 exp. 1, Rómulo Morales to SG, June 30, 1926.
313 Rionda Ramírez, *El conservadurismo popular guanajuatense y el movimiento sinarquista*, 15.
314 López Guzmán, "La cuestión educativa," 182.
315 Newcomer, *Reconciling Modernity*, 136, 266n18.
316 Nathan Whetten, *Rural Mexico* (Chicago: University of Chicago Press, 1948), 260–62. Real wages actually dropped nationally after 1935 due to inflation, meaning workers in Guanajuato probably experienced an even more precipitous decline in real wages.
317 Ibid., 364.
318 Ibid., 418.
319 Ibid., 488.
320 Serrano Álvarez, *La batalla del espíritu*, 2:70–71.
321 Vázquez Soriano, *Signos de identidad*, 160–61.
322 David Shirk, *Mexico's New Politics: The PAN and Democratic Change* (Boulder, CO: Lynne Reiner, 2005), 59–71.
323 Donald Mabry, *Mexico's Acción Nacional: A Catholic Alternative to Revolution* (Syracuse, NY: Syracuse University Press, 1973), 34–36.
324 Almazán ran as the candidate of the Partido Revolucionario de Unificación Nacional (Revolutionary Party of National Unification), which disappeared after he was defeated at the ballot box and his coup fizzled. Both Almazán and the PAN later regretted the tacit alliance, and outside of the north, the PAN largely dropped support for Almazán. See ibid., 37–38.
325 Rossana Almada, *El vestido azul de la sultana: La construcción del PAN en Zamora 1940–1995* (Zamora, Mexico: Colegio de Michoacán, 2001), 43–44, 50–51. While some analysts of the PAN see the contemporary party as markedly different from the party at its foundation due to intraparty struggles in the 1960s and 1970s between more and less religious factions, Almada finds that the PAN's fundamentally religious orientation did not change in Zamora. See ibid., 103–82. For another example of the strong Catholic influence over a local chapter of the PAN, see Benjamin Smith, "'The Priest's Party': Local Catholicism and Panismo in Huajuapam de León," in *Faith and Impiety in Revolutionary Mexico*, ed. Matthew Butler (New York: Palgrave Macmillan, 2007), 261–77.
326 Shirk, *Mexico's New Politics*, 59–71, 231. Bernardo Barranco notes the "constant and significant flow of militants from the ACM to the PAN." See his "Posiciones políticas en la historia de la Acción Católica Mexicana," in *El pensamiento social de los católicos mexicanos*, ed. Roberto Blancarte (Mexico City: Fondo de Cultura Económica, 1996), 39–70.

Conclusion

1. In Durango, another Callista, Governor Carlos Real (1932–35), relied on Catholic middlemen to build a political base. See AHPEC 64/81/4766/exp. 1; AGN DGG 2.311G caja 228 vol. 1, T. de D. A. Torres Estrada to SG, June 13, 1932; AGN DGG 2.384 caja 8 exp. 5.
2. AHAM, LMM, carpeta 83 "Gobierno civil y memorandums" exp. 2, Julio Vertiz, Memorandum to Luis M. Martínez, August 19, 1939.
3. Adrian Bantjes, "Idolatry and Iconoclasm in Revolutionary Mexico: The De-Christianization Campaigns, 1929–1940," *Mexican Studies/Estudios Mexicanos* 13:1 (winter 1997), 87–120
4. Kristina Boylan, "Revolutionary and Not-So-Revolutionary Negotiations in Catholic Annulment, Bigamy and Divorce Trials: The Archdiocese of Mexico, 1929–40," in *Faith and Impiety in Revolutionary Mexico*, ed. Matthew Butler (New York: Palgrave Macmillan, 2007), 167–83, esp. 167, 174, 178.
5. Alan Knight, "Revolutionary Project, Recalcitrant People: Mexico, 1910–1940," in *The Revolutionary Process in Mexico: Essays on Political and Social Change, 1880–1940*, ed. Jaime Rodríguez (Los Angeles: UCLA Latin American Center Publications and Mexico/Chicano Program of the University of California, Irvine, 1990), 227–64, 230, 259–61.
6. Antonio Avitia Hernández, *El caudillo sagrado: Historia de las rebeliones cristeras en el estado de Durango* (Mexico City: Impresos Castellanos, 2000), 188–90. Mary Kay Vaughan finds a similar dynamic in Sonora and Puebla in *Cultural Politics in Revolution: Teachers, Peasants, and Schools in Mexico, 1930–1940* (Tucson: University of Arizona, 1997).
7. RDSRIAM 1930–39 reel 5, Josephus Daniels to SOS, October 16, 1936, and reel 44, Josephus Daniels to SOS, July 14, 1936; AHSSEM DECP, "Declaraciones del Comité Ejecutivo Episcopal," July 1936.
8. Stephen Lewis, "Efrain Gutiérrez of Chiapas: The Revolutionary Bureaucrat," in *State Governors in the Mexican Revolution, 1910–1952: Portraits in Conflict, Courage, and Corruption*, ed. Jurgen Buchenau and William Beezley (Lanham. MD: Rowman & Littlefield, 2009), 139–55, esp. 144–47.
9. On Sonora, see Adrian Bantjes, *As If Jesus Walked on Earth: Cardenismo, Sonora and the Mexican Revolution* (Wilmington, DE: Scholarly Resources, 1998), esp. 69; Armando Chávez Camacho, *Juan Navarrete: Un hombre enviado por Dios* (Mexico City: Editorial Porrua, 1983), 123.
10. Jesús Márquez, "La oposición contrarevolucionaria de derecha en Puebla," in *Religión, política y sociedad. El sinarqusimo y la iglesia en México (nueve ensayos)*, ed. Rubén Aguilar V. and Guillermo Zermeño Padilla (Mexico City: Universidad Iberoamericana, 1992), 31–54, esp. 36–44.
11. AGN DGG 2.311G caja 309 exp. 32106, "Caso Político de Sinaloa."
12. Pablo Moreno, *Torreón: Biografía de la mas joven de las ciudades mexicanas* (Salt-

illo, Mexico: Talleres Gráficos Coahuila, 1951), 274–76; AGN DGG 2.347(2) caja 1 bis exp. 24, governor to SG, February 24, 1936.

13 AHAM, LMM carpeta 83 "Gobierno civil y memorandums," exp. 2, Rafael Dávila Vilchis to Luis M. Martínez, April 20, 1937; RDSRIAM reel 10, Consul Torreón to SOS, December 2, 1937, December 12, 1937, October 1, 1938; José Gutiérrez Casillas, *Jesuitas en México durante el siglo XX* (Mexico City: Editorial Porrua, 1981), 218, 222, 255; Jesús Sotomayor Garza, *Anales laguneros* (Torreón, Mexico: Ayuntamiento de Torreón, 1992), 125–28.

14 Thomas Rath," 'Que el cielo un soldado en cada hijo te dio . . . ': Conscription, Recalcitrance and Resistance in Mexico in the 1940s," *Journal of Latin American Studies* 37, no. 3 (August 2005): 507–31, esp. 508–9, 517; Tanalís Padilla, *Rural Resistance in the Land of Zapata: The Jaramillista Movement and the Myth of the Pax Priísta, 1940–1962* (Durham, NC: Duke University Press, 2008).

15 On Gramsci's distinction between domination, or coercion by the state, and hegemony, created by consent from civil society, see Perry Anderson, "The Antinomies of Antonio Gramsci," *New Left Review* 100 (1976–77): 5–78, esp. 22, and Ranajit Guha in *Dominance without Hegemony: History and Power in Colonial India* (Cambridge, MA: Harvard University Press, 1997). Gramsci insisted that if the "economic nucleus" were not secured, then hegemony would not be won. Stuart Hall, "Antonio Gramsci," in *The Routledge Dictionary of Twentieth-century Political Thinkers*, ed. Robert Benewick and Philip Green (London: Routledge, 1992), 80–82.

16 Paul Gillingham and Benjamin Smith, eds., *La Dictablanda: Soft Authoritarianism in Mexico, 1938–1968* (Durham, NC: Duke University Press, forthcoming).

17 Benjamin Smith, *Pistoleros and Popular Movements: The Politics of State Formation in Postrevolutionary Oaxaca* (Lincoln: University of Nebraska Press, 2009), 282, 343, 347.

18 I am indebted to Terry Rugeley for this observation.

Bibliography

Archival Materials

Archivo General de la Nación
Archivo General del Estado de Yucatán (AGEY)
    Poder Ejecutivo (PE)
Archivo Histórico Arzobispado de México (AHAM)
    Archivo Pascual Díaz (APD)
    Archivo Luis María Martínez (LMM)
Archivo Histórico de Secretaría Educación Pública
    Dirección General de Misiones Culturales (DGMC)
    Dirección de Educación Federal Campeche (CAM)
    Dirección de Educación Federal Guanajuato (GTO)
    Dirección de Educación Federal Guerrero (GRO)
    Dirección de Educación Federal Hidalgo (HGO)
Archivo Histórico Secretariado Social Mexicano (AHSSM)
Archivo del Instituto Nacional de Antropología e Historia (AINAH)
    Conflicto Religioso (CR)
    Conflictos Religiosos por Diócesis (CRD)
    Documentos Episcopales, Cartas Pastorales (DECP)
    Fideicomiso Archivo Plutarco Elías Calles y Fernando Torreblanca
        Archivo Plutarco Elías Calles, Fondo Plutarco Elías Calles (PEC)
        Archivo Personal Joaquín Amaro (APJA)
        Archivo Personal Fernando Torreblanco (FPEC)
Archivo Personal de Tomas Garrido Canabal (APTGC)
Dirección General de Gobierno (DGG)
    Colección Abelardo Rodríguez (AR)
    Colección Alvaro Obregón y Plutarco Elías Calles (OyC)
    Colección Lázaro Cárdenas (LC)
    Oficina de Información Política y Social (IPS)

Paul Murray's Survey of Mexican Dioceses (MS)
Records of the Department of State Relating to the Internal Affairs of Mexico (RDSRIAM)
Universidad Iberoamericana, Biblioteca Francisco Xavier Clavijero, Archivo Acción Católica (AAC)

Periodicals

Boletín de Guerra
El Centro
Diario de Yucatán
Diario Oficial
Excelsior
Hombre Libre
El Nacional
Omega
La Prensa
Pro-Patria
Reconquista
La Revista de Yucatán
Siglo de Torreón
Time
El Universal
La Verdad
La Voz de la Revolución

Books, Articles, and Online Sources

Abud Flores, José. *Campeche: Revolución y movimiento social (1911–1923)*. Campeche, Mexico: INEHRM, Secretaría de Gobernación, and Universidad Autónoma de Campeche, 1992.

Aguilar, Roger, and Guillermo Zermeño. *Hacia una reinterpretación del sinarquismo actual. Notas y materiales para su estudio*. Mexico City: Universidad Iberoamericana, 1988.

Ahumada Medina, Albino. *Organización campesina y lucha agraria en el estado de Hidalgo, 1917–1940*. Pachuca, Mexico: Universidad Autónoma del Estado de Hidalgo, 2000.

Alcocer Bernes, Manuel. *Historia del ayuntamiento del Campeche, 1540–1991*. Campeche, Mexico: Ayuntamiento de Campeche, 1991.

Almada, Rossana. *El vestido azul de la sultana: La Construcción del PAN en Zamora 1940–1995*. Zamora, Mexico: Colegio de Michoacán, 2001.

Alonso Alcocer, Primitivo. *Cuando Quintana Roo fue desmembrado (1931–1935)*. Chetumal, Mexico: Congreso del estado de Quintana Roo, AOP, 1992.

Álvarez Flores, Luis, Andrés Barquin y Ruiz, José Castañedo, José de la Luz León, Jorge Nuñez, Miguel Palomar y Vizcarra, Mario Resendes Martínez, Ramón Ruiz y Rueda, Rosendo Octavio Sandoval, José Serrano Orozco, Luis Vargas Varela, Manuel Velázquez Morales. *J. de Jesús Manríquez y Zárate, Gran Defensor de la Iglesia.* Mexico City: Editorial Rex-Mex, 1952, 346.

Amendolla, [Luis]. *La revolución comienza a los cuarenta.* Mexico City, n.d.

Angeles Contreras, Jesús. *Monografía del municipio de Molango.* Pachuca, Mexico: Gobierno del estado de Hidalgo and Instituto Hidalguense de la Cultura, 1993.

Aranda González, Mario. *Apuntaciones históricas y literarias del municipio de Hopelchen, Campeche.* Mérida, Mexico: Maldonado, 1985.

———. *Hecelchakán: Historia, Geografía, Cultura.* Campeche, Mexico: CONACULTA and INAH, 2003.

———. *Masonería en el Estado de Campeche.* Campeche, Mexico: Instituto Campechano, 1990.

———. *El municipio de Calkiní.* Campeche, Mexico, 1981.

Archer, Christon I. "Death's Patriots: Celebration, Denunciation, and Memories of Mexico's Independence Heroes: Miguel Hidalgo, José María Morelos, and Agustín de Iturbide." In *Body Politics: Death, Dismemberment, and Memory in Latin America*, ed. Lyman L. Johnson. 63–104. Albuquerque: University of New Mexico Press, 2004.

Arias, Patricia. *Irapuato: El bajío profundo.* Guanajuato, Mexico: Archivo General del Gobierno del estado de Guanajuato, 1994.

Arrom, Silvia. *The Women of Mexico City, 1790–1857.* Stanford, CA: Stanford University Press, 1985.

Arteaga, Belinda. *A gritos y sombrerazos. Historia de los debates sobre educación sexual en México, 1906–1946.* Mexico City: UPN and Miguel Angel Porrua, 2002.

Aspe Armella, María Luisa. *La formación social y política de los católicos mexicanos: La Acción Católica Mexicana y la Unión Nacional de Estudiantes Católicos, 1929–1958.* Mexico City: Universidad Iberoamericana, 2008.

Aston, Nigel. *The End of an Elite: The French Bishops and the Coming of the French Revolution, 1786–1790.* Oxford: Clarendon Press, 1992.

Avitia Hernández, Antonio. *El caudillo sagrado: Historia de las rebeliones cristeras en el estado de Durango.* Mexico City: Impresos Castellanos, 2000.

Báez-Jorge, Félix. *Olor de santidad. San Rafael Guízar y Valencia: Articulaciones históricas, políticas y simbólicas de una devoción popular.* Xalapa, Mexico: Universidad Veracruzana, 2006.

Bantjes, Adrian. *As If Jesus Walked on Earth: Cardenismo, Sonora and the Mexican Revolution.* Wilmington, DE: Scholarly Resources, 1998.

———. "Burning Saints, Molding Minds: Iconoclasm, Civic Ritual, and the Failed Cultural Revolution." In *Rituals of Rule, Rituals of Resistance: Public Celebrations and Popular Culture in Mexico*, ed. William H. Beezley, Cheryl English Martin, and William French. 261–84. Wilmington, DE: Scholarly Resources, 1994.

———. "Idolatry and Iconoclasm in Revolutionary Mexico: The De-Christianization

Campaigns, 1929–1940." *Mexican Studies/Estudios Mexicanos* 13, no. 1 (1997): 87–120.

———. "Politics, Class and Culture in Post-Revolutionary Mexico: Cardenismo and Sonora, 1929–1940." PhD diss., University of Texas Press, 1991.

———. "Saints, Sinners and State Formation." In *The Eagle and the Virgin: Nation and Cultural Revolution in Mexico, 1920–1940*, ed. Stephen E. Lewis and Mary Kay Vaughn. 137–56. Durham, NC: Duke University Press, 2005.

———. "The War against Idols: The Meanings of Iconoclasm in Revolutionary Mexico, 1910–1940." In *Negating the Image: Case Studies in Iconoclasm*, ed. Jeff Johnson and Anne McClanan. 41–66. Burlington, VT: Ashgate, 2005.

Barranco V., Bernardo. "Posiciones políticas en la historia de la Acción Católica Mexicana." In *El Pensamiento Social de los Católicos Mexicanos*, ed. Roberto Blancarte. 39–70. Mexico City: Fondo de Cultura Económica, 1996.

Becker, Marjorie. *Setting the Virgin on Fire: Lázaro Cárdenas, Michoacán Peasants, and the Redemption of the Mexican Revolution*. Berkeley: University of California Press, 1995.

———. "Torching La Purísima, Dancing at the Altar: The Construction of Revolutionary Hegemony in Michoacán, 1934–40." In *Everyday Forms of State Formation: Revolution and the Negotiation of Rule in Modern Mexico*, ed. Gilbert M. Joseph and Daniel Nugent. 247–64. Durham, NC: Duke University Press, 1994.

Berrueto Ramon, Federico. *Obras completas*. Saltillo, Mexico: Universidad Autónoma de Coahuila, 1984.

Berzunza Pinto, Ramón. *Una chispa en el sureste (Pasado y futuro de los indios mayas)*. Mexico City: Talleres de la Cooperativa, 1942.

Besserer, Federico, Victoria Novelo, and Juan Luis Sariego. *El sindicalismo minero en México, 1900–1952*. Mexico City: Ediciones Era, 1983.

Blancarte, Roberto. *Historia de la iglesia católica en México*. Mexico City: Colegio Mexiquense y Fondo de Cultura Económica, 1992.

———. *El pensamiento social de los católicos mexicanos*. Mexico City: Fondo de Cultura Económica, 1996.

Blanco, Mónica. *Revolución y contienda política en Guanajuato: 1908–1913*. Mexico City: El Colegio de México, 1995.

Bliss, Katherine. *Compromised Positions: Prostitution, Public Health, and Gender Politics in Revolutionary Mexico City*. University Park, PA: Penn State University Press, 2001.

Bolivar, Juan J. *Compendio de historia de ciudad de Carmen, Campeche*. Mexico City: Ediciones Contraste, 1989.

Borja, Desiderio. *Perfil suriano*. Mexico, 1929.

Bottomore, Tom, and William Outhwaite, eds. *The Blackwell Dictionary of Twentieth-Century Social Thought*. Cambridge: Blackwell, 1993.

Boyer, Chris. *Becoming Campesinos: Politics, Identity, and Agrarian Struggle in Postrevolutionary Michoacán, 1920–1935*. Stanford, CA: Stanford University Press, 2003.

Boylan, Kristina. "The Feminine 'Apostolate in Society' versus the Secular State: The Unión Femenina Católica Mexicana, 1929–1940." In *Right Wing Women: From Conservatives to Extremists Around the World*, ed. Paola Bacchetta and Margaret Power. 167–83. London: Routledge, 2002.

———. "Mexican Catholic Women's Activism, 1929–1940." PhD. diss., Oxford University Press, 2000.

———. "Revolutionary and Not-So-Revolutionary Negotiations in Catholic Annulment, Bigamy and Divorce Trials: The Archdiocese of Mexico, 1929–40." In *Faith and Impiety in Revolutionary Mexico*, ed. Matthew Butler. 167–83. New York: Palgrave Macmillan, 2007.

Brading, David. *Church and State in Bourbon Mexico: The Diocese of Michoacán 1749–1810*. New York: Cambridge University Press, 1994.

———. *The First America: The Spanish Monarchy, Creole Patriots, and the Liberal State 1492–1867*. New York: Cambridge University Press, 1991.

———. *Haciendas and Ranchos in the Mexican Bajío: León 1700–1860*. New York: Cambridge University Press, 1978.

———. *Mexican Phoenix, Our Lady of Guadalupe: Image and Tradition across Five Centuries*. New York: Cambridge University Press, 2001.

Bravo Ugarte, José. *Diocesis y obispos de la iglesia Mexicana (1919–1965)*. Mexico City: Editorial Jus, 1965.

Brown, Denise. "Yucatec Maya Settling, Settlement and Spatiality." PhD diss., University of California–Riverside, 1993.

Brown, Lyle C. "Mexican Church-State Relations, 1933–1940." *Journal of Church and State* 6, no. 2 (1964): 202–22.

Brunk, Samuel. *The Posthumous Career of Emiliano Zapata: Myth, Memory, and Mexico's Twentieth Century*. Austin: University of Texas Press, 2008.

Buenrostro, Efrain. *Geografía económica del estado de Hidalgo*. Mexico City: Secretaría de la Economía Nacional, 1939.

Burke-Young, Francis. *Passing the Keys: Modern Cardinals, Conclaves, and the Election of the Next Pope*. Lanham, MD: Madison Books, 1999.

Burns, Kathryn. *Colonial Habits: Convents and the Spiritual Economy of Cuzco, Peru*. Durham, NC: Duke University Press, 1999.

Bustamante Álvarez, Tomás. "Periodo 1934–1940." In *Historia de la cuestión agraria mexicana. Estado de Guerrero 1867–1940*, ed. Jaime Salazar Adame, Renato Rabelo Lecuona, Daniel Molina, and Tomás Bustamante. 337–534. Mexico City: Gobierno del estado de Guerrero, 1987.

Butler, Matthew. "La consagración nacional del Sagrado Corazón de Jesús en la Arquidiócesis de México, 6 de enero de 1914." In *Memoria del IV Seminario de Historia Regional*, ed. Yolanda Padilla Rangel. Aguascalientes, Mexico: Universidad Autónoma de Aguascalientes, 2010.

———. "Father Perez's Revolution: Or, Making Catholicism 'Mexican' in 20th-Century Mexico." Albuquerque: University of New Mexico Press, forthcoming.

———. "God's Campesinos? Mexico's Revolutionary Church in the Countryside." *Bulletin of Latin American Research* 28, no. 2 (April 2002): 165–84.
———. "The 'Liberal' Cristero: Ladislao Molina and the Cristero Rebellion in Michoacán, 1927–9." *Journal of Latin American Studies* 31, no. 3 (1999): 641–72.
———. *Popular Piety and Political Identity in Mexico's Cristero Rebellion: Michoacán, 1927–29.* Oxford: Oxford University Press, 2004.
———. "A Revolution in Spirit? Mexico, 1910–1940." In *Faith and Impiety in Revolutionary Mexico*, ed. Matthew Butler. 1–20. New York: Palgrave Macmillan, 2007.
Camacho Sandoval, Salvador. *Controversia educativa entre la ideología y la fe. La educación socialista en la historia de Aguascalientes. 1876–1940.* Mexico City: Consejo Nacional para la Cultura y las Artes, 1991.
Cámara de Diputados. http://cronica.diputados.gob.mx/DDebates/36/1er/Ord/19340 824.html (accessed August 8, 2008).
Campos Rodríguez, Patricia. "Salvatierra en el Tiempo y en el Espacio." In *Ciudades guanajuatenese a la orilla del milenio*, ed. Patricia Campos Rodríguez. 11–24. Guanajuato, Mexico: Universidad de Guanajuato y Ayuntamiento de Allende, 1996.
Canabal Cristiani, Beatriz, and José Joaquín Flores Félix. *Montañeros: Actores sociales en la montaña del estado de Guerrero.* Mexico City: UAM, UA–Chapingo, and El Atajo Ediciones, 2004.
Canudas, Enrique. *Trópico Rojo: Historia política y social de Tabasco. Los años garridistas 1919/1934.* Vol. 2. Villahermosa, Mexico: Gobierno del Estado de Tabasco and ICT, 1982.
Carreño, Alberto María. *Paginas de Historia Mexicana.* Mexico City: Ediciones Victoria, 1936.
Carrera Quezada, Sergio Edmundo. *A son de campana: La fragua de Xochiatipan.* Mexico City: CIESAS, Colegio de San Luis, UAEH, 2007.
Casteñada, Quetzil. "'We Are Not Indigenous!': An Introduction to the Maya Identity of Yucatán." *Journal of Latin American Anthropology* 9, no. 1 (spring 2004): 36–63.
Castillo Torre, José. *A la luz de relámpago. Ensayo de biografía subjectiva de Felipe Carrillo Puerto.* Mexico City: Ediciones Botas, 1934.
Ceballos Ramírez, Manuel. *El catolicismo social: Un tercero en discordia. Rerum Novarum, la "cuestión social" y la mobilización de los católicos mexicanos (1891–1911).* Mexico City: El Colegio de México, 1991.
Cervantes, Beatriz. "La educación y el conflicto iglesia-estado." In *IV Jornadas de historia*, 79–100. Jiquilpan: CERM, 1982.
Cervantes, Beatriz, Ana María Crespo, Luz María Flores, and Alfredo Guerrero Tarquín. *La vida airada: imágenes del agrarismo en Guanajuato.* Guanajuato, Mexico: Gobierno del Estado del Estado de Guanajuato, 1989.
Chávez, Gabino. *Novísimo catecismo de los diezmos: Su naturaleza y origen, su obligación y legislación, su sanción y práctica.* Mexico City: Talleres J. de Elizalde, 1901.
Chávez Camacho, Armando. *Juan Navarrete: Un hombre enviado por Dios.* Mexico City: Editorial Porrua, 1983.

Cheney, David. "The Hierarchy of the Catholic Church." http://www.catholic-hierarchy.org/diocese/dtula.html (accessed December 11, 2007).

Clark, Christopher. "The New Catholicism and the European Culture Wars." In *Culture Wars: Secular-Catholic Conflict in Nineteenth Century Europe*, ed. Christopher Clark and Wolfram Kaiser. 11–46. Cambridge: Cambridge University Press, 2003.

Clarke, Nathan. "Modernizing the Countryside: Agrarian Education, the Mexican Revolution and the Hacienda de Roque, Celaya, Guanajuato." Master's thesis, University of California–San Diego, 2001.

Coatsworth, John. "Obstacles to Economic Growth in Nineteenth-Century Mexico." *American Historical Review* 83, no. 1 (1978): 80–100.

Conger, Robert. "Porfirio Díaz and the Church Hierarchy, 1876–1911." PhD diss., University of New Mexico, 1985.

Contreras Valdez, José Mario. *Reparto de tierras en Nayarit, 1916–1940: Un proceso de ruptura y continuidad*. Mexico City: INEHRM and Universidad Autónoma de Nayarit, 2001.

Crehan, Kate. *Gramsci, Culture and Anthropology*. Berkeley: University of California Press, 2002.

Cuervo, Tomás. *El poema de los niños*. Mexico City: n.p., 1964.

Cuevas, Mariano. *Historia de la iglesia en México*. Vol. 5, *1700–1800*. 5th ed. Mexico City: Editorial Patria, 1947.

Curley, Robert. "Slouching towards Bethlehem: Catholics and the Political Sphere in Revolutionary Mexico." PhD diss., University of Chicago Press, 2001.

Dawson, Alexander. *Indian and Nation in Revolutionary Mexico*. Tucson: University of Arizona Press, 2004.

Dehouve, Danièle. *Cuando los banqueros eran santos: Historia economía y social de la provincia de Tlapa, Guerrero*. Trans. Bertha Chavelas Vásquez. Mexico City: Universidad Autónoma de Guerrero and CFEMC, 2002.

———. "The 'Money of the Saint': Ceremonial Organization and Monetary Capital in Tlapa, Guerrero, Mexico." In *Manipulating the Saints: Religious Brotherhoods and Social Integration in Postconquest Latin America*, ed. Albert Meyers and Diane E. Hopkins. 149–174. Hamburg, Germany: Wayasbah, 1988.

de la Cueva, Julio. "The Assault on the City of the Levites: Spain." In *Culture Wars: Secular-Catholic Conflict in Nineteenth Century Europe*, ed. Christopher Clark and Wolfram Kaiser. 11–46. New York: Cambridge University Press, 2002.

de la Luz Mena, José. *La escuela socialista. Su desorientación y fracaso. El verdadero derrotero*. Mexico City, 1941.

de la Peña, Moisés T. *Campeche económico*. Vol. 1. Campeche, Mexico: Gobierno constitucional del estado de Campeche, 1942.

———. *Guerrero económico*. 2 vols. Mexico City: Gobierno del estado de Guerrero, 1949.

———. *Zacatecas económico*. Mexico City: Revista de economía, 1948.

del Llano Ibáñez, Ramón. *El Partido Católico y el primer Gobernador de la Revolución en Querétaro*. Querétaro, Mexico: Universidad Autónoma de Querétaro, 2005.

Diaz Figueroa, Febronio. "Lo dulce y amargo de la tierra." In *Historia de las ligas de communidades agrarias y sindicatos campesinos primer concurso estatal*. Vol. 3: *Centro Sur*, ed. Bertha Beatriz Martínez G., 261–340. Mexico City: CNC and CEHAM, 1988.

Díaz Ordaz, Gustavo, and Rubén Rodríguez Lozano. *Los Gobiernos de la revolución contra la ignorancia*. Mexico City: Instituto Nacional de la Juventud Mexicana, 1965.

Diccionario manual e ilustrado de la Lengua Española. Madrid: Espasa-Calpe, 1927.

Diócesis de Campeche. http://orbita.starmedia.com/diocesis_de_campeche/Obispo51.htm (accessed August 22, 2006).

Dirección General de Crónica Parlamentaria, http://cronica.diputados.gob.mx/DDebates/35/2do/CPerma/19340517.html (accessed July 31, 2007).

Donham, Donald. *Marxist Modern: An Ethnographic History of the Ethiopian Revolution*. Berkeley: University of California Press, 1999.

Dow, James. "Saints and Survival: The Functions of Religion in a Central Mexican Indian Society." PhD diss., Brandeis University Press, 1973.

Dromundo, Baltasar. *Rojo Gómez: Bosquejo de un hombre*. Mexico City: Federación de Escritores de México, 1946.

Dussel, Enrique. *A History of the Church in Latin America: Colonialism to Liberation (1492–1979)*. Trans. Alan Neely. Grand Rapids, MI: William B. Eerdmans, 1981.

Dwyer, John. *The Agrarian Dispute: The Expropriation of American-Owned Rural Land in Postrevolutionary Mexico*. Durham, NC: Duke University Press, 2008.

Eiss, Paul. "Hunting for the Virgin: Meat, Money and Memory in Tetiz, Yucatán." *Cultural Anthropology* 17, no. 3 (August 2002): 291–330.

"Emilio Portes Gil: ¿Quién los mando matar?: No se sabe." In *La Sombra de Serrano: De la Matanza de Huitzilac a la Expulsión de Calles por Cárdenas*, ed. Federico Campbell. 39–42. Mexico City: Proceso, 1981.

Enciclopedia de los Municipios de México. http://www.e-local.gob.mx/work/templates/enciclo/guerrero/municipios/12026a.htm (accessed May 11, 2004).

———. INF and Gobierno del Estado de Hidalgo. http://www.e-local.gob.mx/work/templates/enciclo/hidalgo/municipios/13014a.htm (accessed July 27, 2008).

Erwin, Michael. "The 1930 Agrarian Census in Mexico: Agronomists, Middle Politics, and the Negotiation of Nationalism." *Hispanic American Historical Review* 87, no. 3 (2007): 539–72.

Escobar Ohmstede, Antonio, and Frans Schryer. "Las sociedades agrarias en el norte de Hidalgo, 1856–1900." *Mexican Studies/Estudios Mexicanos* 8, no. 1 (1992): 1–21.

Escobedo, M. Rodolfo. *La Diócesis de Saltillo: Notas Históricas*. Saltillo, Mexico: Gobierno eclesiástico del obispado de Saltillo, 1989.

Espejel López, Laura, and Salvador Rueda Smithers. *Reconstrucción histórica de una comunidad del norte de Guerrero: Ichcateopan*. Mexico City: DEHINAH, 1979.

Espinosa, David. "Jesuit Higher Education in Post-revolutionary Mexico: The Iberoamerican University, 1943–1971." PhD diss., University of California–Santa Barbara, 1998.

Estrada Castañón, Alba Teresa. *Guerrero: Sociedad, economía, política y cultura* (Mexico City: Universidad Autónoma de México, 1994).

Fabila, Alfonso. *Valle de el Mezquital*. Mexico City: Ediciones Culturales, 1938.

Fallaw, Ben. *Cárdenas Compromised: The Failure of Reform in Postrevolutionary Yucatán*. Durham, NC: Duke University Press, 2001.

———. "From Acrimony to Accommodation: Church-State Relations in Revolutionary-era Yucatán, 1915–1940." In *Peripheral Visions: Politics, Society, and the Challenges of Modernity in Yucatán*, ed. Edward Terry, Ben Fallaw, Gilbert Joseph, and Edward Moseley. 227–53. Tuscaloosa: University of Alabama Press, 2010.

———. "Rethinking Mayan Resistance: Changing Relations between Federal Teachers and Mayan Communities in Eastern Yucatán, 1929–1935." *Journal of Latin American Anthropology* 9, no. 1 (spring 2004): 151–78.

Farriss, Nancy. *Maya Society under Colonial Rule: The Collective Enterprise of Survival*. Princeton, NJ: Princeton University Press, 1984.

Favier Orendáin, Claudio. *Ruinas de utopia. San Juan de Tlayacápan. Espacio y tiempo en el encuentro de dos culturas*. Mexico City: Gobierno del estado de Morelos, IIE, UNAM, and FCE, 1989.

Fernández Repetto, Francisco, and Genny Negroe Sierra. "Caminando y 'paseando' con la Virgen. Prácticas de la religión popular e identidades sociales en el noroccidente de Yucatán." In *Identidades Sociales en Yucatán*, ed. María Cecilia Lara Cebada. 99–132. Mérida, Mexico: Facultad de Ciencias Antropológicas, 1997.

———. "Resistencia cultural a través de la religion popular. Los gremios y las fiestas de Yucatán." In *Persistencia cultural entre los Mayas frente al cambio y la modernidad*, ed. Ramón Arzápalo Marín and Ruth Gubler. 99–132. Mérida, Mexico: Universidad Autónoma de Yucatán, 1997.

Fernández Trejo, Isabel, and Carmen Nava Nava. "Images of Independence in the Nineteenth Century: The Grito de Dolores, History and Myth." In *Viva México! Viva Independencia: Celebrations of September 16*, ed. William Beezley and David Lorey. 1–42. Wilmington, DE: Scholarly Resources, 2001.

Figueroa Uriza, Arturo. *Andrés Figueroa. Biografia*. Mexico City, 2000. 1–42.

Flores Arellano, Nédila, and América Wences Román. *Doña María de la O. Una mujer ejemplar*. Mexico City: UA-Guerrero and CEHAM, 1992.

Flores Maldonado, Effraín, and Carlos Klimek Salgado. *Gobernadores del estado de Guerrero*. 4th ed. Mexico City: Sanley, 2005.

Foley, John. "Colima, Mexico and the Cristero Rebellion." PhD diss., University of Chicago, 1979.

Friedrich, Paul. *Agrarian Revolt in a Mexican Village*. Austin: University of Texas Press, 1979.

Gabbert, Wolfgang. *Becoming Maya: Ethnicity and Social Inequality in Yucatán since 1500*. Tucson: University of Arizona Press, 2004.

Galindo Mendoza, Alfredo. *Apuntes geográficos y estadísticos de la Iglesia Católica en México*. Mexico City: La Cruz, 1954.

Gill, Anthony. *Rendering Unto Caesar: The Catholic Church and the State in Latin America*. Chicago: University of Chicago Press, 1998.

Gill, Mario (Mario Velasco Gil). *Sinarquismo. Su Origen, Su Esencia, Su Misión*. 2nd ed. Mexico City: Comité de Defensa de la Revolución, 1944.

Gillingham, Paul. "Ambiguous Missionaries: Rural Teachers and State Facades in Guerrero, 1930–1950." *Mexican Studies/Estudios Mexicanos* 22, no. 2 (2006): 331–60.

Gillingham, Paul, and Benjamin Smith, eds. *La Dictablanda: Soft Authoritarianism in Mexico, 1938–1968*. Durham, NC: Duke University Press, forthcoming.

Gobierno del Estado de Hidalgo. http://sistemas.e-hidalgo.gob.mx:8585/DirEscuelas./dir_escuela.jsp?municipio=SAN+FELIPE+ORIZATLAN&nivel=Preescolar+General (accessed May 30, 2008).

Gómez Montejo, Alicia. *Las H. juntas municipales del estado de Campeche. Una breve descripción*. Campeche, Mexico: Congreso del estado de Campeche, 2002.

González, Fernando. *Matar y morir por Cristo Rey: Aspectos de la cristiada*. Mexico City: Instituto de Investigaciones Sociales, UA-México, 2001.

González, Luis. *San José de Gracia: Mexican Village in Transition*. Translated by John Upton. Austin: University of Texas Press, 1974.

González Navarro, Moisés. *Cristeros y agraristas en Jalisco*. 5 vols. Mexico City: El Colegio de México, 2000.

Gorenstein, Shirley, ed. *Acambaro: Frontier Settlement on the Tarascan-Aztec Border*. Nashville, TN: Vanderbilt University Publications in Anthropology, 1985.

Gotshall, Elwood. "Catholicism and Catholic Action in Mexico, 1929–1941: A Church's Response to a Revolutionary Society and the Politics of the Modern Age." PhD diss., University of Pittsburgh Press, 1970.

Gould, Jeffrey. *To Die in This Way: Nicaraguan Indians and the Myth of the Mestizaje, 1800–1965*. Durham, NC: Duke University Press, 1998.

———, and Aldo A. Lauria-Santiago. *To Rise in Darkness: Revolution, Repression, and Memory in El Salvador*. Durham, NC: Duke University Press, 2008.

Granados Chapas, Miguel Angel. *Fox y Co.: Biografía no autorizada*. Mexico City: Grijalbo, 2000.

Guadalupe Romero, José. *La historia y la estadistica del obispado de Michoacán*. Mexico City: Vicente García Torres, 1862.

Greene, Graham. *The Lawless Roads*. London: Eyre & Spottiswoode, 1950.

Guadarrama Gómez, Román Juan. *Notas eclesiásticas del estado de Guerrero*. Mexico City, 1992.

———. *Reseña histórica del Templo Parroquial de San Francisco de Asís. Iguala, Guerrero*. Iguala, Mexico: GCPAH de Iguala, 1988.

Guanajuato en la voz de sus gobernadores. Compilación de informes de Gobierno, 1917–1991. Vol. 1. Guanajuato, Mexico: Gobierno de estado de Guanajuato, 1991.

Guerra Manzo, Ernesto. "El fuego sagrado. La segunda cristiada y el caso de Michoacán. (1931–1938)." *Historia Mexicana* 40, no. 2 (2005): 513–75.

Guerrero Tarquín, Alfredo. *Memorias de un agrarista: Pasajes de la vida de un hombre y de toda una región del estado de Guanajuato (1913–1938)*. Mexico City: INAH, 1987.

Guha, Ranajit. *Dominance without Hegemony: History and Power in Colonial India.* Cambridge, MA: Harvard University Press, 1997.

Gutiérrez Ávila, Miguel Angel. *Nabor Ojeda, el batallador del sur.* Mexico City: CEHAM and CNC, 1991.

Gutiérrez Casillas, José. *Jesuitas en México durante el siglo XX.* Mexico City: Editorial Porrua, 1981.

Gutiérrez Mejía, Irma Eugenia. *Hidalgo: Sociedad, economía, política y cultura.* Mexico City: UNAM, 1990.

Guzmán Flores, Guillermo. "El Cardenismo y la nueva democracia." In *Historia de la cuestión agraria mexicana, estado de Zacatecas,* ed. Ramón Vera Salvo. vol. 2, 237–67. Mexico City: Juan Pablo, 1992.

Guzmán Urióstegui, Jesús. *Evila Franco Nájera, a pesar del olvido.* Mexico City: INEHRM and Secretaría de Gobernación, 1995.

Hall, Stuart. "Antonio Gramsci." In *The Routledge Dictionary of Twentieth-Century Political Thinkers,* ed. Robert Benewick and Phillip Green. 80–82. London: Routledge, 1992.

Hanley, Timothy. "Civilian Leadership of the Cristero Movement: The Liga Nacional Defensora de la Libertad Religiosa and the Church-State Conflict in Mexico, 1924–1938." PhD diss., Columbia University Press, 1977.

Hanson, Randall. "Day of Ideals: Catholic Social Action in the Age of the Mexican Revolution, 1867–1929." PhD diss., Indiana University Press, 1994.

Harline, Craig, and Eddy Put. *A Bishop's Tale: Mathias Hovius among His Flock in Seventeenth-Century Flanders.* New Haven, CT: Yale University Press, 2000.

Hernández Castillo, Rosilva Aída. *Histories and Stories from Chiapas: Border Identities in Southern Mexico.* Translated by Martha Poulos. Austin: University of Texas Press, 2001.

Herrera Cabañas, Arturo. "Poder y familia en el mezquital." In *Nos queda la esperanza. El valle del mezquital,* ed. Carlos Martínez Assad and Sergio Sarmiento. 135–47. Mexico City: Consejo Nacional para la Cultura y las Artes, 1991.

Herrera Pech, Manuel. *Apuntes para la historia de Calkiní.* Calkiní, Mexico, 1966.

Hidalguia. "Política en Xochiatipan." http://www.hidalguia.com.mx/xochiatipan/politica.htm (accessed March 28, 2008).

Hurtado, Javier. *Familia, política y parentesco: Jalisco 1919–1981.* Mexico City: Fondo de Cultura Económica and Universidad de Guadalajara, 1993.

Ibarra Grande, Jesús. *Jaral de Berrio y su marquesado. Monografía histórica.* León, Mexico, 1973.

Igualaonline.com. http://igualaonline.com/nuestra-historia./informacion-general/cronologia-de-hechos-historicos/los-cristeros (accessed June 5, 2007).

Instituto Nacional para el Federalismo/DMGEG. http://www.e-local.gob.mx/wb2/ELOCAL/EMM_guanajuato (accessed July 14, 2009).

Instrucciones de los ilmos.y rvmos. Prelados de la provincia mexicana a los señores vicarios foráneos y sus respectivas dióceses sobre los puntos que deben informar anualmente. Mexico City: Escuela Tipografica Salesiana, 1924.

Isidore Sánchez, George. *Mexico: A Revolution by Education*. New York: Viking Press, 1936.
Iverleigh, Austen. "The Politics of Religion in an Age of Revival." In *The Politics of Religion in an Age of Revival: Studies in Nineteenth-Century Europe and Latin America*, ed. Austen Iverleigh. 1–21. London: Institute of Latin American Studies, 2000.
Jacobs, Ian. *Ranchero Revolt: The Mexican Revolution in Guerrero*. Austin: University of Texas Press, 1982.
Jacoby, Susan. *Freethinkers: A History of American Secularism*. New York: Metropolitan Books, 2004.
Jiménez, Blanca M., and Samuel Villela. *Los Salmerón: Un siglo de fotografía en Guerrero*. Mexico City: INAH, 1998.
Joseph, Gilbert, and Daniel Nugent, eds. *Everyday Forms of State Formation: Revolution and the Negotiation of Rule in Modern Mexico*. Durham, NC: Duke University Press, 1994.
Juárez, José Roberto. *Reclaiming Church Wealth: The Recovery of Church Property after Expropriation in the Archdiocese of Guadalajara, 1860–1911*. Albuquerque: University of New Mexico Press, 2004.
Kellogg, Susan. *Law and the Transformation of Aztec Culture, 1500–1700*. Norman: University of Oklahoma Press, 1995.
Knight, Alan. "The Mentality and Modus Operandi of Revolutionary Anticlericalism." In *Faith and Impiety in Revolutionary Mexico*, ed. Matthew Butler. 21–56. New York: Palgrave Macmillan, 2007.
———. *The Mexican Revolution*. Lincoln: University of Nebraska Press, 1986.
———. *Mexico: The Colonial Era*. Cambridge: Cambridge University Press, 2002.
———. "Popular Culture and the Revolutionary State in Mexico, 1910–1940." *Hispanic American Historical Review* 74, no. 3 (1994): 393–444.
———. "Revolutionary Project, Recalcitrant People: Mexico, 1910–1940." In *The Revolutionary Process in Mexico: Essays on Political and Social Change, 1880–1940*, ed. Jaime Rodríguez, 227–64. Los Angeles: UCLA Latin American Center Publications and Mexico/Chicano Program of the University of California–Irvine, 1990.
———. "Subalterns, Signifiers, and Statistics: Perspectives on Mexican Historiography." *Latin American Research Review* 37, no. 2 (2002): 136–158.
Kouri, Emilio. *Business, Property, and Community in Papantla, Mexico*. Stanford, CA: Stanford University Press, 2004.
LaFrance, David. *Revolution in Mexico's Heartland: Politics, War, and State Building in Puebla, 1913–1920*. Wilmington, DE: Scholarly Resources, 2003.
Las Misiones Culturales en 1927: Las Escuelas Normales Rurales. Mexico City: SEP, 1928.
Lerner, Victoria. *La educación socialista. Historia de la Revolución Mexicana 1934–1940*. Mexico City: El Colegio de México, 1979.
Lewis, Stephen. "Efrain Gutiérrez of Chiapas: The Revolutionary Bureaucrat." In *State Governors in the Mexican Revolution, 1910–1952: Portraits in Conflict, Courage, and Corruption*, ed. Jurgen Buchenau and William Beezley. 139–55. Lanham, MD: Rowman & Littlefield Publishers, 2009.

———. "A Window into the Recent Past in Chiapas: Federal Education and Indigenismo in the Highlands, 1921–1940." *Journal of Latin American Anthropology* 6, no. 1 (2001): 58–83.
Ley reglamentaria de cultos del estado de Campeche. Campeche, Mexico: Gobierno del estado, 1934.
Loewe, Ronald. "Marching with San Miguel: Festivity, Obligation, and Hierarchy in a Mexican Town." *Journal of Anthropological Research* 59, no. 4 (2003): 463–86.
Lomnitz-Adler, Claudio. *Exits from the Labyrinth: Culture and Ideology in the Mexican National Space*. Berkeley: University of California Press, 1992.
López Beltrán, Lauro. *Manríquez y Zárate, primer obispo de Huejutla. Sublimador de Juan Diego. Heroico defensor de la Fe*. Mexico City: Editorial Tradición, 1974.
López Espínola, Salvador. *Nuestras huellas recientes: Las sucesiones gubernamentales en Campeche de 1939 a 1991*. Mexico City: Editorial Cumbres, 1999.
López Guzmán, Jorge. "La cuestión educativa en Guanajuato. Proceso de modernización y cambio político 1915–1939." Master's thesis, Universidad Iberoamericana, 2004.
López Sosa, Rodolfo. *Tarjeta Presidencial*. Merida, Mexico: Guerra, 1952.
Low, Seth. *On the Plaza: The Politics of Public Space and Culture*. Austin: University of Texas Press, 2000.
Lynch, John. "The Catholic Church in Latin America, 1830–1930." In *Cambridge History of Latin America*, ed. Leslie Bethell. 527–95. Cambridge: Cambridge University Press, 1986.
Mabry, Donald. *Mexico's Acción Nacional: A Catholic Alternative to Revolution Accion Nacional: A Catholic Alternative to Revolution*. Syracuse: Syracuse University Press, 1973.
MacFarland, Charles. *Chaos in Mexico: The Conflict of Church and State*. New York: Harper and Brothers, 1935.
Mallon, Florencia. *Peasant and Nation: The Making of Postcolonial Mexico and Peru*. Berkeley: University of California Press, 1995.
———. "Time on the Wheel: Cycles of Historical Revisionism and the 'New Cultural History.'" *Hispanic American Historical Review* 79, no. 2 (1999): 331–51.
Manríquez y Zarate, José de Jesús. *El socialismo*. Mexico City: PAGF, 1936.
Manzano, Maria de los Ángeles. *Cuajinicuilapa, Guerrero: Historia oral (1900–1940)*. Mexico City: Ediciones Artesa, 1991.
Manzano, Teodomiro. *Anales del estado de Hidalgo: Desde los tiempos mas remotos hasta nuestros días*. 2 vols. Pachuca, Mexico: Gobierno del estado de Hidalgo, 1927.
Marak, Andrae M. "Federalization of Education in Chihuahua." *Paedagógica Histórica* 41, no. 3 (2005): 357–75.
Marcilla, Alberto. *Resumen histórico del obispado de Campeche*. Mérida, Mexico: Imprenta del Colegio San José Artes y Oficios,1908.
Márquez, Jesús. "La oposición contrarevolucionaria de derecha en Puebla." In *Religión, política y sociedad. El sinarqusimo y la iglesia en México (nueve ensayos)*, ed. Rubén

Aguilar and Guillermo Zermeño Padilla. 31–54. Mexico City: Universidad Iberoamericana, 1992.

Márquez, Octaviano. *Monseñor Ibarra. Biografía del excmo. Sr. Dr. y Maestro D. Ramón Ibarra y González, Cuarto obispo de Chilapa, Ultimo obispo y primer Arzobispo de Puebla*. Mexico City: Editorial Jus, 1962.

Martínez Assad, Carlos. *A dios lo que es de dios*. Mexico City: Aguilar, Nuevo Siglo, 1994.

——. *El laboratorio de la revolución: El tabasco garridista*. Mexico City: Siglo XXI, 1979.

——, ed. *Los lunes rojos. La educación racionalista en México*. Mexico City: SEP and El Caballito, 1986.

McFarland Correa, Phyllis. "Changing Patterns of Sharecropping Arrangements in the Municipio of Allende, State of Guanajuato." PhD diss., State University of New York–Stony Brook, 1991.

——. "Otomí Rituals and Celebrations: Crosses, Ancestors, and Resurrection." *Journal of American Folklore* 113, no. 450 (2000): 436–50.

Mecham, J. Lloyd. *Church and State in Latin America: A History of Politico-Ecclesiastical Relations*. Chapel Hill: University of North Carolina Press, 1966.

Menéndez Rodríguez, Hernán. *Iglesia y poder. Proyectos sociales, alianzas políticas y económicas en Yucatán (1857–1917)*. Mexico City: Editorial Nuestra América and CNCA, 1995.

——. "The Resurgence of the Church in Yucatan: The Olegario Molina-Crescencio Carrillo Alliance, 1867–1901." In *Peripheral Visions: Politics, Society, and the Challenges of Modernity in Yucatan*, ed. Edward Terry, Ben Fallaw, Gilbert Joseph, and Edward Moseley. 213–26. Tuscaloosa: University of Alabama, 2010.

Menes Llaguno, Juan. *Javier Rojo Gómez (Apuntes biográficos)*. Mexico City: Editorial Penelope, 1980.

——. *Pachuca: diez décadas de su historia*. Itzmiquilpan, Mexico: Presidencia Municipal de Pachuca, 1999.

Mercadillo Miranda, José. *Anecdotas sin importancia*. San Miguel Allende, Mexico: Impresa San Miguel, 1960.

Meyer, Jean. "El anticlerical revolucionario, 1910–1940. Un ensayo de empatía histórica." In *Las Formas y Las Políticas del Dominio Agrario: Homenaje a Francois Chevalier*, ed. Ricardo Ávila Palafox, Carlos Martínez Assad, and Jean Meyer. 284–304. Guadalajara, Mexico: Universidad de Guadalajara, 1992.

——. *The Cristero Rebellion: The Mexican People between Church and State*. Trans. Richard Southern. Cambridge: Cambridge University Press, 1976.

——. *La Cristiada*. 8th ed. 3 vols. Mexico City: Siglo XXI, 1983.

——. "La cuestión religiosa en las revoluciones francesa y mexicana." In *México y Francia: dos perspectivas revolucionarias*, ed. Carlos R. Martínez Assad, Carmen Castañeda Garcia, Jean Meyer, and Ricardo Ávila Palafox. 68–79. Guadalajara, Mexico: Editorial Universidad de Guadalajara, 1992.

———. *Historia de la revolución mexicana: Periodo 1928–1934*. Vol. 11. Mexico City: Colegio de México, 1977.
Meyer, Lorenzo. *Historia de la revolución mexicana: Periodo 1928–1934*. Vol. 12. Mexico City: Colegio de México, 1978.
———. *El sinarquismo, el cardenismo y la iglesia (1937–1941)*. Mexico City: Tiempo de Memoria TusQuets, 2003.
Meyer Cosío, Francisco Javier. *Tradición y progreso: La reforma agraria en Acámbaro, Guanajuato (1915–1941)*. Mexico City: INEHRM and Secretaría de Gobernacíon, 1992.
Michaels, Albert. "The Modification of the Anti-Clerical Nationalism of the Mexican Revolution by General Lázaro Cárdenas and Its Relationship to the Church-State Detente in Mexico." *The Americas* 26, no. 1 (July 1969): 36–53.
Millsap, William. "An Otomi Village in the Mezquital Valley: A Study of History and Cultural Adaptation in Mexico." PhD diss., University of Missouri, 1976.
Misioneros Claretianos de México. http://www.claret.org.mx/sola/sola.htm (accessed August 5, 2009).
Moctezuma Barragán, Javier, ed. *Francisco J. Múgica: Un romántico rebelde*. Mexico City: FACE, 2001.
Molina, Silvia. *Imagen de Héctor*. Mexico City: Cal y Arena, 1990.
Monsivais, Carlos. *El estado laico y sus malquerientes (crónica/antología)*. Mexico City: UNAM, 2008.
Montes de Oca, Elvia. *La educación socialista en el Estado de México 1934–1940. Una historia olvidada*. Zinacantepec, Mexico: El Colegio Mexiquense, 1998.
Montoya Briones, José de Jesús. *Etnografía de la dominación en México. Cien años de violencia en la Huasteca*. Mexico City: INAH, 1996.
Moreno, Manuel. *Guanajuato: Cien años de historia (1867–1967)*. Guanajuato, Mexico: Gobierno del estado de Guanajuato, 1989.
Negrín Muñoz, Alejandro. *Campeche: Una historia compartida*. Mexico City: Gobierno del estado de Campeche and IIDJMLM, 1991.
Nesvig, Martin, ed. *Religious Culture in Modern Mexico*. Lanham, MD: Rowan & Littlefield, 2007.
Newcomer, Daniel. *Reconciling Modernity: Urban State Formation in 1940s León, Mexico*. Lincoln: University of Nebraska Press, 2004.
Ochoa Campos, Moisés. *Historia del estado de Guerrero*. Mexico City: Porrua, 1968.
Octava carta pastoral que el Ilmo. Sr. Dr. D. Ramón Ibarra y González dirige al clero y fieles de la diócesis de Chilapa dando a conocer las letras apostólicas del santo padre y el nuevo Instituto de misioneros Guadalupanos. Puebla, Mexico: Colegio Pio de Artes y Oficios, 1895.
Olcott, Jocelyn. *Revolutionary Women in Postrevolutionary Mexico*. Durham, NC: Duke University Press, 2005.
Ortoll, Servando. "Catholic Organizations in Mexico's National Politics and International Diplomacy (1926–1942)." PhD diss., Columbia University, 1986.

Overmayer-Velázquez, Mark. *Visions of the Emerald City: Modernity, Tradition, and the Formation of Porfirian Oaxaca, Mexico*. Durham, NC: Duke University Press, 2006.

Padilla, Juan Ignacio. *Sinarquismo: Contrarevolución*. Mexico City: Editorial Polis, 1948.

Padilla, Tanalís. *Rural Resistance in the Land of Zapata: The Jaramillista Movement and the Myth of the Paz Priista, 1940–1962*. Durham, NC: Duke University Press, 2008.

Parsons, Wilfrid. *Mexican Martyrdom*. 2nd ed. Rockford, IL: Tan Books and Publishers, 1987.

Pastrana, Catalina. *Remembranzas históricos de Iguala y apuntes de su tradición*. Chilpacingo, Mexico: Ayuntamiento municipal constitucional de Iguala, 1990.

Perez-Rayón, Nora. "The Capital Commemorates Independence at the Turn of the Century." In *Viva México! Viva Independencia!: Celebrations of September 16*, ed. William Beezley and David Lorey. Wilmington, DE: Scholarly Resources, 2001.

Peterson, Anna. *Seeds of the Kingdom: Utopian Communities in the Americas*. New York: Oxford University Press, 2005.

Phelan, John Leddy. *The Millennial Kingdom of the Franciscans in the New World: A Study in the Writings of Gerónimo de Mendieta, (1525–1604)*. Berkeley: University of California Press, 1956.

Pilcher, Jeffrey. *¡Que Vivan los Tamales!* Wilmington, DE: Scholarly Resources, 1998.

Piña Chán, Román. *Enciclopedia histórica de Campeche*. 4 vols. Mexico City: Porrua and Gobierno de Campeche, 2003.

Pinto Ávila, Baltazar. "Carretero historiador y crítico." http://www.calkini.net/notas/febrero2005/carretero.htm (accessed September 9, 2006).

Plascencia de la Parra, Enrique. "Adolfo de la Huerta en el Exilio." *Boletín del Fideicomiso Archivos Plutarco Elías Calles y Fernando Torreblanca* 41 (September–December 2002): 1–32.

Prado, Juan José, and Manuel Leal. *Leyendas y Tradiciones Guanajatenses en prosa*. Guanajuato, Mexico: Prado Hermanos, 1955.

Purnell, Jennie. *Popular Movements and State Formation in Revolutionary Mexico: The Agraristas and Cristeros of Michoacán*. Durham, NC: Duke University Press, 1999.

Quintanilla, Luis. *The Other Side of the Mexican Church Question*. Washington, DC: Luis Quintanilla, 1935.

Quirk, Robert. *The Mexican Revolution and the Catholic Church, 1910–1929*. Bloomington: Indiana University Press, 1973.

Raby, David. *Educación y revolución social en México (1921–1940)*. Trans. Roberto Gómez Ciriza. Mexico City: Sep-Setentas, 1974.

Ramírez Rancaño, Mario. *El patriarca Pérez. La Iglesia católica apostólica mexicana*. Mexico City: UNAM, Instituto de Investigaciones Sociales, 2006.

Rangel Camacho, Manuel. *D. Emeterio Valverde Téllez. VI obispo de León y asistente al sacro solio pontificio: Algo sobre su vida y su obra*. León, Mexico, 1950.

Rath, Thomas. "'Que el cielo un soldado en cada hijo te': Conscription, Recalcitrance and Resistance in Mexico in the 1940s." *Journal of Latin American Studies* 37, no. 3 (August 2005): 507–31.

Redfield, Robert. *The Folk Culture of Yucatán*. Chicago: University of Chicago Press, 1941.
———. *A Village That Chose Progress*. Chicago: University of Chicago Press, 1957.
Reed, Alma. *Peregrina: Love and Death in Mexico*. Austin: University of Texas, 2007.
Reich, Peter. *Mexico's Hidden Revolution: The Catholic Church in Law and Politics since 1929*. Notre Dame, IN: University of Notre Dame Press, 1995.
Rionda Ramírez, Luis Miguel. *El conservadurismo popular guanajuatense y el movimiento sinarquista*. Guanajuato, Mexico: Universidad de Guanajuato and CICS, 1997.
———. "Enrique Fernández Martínez: Un gobernador de la vorágine. El cardenismo y la ruptura generacional revolucionaria." http://www.cicsug.ugto.mx/Publico/Libros/Luis/FdezMrtz.pdf (accessed February 2006).
———. *Movimientos populares y lucha de la Izquierda en Guanajuato 1900–1994*. Guanajuato, Mexico: CICS and Universidad de Guanajuato, 2001.
———. *Origen y evolución de los partidos políticos en el estado de Guanajuato*. Guanajuato, Mexico: Instituto Electoral del Estado de Guanajuato, 1998.
———. *Primer acercamiento a una historia política contemporánea de Guanajuato siglo XX*. Guanajuato, Mexico: CICS–Universidad de Guanajuato, 1997.
Ríos Figueroa, Julio. *Siglo XX: Muerte y resurrección de la iglesia católica en Chiapas. Dos estudios historicos*. Mexico City: PIMMS, 2002.
Rius Facius, Antonio. *De don Porfirio a Plutarco; historia de la A.C.J.M.* Mexico City: Editorial Jus, 1958.
Rodríguez, Alberto A. *El proceso de la religion en Mexico*. Jalapa, Mexico: Talleres del gobierno del estado, 1930.
Rodríguez, Cristobal. *La influencia del clero en la América Latina*. Mexico City: Talleres Gráficos de la Nación, 1931.
Rodríguez, Esteban David. *Derecho de sangre: Historias familiares de herencia del poder público en México*. Mexico City: El Colegio de México, FHA, and FCE, 2000.
Rodríguez Herrera, Emilio. *Legislaturas Campechanas: Compendio histórico (1861–1998)*. Campeche, Mexico: Congreso del estado de Campeche, 1999.
Rodríguez López, María Teresa, and Pablo Valderrama Rouy. "The Gulf Coast Nahua." In *Native Peoples of the Gulf Coast of Mexico*, ed. Alan Sandstrom and E. Hugo Garcia Valencia. 158–86. Tucson: University of Arizona Press, 2006.
Rodríguez Lozano, Rubén. *Maestros revolucionarios*. Mexico City: Instituto Nacional de Juventud Mexicana, 1963.
———. *San Luis Potosí en su lucha por la libertad*. Mexico City, 1938.
Rodríguez Piña, Javier. "Conservatives Contest the Meaning of Independence, 1846–1855." In *Viva México! Viva Independencia!: Celebrations of September 16*, ed. William Beezley and David Lorey. 101–30. Wilmington, DE: Scholarly Resources, 2001.
Rodríguez Ramírez, Eliseo. "El agrarismo en Guanajuato." In *Historia de las ligas de comunidades agrarias y sindicatos campesinos: primer concurso estatal*. Vol. 2: *Centro*, ed. Julián Rodríguez Sesma. 73–149. Mexico City: Confederación Nacional Campesina, 1988.

Rojas, Pedro. *Acámbaro colonial: Estudio histórico, artístico e iconográfico*. Mexico City: Universidad Nacional Autónoma de México, 1967.

Romero, Jorge J. "Contra la estupidez, los propios dioses luchan en vano." http://jorgejavierromero.blogspot.com/2007_09_23_archive.html (accessed September 1, 2009).

Rubenstein, Anne. *Bad Language, Naked Ladies, and Other Threats to the Nation: A Political History of Comic Books in Mexico*. Durham, NC: Duke University Press, 1998.

Rugeley, Terry. *Of Wonders and Wise Men: Religion and Popular Culture in Southeast Mexico, 1800–1876*. Austin: University of Texas Press, 2001.

———. *Rebellion Now and Forever: Mayas, Hispanics, and Caste War Violence in Yucatán, 1800–1880*. Stanford, CA: Stanford University Press, 2009.

Ruiz de Barrera, Rocío. *Breve historia de Hidalgo*. Mexico City: El Colegio de México, FHA and FCE, 2000.

Samuels, Richard. *Machiavelli's Children: Leaders and Their Legacies in Italy and Japan*. Ithaca, NY: Cornell University Press, 2003.

Sánchez, José. *Anticlericalism: A Brief History*. Notre Dame, IN: University of Notre Dame Press, 1972.

Sánchez Díaz, Alfonso, ed. *La guerra cristera en Guanajuato. Apuntes para la historia regional*. Mexico City: La Rana, 2005.

Sánchez García, Alfonso. *El círculo rojinegro*. Mexico City: Universidad Autónoma del Estado de México, 1984.

Sánchez Maldonado, María Isabel. *Diezmos y crédito e eclesiástico. El diezmatorio de Acámbaro, 1724–1771*. Morelia, Mexico: El Colegio de Michoacán, 1994.

Sánchez Medal, Ramón. *En defensa del derecho de los padres de familia*. Mexico City: Editorial Jus, 1964.

Sandstrom, Alan. *Corn Is Our Blood: Culture and Ethnic Identity in a Contemporary Aztec Indian Village*. Norman: University of Oklahoma Press, 1991.

San Luis de la Paz Online. http://www.sanluisdelapaz.com/cmsdreamer2/index.php?categoryid=15 (accessed August 3, 2005).

Santiago, Myrna. *The Ecology of Oil: Environment, Labor, and the Mexican Revolution, 1900–1938*. Cambridge: Cambridge University Press, 2006.

Santiago Sierra, Augusto. *Las Misiones Culturales (1923–1973)*. Mexico City: Sep-Setentas, 1973.

Santos, Gonzalo N. *Memorias*. Mexico City: Grijalbo, 1986.

Savarino Rogerro, Franco. *Pueblos y nacionalismo, del régimen oligárquico a la sociedad de masas en Yucatán, 1894–1925*. Mexico City: INEHRM, 1997.

Schell, Patience. *Church and State Education in Revolutionary Mexico*. Tucson: University of Arizona Press, 2003.

———. "Of the Sublime Mission of Mothers of Families: The Union of Mexican Catholic Ladies in Revolutionary Mexico." In *The Women's Revolution in Mexico, 1910–1953*, ed. Stephanie Mitchell and Patience Schell. 99–123. Boulder, CO: Rowman & Littlefield, 2007.

Schroeder, Michael. "From Horse Thieves to Rebels to Dogs: Political Gang Violence and the State in the Western Segovias, Nicaragua, in the Time of Sandino, 1926–1934." *Journal of Latin American Studies* 28, no. 2 (May 1996): 383–434.

Schryer, Frans. "Discussion and Conclusions: Agrarian Conflict and Pilgrimage." In *Pilgrimage in Latin America*, ed. N. Ross Crumrine and Alan Morinis, 357–68. New York: Greenwood Press, 1991.

———. *Ethnicity and Class Conflict in Rural Mexico*. Princeton, NJ: Princeton University Press, 1990.

———. "Peasants and the Law: A History of Land Tenure and the Conflict in the Huastecas." *Journal of Latin American Studies* 18, no. 2 (1986): 283–311.

Schuler, Friedrich. *Mexico between Hitler and Roosevelt: Mexican Foreign Relations in the Age of Lázaro Cárdenas, 1934–1940*. Albuquerque: University of New Mexico Press, 1998.

Schuren, Ute. "La revolución tardía: Reforma agraria y cambio político en Campeche (1910–1940)." In *Yucatán a través de los siglos*, ed. Ruth Gubler and Patricia Maskel. 285–318. Mérida, Mexico: Universidad Autónoma de Yucatán, 2001.

Scott, James C. *Domination and the Arts of Resistance: Hidden Transcripts*. New Haven, CT: Yale University Press, 1990.

Secretaría de Gobernación. http://www.gobernacion.gob.mx/transparencia/docum entos (accessed August 5, 2005).

Sepúlveda Garza, Manola. "Paradojas de la Historia Ejidal: El Llanito, Dolores Hidalgo, Guanajuato, 1930–1960." *Cuicuilco* 11, no. 31 (2004): 1–21.

———. *Políticas agrarias y luchas sociales: San Diego de la Unión, Guanajuato, 1900–2000*. Mexico City: Procuraduría Agraria and INAH, 2000.

Serna Alcántara, Gonzalo Aquiles. "La escuela normal libre de Huejutla (1925–1935): Una Historia para Preservar." Consejo Mexicano de Investigación Educativa. http://www.comie.org.mx/congreso/memoria/v9/ponencias/at09/PRE1177698825.pdf (accessed March 27, 2008).

Serrano Álvarez, Pablo. *La batalla del espíritu: El movimiento sinarquista en el Bajío (1932–1951)*. 3 vols. Mexico City: Consejo Nacional Para la Cultura y las Artes, 1992.

Sewell, William, Jr. "Towards a Post-materialist Rhetoric for Labor History." In *Rethinking Labor History*, ed. Leonard Berlangstein. 15–38. Champagne: University of Illinois Press, 1993.

Shirk, David. *Mexico's New Politics: The PAN and Democratic Change*. Boulder, CO: Lynne Reiner, 2005.

Sierra, Carlos. *Acción gubernamental en Campeche 1857–1960*. Mexico City: Talleres de Impresión de Estampillas y Valores, 1972.

———. *Diccionario biográfico de Campeche*. Mexico City: La Muralla, 1997.

Simpson, Eyler. *The Ejido Mexico's Way Out*. Chapel Hill: University of North Carolina Press, 1937.

Smith, Benjamin. "Anticlericalism, Politics, and Freemasonry in Mexico." *The Americas* 65, no. 4 (2009): 559–88.

———. "Inventing Tradition at Gunpoint: Culture, Caciquismo, and State Formation in the Región Mixe, Oaxaca (1930–1959)." *Bulletin of Latin American Research* 27, no. 2 (2008): 215–34.

———. "The Politics of Anticlericalism and Resistance: The Diocese of Huajuapam de Leon 1930–1940." *Journal of Latin American Studies* 37, no. 3 (2005): 469–506.

———. "'The Priest's Party': Local Catholicism and Panismo in Huajuapam de León." In *Faith and Impiety in Revolutionary Mexico*, ed. Matthew Butler. 261–77. New York: Palgrave Macmillan, 2007.

———. *Pistoleros and Popular Movements: The Politics of State Formation in Postrevolutionary Oaxaca*. Lincoln: University of Nebraska Press, 2009.

Smith, Michael. "The Strategic Provinces." In *Aztec Imperial Strategies*, ed. Frances Berdan, Richard Blanton, Elizabeth Boone, Mary Hodge, and Michael Smith. 137–79. Washington, DC.: Dumbarton Oaks Research Library and Collection, 1996.

Sol, Hugo. *Bolchevismo criminal de Yucatán. Documentos y apuntes para la historia trágica del estado*. Mexico City, 1921.

Sosa Elízaga, Raquel. *Los códigos ocultos del cardenismo: Un estudio de la violencia política, el cambio social y la continuidad institucional*. Mexico City: Universidad Nacional Autónoma de México and Plaza y Valdés, 1996.

Spenser, Daniela. *The Impossible Triangle: Mexico, Soviet Russia, and the United States in the 1920s*. Durham, NC: Duke University Press, 1999.

Tapia Gómez, José. "Episodio Almazanista en Tlapa: Elecciones presidenciales, 1939–1940." In *Tlapa: Origen y Memoria Histórica*, ed. Mario Martínez Rescalvo. 207–38. Chilpancingo, Mexico: Universidad Autónoma de Guerrero and AMTC, 2000.

———. *Feliciano Radilla, un líder natural costeño*. Chilpancingo, Mexico: UAG and CEHAM, 1992.

Taracena, Alfonso. *La verdadera revolución mexicana. Decimaséptima etapa (1931): La Familia Revolucionaria*. Mexico City: Editorial Jus, 1965.

Taylor, William. *Drinking, Homicide, and Rebellion in Colonial Mexican Villages*. Stanford, CA: Stanford University, 1979.

Tejeda de León, Francisca. *Chilapa: Tierra de novela y ensoñación poética*. Mexico City: Costa-Amic Editores, 1999.

Torres Septién, Valentina. *La educación privada en México (1903–1976)*. Mexico City: El Colegio de México and Universidad Iberoamericana, 1997.

Torres Vera, María Trinidad. *Mujeres y utopía: Tabasco garridista*. Villahermosa, Mexico: Universidad Juárez Autónoma de Tabasco, 2001.

Tostado Gutiérrez, Marcela. *El intento de liberar a un pueblo. Educación y magisterio tabasqueño con Garrido Canabal: 1924–1935*. Mexico City: INAH, 1991.

Tresierra, Julio. "Mexico: Indigenous Peoples and the Nation-State." In *Indigenous Peoples and Democracy in Latin America*, ed. Donna Lee Van Cott. 187–210. New York: St. Martin's Press, 1994.

Uc Dzib, Andrés. "La escuela rural, una nueva escuela de la época de oro de la educación en México." In *Los maestros y la cultura nacional, 1920–1952*, ed. Cecilia Greaves, Engracia Loyo, and Valentina Torres. Vol. 5, 17–25. Mexico City: SEP, 1987.

Vadillo López, Claudio. *Campeche: Sociedad, economía, política y cultural*. Mexico City: UNAM, 2000.
Valdez, Norerto. *Ethnicity, Class and the Indigenous Struggle for Land in Guerrero, Mexico*. New York: Garland, 1998.
Valencia García, Guadalupe. *Guanajuato: Sociedad, economía, política y cultura*. Mexico City: UNAM, 1998.
Valle Basilio, Sabas, Salvador Rebolledo Orbe, and Filimón Vázquez Moreno. *Tlapa de Comonfort: primer centenario, 1890–1990*. Chilpancingo, Mexico: Gobierno del Estado de Guerrero, 1990.
Vallier, Ivan. *Catholicism, Social Control, and Modernization in Latin America*. Englewood Cliffs, NJ: Prentice-Hall, 1970.
Vanderwood, Paul. "Religion: Official, Popular and Otherwise." *Mexican Studies/Estudios Mexicanos* 16, no. 2 (2000): 411–41.
Van Oosterhout, Aaron, and Benjamin T. Smith. "The Limits of Catholic Science and the Mexican Revolution." *Endeavor* 34, no. 2 (2010): 55–60.
Van Oss, Adrian. "La iglesia en Hidalgo hacia 1930." *Historia Mexicana* 29, no. 2 (1979): 301–24.
Van Young, Eric. "Are Regions Good to Think?" In *Mexico's Regions: Comparative History and Development*, ed. Eric Van Young. 1–36. San Diego: University of California–San Diego, 1992.
Vásquez Soriano, Mario Armando. *Signos de identidad: los espacios simbólicos de Dolores Hidalgo*. Mexico City: Instituto Mora, 1999.
Vaughan, Mary Kay. "The Construction of the Patriotic Festival in Tecamachalco." In *Rituals of Rule, Rituals of Resistance: Public Celebrations and Popular Culture in Mexico*, ed. William Beezley, Cheryl English Martin, and William French. 213–46. Wilmington, DE: Scholarly Resources, 1994.
———. *Cultural Politics in Revolution: Teachers, Peasants, and Schools in Mexico, 1930–1940*. Tucson: University of Arizona Press, 1997.
Verástique, Bernardino. *Michoacán and Eden: Vasco de Quiroga and the Evangelization of Western Mexico*. Austin: University of Texas Press, 2000.
Voss, Stuart. *Latin America in the Middle Period, 1750–1929*. Wilmington, DE: Scholarly Resources, 2002.
Waters, Wendy. "Revolutionizing Childhood: Schools, Roads, and the Revolutionary Generation Gap in Tepoztlán, Mexico, 1928–1944." *Journal of Family History* 23, no. 3 (1998): 292–311.
Weiner, Richard. *Race, Nation and Market: Economic Culture in Porfirian Mexico*. Tucson: University of Arizona Press, 2004.
Weldon, Jeffrey. "El Congreso, Las Maquinarias Políticas Locales y el Maximato: Las Reformas No-Reeleccionistas de 1933." In *El Legislador a Examen: El debate sobre la reelección legislativa en México*, ed. Fernando F. Dworak. 33–53. Mexico City: Cámara de Diputados and FACE, 2003.
Whetten, Nathan. *Rural Mexico*. Chicago: University of Chicago Press, 1948.

Wilkie, James. "Statistical Indicators of the Impact of National Revolution on the Catholic Church in Mexico, 1910–1967." *Journal of Church and State* 12 (Winter 1970): 89–106.

Williman, John. *La iglesia y el estado en Veracruz, 1800–1940*. Mexico City: Sep-Setentas, 1976.

Wright-Rios, Edward. "A Revolution in Local Catholicism? Oaxaca, 1928–1934." In *Faith and Impiety in Revolutionary Mexico*, ed. Matthew Butler. New York: Palgrave Macmillan, 2007.

———. *Revolutions in Mexican Catholicism: Reform and Revelation in Oaxaca, 1887–1934*. Durham, NC: Duke University Press, 2009.

Wuhs, Steven. *Savage Democracy: Institutional Change and Party Development in Mexico*. University Park: Pennsylvania State University Press, 2008.

Yañez Rizo, Emma. *Vida y muerte de Fidelita, la novia de Acámbaro: Una historia social de la tecnología en los años cuarenta: El caso de los Ferrocarriles Nacionales de México*. Mexico City: Consejo Nacional para la Cultura y las Artes, 1991.

Yescas Martínez, Isidoro. "El sacerdote que desafió la voluntad de Dios: El caciquismo de Cornelio Bourget en Oaxaca." In *A dios lo que es de dios*, ed. Carlos Martínez Assad. Mexico City: Aguilar, Nuevo Siglo, 1994.

Index

Acámbaro: agrarian reform in, 211, 214; anticlericalism in, 198–99; Ayala's Catholic cacicazgo in, 197; Cardenista politics in, 212; Church presence in, 194, 195, 197; indigenous population around, 214; opposition to SEP, 199–200; Segunda in, 204–5; Sinarquism in, 212; violence against Protestants in, 203; voto morado in, 161–62
Acapulco: agrarian struggle in, 114, 128, 140–42, 146; history of, 103, 106; radical tradition in, 105; religious question in, 111, 117
acerba animi, 2, 17
ACJM (Asociación Católica de la Juventud Mexicana), 25–27; in Guanajuato, 160, 163, 187, 192
ACM (Acción Católica Mexicana), 10–11, 25–28, 30; in Campeche, 44, 49, 50, 59; and civic action, 16, 25, 90, 160; and the Cristero War, 25; and elections, 16, 26, 30–31, 160; in Guanajuato, 160–61, 187; in Guerrero, 145, 148, 153, 156; in Hidalgo, 66, 90, 98; organizational debility of, 57, 59, 111, 194; promotion of liturgical orthodoxy, 55, 60; role in radial strategy, 13, 28, 44, 110, 196; and Segunda, 27, 160; social Catholic outreach, 66, 132, 190, 209; state repression of, 53, 59, 167; tactics to oppose SEP, 181, 187, 206; women leaders of, 28, 73, 111, 206
agrarian reform, 6, 220, 224–25, 228n7; in Guanajuato, 157–58, 162, 166, 183, 188–91, 201, 211–12; in Guerrero, 114, 129, 142, 148, 155; in Hidalgo, 65, 73–74, 95–96
Aguilera, Ezequiel, 173–74, 182
Almazán, Juan Andreu: Catholic support for the presidency, 109, 208, 213, 217, 220; and the Church, 2, 154, 217
Altamirano y Bulnes, José Luis María, 90, 97
Amaro, Joaquín: Cristiada service, 169, 178; forcible relocation of Iguala's cemetery, 115; in Guerrero politics, 102, 104, 106, 140
Amuzgos, 7, 103, 122; compadrazgo with mestizos, 125; and Costa Chica segundita, 121, 124, 125; landholding patterns, 122; religious practices of, 123, 124, 125; and SEP, 122, 123; and Zapatismo, 122
Angli Lara, Fernando, 36–38, 47–49, 57–58
Añorve, Pantaleón, 124–26

anticlericalism: among agraristas, 17, 132, 201, 212; ideological sources of, 38; among local organizations, 153; in oaths required of teachers, 80; patriotism and, 93; as theme of murals, 40, 81. *See also* defanaticization; iconoclasm; ley de cultos

Apango, 133–34

Arcelia: opposition to SEP in, 118, 127, 141; priests in, 151; SEP anticlericalism in, 127

army: challenge of protecting teachers, 74, 119, 183; fighting segunderos, 182–83, 147, 189; officers' repression of agraristas, 120, 125–26, 142, 183, 189

Arreglos, 15, 16; failure to demobilize, disarm, and reintegrate many cristeros, 160, 204

Article 130, 15, 43, 80

Assembly of God. *See* Protestantism

Atoyac, 140–41, 153

Austria, Honorato, 95–96, 261n205

Ávila Camacho, Manuel: presidential campaign, 151, 154, 156, 220, 222; and the religious question, 2, 21

Ayala, David: Catholic cacicazgo, 158, 196, 215, 216; and Catholics, 163, 193, 197, 198; and Melchor Ortega's election, 163; political career, 197–98; and SEP teachers, 199; and white terror, 201, 209

Azanza, Salvador, 11; alliance with Melchor Ortega, 170, 171, 172, 181; assault on Arnulfo Ochoa, 157, 182; assassination of Ezequiel Aguilera, 173–74, 182; Catholic cacicazgo, 157–58, 169–74, 181–82, 222; as Catholic electoral broker, 163, 170, 171; and the Church, 174, 181; clientele, 174; as a cristero, 169–70, 192; incarceration, 170, 182; as landowner, 169, 171, 172; as a "political amphibian," 172, 182; and Genovevo Rivas Guillén, 173–74, 182, 222; and Segunda, 171, 172, 182; ties to Luis Martínez Vértiz, 157, 169, 170, 181; use of white terror, 173, 179, 222

Bantjes, Adrian, 9, 41, 146, 221
Barbosa, Juan, 48–50, 246n80
Berber, Alfredo: and the clergy, 134, 153; election to governor, 147; as federal congressman, 147; links to landowners and anti-agrarian violence, 126, 147; and the Ranchero group, 104; and the religious question, 104, 147, 150–51; and SEP, 152

bishops. *See* episcopate and bishops by name

Blancarte, Roberto, 31, 32

Bonilla Segura, Guillermo, 119, 123, 139, 269n117

Borja, Desiderio, 105, 128, 139

Boylan, Kristina, 5, 28, 111, 221

Butler, Matthew, 9–10, 25, 173, 195, 243n33

caciquismo: and agrarian reform, 131–32, 148, 179; in Campeche, 35, 49, 50, 51, 60; and the clergy, 84, 177; in Guanajuato, 157, 158, 171, 187, 193, 215, 275n3; in Hidalgo's upstate, 87, 95; in middle politics, 5; PSA's reliance on, 48, 57; Matías Rodríguez's support for, 65, 70, 91, 93; SEP opposition to, 47, 83, 89, 96, 97; and state formation, 216, 224, 225

Calles, Plutarco Elías: and Honorato Austria, 95; break with Lázaro Cárdenas, 20, 89, 90; and Campeche politics, 46; and the Great Depression, 224; as Jefe Máximo, 4, 15, 17; pressure on governors to crack down on the Church, 3, 117; and the religious question, 64, 225; selection of Gabriel Guevara for governor, 102; support for Melchor Ortega for governor, 163;

318 INDEX

support for the Red Party, 162. *See also* Psychological Revolution

Calnalí, 78, 83–85

Campeche: economy, 37–38; geography of, 44–45; governmental weakness, 37; gubernatorial election of 1935, 67, 147–61; gubernatorial election of 1939, 59; subregional differences, 45–46

Campeche, Diocese of, 32, 51–57, 60

Cárdenas, Lázaro: and agrarian reform, 21, 225; anticlericalism, 2; break with Plutarco Elías Calles, 20, 89, 130; and Campeche, 58–59; and Catholics, 20–22, 158, 188–89, 221; and Ciudad González violence, 11, 21, 183, 215; as governor of Michoacán, 106, 196; and Guanajuato, 183, 188, 190, 215; and Guerrero, 107, 117, 145, 147, 153; and Hidalgo, 94; and Luis María Martinez, 21; and the religious question, 2, 8, 12, 20–21, 58, 96, 117, 156, 220–21; rightward tilt after 1937, 2, 21; romance with oil, 224; support for SEP, 21, 89; visit to ENR-H, 42

cargo system. *See* confraternities

Carranza, Venustiano, 15, 29, 106, 138

Castillo Lanz, Angel, 48, 59

Castrejón, Adrían: and Amaro, 102, 106; attempt to impose Ezequiel Padilla as successor, 101, 102, 107; background, 106, 113, 148; creation of the PSG, 105, 106; in the Cristero War, 107; nomination by Claudio Fox, 106; Pascual Ortíz Rubio's backing, 102, 106

Catholics: double militancy and partisan politics, 3, 196, 217, 223; moral panic over the revolutionary project, 97, 99, 127, 143, 203, 207; opposition to agrarian reform, 4, 7, 106–7, 193, 209; opposition to SEP, 5, 10, 45–46, 134, 202–3, 210; residual antistate resentment after the religious question, 146, 217. *See also* Catholic women activists; Church; gremio

Catholic women activists, 5–6, 11, 14, 25–28, 224; in Campeche, 43, 45, 51, 53, 56, 57; Cárdenas's disparagement of, 188; in Guanajuato, 174, 195, 200, 202, 228; in Guerrero, 101–2, 111–12, 148–49, 152; in Hidalgo, 66, 71, 77, 90; in Oaxaca, 223; and Segunda, 149; in Sinaloa, 224

Cedillo, Saturnino: Catholic lack of support for his revolt, 21, 223; ouster by Cárdenas, 73; paramilitary, 160; protection of Manríquez's family, 95; ties to Honorato Austria, 95

Chamácuaro, 201

Chichihualco, 110–11, 130

Chilapa: conflicts over SEP in, 118, 127, 143, 144; defensive violence in, 121; Sinarquism in, 151; voto morado in, 101

Chilapa, Diocese of, 107–9, 115, 146, 148, 156

Christianity by fear, 138–41

Christian socialism, 40–42

Chupícuaro, 201–2, 210, 212

Church: and Plutarco Elías Calles, 2, 8; and Lázaro Cárdenas, 2, 8, 12, 22, 158, 222–23; and Cristero War, 15, 19, 25; and electoral politics, 3, 14, 16; indigenism and indigenous people, 7, 68; and oil nationalization, 2, 8; opposition to agrarian reform, 2, 6, 21, 25, 67, 110, 142, 144, 209, 215; opposition to SEP, 2, 20, 28, 110, 151; relationship with agraristas, 21, 145, 151–53, 162, 192, 199, 223; and Segunda, 2, 6, 12, 19, 23, 204; ties to upper class, 23, 51, 53. *See also* Catholics; clergy; episcopate

Ciudad González: agrarian reform in, 184, 188–91; Hernández Alcocer's cacicazgo in, 186; Cárdenas's visit to, 188; Catholic resistance to the revolutionary project in, 186–87; clash of

INDEX 319

Ciudad González (*cont.*)
March 28, 1936, 183–85, 188, 215; Lámbarri cacicazgo in, 171; Segunda in, 172, 185

civic action: and the ACM, 25, 90, 160; in Campeche, 44; in Church's political strategy, 16, 146, 176, 222

civil society: Catholic organizations' strong presence in, 6, 14, 28–29, 127, 144, 158, 166, 174, 219, 220; concept of, 1; and state formation, 11, 12, 14, 145, 151, 177

clergy: discipline of, 23, 109–10; and indigenous Catholics, 52, 68, 75, 84; influence of Roman education on, 14; opposition to agrarian reform, 110, 143, 153, 171, 175, 192, 207, 209, 270–71n147; opposition to SEP, 19, 77, 110, 143, 177, 184, 203; and politics, 9; reduction due to persecution, 43, 164, 192; and segunderos, 119, 154; ties to the upper class, 6, 14–15, 24, 52, 110, 128, 192, 208. *See also* tithes

Coahuayutla, 138

Cochoapa, 124–26

coeducation, 18, 118, 211

Colunga, Enrique, 162, 169, 207, 209

compadrazgo (godparentage): and mestizo-Amuzgo ties, 121, 125, 126; and mestizo-indigenous ties in la Montaña, 113, 269–70n130; and mestizo-Maya ties, 39, 50; and priests in Hidalgo's upstate, 84; and segundita in the Costa Chica, 121, 122–26, 155; as a source of social capital, 51

confraternities: among Amuzgos, 123, 125; anticlerical threat to, 114, 178; in Campeche, 51, 54; expenses of, 55; foundation in modern times, 112; in Hidalgo, 70–71; in Iguala, 116; landowning by, 114; maintenance of chapel by, 112, 113; political role of, 113; and syncretism, 112; in upstate Hidalgo Nahua, 67, 69. *See also* gremios

cooperatives: ACM's use to appeal to the poor, 27, 60; in the Diocese of Huejutla, 66, 69; Melchor Ortega and Salvador Azanza's, 171; PSA-run in Campeche, 48; SEP-run in Campeche, 10, 37–39, 46, 50, 52, 56, 59

Coroneo, 210–11, 215

Cortés, Claudio, 37–39, 41–42

Corzo, Federico, 73, 74, 79, 80, 81

countercorporatism. *See* voto morado

Cristero War: communal support for, 9–10, 162, 213–14; in Guanajuato, 159–60, 162, 167–70, 177–78, 186–87, 191, 205; in Guerrero, 106, 108, 114, 136, 140; in Hidalgo, 65; leadership of, 8. *See also* clergy; LNDL; recristeros

CROM: and agrarian reform, 176, 179, 207; and anticlericalism, 205; and the Knights of Guadalupe, 162; and the Red Party, 206; repression in Guanajuato, 182, 207

Cuervo, Tomás: admiration for Garrido Canabal, 165; in Guerrero, 127; in Guanajuato, 165–66, 176, 203

Cuetzala, 113–14, 150

cultural missions: origins of, 41; in Acámbaro, 212; in Campeche, 42; in Ciudad González, 183–84, 188, 215; in Guerrero, 127; in Hidalgo's upstate, 72; in León, 166, 183; in the Mezquital, 92; in Tarimoro, 209

Damas Católicas, 25–28; and electoral politics, 48; in Guanajuato, 160–61; in Guerrero, 111; and Martínez Vértiz, 180; repression of, 26, 160; in Salvatierra, 206–7; opposing SEP, 29, 148, 177, 196

Daughters of Maria (*Hijas de María*): Guanajuato, 184, 196, 224; in Guerrero, 111, 118, 126, 137, 148 defanaticization, 18; in Campeche, 37–38, 40, 46, 59; Cárdenas's strategy of structural reform to achieve it, 20–21, 96, 144, 148, 188, 220; in Guanajuato, 176, 207, 215; in Guerrero, 117, 119, 122, 129, 135, 140; in Hidalgo, 63, 72–83, 89–90, 96–97; SEP doctrine of, 36; and structural change, 86. *See also* science

defensive violence. *See* Segunda

Díaz, Pascual: and the Arreglos, 22; and revolutionary politicians, 3; strategy to regain social and political influence, 16, 19–20

Díaz Escudero, Leobardo: and Almazán's campaign, 154; as bishop, 105, 108; defense of family's land from agraristas, 108, 129; discipline of clergy, 109–10; moralization of society, 110; opposition to revolutionary project, 109; opposition to SEP, 148, 161–62; pact with Lugo, 105, 146; rechristianization strategy in the late 1930s, 146, 147; return from exile, 102; suppression of Segunda, 109; and the UNPF, 111

Dolores Hidalgo: agrarian reform in, 170, 188, 191–92; Azanza's cacicazgo in, 170–71; Cardenistas in, 173–74, 182; conflict over SEP schools in, 174, 176–77, 178, 191–92; hero cult of Miguel Hidalgo in, 180; military abuses in, 177; Segunda in, 172, 189, 192

ejido. *See* agrarian reform; *communities by name*

elections, 2, 4, 5; and the Church, 114, 116, 131; fraud in, 57, 222; presidential race of 1924, 161, 205; presidential race of 1940, 21, 95, 109, 154, 208, 215, 217, 220; presidential race of 2000, 216; and SEP, 10. *See also elections by individual states*

ENR-H (Escuela Normal Rural de Hecelchakán), 37–38, 41–42, 49–50

episcopate, 13; and the ACM, 27; and the Almazán campaign, 109; and the Arreglos, 13, 16; and Cárdenas, 21; and conflict over Manríquez, 100; divisions over the Cristero War, 15, 22; exile during the Cristero War, 52, 160, 195; exile during the Maximato, 17; family origins, 22; geographical origins, 159; imposing religious orthodoxy, 60; leadership of, 8; position on violence, 19, 22, 148; and priests' discipline and training, 23; Roman education, 14; and Segunda, 22–23. *See also* Church; clergy

EPL (Ejército Popular Libertador), 19, 199

Escuela Magnética Espiritual de la Comuna Universal. *See* spiritism

Fernández Martínez, Enrique: and agrarian reform, 189, 211; and cacicazgos, 212; as gubernatorial candidate, 183; as interim governor, 182; and Segunda, 168

Foucault, Michael, 7

Fox, Claudio: and counterinsurgency, 106–7; execution of priests, 115, 118; intervention in politics, 106

Freemasons: in Acámbaro, 195, 198, 199; in Acapulco, 141; and anticlericalism, 38, 93, 141, 162; in Calkiní, 49; demonization by Catholics, 24, 77, 135, 168, 181; in Molango, 89; and political careerism, 3, 112; Revolutionary Lodge of Tlacotepec, 130–32; ritual of, 40; in Salvatierra, 205–6

Gallegos, Rodolfo, 170, 205

Garrido Canabal, Tomás: and anticlerical pressure on other governors, 17; Berber's admiration for, 147; Catholic fears of, 36, 116, 135, 146, 164, 166, 203; export of teachers to Hidalgo, 78;

Garrido Canabal, Tomás (*cont.*)
  influence in Campeche, 38, 41, 48, 49; as inspiration for some SEP leaders, 119, 121, 165; removal from cabinet by Cárdenas, 89. *See also* Red Shirts
Giles, Antonio, 136–37, 143, 149
Gramsci, Antonio, 1, 3, 227. *See also* hegemony; state formation
Green Party: in Acámbaro, 197, 209; and agrarian reform, 162, 169, 176, 189, 200, 207; and Cárdenas, 182, 183, 212; in Ciudad González, 186–87, 189; corruption in, 163; in Jerécuaro, 210, 212; origins, 161; and the religious question, 161, 189; in Salvatierra, 196; support for cristeros, 162; and voto morado, 162, 170, 196, 208
gremios: caciques's leadership of, 50, 60; history of, 50, 54, 55, 60; opposition to the revolutionary project, 10, 55–56, 224; SEP suppression of, 56; social inequality in, 46, 54, 55; as source of social capital, 50
Guadalupe, Virgin of: and the canonization of Juan Diego, 100, 262n229; Catholic cult of, 17, 194; confraternities dedicated to, 112–13; and cult of Miguel Hidalgo, 283n135; Knights of Guadalupe, 162; Manríquez's advocacy of, 64, 66, 69; as symbol of rejection of the revolutionary project, 71, 131, 191, 223
Guanajuato: geography, 192–93; gubernatorial election of 1927, 162; gubernatorial election of 1931, 162–63, 197, 208; gubernatorial election of 1932, 163, 197; gubernatorial election of 1935, 175; gubernatorial election of 1937, 183; gubernatorial election of 1939, 183; haciendas in, 175, 176, 195; indigenous population of, 214; landholding patterns in, 189, 191, 207, 211, 214; municipal elections of 1934, 169; religious geography of, 192–93; subregions of, 159
Guerrero (state of): geography of, 103–4; gubernatorial election of 1932, 101–2, 111; gubernatorial election of 1936, 147; history of, 103; municipal elections 1932–34, 104–6; religious geography of, 108, 132, 134; social segmentation in, 156; subregions of, 104
Guerrero, Francisco, 133–34, 153
Guerrero Tarquín, Alfredo, 174, 178, 189–90
Guevara, Gabriel: background, 102; and Calles, 102; and Catholics, 103, 107, 114, 132, 135; election of, 101, 219; and Ranchero group, 104; and the religious question, 117–18, 128, 130, 143; removal by Cárdenas, 145; repression of agraristas, 114, 118, 133, 135; and Segunda, 129, 130
Guízar, Luis, 22, 52, 57

Hecelchakán: anticlericalism in, 39; opposition to ENR-H in, 49–50; reopening of its church, 50; Reyes Ortega's attack on, 59; support for ENR-H in, 58; violent demonstration against ley de cultos in, 44. *See also* ENR-H
hegemony: and the Catholic response to state formation, 5, 12, 156, 220, 222–25; conceptual indeterminacy, 220; contrasted with dominance, 223
Hernández Alcocer, Enrique, 186
Herrera, Miguel, 139–143
Hidalgo (state of): 10; geography, 64, 72, 249–50n4; geostrategic position, 72, 95; gubernatorial election of 1936, 94–95; socioeconomic inequalities in, 64, 67, 71–72, 76
Hidalgo, Manuel, 135–36

Hidalgo, Miguel: Catholic hero cult of, 180–82; CROM's use of, 179; in liberal patriotic history, 181; SEP's hero cult of, 41, 56
Hijas de María. *See* Daughters of Maria
Huajuapan de León, Diocese of, 52, 66, 69
Huejutla: Día de la Raza demonstration in, 80; elite's educational and social ties to the Church, 70; elite's resistance to the revolutionary project, 74; quemasantos in, 86; religious dissidents in, 79; Zárate's scandal, 87–88
Huejutla, Diocese of: anticlerical legislation's impact on, 80; foundation and early history, 66–70; lack of clergy, 32, 98
Huitzuco, 135–37, 156

ICAM (Iglesia Católica Apostólica Mexicana), 71, 109, 259n179
iconoclasm: agraristas in, 116; and Almazán's campaign, 154; and Catholic countercorporatism in, 126, 224; Iguala, 104; in levitical nature of, 108; military atrocities in, 115, Nunkiní, 35–36, 38; as social Catholic laboratory, 115; in upstate of Hidalgo, 81, 86–87; voto morado in, 105, 115–16, 155
indigenism, 7; in Campeche, 42; in Huasteca of Hidalgo, 72, 77
Iturbide, Agustín, 120, 181

Jerécuaro: conservative restoration in, 212; indigenous communities in, 225; revolutionary project's success in, 209–10; Segunda in, 203, 205, 213
Jesuits, 231; in León, 159; in the Laguna, 223; missions in la Montaña, 146
Joseph, Gilbert M., 3, 227n3

Knight, Alan: critique of the cultural turn, 227nn2,3; on rancheros' Jekyll and Hyde character, 105; on religion, regionalism, and state formation, 31, 44
Knights of Columbus: in Acámbaro, 196–97; in Celaya, 167; in Ciudad González, 186–87; in Dolores Hidalgo, 177; foundation of, 25; and hero cult of Iturbide, 181; incorporation into ACM, 26, 160–61; and Melchor Ortega, 170; persecution during Cristiada, 26, 160; UNPF's creation, 29; in Valle de Santiago, 164

labor drafts: Church's reliance on, 67, 84, 110, 113, 114, 152; in Hidalgo's upstate, 71–76; SEP's reliance on, 113, 114, 152
Lámbarri, Jorge: as Catholic cacique, 171, 186, 193, 215; role in anti-agrarian violence, 186, 188; and violence in Ciudad González, 187–88
León, Diocese of, 26, 159–61, 167
León Montero, José, 50, 52, 56, 58
ley de cultos, 4, 15, 17, 20; in Campeche, 35, 43, 45; in Chihuahua, 21; in Guanajuato, 163–65, 196; in Guerrero, 107, 113, 117, 118; in Hidalgo, 65, 66, 79, 95; impact on priests' numbers, 24, 65. *See also* anticlericalism
Llanito, El, 178–80, 192
LNDL (Liga Nacional Defensora de la Libertad), 19, 25, 30, 31
LNDLR (Liga Nacional Defensora de la Libertad Religiosa), 105, 200
Lomnitz-Adler, Claudio, 68, 230n28
López, Héctor F.: and the Almazán campaign, 154; and Alfredo Berber, 147; and the Church, 105, 138, 140; opposition to agrarian reform, 131, 138; and the Ranchero group, 104, 145; ties to landowners, 138–43
Lugo, José Inocencio, 128; and Cárdenas, 145; links to landowners, 128; opposition

INDEX   323

Lugo, José Inocencio (*cont.*)
to agrarian reform, 146; pact with Bishop Díaz, 105, 156; and the Ranchero group, 104, 145; selection as interim governor, 145; and SEP, 135–36, 152

Manríquez Zárate, José de Jesus, 10, 63–64; anti-Semitism, 77, 78; and Catholic indigenism, 11, 66–70, 77–78, 97; conflict with episcopate, 80, 98, 109; and cristeros, 22, 63; exile in Texas, 77; and Guadalupanism, 64, 66, 69, 100; opposition to SEP, 78, 87, 97, 99; pastoral letters as incitement to violence, 180; and Segunda, 99–100, 180
Manuel Ocampo: agrarian struggle in, 176, 211; Segunda in, 171; social hierarchy in, 175
Marín, Luis: conflict with Zárate, 83–85, 87; conflict with Francisco Austria, 95; opposition to socialist education, 77
Martínez, Luis María, 8, as head of episcopate, 21; and Lázaro Cárdenas, 21
Martínez Vértiz, Luis: alliance with Salvador Azanza, 157, 169, 170, 181; alliance with Melchor Ortega, 170, 171, 174; and assassination of Ezequiel Aguilera, 174; and assassination of Guadalupe Olvera, 190; assault on Arnulfo Ochoa, 157, 182; association with Gonzalo Santos, 170; as Catholic electoral broker, 170, 171; economic portfolio, 170; as organizer of Catholic lay groups, 170; as rancher, 170
Marxist historiography, 2
Maya: exclusion from clergy, 52; religious practices of, 36, 52, 56; resentment of anticlericalism, 56; social subordination of, 39, 46–48, 55; support for SEP, 35, 39, 55, 56. *See also* syncretism
mayordomías (stewardships). *See* confraternities

Mena Córdoba, Eduardo: as governor, 57–59; gubernatorial campaign, 48–51
mestizaje: in Amuzgo communities, 122; as nationalist trope, 42; promotion of white-*mestiza* unions, 258n152; SEP advocacy of, 75; in José Vasconcelos's Cosmic Race, 42
middle politics, 5
Mixtecs: and defensive violence, 123; in Diocese of Huajuapan de León, 66, 68; in la Montaña, 104, 112, 122
Molango, 70, 76, 78, 89
Morelia, Archdiocese of, 27, 32, 195–96, 204, 209
Múgica, Francisco: in Campeche, 38, 42–44, 48; as governor of Michoacán, 214

Nahua, 64, 72; and the Church, 63, 66; electoral participation, 113, 224; elites, 67, 70, 71, 72, 113, 114; gender, 82, 87, 113, 114, 134; intracommunal conflicts, 74–75, 82, 103, 104, 112–14, 133; religious practices, 66, 68–70, 71, 81, 82, 84, 87, 97, 112, 113; zahorines, 96. *See also* labor drafts; SEP; syncretism
natural right: and education, 19, 21, 175; and private property, 6, 21, 24, 26, 141, 191, 215; and violent resistance to tyranny, 19, 191
Noxtepec, 135–36, 150, 151
Nunkiní, 35–36, 49

Obrajuelos, 201, 215
Obregón, Álvaro, 15, 29, 46, 64, 161, 205; hero cult of, 41, 76
Ocampo, Gabriel, 131, 149, 151
Ochoa, Arnulfo: assault on, 157, 182; and the revolutionary project, 157, 177; struggle against "fanaticism," 174, 207
Ochoa, Mateo, 68, 85–86, 224
offensive violence. *See* Segunda
oil, nationalization of, 2, 8, 224

Ojeda, Nabor, 126, 146–47, 153
Ometepec, 108, 124–26, 153
Orizatlán, 72, 74, 78, 86
Ortega, Melchor: camarilla, 185; and Catholics, 163–69, 170–71, 176, 198–200, 205, 219; election to governor, 162–63; in Michoacán, 163; negotiations with Bishop Valverde, 196; opposition to agrarian reform, 171–207; ouster by Cárdenas, 183; reliance on David Ayala, 197; and Segunda, 171–72; ties to Salvador Azanza, 170–72
Ortiz Rubio, Pascual, 16, 17, 102
Otomí: in Guanajuato's Laja river valley, 178–79, 214; in Hildago, 7, 64, 91, 92; and SEP project in the Mezquital, 92–93. *See also* Llanito, El; syncretism

Padilla, Ezequiel, 101–3, 105, 107
PAN (Partido de Acción Nacional), 216–17
parents' groups. *See* UNPF
Party of the Institutionalized Revolution (PRI), 1
Patiño, Rafael, 205–8
patriarchy: in Amuzgo society, 125; in the Church, 14, 21, 111, 146, 150, 221; defense by conservative press, 18; in Nahua society, 82, 87, 113, 134; in SEP, 18, 88, 200; threatened by sports, 125; undermined by female literacy, 211
Peña, León: as Catholic cacique, 191, 193, 215; evasion of agrarian reform, 19; as landowner, 175; support for Segunda, 191–92, 225; use of Catholic ideology, 191
Piedra Hincada, 74, 86
Pius IX, 14, 17, 19, 28, 156
PNR (Partido Nacional Revolucionario). *See* PRI
POA (Partido Obrero de Acapulco), 105, 140
Portes Gil, Emilio, 15, 57, 94

press: and civil society, 8; coverage of Ciudad Gónzalez clash, 189; coverage of Zárate scandal, 88; criticism of SEP, 29; criticism of sports, 125; opposition to Cárdenas, 189; reflecting Catholic sensibilities, 8; reporters in Chilapa, 144
PRI (Partido Revolucionario Institutional): origins, 227n1; and organized labor, 95
PRM (Partido Revolucionario Mexicano). *See* PRI
Protestantism: and anticlericalism, 79, 96, 133; Assembly of God, 91; Catholic antipathy toward, 24, 93, 181, 203; conversion to, 91, 112, 214; and radicalism, 79, 141, 214; repression of, 79, 126; and SEP, 61, 121
PSA (Partido Socialista Agrario): and caciques, 47–51; conflict against Carmen and Palizada elite, 46; during Mena Córdoba administration, 57–59; and the PNR, 241n5; and the religious question, 43–44
PSG (Partido Socialista Guerrerense), 105, 106
Psychological Revolution: Calles's proclamation of, 18, 79, 117; Catholic reaction against, 77, 203; rejection by Cárdenas, 20, 183, 215; and repression of Catholics, 26, 119, 147, 164; and SEP, 144
Puebla: Diocese of, 32; export of clergy, 22, 51; gubernatorial election of 1936, 222; loss of la Montaña, 104, 107; Segunda in, 19; SEP scandal in, 88
Purnell, Jennie, 9–10, 208, 213
Puroagua, 203, 205, 210, 213

Quechultenango, 108, 118, 150

Radial Strategy, 6, 28, 126, 156; and the ACM, 44; in Campeche, 33; and control

Radial Strategy (*cont.*)
of popular Catholic mobilizations, 156, 225; in denial of postrevolutionary state's legitimacy, 13, 225; in opposition to SEP, 31, 55, 127, 177, 195, 199, 204, 206; and penetration of civil society, 146, 166, 220; Pius IX's proclamation of, 28; unintended facilitation of Segunda, 30, 143, 148, 167, 186, 192; unintentional weakening of Church's authority by, 30, 44, 110–11, 148, 167, 220; and the UNPF, 30–31, 112; and the upper class, 55; and violence in Ciudad González, 186

Radilla, Feliciano: and agrarian reform, 153; and agrarian violence, 142, 153; anticlericalism, 141–42; assassination of, 153; and Cárdenas, 146

Ranchero group: and Cárdenas, 145–47, 155; and Christianity, 141; and the clergy, 110; and nomination of Guevara, 102; opposition to agrarian reform, 106, 126; opposition to SEP, 118; origins of, 104; reliance on Catholic support, 101–3, 106, 130, 135; and the religious question, 104, 116, 146

Ramírez, Rafael, 72

Recristeros, 18; in Segunda in Guanajuato, 160, 167–68; in Segunda in Guerrero, 120, 135–36, 150

Red Party: in Acámbaro, 193, 196, 214, 215; attraction of the voto morado, 163–64, 171; in gubernatorial election of 1931, 163; local congressmen of, 172, and the religious question, 161–62; in Salvatierra, 205

Red Shirts: Catholic reaction to, 107, 155, 203; donned by Campeche's federal teachers, 38, 49; in Guerrero's Tierra Caliente, 127, 165. *See also* Garrido Canabal, Tomás

regional culture, concept of, 68

Reich, Peter, 9, 235–36n53

religious question, 2; ambiguous resolution of, 21–22, 97, 126; Cárdenas's concessions on, 99, 144, 156, 158, 180, 183, 188–89, 215, 220–21; Cárdenas's strategy to resolve, 20, 58, 96, 215; similarities between Calles and Cárdenas, 21, 183, 225

revisionist historiography of Mexico, 1

Revolutionary Family, 4, 138, 154, 163

revolutionary project, 4, 16, 36, 114. *See also* state formation

Reyes Ortega, Ignacio: as cacique of Calkiní, 48–49; support for clergy, 52, 58, 224

Rionda Ramírez, Luis Miguel, 277n23

Rivas Guillén, Genovevo: alliance with Salvador Azanza, 173–74, 182, 222; anticlericalism, 173; in Cristiada, 178; and landowners, 173; in Segunda, 172–74, 187

Rocha, Laura, 18, 19

Rodríguez, Abelardo, 17, 73, 106

Rodríguez, Enrique "El Tallarín," 19, 129

Rodríguez, Luis I., 183, 189, 212

Rodríguez, Matías, 64–65, 70, 92–95

Rodríguez Lozano, Rubén: as adviser to Díaz Ordaz, 73; background of, 73; clash with Manríquez, 77–78; confrontation with mestizo elites in upstate Hidalgo, 74–76; in downstate Hidalgo, 89, 92–94; relationship with Nahua, 76–77; in San Luis Potosí, 93

Rojo Gómez, Javier, 94–96

Romero Esquivel, Benjamín, 43–44, 48, 58

Rugeley, Terry, 9, 54

Ruiz, Leopoldo: as archbishop of Morelia, 163, 196, 198; as co-leader of national episcopate, 16, 19, 22; exile of, 17; integralism of, 195; opposition to Segunda, 203, 205

Salgado, David, 130–32, 149, 225
Salgado, Macario Roman, 109, 115–16
Salvatierra: agrarian conflict, 207–8, 212; Catholic resistance to revolutionary project in, 206, 214; cult of Iturbide in, 181; Rafael Patiño's cacicazgo in, 205; politics in, 196, 212
Sandoval, Fermín, 168–69, 172, 186
San Miguel Allende: agrarian reform in, 188, 191; recristeros in, 168, 189; Segunda in, 189; SEP in, 192
Santos, Gonzalo, 170, 175, 178
science: in Catholic education, 107; Nahua notions of, 82, 256n117; in SEP anticlerical oaths, 80; in SEP defanaticization, 77, 92, 96, 129, 135, 165, 202, 213
Segunda: army's links to, 119, 203; in the Bajío, 158; casualties of, 18, 120, 142, 172–73, 189, 222, 223; causes and local variations, 91; in Chiapas, 221; chronology of, 18, 221, 223; defensive violence, 6, 11, 120–23, 128, 142, 202–4; end of, 12, 213, 221; in Guanajuato's north, 166–69, 183, 172, 191–93; in Guanajuato's southeast, 202, 204–5, 213; in Guerrero's Costa Chica, 122–26; in Guerrero's Costa Grande, 138–42; in Guerrero's northern and central valleys, 129–38, 149, 151; in Guerrero's Tierra Caliente, 127–28, 151; hacendados' links to, 193; in Hidalgo's downstate, 91–93; offensive violence, 7, 11, 120, 140, 142, 156, 204; and socialist education, 18, 30, 143, 168, 180, 203, 204; women's role in, 6. *See also* Church; LNDL; white terror
SEP (Secretaría de Educación Pública), 5; and anticlericalism, 17, 35, 42, 77, 79, 80, 97, 117–18, 135–37; in Campeche, 35–39, 45–47; Cárdenas's cutbacks 1937–40, 205, 211; conflicts with teachers over religion, 45, 80, 203; conservative turn, 95–96, 111, 144, 155, 220; in Guanajuato, 159, 162, 165–66, 176, 178, 192, 208; in Guerrero, 106, 113–14; in Hidalgo, 72–73, 79–80, 89–92, 95–96; and indigenous people, 10–11, 37–38, 72–73, 74, 96–97, 178–79; involvement in elections, 47, 59, 94; language policy, 40, 75, 83, 118, 122; promotion of mestizaje, 122; recruitment and retention of teachers, 37, 78, 80, 89, 121, 176; sex scandals in its ranks, 88, 258n159. *See also* cultural missions
Sepúlveda Garza, Manola, 170
sexual education: Catholic campaign against, 29–30; Catholic fears of, 18, 89, 139, 206, 207; local controversies over, 87, 127
Sinarquismo: in Church's global strategy, 145; in Guanajuato, 158, 180–81, 212–13, 216; in Guerrero, 125, 145, 150, 151; in Hidalgo, 98; ideology of, 98; politicalization of, 151; suppression of, 213
Singuilucan, 92
Smith, Benjamin, 40, 198
Social Catholicism, 14, 67; in Diocese of Huejutla, 10, 66; in Huasteca revolt of 1879–82, 67; importance of women in implementation of, 14, 25; and state formation, 28, 115
socialist education: Catholic fears of, 29, 78; Catholic national strategy against, 6, 18–20, 29, 45, 90, 200, 206; conflation with sexual education and immorality, 30, 125, 142, 207; opposition by regional politicians, 163, 165–67, 216, 222; SEP abandonment of, 12, 145; SEP's adoption of, 18, 36; SEP dismissal of teachers who refused to implement it, 165, 202; SEP's struggles to define, 38, 83, 165. *See also* Segunda
spiritism: and anticlericalism, 38, 79, 133, 224; Escuela Magnética Espiritual de la

spiritism (*cont.*)
  Comuna Universal, 79; recruitment of teachers among, 79
sports: Catholic fear of, 124–25; female participation in, 125; to reform indigenous people, 84; in the revolutionary project, 42; in SEP's philosophy, 125, 165
state formation, 2; Catholics' role in, 2, 3, 4–7, 60, 102, 222; definition of, 156, 220; and everyday life, 3, 223, 224; impeded by caciques, 216, 224, 225
syncretism: and the Church, 52, 56, 70, 107, 110, 115, 116, 215; economic impact, 60; fostered by confraternities, 112, 113; in Maya Catholicism, 38, 54, 68; in Nahua Catholicism, 66, 69, 112; in Otomí Catholicism, 178–79, 214; in Tlapanec Catholicism, 112

Tabascanization. *See* Garrido Canabal, Tomás
Tabasco, 10, 18, 32. *See also* Garrido Canabal, Tomás; Red Shirts
Tarandacuao, 193, 196, 208, 212
Tarimoro, 201, 208–9
Taxco, 104; ACM in, 148; Catholic women activists in, 147, 156; conflict over SEP in, 135–37; Segunda in, 173
Taylor, William, 125
Tenango de Doria, 91–92
Tepeji del Rio, 91, 92
Terciarios, 160, 170, 194, 196–97, 213
Tetipac, 135–36, 149–51
tithes: in the anticlerical imagination, 131; and agraristas, 152, 176, 194, 212, 213; economic necessity for Church, 24, 60, 107; imposition on indigenous communities, 10, 69, 84; persistence and restoration of, 110, 150, 153, 161, 187, 212; as proxy for support for the Church, 110, 208; regulation of, 24, 159; and speculation in grain, 69, 110, 116; threatened by agrarian reform, 24; widespread collection, 6
Tlacoachistlahuaca, 122, 124
Tlacotepec: Catholic campaign against SEP schools in 1938–40, 149; Catholicism's strength in, 132, 134; hybrid Segunda violence in, 121; segundita of 1935–36 in, 129–32
Tlapam 112, 113, 128, 146
Tlapanec (Me'phaa), 103, 104, 112; confraternities, 113; religious practices, 112
Torres, Francisco G., 122; and defanaticization, 123–24, 153; denunciation of segunderos, 125–26
Tritschler y Córdoba, Martin, 15, 16, 22, 42, 43
Tulancingo, Diocese of, 64, 90, 92, 98

UFCM (Unión Feminina Católica Mexicana). *See* Damas Católicas
UNPF (Unión Nacional de Padres de Familia), 10, 30; in Campeche, 53; covert ties to the Church, 29, 30, 196, 199, 206; in Guanajuato, 164, 167, 180, 196, 198, 206, 207; in Guerrero, 111; history, 29; opposition to SEP, 29, 143, 180, 182, 199, 206; politicalization, 31; and Segunda, 143, 180, 182; similar parents' groups, 30, 31, 90, 111, 143, 203
Uribe Velázquez, David: beatification of, 115; execution of, 107

Valverde Téllez, Emeterio, 159; alliance with Melchor Ortega, 196; covert opposition to SEP, 167, 216; evasion of ley de cultos through pacts with governors, 16, 164; exile during Cristiada, 160; and Mother's Day, 216; suppression of Segunda, 163, 167, 168; ties to Luis Martínez Vértiz, 164
Vaughan, Mary Kay, 5, 9, 36, 125

Vasconcelos, José, 41, 42, 99
Vértiz, Mariano, 170, 197, 199
Viveros, Ernesto, 65, 79, 80, 93
voto morado, 2, 5, 229–230n18; Callistas' reliance on, 216, 219; in Calnalí, 83–85; in Campeche's 1935 gubernatorial election, 48, 51, 55, 57; in Campeche's 1936 municipal elections, 58; Cardenistas' reliance on, 216, 222; depression of, after Calles-Cárdenas break, 95; and the Green Party, 162, 170, 196, 208; in Guanajuato's 1931 and 1932 gubernatorial elections, 17, 163, 169, 170; in Guerrero's 1932 gubernatorial election, 101–7; in Guerrero's 1936 gubernatorial election, 147; in Hidalgo's 1929 gubernatorial election, 93; in Iguala, 115–16; in León, 163, 169; limits of, 222; in Puebla, 222; and the Ranchero group, 155; and the Red Party, 171

white terror, 6, 26; in Acámbaro, 204, 213; in Ciudad Gónzalez, 186–87, 207; and the clergy, 155, 224–25; in the Costa Grande, 138–43; in Dolores Hidalgo, 171–73; legitimized as fighting "banditry," 114, 131, 201, 207–9; and recristeros in Guanajuato, 168, 187, 201; in San Miguel Allende, 168, 189; and Segunda, 120–21, 210–11

Xochiatipan, 85, 86, 87
Xochistlahuaca, 122

Yahualica, 76, 87
Yañez Maya, José Jesús, 164, 171, 182
Yextla, 130, 132
Yoloxóchitl, 123

Zapata: limited symbolic appeal in the 1930s, 267n81; SEP's promotion of the hero cult of, 40
Zapatismo: in Guanajuato, 161; in Guerrero, 104, 105, 122, 133
Zapatista veterans: and Adrián Castrejón, 113; support for the revolutionary project in Guerrero, 114, 116, 129, 131, 133; support for the revolutionary project nationally, 226
Zárate González, Francisco, 11, 63, 97; in Calnalí, 83–85; iconoclasm in Huejutla, 86–87; scandal over sexual assault charges, 87–89, 97, 99; training in Yucatán, 83

BEN FALLAW has taught Latin American history at Colby College since 2000. He is the author of *Cárdenas Compromised: The Failure of Reform in Postrevolutionary Yucatán*, published by Duke University Press (2001), and is coeditor of *Forced Marches: Soldiers and Military Cacicazgos in Modern Mexico* (2012). He has published articles in the *Hispanic American Historical Review*, *Latin American Research Review*, *The Americas*, *Ethnohistory*, and the *Journal of Latin American Studies*.

❊ ❊ ❊

Library of Congress Cataloging-in-Publication Data
Fallaw, Ben.
Religion and state formation in postrevolutionary Mexico /
Ben Fallaw.
p. cm.
Includes bibliographical references and index.
ISBN 978-0-8223-5322-5 (cloth : alk. paper)
ISBN 978-0-8223-5337-9 (pbk. : alk. paper)
1. Church and state—Mexico—History—20th century.
2. Catholic Church—Political activity—Mexico—20th century.
3. Mexico—History—Revolution, 1910–1920—Religious aspects.
4. Mexico—History—1910–1946. I. Title.
BR610.F35 2012
322.'109720904—dc23
2012011623

www.ingramcontent.com/pod-product-compliance
Lightning Source LLC
Chambersburg PA
CBHW070745020526
44116CB00032B/1976